A STORM
OVER THIS
COURT

Constitutionalism and Democracy

GREGG IVERS AND
KEVIN T. MCGUIRE,
EDITORS

A STORM OVER THIS COURT

LAW, POLITICS, AND SUPREME COURT DECISION MAKING IN *BROWN V. BOARD OF EDUCATION*

Jeffrey D. Hockett

University of Virginia Press
Charlottesville and London

University of Virginia Press
© 2013 by the Rector and Visitors of the University of Virginia
All rights reserved
Printed in the United States of America on acid-free paper

First published 2013

9 8 7 6 5 4 3 2 1

LIBRARY OF CONGRESS CATALOGING-IN-PUBLICATION DATA
Hockett, Jeffrey D.
   A storm over this court : law, politics, and Supreme Court decision making in Brown
v. Board of Education / Jeffrey D. Hockett.
         p. cm. — (Constitutionalism and democracy)
   Includes bibliographical references and index.
   ISBN 978-0-8139-3374-0 (cloth : alk. paper) — ISBN 978-0-8139-3375-7
(e-book)
   1. Brown, Oliver, 1918–1961—Trials, litigation, etc. 2. Topeka (Kan.). Board
of Education—Trials, litigation, etc. 3. Segregation in education—Law and legislation—United States. 4. School integration—United States. 5. Discrimination in
education—Law and legislation—United States. 6. African Americans—Civil rights.
I. Title.
   KF228.B76H63 2013
   344.73'0798—dc23
                                                                            2012035954

For Aaron

CONTENTS

Acknowledgments   *ix*

Introduction   *1*

1 Barriers to Desegregation   *15*

2 The Attitudes of the Justices   *36*

3 Law, Anticipated Violence, and Loyalty to the Court   *59*

4 A Sense of the Court's Mission   *92*

5 The Relevance of Foreign Affairs   *127*

6 Domestic Political Considerations   *148*

Conclusion   *178*

Notes   *197*

Bibliography   *235*

Index   *251*

ACKNOWLEDGMENTS

While writing this book, I accumulated a number of debts that it is my pleasure to acknowledge. Bill Caferro and Megan Weiler kindly invited me into their home during one of my numerous research trips. Justin and Rosa Byrne provided companionship during another research-related excursion. David O'Brien, Jeff Oldham, and Step Feldman read an early version of my argument and offered valuable counsel. Step also suggested that I consider developing the piece into a book-length study. After I did so, Jacob Howland read a first draft of the manuscript and offered a number of helpful stylistic and substantive suggestions. Elvin Lim and Cornell Clayton likewise provided valuable comments and suggestions after they read an expanded version of the manuscript. I had the good fortune to have extended conversations with Howard Gillman and Gerald Rosenberg during their respective visits to the University of Tulsa for the Lectureship in Politics and Law. I also had a brief but informative discussion with Mark Graber during his visit to the University of Tulsa College of Law, and I benefited greatly from conversations that I had with Ron Jepperson. I thank Lee Epstein for bringing her recent work on ideological drift to my attention, and I appreciate Kevin Quinn's willingness to respond to my questions regarding the same subject. I am grateful to Andy Burstein for encouraging me to send the completed manuscript to the University of Virginia Press and for contacting the press on my behalf.

I extend a special thank you to Bill Schabas, Director of the Irish Centre for Human Rights, National University of Ireland, Galway, for his generosity and support during my sabbatical semester in 2006. The faculty, staff, and students at the Centre could not have been more welcoming to my family and me. The Centre provided a truly hospitable environment in which to research and write.

My colleagues in the Department of Political Science at the University of Tulsa are deserving of thanks for their collegiality and encouragement.

I am especially grateful to Michael Mosher, Chair of the Department of Political Science, and Tom Benediktson, Dean of the Henry Kendall College of Arts and Sciences, for their support. The Office of Research and Sponsored Programs at the University of Tulsa afforded valuable support regarding the publication of the manuscript. Keith Schoenefeld provided software expertise at critical moments, while Toy Kelley helped me with the department's computer hardware and otherwise aided in the book's production. Katy Barr, Vanessa Metzner, and especially Anna Gann patiently accommodated my endless requests for articles and documents.

An Earhart Foundation Fellowship enabled me to extend a sabbatical leave, providing valuable time to research and write. A Henry M. Phillips Research Grant in Jurisprudence from the American Philosophical Society provided funds to visit libraries housing the collections of various Supreme Court justices. The staff of the manuscript division of the Library of Congress was immensely helpful. Michael Widener, Head of Special Collections at the Tarlton Law Library of the University of Texas at Austin, afforded valuable assistance. Portions of chapter 4 appeared in the 1989 *Journal of Supreme Court History* (copyright 1989 by The Supreme Court Historical Society. All rights reserved).

I am especially grateful to the editors, staff, and readers of the University of Virginia Press. In particular, Dick Holway was patient and very helpful while I revised the manuscript before publication, and it was a pleasure to work with Raennah Mitchell, Mark Mones, Morgan Myers, Margie Towery, and Margaret Hogan. Ronald Kahn and Thomas Keck provided detailed comments, criticisms, and suggestions that substantially improved the book.

Finally, I would like to thank my wife Laura and my sons Evan and, especially, Aaron for their patience and encouragement. Laura tolerated me on countless occasions when I felt compelled to work through book-related problems in the evening, and Evan offered his Luddite of a father much-needed aid regarding the mysteries of Microsoft Paint. Aaron grew quite a bit (and much too quickly, I might add) during the time that it took to write this book. With good humor, he endured the competition that this project presented to significantly more important matters such as roofball, hockey behind the garage, soccer, baseball, hoops, hurling, and tennis. He also graciously agreed (although he may have been watching television at the time) to assume full responsibility for any errors and omissions in the manuscript. Although I think Aaron would understand if the dedication page referenced Jonathan Toews and the 2009–10 Chicago Blackhawks, it is with much love (and gratitude) that I dedicate this book to him.

A STORM
OVER THIS
COURT

Introduction

On May 17, 1954, the U.S. Supreme Court ruled unanimously in *Brown v. Board of Education of Topeka, Kansas*—the lead case in a group of four consolidated state cases—that racial segregation in public schools violated the equal protection clause of the Fourteenth Amendment to the U.S. Constitution.[1] The Court maintained that the separate-but-equal principle enunciated at the end of the nineteenth century in *Plessy v. Ferguson* was a contradiction in terms as applied to education.[2] Justice Hugo Black's admonition to his brethren during the Court's deliberations in *Brown*—that rash action regarding enforcement would bring a "storm over this Court"—indicates that the justices understood that their behavior would be carefully scrutinized.

In spite of the justices' awareness of the sensitive nature of the case at hand, the rationale that they adopted for their desegregation order generated enormous controversy. Speaking for all of his brethren, Chief Justice Earl Warren made no pretense that the Court's ruling rested on the intentions of the framers and ratifiers of the Fourteenth Amendment. The historical sources that were the focus of reargument of the case in 1953, he suggested, were, "at best, . . . inconclusive." The chief justice followed this comment with the observation that "the most avid proponents of the post-War Amendments undoubtedly intended them to remove all legal distinctions among 'all persons born or naturalized in the United States,'" while "their opponents, just as certainly, were antagonistic to both the letter and the spirit of the Amendments and wished them to have the most limited effect." "What others in Congress and the state legislatures had in mind," he said, "cannot be determined with any degree of certainty."[3] Given the powerful historical defense of segregation that the lawyers for the respondents (i.e., the school boards) had presented to the Court at the rehearing, however, Warren's claim regarding the indeterminacy of the framers' intentions appeared rather disingenuous.[4]

The Court based its holding in *Brown* on the empirical proposition that racial segregation in public schools "generates a feeling of inferiority [in black children] as to their status in the community that may affect their hearts and minds in a way unlikely ever to be undone." For this reason, Warren stated, "separate educational facilities are inherently unequal." "Whatever may have been the extent of psychological knowledge at the time of *Plessy v. Ferguson*," he declared, "this finding is amply supported by modern authority." At this point in the opinion, the chief justice made reference to social science studies that Thurgood Marshall and the lawyers of the NAACP Legal Defense and Educational Fund (LDF) introduced on behalf of the petitioners in the case.[5] Given that this was the first time the Court had turned to modern social science evidence to invalidate governmental action—and given that counsel for the school boards had thoroughly critiqued the evidence on which the Court relied—the Court's rationale appeared dubious even to those sympathetic to desegregation.[6]

Bolling v. Sharpe, a companion case to *Brown* that involved the public schools of the District of Columbia, was no less controversial. Since the Fourteenth Amendment applies only against the states, the Court held in *Bolling* that racial segregation in the District's public schools violated the due process clause of the Fifth Amendment. Specifically, Warren contended in his opinion for the Court that the federal government failed to satisfy the requirement that a rational relationship exist between a legislative goal and the means chosen to effectuate that goal. The chief justice courted controversy by failing to explain his statement that "segregation in public education is not reasonably related to any proper governmental objective and thus . . . imposes on Negro children of the District of Columbia a burden that constitutes an arbitrary deprivation of their liberty in violation of the Due Process Clause."[7] Warren entirely ignored the primary argument that segregationists offered in support of the practice—that it provides for the welfare of blacks and whites alike by preserving racial harmony.

Because of the sensitive nature of the issue that the Court addressed in *Brown* and *Bolling*, and because of the difficulty that Warren had in articulating a compelling legal basis for the Court's holdings, the desegregation decisions were controversial in their day and for some time thereafter. Yet, in spite of the vulnerability of the arguments that Warren offered, *Brown* eventually became one of the Supreme Court's most celebrated rulings. As Michael J. Perry observes, *Brown* "is generally thought to represent the Court at its best." Scholars of all ideological stripes agree that "*Brown* was a great and correct decision," "perhaps the most important judgment ever handed down by an American Supreme Court."[8] In an attempt to explain the widespread sentiment that "*Brown* may be the most important political, social, and legal event in America's twentieth-century history," J. Harvie Wilkinson III does not suggest that, with the passage of time, jurists and scholars developed an appreciation for Warren's logic. Indeed, he contends not only that the Court "spoke *without* eloquence" in *Brown;* he charges that it "never attempted to reason much at all." Wilkinson observes that *Brown's* "greatness" lay not in the substance of the Court's argument, but "in the enormity of injustice it condemned, in the entrenched sentiment it challenged, in the immensity of law it both created and overthrew."[9] In other words, televised images of the brutality that segregationists directed at peaceful civil rights protestors in the 1960s deprived southerners of the rationalization that segregation was intended to benefit blacks as well as whites. As a consequence, and as Charles L. Black had predicted in 1960, "in the end the [desegregation] decisions [were] accepted by the profession" not because southern whites had inadvertently made black children feel inferior, but for a powerful reason about which Warren and his brethren said nothing: "that the segregation system [was] actually conceived and . . . actually function[ed] as a means of keeping the Negro in a status of inferiority."[10]

Although *Brown* became one of the Supreme Court's most respected decisions, the ruling ushered in one of the most contentious periods in the Court's history. Under Earl Warren, the Court generated enormous controversy across a range of areas of constitutional law, including the First Amendment's freedoms of speech, press, and religion, and the procedural protections contained in other provisions of the Bill of Rights. The Court's use of the due process clause of the Fourteenth Amendment to apply many of the provisions of the Bill of Rights against the states; its recognition of a general, unenumerated right of privacy; and its use of the equal protection clause of the Fourteenth Amendment to restructure the electoral systems of the states were no less controversial.[11] The Warren Court even sustained criticism in the area in which it achieved its greatest constitutional victory—equal protection and race. In a unanimous ruling handed down fourteen years after *Brown,* the justices set the stage for judicial involvement in the controversial issue of busing when they held that desegregation would be measured by actual results. The Court obliged southern states to eliminate (presumably through "benign" racial classifications) the racial imbalance in public schools that remained after the legal framework of segregation was dismantled.[12]

As a consequence of *Brown*'s eventual rise to iconic status in American political culture and the controversial rulings that followed in its wake, there is no shortage of histories of the LDF's direct attack on school segregation.[13] Scholars have also given considerable attention to the process by which the members of the Supreme Court reached the holding in *Brown*.[14] But, in view of the problematic nature of Chief Justice Warren's legal argumentation, the aspect of *Brown*'s origin to receive perhaps the most attention involves the justices' reasons for declaring public school segregation unconstitutional. Students of *Brown* have borrowed from important work on Supreme Court decision making that political scientists contributed in the half-century since the Court ruled against segregation. One group of scholars—those who believe that institutional considerations are central to any accurate account of *Brown*'s basis—can be subdivided into instrumentalists, who regard institutions merely as potential impediments to the justices' efforts to use law as an *instrument* to realize their personal policy preferences, and noninstrumentalists, who contend that institutions may constitute justices' decisions by providing information concerning normatively appropriate judicial behavior. The former subgroup includes scholars who have related the justices' desegregation votes to the policy preferences of either the leaders of the dominant national alliance of the mid-twentieth century or to elements of the New Deal political coalition.[15] For their part, noninstrumentalists have characterized the ruling as an executive-inspired Cold War imperative, a reflection of the policy preferences of the Eisenhower administration, a response to politicians' requests to remove the volatile issue of segregation from the political landscape, or an effort to complete Franklin Roosevelt's attempt to alter the nature of the Democratic party by undermining the segregationist element of the New Deal coalition for the more fundamental purpose of shifting the balance of power toward the national executive.[16]

But institutional accounts of *Brown* compete with the most commonly held view, which appeared immediately after the decision was announced—that the ruling represented an especially flagrant instance of instrumental decision making by judges. In other words, *Brown* was and is regarded as an *institutionally unrestrained* infusion of the justices' attitudes or personal policy preferences into the abstract language of the Fourteenth Amendment.[17] Senator Burnet Maybank of South Carolina spoke for many southerners in 1954 when he characterized *Brown* as "a shamefully political rather than a judicial decision." It is not surprising that southern politicians considered *Brown* a manifest instance of judicial usurpation of the legislative function. In view of the daunting and seemingly insurmountable impediments that constitutional history and precedent presented to the LDF's direct attack on the separate-but-equal principle, even those sympathetic to the petitioners' cause characterized *Brown* as an instance of unrestrained judicial activism. Wesley Sturges, the dean of Yale Law School, for example, described the decision as "very humane"; "the court," he concluded, "had to make the law" in the case.[18]

This starkly instrumental, or attitudinal, interpretation of the *Brown* decision figures prominently in contemporary conservative criticism of the jurisprudence of the Warren Court. In the decades following *Brown,* these critiques functioned merely as laments against what seemed an unrelenting expansion of civil rights and liberties across a range of issue areas.[19] Since the 1980s, however, when conservative politicians and jurists began a concerted effort to roll back the supposed excesses of the Warren Court by altering the composition of the federal judiciary, these works have served as blueprints for change.[20] In perhaps the most publicized effort to promote such a jurisprudential shift, Robert H. Bork, echoing the substance of earlier conservative critiques of the Warren Court, contends that the *Brown* decision, while one of the Supreme Court's "great triumphs," had "a calamitous effect upon the law." He explains that the non-originalist basis of Chief Justice Warren's opinion for the Court, combined with "the obvious moral rightness of [*Brown's*] result," led the Court to believe mistakenly that the achievement of justice in any situation depends on decision making that is divorced from the original intentions of the Constitution's framers. Bork argues that "the catalogue of the Warren Court's legislative alterations of the Constitution"—*Brown's* unfortunate legacy—"is a thick one and is organized by the theme of egalitarianism." "It is no answer to say that we like the results, no matter how divorced from the intentions of the lawgivers," he declares; to embrace the "unprincipled activism" of the Warren Court is merely to substitute the values of liberal judges who disregarded the law for the policy preferences of political majorities that adhered to constitutionally prescribed methods of lawmaking.[21]

This book challenges the empirical basis of this normative assessment of the Warren Court's constitutional jurisprudence by demonstrating the problematic nature of an attitudinal account of the *Brown* decision. If, as conservative opinion suggests, *Brown* was the crucible in which the Court formulated the interpretive strategy that would inform its civil rights and civil liberties rulings for the next two decades, then critics of the

Warren Court's constitutional decision making must abandon the charge that the individual justices necessarily acted on a liberal preference for egalitarianism in this and subsequent cases. While all of the justices engaged in non-originalist decision making, and some of them based their votes on a policy preference for desegregation, it is necessary to consult the insights of institutional—primarily *noninstrumental*—approaches to Supreme Court decision making in order to explain the behavior of *most* of the justices in *Brown.* One cannot conclude on the basis of this case study that the Warren Court justices' votes in cases other than *Brown* and related racial equality controversies were noninstrumental in nature. But this analysis of *Brown* reveals that instrumental decision making—the self-interested pursuit of a favored policy preference—is not an inevitable consequence of a justice's conviction that the proper resolution of a controversy requires reference to something other than the intentions of the framers of the particular constitutional provision at issue. As important, this study demonstrates that the noninstrumental factors that informed the desegregation votes of certain members of the Court prompt important critical inquiries regarding the nature of American racial politics. These inquiries contrast sharply with the uncritical professions of faith in existing political arrangements that Bork and other critics of the Warren Court combine with their charges of judicial legislation.

In contrast to earlier works on the desegregation decision, this study demonstrates that the puzzle regarding *Brown*'s basis defies an elegant solution. While most general studies of Supreme Court decision making emphasize the degree to which a single (usually instrumental) factor affords predictive success for many decisions across numerous issue areas, such a focus is of limited value, especially if the task is to explain the votes of nine justices in one case. Scholars must recognize that all Supreme Court decisions are combinations of instrumental and noninstrumental factors, and should take to heart Rogers M. Smith's admonition that the most productive inquiries into the Court's decision-making process are those that "focus on the interplay of specified [instrumental and noninstrumental] structures and decisions."[22] While Smith could not realistically expect, at least in the short term, that his observation would do more than provoke thought and perhaps promote a degree of methodological tolerance among scholars whose interest is to develop and test decision-making theories, those who seek to explain the behavior of the nine individuals who voted in *Brown* should regard his point as indisputable.

A thorough, accurate account of *Brown* requires reference to published studies that apply a particular model of Supreme Court decision making to the case and to approaches that have not been utilized for this purpose. Such an account demands a critical analysis of existing studies, since some elegant arguments that employ one model to explain the votes of most or all of the justices are overly broad in their application, while others are either unconvincing or require strengthening. And more than one model may be required to explain a particular vote, since individual justices might have had multiple goal orientations in the case.

This case study uses the various models of Supreme Court decision making as a framework for analysis. Each chapter, save for the first, views *Brown* through the lens of a particular decision-making model, and the chapter titles alert the reader to the explanatory factors to which each model points. The analysis of *Brown*'s basis begins with an assessment of the contribution of an attitudinal understanding of Supreme Court decision making—the strongly instrumental model that supports the conventional view that *Brown* was the product of the justices' liberal value preferences[23]—and then moves to consider the insights that institutional approaches to the Court afford. As noted, institutional decision-making models are of two types: instrumental and noninstrumental. Scholars refer to the former as the strategic or rational choice approach, while the latter type includes both the constitutive and "political regimes" approaches. The strategic approach shares the attitudinalist assumption that policy goals are the primary influence in Supreme Court decision making but avers that constraints, both internal and external to the Court, may impede judicial policy making.[24] The noninstrumental institutional approaches, by contrast, posit that institutions *provide the norms* upon which justices base their decisions. These noninstrumental approaches differ in that the constitutive model puts forth an abstract conception of institutions and places particular emphasis on the notion of a sense of mission or duty that is transmitted through the somewhat indistinct process of judicial socialization.[25] By contrast, the "political regimes" approach locates the Court within the political system or regime and identifies specific political actors (such as executive branch officials) whose own senses of the Court's mission or, more broadly, whose own constitutional views or concerns serve as a source of judicial norms.[26]

The unevenness of the documentary record ensures that a comprehensive analysis of the justices' votes in *Brown,* even one that guards against oversimplification, will yield varying levels of certainty. That said, the present study marshals ample evidence to demonstrate the relevance of noninstrumental approaches to a majority of the justices in *Brown,* and thus reveals the problematic nature of the claim that the ruling set the stage for value-based decision making on the part of the Warren Court.

In order to appreciate the claim that *Brown* was merely a reflection of the values of the justices, it is necessary to come to terms with the significant barriers that the LDF and the petitioners faced when their cases came before the Court in 1952 and again the following year for reargument. These barriers were formidable, especially considering that seven of the nine justices who decided *Brown* had been active participants in the New Deal before joining the Court. As harsh critics of the anti–New Deal decisions that the Supreme Court rendered before Franklin Roosevelt was able to alter the composition of that body through presidential appointment, the New Deal justices were sensitive to the charge of judicial policy making.[27] To provide a sense of the Court's vulnerability to this charge, chapter 1 illuminates the respondents' powerful answers to the arguments that the LDF made on behalf of the petitioners in the case. The lawyers for the school boards emphasized the force of precedent, provided a thorough critique of the social science evidence that the petitioners offered as reason to overturn the line of cases that placed the Court's imprimatur on segregation, noted that courts typically deferred under the Fourteenth Amendment to state determinations of the need for the classifications employed, and offered considerable evidence that the framers of that amendment accepted school segregation. In view of the legal obstacles that the Court faced in *Brown,* supporters as well as opponents of desegregation characterized the ruling as the product of the justices' personal policy preferences.

The development in political science of an attitudinal model of Supreme Court decision making lent credence to the charges of judicial policy making that greeted the *Brown* decision in 1954. As chapter 2 notes, defenders of an attitudinal model contend that judicial independence enables the justices to take advantage of the indeterminacy inhering in legal language and to use law as an instrument for the pursuit of their personal policy preferences. In support of an attitudinal understanding of Supreme Court decision making, and of *Brown* in particular, Michael J. Klarman suggests that the Supreme Court almost inevitably reflects the broader social and political context of the times because the justices are embedded in majoritarian culture.[28] As perhaps the most famous example of this proposition, he argues, *Brown* was rendered at a time when important historical events, such as the fight against a genocidal regime during the Second World War, brought about significant changes in American racial attitudes.

Instructive as it may be to consider the context in which the Court rendered *Brown,* aggregate data cannot provide definitive conclusions about individual behavior. Klarman's strongly instrumental account of *Brown* is incomplete in that he only provides evidence of desegregation policy preferences for Felix Frankfurter, William Douglas, and Robert Jackson. An attitudinal account of *Brown* is also complicated by the fact that the methods scholars have developed for measuring the values of past justices indicate, if anything, that the members of the Court were deeply divided over the issue of elementary school segregation and that certain justices, in voting against segregation, acted contrary to their personal policy preferences. Finally, studies of ideological drift suggest that, relative to their respective first years on the Court, a majority of the justices had become significantly more conservative before they decided *Brown.* While this evidence does not prove that noninstrumental goals informed the desegregation votes of these men, it suggests we cannot assume the justices were part of the current of history that was beginning to liberalize American racial attitudes at midcentury.

A review of the documents regarding the justices' deliberations in the case, featured in chapter 3, further suggests an attitudinal account of *Brown* may be incomplete. Given that *Brown* was a unanimous ruling, attitudinalists would regard as mere hand-wringing the legal objections to desegregation that several members of the Court raised, and they would question whether other justices' legal arguments supporting desegregation were sufficiently strong to explain their votes. But the policy defenses of segregation that two of the southerners, Stanley Reed and Tom Clark, advanced suggest that these justices may have voted for desegregation for reasons other than the satisfaction of their personal policy preferences. And, even assuming that the members of the Court were simply following their policy preferences in *Brown,* nearly all of the justices expressed a willingness to postpone, if not deny, the satisfaction of those preferences by calling for the delay of desegregation in order to minimize the threat of social disorder or violence.

A strategic or rational choice model of Supreme Court decision making helps to compensate for some of the shortcomings of an attitudinal account of *Brown.* The willingness of the justices to delay the implementation of *Brown* fits comfortably within the framework of a strategic understanding of Supreme Court decision making, since the model acknowledges that justices might behave insincerely (i.e., in a manner that is not an accurate reflection of their preferences) in response to external threats to judicial prestige. By examining the constraints that are internal as well as external to the Court, the strategic model also provides a framework for analyzing the process by which the justices resolved their differences over the rule of law and the implementation of a desegregation ruling. The story of the justices' resolution of their differences is significant because, as Chief Justice Warren understood, anything other than unanimity in this case would have borrowed enormous trouble. Ironically, the upshot of Warren's efforts to achieve unanimity was a social science–based rationale regarding the psychological harms of segregation to which certain members of the Court objected, that none of the justices demanded or even defended, and that proved unconvincing to racial progressives and segregationists alike. Finally, by acknowledging the receptiveness of justices to professional considerations, the strategic model provides an explanation of the willingness of Justice Reed to vote against his policy preferences. Failing to secure Reed's vote through bargaining, Warren ultimately achieved unanimity by emphasizing his colleague's isolation and appealing to his sense of loyalty to the Court as an institution.

But a strategic interpretation of *Brown* is not entirely satisfactory either. Since the strategic model acknowledges only limited instances of noninstrumental judicial behavior, it cannot account for justices who did not possess desegregation policy preferences but whose voting behavior revealed a marked commitment to civil rights. As chapter 4 demonstrates, Justice Hugo Black, the erstwhile member of the Ku Klux Klan, was not the only member of the Court (apart from Reed and Clark) who could be classified as something other than a racial progressive. While Justice Jackson was not a defender of segregation, his correspondence demonstrates (contrary to Michael Klarman's suggestion) that he was not an avid reformer of race relations. In spite of the presence of strong incentives and few disincentives for Earl Warren to support desegregation as a national political figure, the public statements that he made before he joined the Court included only references to the importance of avoiding federal oversight of the nation's public schools. The strong support for civil rights that Warren and Black demonstrated over the course of their judicial careers (Jackson died shortly after the Court rendered *Brown*) reveals the limitations of instrumental decision-making models.

In order to understand the desegregation votes of Warren, Black, and Jackson, it is important to consider the insights of the constitutive model, which locates the source of Supreme Court rulings in something other than the justices' personal policy preferences. A constitutive understanding of Supreme Court decision making emphasizes that the process of judicial socialization—through, among other things, legal training, deliberations while on the bench, and the internalization of the social expectation that judges must base their rulings on something other than personal preference—serves as a source of standards for normatively appropriate judicial behavior, that is, for a proper sense of judicial obligation, duty, or mission. With regard to Warren, Black, and Jackson, the documentary record reveals both the operative standards that informed their behavior in *Brown* and a specific source from which they adopted these rules of appropriateness. The justices found compelling the historical argument that informed the petitioners' legal position that, under the Fifth and Fourteenth Amendments, the Court's role or mission in racial discrimination cases should be to afford considerable protection to minorities. The petitioners demonstrated that segregation was predicated not on a desire to promote racial harmony (as the respondents would have it) but on the principle of racial inferiority.

The relevance of the constitutive understanding of Supreme Court decision making to a thorough account of the *Brown* decision extends beyond the desegregation votes of Chief Justice Warren and Justices Black and Jackson. Recent studies of *Brown,* which partly reflect or draw on this model, are especially potent in that they, like the argument in chapter 4, avoid the imprecision to which a decision-making model that posits an abstract notion of legal institutions is prone. The authors of these studies identify concrete sources of political activity that affect judicial decision making (especially the constitutional views or concerns of executive branch officials), but they contend that these institutional influences shape or constitute judicial behavior and do not function merely as potential impediments to instrumental decision making on the part of the justices. As such, these works, which illuminate the constitutional relevance of the Court's connections to elements within the broader political system or regime, are more accurately characterized as part of a "political regimes" approach to Supreme Court decision making.

Mary L. Dudziak, whose scholarship is the focus of chapter 5, emphasizes the relevance to *Brown* of the executive's foreign policy concerns at midcentury. Dudziak suggests that the desegregation decision was a "Cold War imperative," that is, a decision that was intended to serve as an important symbol at a time when the Soviet Union effectively exploited the existence of segregation in the United States in its propaganda campaign against its chief international rival. As evidence for her claim, she focuses on the Truman administration's extended treatment of the Cold War implications of segregation in its *amicus curiae* brief to the Court during the initial hearing of *Brown.*[29] Social expectations for the judiciary precluded the Court from indicating that such extralegal considerations influenced its decision, Dudziak argues, but the seriousness of the international dimension of segregation makes it likely that the justices shared and acted on the executive's foreign policy concerns.

While Dudziak cannot claim that all of the justices viewed desegregation as a Cold War imperative, this chapter points to remarks and voting behavior that indicate foreign policy considerations may have been an additional factor in the desegregation votes of Justices Douglas, Reed, Jackson, and Frankfurter. But the justices who proved most receptive to the international implications of segregation were those who had been appointed by the administration that brought these matters to the Court's attention—Harold Burton, Sherman Minton, and, especially, Harry Truman's former attorney general, Tom Clark. Unlike Clark, who revealed in his spoken and written remarks that he was deeply torn over segregation as a matter of policy, neither Burton nor Minton left sufficient documentation to ascertain their preferences regarding the practice. Like Clark, however, each man was nominated to the Supreme Court by President Truman, whose administration responded to communism in part by combining an illiberal approach to civil liberties (to meet the ostensible threat that domestic radicals posed to national security) with a more permissive approach to civil rights (to prevent the Soviet Union from using racial discrimination in the United States as a propaganda weapon). All three justices had voting records that reflected the administration's posture toward civil liberties and civil rights.

Chapter 6 likewise considers the relevance of the executive branch to the *Brown* decision but focuses instead on the justices' responsiveness to *domestic* political considerations. A thorough account of *Brown*'s basis must address scholarship that points to the relevance of the leadership of the dominant national alliance at that time. Specifically, scholars draw attention to the Truman administration's decision to submit an *amicus* brief for the initial hearing, which followed a substantial increase in the influence of African Americans within the New Deal coalition, and the Eisenhower administration's participation as *amicus curiae* in the rehearing.[30] But critical analysis reveals that the most promising effort to situate *Brown* in the politics of that era is Kevin J. McMahon's argument that the seven members of the Court who were New Deal justices sought to help alter the nature of the Democratic party by weakening the power of southern conservatives.[31] McMahon locates this understanding of *Brown* in the connection between that decision and the efforts of the executive—in particular, the administration of Franklin Roosevelt—to remove the barrier that the southern element of the New Deal coalition presented to the president's progressive constitutional vision of an empowered national executive.

McMahon, however, underestimates the impact on the New Dealers of the unanticipated consequences of Roosevelt's efforts to alter the nature of the Democratic party. Dwight Eisenhower's electoral success in the South in 1952, and, prior to that, the Dixiecrat Revolt at the Democratic convention in 1948, revealed as unfounded the long-standing assumption that southern conservatives were captives of the Democratic party. These events demonstrated that demands for civil rights measures, which a desegregation ruling could inspire, would contribute to the dismemberment of the New Deal coalition, the loss of the Democratic party's majority status, and, ultimately, the *sacrifice* of Roosevelt's constitutional vision.

After critically analyzing Mark A. Graber's suggestion that the justices acted because they believed politicians, including segregationists, had invited them to remove the divisive issue of segregation from the national political landscape in order to preserve existing partisan alignments, chapter 6 reveals that the New Dealers' willingness to risk the negative consequences associated with the destruction of the Democratic coalition stemmed not from a desire to preserve the political status quo (as Graber would have it) but from a belief in the fluidity of the southern political situation.[32] The justices recognized social and political forces that were altering race relations in the South, and their comments regarding these changes reflected a faith that the expansion of liberalism in the region—especially the development of a mutually beneficial relationship between racial minorities and labor, which the New Dealers promoted in their rulings—would at some point offset the loss of southern conservatives to the Republican party. The justices' comments and voting records are consistent with, although they do not prove, McMahon's effort to link *Brown* to Roosevelt's constitutional vision. Yet the New Dealers believed they had contributed to this goal not by taking a progressive stance in an intraparty dispute (as McMahon suggests) but by helping to alter significantly the partisan landscape of the South.

The conclusion summarizes the multiple factors that influenced the justices in *Brown* and emphasizes that the most productive inquiries into Supreme Court decision making are those that focus on the interplay of instrumental and noninstrumental factors. Although one cannot argue on the basis of this case study that Warren Court decisions beyond the area of racial equality were noninstrumental in nature, this analysis of *Brown* demonstrates that instrumental decision making is not a necessary consequence of a justice's determination that the proper resolution of a constitutional controversy demands reference to a standard other than the framers' intentions. Given the centrality of *Brown* to contemporary, conservative criticisms of the jurisprudence of the Warren Court, the implications of the study's narrow focus become consequential when we move beyond the matter of describing the process of Supreme Court decision making. The demonstrated relevance of *noninstrumental* decision-making models to the behavior of *most* of the justices in *Brown* raises— and obliges the Warren Court's critics to confront—important critical inquiries regarding the nature of American racial politics. For example, the point that Chief Justice Warren's desegregation vote was informed by a profound sense of civic obligation, as opposed to the crass pursuit of his personal values, compels us to consider his sympathetic critique of American democracy, which for strategic reasons he excluded from his opinion in *Brown*. Indeed, notwithstanding the significance of Warren's acknowledgment of institutionalized racism in this country, it is necessary to entertain the possibility that his equal protection analysis was superficial in that he failed to recognize more informal and insidious forms of discrimination, such as gender or economic inequality. In order to understand how the critics of the Warren Court have been able to avoid these issues by charging that, beginning with *Brown*, the justices merely engaged in liberal policy making, we must examine the formidable barriers to desegregation, legal and extralegal, that the Court faced in that case.

ONE

Barriers to Desegregation

One of the impediments the LDF faced in its litigation campaign against school segregation was that seven of the nine justices who ultimately decided that issue had been active in the Democratic party before joining the Court. As strong proponents of the New Deal—and, therefore, strong critics of the anti–New Deal decisions that the Supreme Court rendered in the 1930s—these justices were sensitive to the charge that they had usurped the legislative function.[1] The accusation of judicial policy making appeared to be particularly applicable in *Brown,* since all of the petitioners' claims, whether related to traditional legal sources or empirical arguments intended to overcome these legal constraints, were open to challenge. Judicial action in the face of such barriers indicated to many commentators, including scholars who favored desegregation, that the justices based their ruling on something other than legal criteria.

The Initial Hearing (1952)

STARE DECISIS

Precedent was the most evident barrier to a desegregation ruling when the LDF's lawyers first argued *Brown* before the Court in 1952. And *Plessy v. Ferguson* was only the most obvious ruling that placed the Court's imprimatur on segregation.[2] In *Gong Lum v. Rice,* the Court held that Mississippi could require a child of Chinese ancestry to attend a black school under a state law that established separate schools for children of "the white and colored races." Speaking for the Court, Chief Justice William Howard Taft dismissed the equal protection challenge: "Were this a new question, it would call for very full argument and consideration, but we think that it is the same question which has been many times decided to be within the constitutional power of the state legislature to settle without intervention of the federal courts under the Federal Constitution."[3]

The LDF's lawyers sought to overcome this barrier by maintaining the irrelevance of *Plessy* and *Gong Lum* to the current controversy. *Plessy* was inapplicable, they argued, because it involved public transportation, not education. And while *Gong Lum* was an education case, it dealt with a narrow question—whether an Asian child had a right to attend a white school. The Court, in other words, merely assumed the constitutionality of educational segregation; it did not give full argument and consideration to the matter. Furthermore, this assumption, *when* fully argued and considered, "w[as] *rejected* in the *McLaurin* [*v. Oklahoma State Regents for Higher Education*] and *Sweatt* [*v. Painter*] cases in relation to racial distinctions in state graduate and professional education."[4]

Paul Wilson, the assistant attorney general of Kansas, emphasized the controversial nature of these points when he declared during oral argument, "It is sheer sophistry to attempt to distinguish [*Plessy* and *Gong Lum*] from the case that is here presented." Wilson and his colleagues suggested in their brief to the Court that *Plessy* rose "above the specific facts in issue and announce[d] a doctrine applicable to any social situation wherein the two races are brought into contact." Indeed, the Court observed in that case that "the most common instance of [segregation] is connected with the establishment of separate schools for white and colored children which has been held to be a valid exercise of the legislative power even by courts of States where the political rights of the colored race have been longest and most earnestly enforced." *Gong Lum* likewise indicated that school segregation presented no threat to constitutional rights. In that case, the Court "cite[d] sixteen [segregation] cases decided by federal courts and state courts of last resort, including *Plessy v. Ferguson*," and thus meant to declare that there was *no need* to give full argument and consideration to the issue of the constitutionality of the practice.[5]

Finally, the respondents contended that their opponents exaggerated the import of *McLaurin* and *Sweatt*. "We find no statement therein," they maintained, "that would cause us to believe the Court intended to reverse or modify its earlier decisions." Indeed, *Sweatt* clearly responded to the LDF's direct attack on segregation. "Broader issues have been urged for our consideration," the Court acknowledged, "but we adhere to the principle of deciding constitutional questions only in the context of the particular case before the Court." The justices stated explicitly that the Court need not "reach the petitioner's contention that *Plessy v. Ferguson* should be reexamined in the light of contemporary knowledge respecting the purposes of the Fourteenth Amendment and the effects of racial segregation." In view of these passages, the respondents concluded, the Court's refusal "to review the *Plessy* and *Gong Lum* doctrines in its later decisions can only be interpreted to support the view that those cases still stand as expressions of the rule established by the Supreme Court upon the question of racial segregation within the public schools."[6]

EMPIRICAL FINDINGS

In response to the argument that precedent supported the respondents, Spottswood Robinson spoke for all of the petitioners when he maintained during oral argument that *stare decisis,* "while . . . persuasive, is not controlling." He reminded the justices that "this Court has not hesitated to change the course of its decision, although of long standing, when error has been demonstrated."[7] In short, Robinson and his colleagues meant to convince the justices that, if they should find *Plessy* and *Gong Lum* applicable to the current controversy, they should nevertheless abandon those rulings because advances in social scientific knowledge rendered untenable the assumptions supporting the constitutionality of segregated schooling.

To demonstrate that new findings required the Court to overturn *Plessy* and *Gong Lum,* the petitioners' briefs recounted the attack that had been leveled in the lower courts at the underpinnings of the separate-but-equal principle as applied to education. The first part of this challenge held that the respondents failed to meet the baseline equal protection requirement—that a rational relationship exist between the trait used as the basis of a classification and the legislative goal—because both of the rationales supporting school segregation could be maintained no longer.[8] With regard to the segregationists' view that black children presented special educational problems, the LDF's initial petition to the Court stated, "There is no difference between Negro children and white children with respect to ability to learn or to absorb knowledge based upon the racial factor alone." To support this assertion and others to follow, the LDF's lawyers attached an appendix to the petitioners' briefs that summarized and augmented the empirical evidence they had produced in the trial courts. The appendix, signed by over thirty leading social scientists, declared, "The available scientific evidence indicates that much, perhaps all, of the observable differences among various racial and national groups may be adequately explained in terms of environmental differences."[9]

Regarding the primary justification for segregated schooling—that racial separation prevents interracial tension and conflict—the appendix referred to examples of integration in other areas of life. "Comprehensive reviews of such instances clearly establish the fact," the report asserted, "that desegregation has been carried out successfully in a variety of situations although outbreaks of violence have been commonly predicted." Indeed, "under certain circumstances desegregation not only proceeds without major difficulties, but has been observed to lead to the emergence of more favorable attitudes and friendlier relations between races." The document made specific reference to relevant studies in the areas of housing, employment, the armed services and merchant marine, recreation, and general community life.[10]

The petitioners' briefs and social science appendix devoted even more attention to the segregationists' assumption that racial separation does not necessarily imply educational inequality. "Even assuming that the segregated schools attended by [the petitioners] are not inferior to other elementary schools in Topeka with respect to physical facilities, instruction and courses of study," the *Brown* brief stated, "unconstitutional inequality inheres in the retardation of intellectual development and distortion of personality which Negro children suffer as a result of enforced isolation in school from the general public school population." After recounting the expert testimony that the petitioners brought to bear on this matter in the lower courts, the brief asserted "that these conclusions are the consensus of social scientists." The appendix to the brief invoked a survey of academic opinion on segregation in which "a large majority (90%)" of those polled agreed "that, regardless of the facilities which are provided, enforced segregation is psychologically detrimental to the members of the segregated group."[11]

In response to the petitioners' arguments for overturning precedent, the respondents suggested, first, that the supposed consensus among social scientists on the matter of the negative effects of segregation was illusory. T. Justin Moore, the main lawyer for the Virginia respondents, informed the justices that "there were some six or eight thousand persons who were eligible to have that questionnaire [i.e., the survey of academic opinion on segregation] sent to them." Unfortunately, "only thirty-two came from south of the Mason and Dixon line."[12]

The brief for the respondents in the South Carolina case added that the petitioners' social science evidence, which supposedly gave a firm empirical basis to their claims regarding the harms of school segregation, suffered from a fundamental shortcoming, namely a failure to isolate the effects of segregation generally (to say nothing of segregation in education, specifically) from the impact of other social phenomena. This methodological flaw, the brief averred, precluded one from definitively attributing to segregation the supposed psychological damage that the petitioners' witnesses identified in the children who served as subjects for their tests and interviews. Social scientists agree, the respondents maintained, that "Negro children are already aware of race and accompanying value judgments at the preschool age." Thus, the argument "that the schools play an initiating role in creating psychological conflicts" is unfounded.[13]

John Davis, the main attorney for the respondents in the South Carolina case, informed the justices that some of the petitioners' empirical research actually contradicted their claims that segregation, or some other aspect of southern culture, harmed black children. Specifically, Kenneth Clark's doll test—in which he offered black children a choice between a black and a white doll—demonstrated that southern black children were *less* inclined than their counterparts in the North to express a preference for the white doll or to identify the black doll as "bad." Southern black children were also *more* inclined to think of black dolls as "nice." Davis asked rhetorically: "With those results compared, what becomes of the blasting influence of segregation to which Dr. Clark so eloquently testifies?" In answer to this question, the respondents' appellate brief stated, "These experiments would seem to indicate that Negro children in the South are healthier psychologically speaking than those in the North. . . . The results obtained in the broader sample of experiments completely explodes any inference that the 'conflicts' from which Professor Clark's Clarendon County subjects were found to suffer are the result of their education in segregated schools."[14]

The attorneys for the South Carolina school board argued that such findings—which, if anything, suggested that educational segregation reduces psychological damage in black children—corroborated claims regarding the reasonableness of the practice. "The age of starting school is a crucial one in the development of the child's ego structure," they elaborated. Furthermore, the child "is especially sensitive to the accepted social values of his larger environment, because he seeks group identification and personal self-esteem." The fact that children possess racial awareness before entering school thus renders doubtful the wisdom of placing a black child with white children whom he regards as superior and who look upon him as inferior.[15]

The prevention of psychological damage to black children, the South Carolina lawyers believed, complemented the primary benefit of school segregation—the avoidance of racial conflict. In defense of this view,

T. Justin Moore and John Davis emphasized the historical experiences of their respective states. As Moore explained to the justices: "The historical background that exists, certainly in this Virginia situation, with all the strife and the history that we have shown in this record, shows a basis, a real basis, for the classification that has been made."[16]

BURDEN OF PROOF

Davis reminded the justices that, even if the empirical case against segregation were not so flawed, the Court would have to rule in favor of the respondents. Under the reasonableness requirement for equal protection, courts deferred to state determinations of the need for the classifications employed. In the current controversy, in other words, those who challenged segregation assumed the burden of proof. In Davis's view, the petitioners obviously failed to meet this burden. "It cannot be said," he declared, "that the testimony will all be one way. Certainly it cannot be said that a legislature conducting its public schools in accordance with the wishes of its people . . . [is] acting merely by caprice or by racial prejudice."[17]

George Hayes and James Nabrit, counsel for the petitioners in the District of Columbia case, challenged the notion that judicial deference was appropriate in segregation cases. They reminded the justices that the Court had said in the wartime Fifth Amendment cases, *Hirabayashi v. United States*[18] and *Korematsu v. United States*,[19] that racial classifications are "suspect" and thus presumed unconstitutional. True, the Court placed its imprimatur in those cases on the curfew and internment orders, respectively, that the federal government directed against Japanese-Californians. But, the attorneys suggested, the import of these rulings was that only the wartime effort "to prevent sabotage and espionage" would justify classifying American citizens according to race.[20]

Spottswood Robinson and Louis Redding sought to give the justices additional reason to believe that judicial deference was unwarranted in cases involving racial classifications. They examined the legislative history behind the laws at issue in the Virginia and Delaware cases to show that, Davis's assurances to the contrary notwithstanding, racial prejudice typically informed race-based laws. Robinson thought it telling that the constitutional convention responsible for Virginia's segregation law also sought to eliminate through suffrage restrictions "every Negro voter who can be gotten rid of legally without materially impairing the numerical strength of the white electorate." He maintained that this fact demonstrated that the purpose of the segregation law was "to limit the educational opportunities of the Negro." Redding detected a similar motivation in Delaware's segregation laws, given that the state "has never, by the normal process of ratification, ratified the Fourteenth Amendment."[21]

On behalf of the respondents in the District of Columbia case, Milton Korman provided an alternate, narrow interpretation of the Japanese curfew and internment cases—that heightened judicial scrutiny is appropriate *only* in instances in which government detains or imprisons persons because of their race. But, if the Court were to agree with the petitioners and regard all racial classifications as suspect, the respondents informed the justices that they faced the politically unpalatable task of giving voice to arguments similar to those that Robinson and Redding put forth. Predictably, the lawyers for the school boards responded to these attacks with righteous indignation and restatements of the view that a concern for the welfare of black and white children alike informed the segregation laws.[22] Such strong denials, coupled with the absence in the Japanese curfew and interment cases of an explanation for according racial classifications suspect status, made it seem essential that any ruling that, in contrast to the Japanese cases, *invalidated* governmental action contain some discussion of the Court's reasons for believing that state and federal officials were no longer deserving of judicial deference.

THE FRAMERS' INTENTIONS

The petitioners may not have been convinced that beneficent intentions informed segregation policies. But, after oral argument, they certainly understood that the respondents' arguments had enormous potential to preserve the status quo. The penetrating questions that certain justices directed at Thurgood Marshall and his colleagues echoed each of the points that the respondents raised. Responding to the petitioners' suggestion of racist motivations on the part of segregationist legislatures (and thus the need to abandon deference in race cases), Chief Justice Fred Vinson asked whether the Congress responsible for proposing the Fourteenth Amendment could have had "the purpose of just punishing the Negro" when it segregated the schools of the District of Columbia. On a number of occasions, Justice Stanley Reed intimated that the need to avoid racial friction seemed a more compelling explanation of the purpose of such laws.[23]

If the justices were to accept Reed's point, and thus decline to place the burden of proof on state and federal officials in race cases, the petitioners' chances for a favorable ruling appeared slim. Through aggressive questioning, Justice Felix Frankfurter pointed up the problematic nature of the petitioners' social science evidence, which supposedly demonstrated the unreasonableness and harms of school segregation. He concluded that such evidence is "a very different thing from . . . things that are weighed and measured and are fungible."[24]

Justice Hugo Black posed the most basic question of the hearings when, during a discussion of the supposed harms of school segregation, he asked the petitioners' lawyers in the Kansas case: "Why do you say that [the issue] in this case depends upon the findings of fact at all?" Black's query reflected the perspective of a justice who would become renowned for his belief that the intentions of the framers of the Constitution represented the only legitimate basis for constitutional interpretation. The petitioners' lawyers answered that they merely followed the logic of the Court's rulings in *Sweatt* and *McLaurin,* which acknowledged the relevance of empirical considerations to equal protection cases involving graduate and professional programs.[25]

By contrast, the brief for the respondents in the South Carolina case took the position that the Court is obliged to adhere to traditional sources of constitutional interpretation. Since historical analysis demonstrates that those responsible for the passage and ratification of the Fourteenth Amendment did not intend to prohibit segregation, the justices should declare the irrelevance of psychological and sociological data to the current controversy. As the brief stated, the background of the Amendment "compels the conclusion that it has no such scope as is claimed by [the] appellants." For "23 [of the 37 states in the Union at the time of the adoption of the Fourteenth Amendment] continued, or adopted soon after the Amendment, statutory or constitutional provisions calling for racial segregation in the public schools." At oral argument, John Davis added, "The same Congress [that proffered the Fourteenth Amendment in June 1866] proceeded to establish, or to continue[,] separate schools in the District of Columbia. . . . From that day to this, Congress has not wavered in that policy."[26]

The Rehearing (1953)

THE FRAMERS' INTENTIONS

The intentions of the framers of the Fourteenth Amendment figured prominently in the reargument order that the Court issued six months after the initial hearing.[27] The surprise that this order must have engendered in the lawyers on both sides of the controversy was exceeded only by the news shortly before the beginning of the Court's next term that

Chief Justice Vinson had died of a heart attack. Earl Warren, who was governor of California at the time, would replace Vinson.[28]

In sharp contrast to their efforts in 1952, the LDF's lawyers would have much to say to the new chief justice and his brethren about the intentions informing the Fourteenth Amendment. Nevertheless, they found the barriers to desegregation as imposing as they had been the preceding year. At best, they could inform the Court that the members of the Thirty-Ninth Congress had not sought to exclude public school segregation from the reach of the Fourteenth Amendment.[29] The framers had neither proscribed nor sought to protect segregated schooling, the petitioners' brief maintained, because "compulsory public education at that time was the exception rather than the rule."[30]

Although they tacitly conceded the absence of evidence that the framers specifically sought to eradicate public school segregation, the LDF's lawyers argued that such a pinched understanding of constitutional intent does not accord with constitutional history. Rather, the framers of the Fourteenth Amendment sought to proscribe *all* forms of racial caste legislation, and thus did not want to limit judges to the particular evils that inspired the amendment.[31] As the petitioners' brief stated,

> The intention of the framers with respect to any specific example of caste state action—in the instant cases, segregated education—cannot be determined solely on the basis of a tabulation of contemporaneous statements mentioning the specific practice. The framers were formulating a constitutional provision setting broad standards for determination of the relationship of the state to the individual. In the nature of things they could not list all the specific categories of existing state activity which were to come within the constitutional prohibitions.[32]

The petitioners, in short, maintained that the provisions of the Fourteenth Amendment were intended to be "living," or to have an open texture, in the sense that judges could make the amendment's concepts relevant to contemporary circumstances.

The notion of a living Constitution as applied to the *powers* of government had been an accepted part of American constitutional jurisprudence since at least the end of the New Deal. Yet no jurisprudential consensus had developed that judges should regard the constitutional *rights* of individuals in a similar manner.[33] In order to address the concerns that the Democratic members of the Court had regarding judicial usurpation of the legislative function, the petitioners argued that, at least with regard to the Fourteenth Amendment, fidelity to constitutional intent obliges judges to expand individual rights as circumstances require. Thus, even if the justices agreed with the respondents' contention that the framers of the Fourteenth Amendment accepted school segregation, they could still invalidate the practice if they embraced the petitioners' argument that the framers championed the notion of a living Constitution. An understanding of constitutional interpretation authorizing judges to prohibit forms of racial caste legislation that the framers *failed to consider* presumably allows judges to invalidate legislation that could be *demonstrated to be* caste legislation, contrary to the framers' assumptions.

As evidence that the framers of the Fourteenth Amendment thought it appropriate for judges to expand the meaning of a constitutional right to apply against instances of governmental behavior that the framers themselves had not considered, or had even regarded as constitutional, the petitioners referred, first, to the Amendment's language: "Congress used broad comprehensive language [as opposed to the more concrete phraseology typical of statutes] to define the standards necessary to guarantee complete federal protection." Such language, they maintained, was chosen deliberately by the members of the Thirty-Ninth Congress, a majority of whom were Radical Republicans and thus "products of the great Abolitionist tradition." Abolitionism, which came into being to address the evils of slavery, was "dedicated to the equalitarian principles of real and complete equality for all men."[34]

The petitioners contended that "the Fourteenth Amendment was actually the culmination of the determined efforts of the Radical Republican majority in Congress to incorporate into our fundamental law the well-defined equalitarian principle of complete equality for all without regard for race or color." Congress's original version of the Civil Rights Act of 1866, for example, "possessed scope sufficiently broad in the opinion of many Congressmen to entirely destroy all state legislation based on race." The House narrowed the scope of the legislation to include only the important but minimal protections of life and property, in part because a majority of its members "believed that so sweeping a measure could not be justified under the Constitution as it stood." They also knew, though, "that the Fourteenth Amendment was in process of preparation and would itself have scope exceeding that of the original draft of the Civil Rights Bill." Indeed, one Democratic opponent of the proposed amendment charged that the measure would destroy all state legislation that distinguished among citizens on the basis of race. Representative John Bingham of Ohio, who introduced the proposed Fourteenth Amendment to the House and had moved to narrow the scope of the original civil rights bill, did not dispute this claim. Senator Jacob M. Howard of Michigan, who opened the debate in the Senate over the proposed amendment, received no challenge to his understanding that the amendment would eradicate all caste legislation in the United States.[35]

The petitioners added that those individuals responsible for ratifying the Fourteenth Amendment demonstrated that they agreed with the framers' broad understanding of the measure. To gain readmission to the Union, the states of the former Confederacy had to ratify the Fourteenth Amendment and "modify their constitutions and laws in conformity therewith." The new constitutions of these states were "without exception . . . free of any requirement or specific authorization of segregated schools." Furthermore, "no law compelling segregated schools was enacted until after it had been readmitted" to the Union. The overwhelming majority of the twenty-two Union states also indicated that the Fourteenth Amendment prohibited educational segregation. Of those states that did not already respect the principle of racial equality in education, five "adjusted their school laws almost simultaneously with their ratification of the Amendment," while eight others merely "deferred attuning their school laws with the keynote of the Amendment until several years after it had become the law of the land." Only two states—West Virginia and Missouri—continued to require segregated schools after ratifying the Fourteenth Amendment.[36]

John Davis provided a powerful indictment of the petitioners' treatment of the intentions informing the Fourteenth Amendment. He directly challenged the claim that the amendment's framers had neither proscribed nor sought to protect segregated schools. The behavior of the Thirty-Ninth Congress, Davis contended, provides the most compelling evidence that the framers accepted school segregation. Returning to a point he had made during oral argument the preceding year, Davis reminded the justices that the very Congress responsible for framing the Fourteenth Amendment established segregated schools in the District of Columbia. In the same year that Congress formulated both the Civil Rights Act and the Fourteenth Amendment, he observed, that body "passed a donation of certain lots [in the District of Columbia] to be given to schools for Negroes only," and then enacted "a second Act . . . dealing with the distribution of funds between the Negro and the white schools" of the District. In Davis's view, "it is no answer to say that Congress is not controlled by the Fourteenth Amendment." He asked, "Is it conceivable to any man that Congress should submit to the states an amendment destroying their right to segregated schools and should contemporaneously and continuously institute a regime of segregated schools in the District of Columbia?"[37]

Davis added that the behavior of the states after ratifying the Fourteenth Amendment revealed a similar understanding of the Amendment's implications for school segregation. "Of the thirty-seven states that were then in existence," he said, "there were [only] about five . . . where there had been segregation, and they contemporaneously discontinued" the practice after ratification. With regard to those Union states that delayed school desegregation for several years after they had ratified the amendment, Davis, in contrast to the LDF's lawyers, emphasized the implications of the delay rather than of the eventual shift to mixed schools. But he reserved his most biting commentary for the petitioners' attempt to link the states of the former Confederacy with an understanding that the Fourteenth Amendment proscribes segregated schools. Where the brief for the petitioners emphasized that none of the constitutions for the eleven Reconstructed states required or authorized educational segregation, and that none of these states enacted school segregation laws until after they had gained readmission to the Union, Davis stressed the composition of the legislatures that ultimately embraced segregation. "Of the reconstructed states who ratified in order to get their . . . congressmen and senators back to Washington," he said, eight "Republican controlled" legislatures "passed statutes continuing or immediately establishing segregated schools." He exclaimed that, if "there was any place where the Fourteenth Amendment and its sponsors would have blown the bugle for mixed schools and asserted that the Fourteenth Amendment had settled the question, surely it would have been those eight states under Reconstruction legislation, sympathetic to the party which was responsible for the submission of the Fourteenth Amendment."[38]

Davis also challenged the petitioners' effort to link the framers of the Fourteenth Amendment with the notion of a living or open-textured Constitution. The "first fallacy" contained in the petitioners' brief, he argued, "is the assumption . . . that the . . . abolitionist crusade . . . was directed not only against slavery but against segregation in schools." "The thrust . . . of the abolitionist crusade," he insisted, "was directed toward one thing, and one thing only: the abolition of slavery, and from that nothing can be deduced which is helpful to the Court in its study of this section of history." Not surprisingly, then, when the Thirty-Ninth Congress debated the Fourteenth Amendment, the "constant claim" of many of those who favored the measure was that "it was intended [merely] to make the [final—i.e., narrow—version of the] Civil Rights Act not only constitutional, but to make it irrepealable." Davis suggested that the LDF's lawyers erred in assuming that broad appeals to racial equality by certain proponents of the amendment reflected an intention on the part of the entire body.[39]

Justice Frankfurter, who was as aggressive in his questioning of the petitioners' view of the history of the Fourteenth Amendment as he was in his examination of their social science evidence, contributed one of the most damaging arguments to their contention that the framers intended to prohibit all forms of race-based legislation. Frankfurter asked Thurgood Marshall whether he thought "the Fifteenth Amendment was redundant, superfluous." Had Marshall persisted in his initial, ill-considered response—that the Fifteenth Amendment was "definitely not" superfluous—he would have found himself in the unenviable position of having to explain how a right to desegregated schooling could be contained in the Fourteenth Amendment if Congress determined that it had to pass a separate amendment to protect a more fundamental interest in equal voting rights. Immediately reversing his position, he responded affirmatively when Frankfurter asked, "So if [the Fifteenth Amendment] had not been there, [the right to suffrage] would have been included in the Fourteenth?" Marshall said he could not bring himself to "say a constitutional amendment is superfluous," but he conceded that his line of reasoning rendered the Fifteenth Amendment "an extra."[40] The LDF's chief litigator apparently preferred the profound awkwardness of relegating the Fifteenth Amendment to the status of a constitutional irrelevance to the devastating implications that arguing otherwise would have had for the petitioners' cases.

The lawyers for the LDF could hope that, if the justices did not find their version of the intentions of the framers and ratifiers of the Fourteenth Amendment compelling, they would regard it as sufficiently powerful to declare the debate between the legal adversaries inconclusive. On behalf of the Eisenhower administration as *amicus curiae,* J. Lee Rankin, assistant attorney general for the United States, championed the idea of the indeterminacy of the history surrounding the Fourteenth Amendment.[41] If the Court accepted this argument, however, the justices still had to reach one more conclusion in order for the petitioners to have any hope of judicial support. The justices had to come to the same conclusion they would have to reach if they determined that the framers supported segregation and did not create an open-textured amendment—that investigation into the specific intentions of those individuals responsible for the Fourteenth Amendment did not exhaust the search for the meaning of that provision.[42]

OTHER LEGAL BARRIERS

In order to provide the justices with an alternative legal basis for a desegregation order, the LDF's lawyers sought, as they had in 1952, to reconcile such a ruling with the Court's earlier decisions. In a departure from their strategy of the preceding year, however, Marshall and his colleagues abandoned their claim that the *Plessy* decision was inapplicable to the present controversy. Instead, they portrayed *Plessy* as a departure from the egalitarianism of the Court's earlier Fourteenth Amendment rulings. In defense of this proposition, the petitioners' brief contended that "all the early cases" had as their thesis "that law must not distinguish between colored and white persons." In "the *Slaughter House Cases* . . .—the first case decided under the Fourteenth Amendment—the Court, drawing on its knowledge of an almost contemporaneous event, recognized that the Fourteenth Amendment secured to Negroes full citizenship rights and prohibited any state action discriminating against them as a class on account of their race." And, in "*Strauder v. West Virginia,* . . . the Court . . . viewed the Fourteenth Amendment in the same light and stated that its enactment was aimed to secure for the Negro all the civil rights enjoyed by white persons." The opinion also "explicitly stated . . . that the Amendment prevented laws from distinguishing between colored and white persons." The petitioners submitted that "there can be no doubt . . . that, had the state regulation approved in *Plessy v. Ferguson* been before the Court that rendered the initial interpretations of the Fourteenth Amendment, the regulation would have been held a violation of the Federal Constitution."[43]

In another departure from their strategy of the previous year, the petitioners conceded that the Court's more recent decisions—the university desegregation rulings—found *Plessy* relevant to the issue of school segregation. They emphasized, instead, that *Sweatt* and *McLaurin* belied the assumption of the *Plessy* majority that segregation is not inherently unequal. In those cases, the Court acknowledged the relevance of intangible considerations to the matter of educational equality and the detrimental effect that segregation has upon learning, even if the educational facilities for each race are physically equal. And the petitioners contended that the empirical evidence they had presented to the Court the preceding year demonstrated that segregation has a similar effect on students at the elementary and secondary school levels.[44]

The petitioners complemented their reference to the social science evidence regarding segregation with a more elaborate rendering of the argument that Spottswood Robinson and Louis Redding had presented to the justices in 1952—that legislatures were undeserving of judicial deference regarding their claims of the need for and the harmlessness of school segregation. In view of the weaknesses in the empirical case against school segregation, which the respondents had emphasized during oral argument the preceding year, it is not surprising that the petitioners' brief for the rehearing sought to shift the burden of proof to the respondents. In this effort, the brief provided considerably more historical evidence that racial hostility, as opposed to a desire for racial harmony, informed the passage of segregation laws. Suggesting that the Court had already accepted the view that oppressive designs typically informed governmental discrimination on the basis of race, the brief also made reference, as had George Hayes and James Nabrit in 1952, to the Japanese curfew and internment cases *Hirabayashi* and *Korematsu,* which identified such classifications as "suspect."[45]

John Davis surely spoke for all of the respondents when, in response to the petitioners' effort to characterize *Plessy* as an anomalous departure from an egalitarian body of case law, he emphasized that "this Court had not once but seven times, I think it is, pronounced in favor of the 'separate but equal' doctrine." While conceding that the Court had never regarded its constitutional rulings as unchangeable, Davis suggested that "somewhere, sometime to every principle comes a moment of repose when it has been so often announced, so confidently relied upon, so long continued, that it passes the limits of judicial discretion and disturbance."[46]

Davis's position had already received a complementary argument from the bench. When Justice Frankfurter questioned Thurgood Marshall, he suggested that broad references to equality in Fourteenth Amendment case law prior to *Plessy* were not necessarily statements of support for desegregation. Specifically, Frankfurter looked skeptically on Marshall's interpretation of the *Slaughter House Cases.* While the justice regarded as uncontroversial the argument "that the . . . target of the Fourteenth Amendment . . . was to give Negroes certain rights," he suggested that "one of the difficulties . . . that ha[d] to be remedied by later cases" was to give concrete meaning to "the intimation of Justice [Samuel] Miller that [the Fourteenth Amendment] related exclusively to equalizing things" for blacks. Frankfurter might have explained that, as even the petitioners noted in their brief, the *Slaughter House Cases* stated that "the evil to be remedied by [the equal protection] clause" was "the existence of laws in the states . . . which discriminated *with gross injustice and hardship* against them as a class." Similarly, in *Strauder* (again, as even the petitioners noted), the Court concluded that the Fourteenth Amendment "was designed to assure the colored race the enjoyment of *all the civil rights that under the law are enjoyed by white persons.*"[47] The petitioners' assertions to the contrary notwithstanding, such language does not demonstrate clearly that the Court that rendered each decision would have regarded the state regulation approved in *Plessy* as a violation of the Fourteenth Amendment.

Justices Frankfurter and Reed also lent support to the respondents by criticizing the petitioners' argument that the university cases maintained the inherent inequality of segregated schooling. The justices emphasized, as had the respondents the preceding year, that the Court explicitly declined in *Sweatt* and *McLaurin* to rule that the separate-but-equal doctrine was a contradiction in terms.[48]

Davis complemented the justices' point by attacking the petitioners' claim that the empirical case against segregation demonstrated the inherent inequality of the practice at the lower levels of education. Reminding the justices of the weaknesses in the social science evidence of the petitioners, Davis concluded that "it was late indeed in the day to disturb [segregation] on any theoretical or sociological basis." Before considering the evidence, which Davis and his colleagues had previously criticized at length, he reminded the Court of the concrete benefits that blacks currently enjoyed under segregation. The state of South Carolina, he said, "has now provided those 2,800 Negro children [of Clarendon School District No. 1] with schools as good in every particular" as those provided to whites. "In fact, because of their being newer, they may even be better. There are good teachers, the same curriculum as in the schools for the [county's] 295 whites." He asked rhetorically, "Who is going to disturb that situation?" Refusing to concede the validity of the petitioners' sociological argument that intangible considerations rendered the state's segregated schools unequal, he posed another question: Would placing black and white children in one school room "make [them] any happier? Would they learn more quickly[?] Would their lives be more serene?" Noting that "children of that age are not the most considerate animals in the world," he intimated that, contrary to the petitioners' expectations, desegregation could have a negative impact on the personalities of black children. He also wondered, in the case of Clarendon School District No. 1 in South Carolina, whether "white children [would] be prevented from getting a distorted idea of racial relations if they sat with [a majority of] Negro children?"[49]

Davis joined T. Justin Moore in challenging the petitioners' argument concerning the inappropriateness of judicial deference to segregationist legislatures. Davis and his colleague insisted, as they had the preceding year, that the burden of proof belonged properly with the petitioners. For it was not racism but a concern for the well-being of the children of both races that informed the school segregation laws before the Court. Putting the matter in terms that should have resonated with the seven members of the Court who had been active in the Democratic party—and thus strong critics of the anti–New Deal decisions of the Court—Moore reminded the justices that the two jurists most respected by contemporary economic liberals, Louis Brandeis and Oliver Wendell Holmes, were themselves strong proponents of judicial deference to legislative decision making. Although Moore conveniently ignored the fact that Holmes and Brandeis did not believe that the principle of judicial deference extended to legislative infringement of the liberties of speech or press, neither he nor Davis received questions from the bench on the issue of burden of proof or, for that matter, on their treatment of the import of case law.[50]

AN EXTRALEGAL BARRIER

The petitioners faced yet another barrier to a desegregation ruling when the justices turned their attention to the practical matter of enforcing such a judgment. Even though two of the five questions in the Court's reargument order dealt with enforcement concerns, the LDF's lawyers devoted a mere 8 pages of their 235-page brief to the issue.[51] Furthermore, those pages dismissed concerns the justices might have had over the prospect of hostility among large segments of the southern population. In a statement that convinced none but the converted, the petitioners informed the Court that "the states in question are inhabited in the main by law-abiding people who up to now have relied upon what they believe—erroneously, as we have demonstrated—to be the law. It cannot be presumed that they will not obey the law expounded by this Court." And, given the respondents' alleged failure to provide compelling reasons for delay, the brief included no suggestions regarding the form that an order for gradual adjustment should take. Instead, the petitioners insisted that the personal nature of constitutional rights necessitated the immediate enforcement of a desegregation order.[52]

Assistant Attorney General J. Lee Rankin endured the brunt of Justice Robert H. Jackson's combative questioning, in spite of the fact that the LDF's lawyers certainly deserved judicial reproach for their apparent insouciance. Toward the end of his presentation, Rankin began his discussion of the government's position, which the Eisenhower administration had adopted from the Truman administration, that the Court should direct the district courts not to demand prompt desegregation but to require the states to dismantle segregated schooling "with deliberate speed." Jackson quickly interrupted with the suggestion that, "even if we said that the state statutes or state constitutional provisions authorizing segregation were unconstitutional, local custom would still perpetuate it in most districts of the states that really want it." Echoing the petitioners' faith in public compliance, Rankin responded, "We do not assume that once this Court pronounces what the Constitution means in this area that our people are not going to try to abide by it and be in accord with it as rapidly as they can." Having none of this, the justice shot back: "I do not think a court can enter a decree on that assumption, particularly in view of the fact that for seventy-five years the 'separate but equal' doctrine has prevailed in the cases that came before us within the recent past, indicating that it still had not been complied with in many cases." After establishing that he anticipated considerable resistance to a desegregation decision, Jackson then took Rankin to task for failing to provide the Court with sufficient guidance on the appropriate form for such a decree.[53]

The Court received no better assistance from the respondents on the question of the appropriate form of a desegregation decree. John Davis's refusal to provide guidance, however, stemmed not from the formidability of the task but from his assessment of the Court's equitable powers. In response to the Court's fourth query,[54] he said, "As to the question of the right of the Court to postpone the remedy, we think that [in]heres in every court of equity." As to "whether the Court should formulate a decree," however, he declared, "Your Honors do not sit, and cannot sit as a glorified Board of Education for the State of South Carolina or any other state. Neither can the District Court." Should the Supreme Court "find that inequality is being practiced in the schools, it can enjoin its continuance." But "neither this Court nor any other court . . . can sit in the chairs of the legislature of South Carolina and mold its educational system. . . . The State of South Carolina must devise the alternative. It establishes the schools, it pays the funds, and it has the sole power to educate its citizens."[55]

After the Announcement (1954)

The only matter about which the respondents felt more strongly than the Court's lack of authority to devise the means by which school districts would make the transition from a segregated to a desegregated system was, of course, the Court's lack of authority even to declare segregation unconstitutional. With a sense of confidence borne of his performance before the Supreme Court, the efforts of his colleagues, and the weight of the legal materials supporting the respondents, John Davis thought that at least seven of the justices were likely to vote to sustain the constitutionality of segregated schooling. Nearly six months after concluding the reargument of *Brown,* however, Davis's confidence gave way to shock and dismay.[56] It would have been enough of a surprise for Davis had a bare majority of the Court voted to end school segregation; the Court's unanimity must have struck him as remarkable.

Surely Governor Herman Talmadge of Georgia gave voice to the thoughts of Davis, and of segregationists generally, when immediately after the ruling he declared bitterly that the Court had reduced the Constitution to a "mere scrap of paper." The justices, he said, had "blatantly ignored all law and precedent and usurped from the Congress and the people the power to amend the Constitution, and from the Congress the authority to make the laws of the land." In sweeping aside eighty-eight years of "sound judicial precedent," he continued, the Court had "repudiated the greatest legal minds of our age and lowered itself to the level of common politics." Such criticisms of form were more common at this time than statements of outright defiance. But Senator James Eastland of Mississippi took Talmadge's sentiment to its logical (and ultimate) conclusion. "The South," he said, "will not abide by nor obey this legislative decision by a political court."[57]

Eastland was one of ninety-six southern congressmen who, in March 1956, signed the "Southern Manifesto," a statement of protest against *Brown.* "Commend[ing] the motives of those States which have declared the intention to resist forced integration by any lawful means," the document excoriated the justices for undertaking "to exercise their naked judicial power and substitute . . . their personal political and social ideas for the established law of the land." Echoing the arguments of the lawyers for the school boards, the document emphasized that "the debates preceding the submission of the 14th amendment clearly show that there was no intent that it should affect the systems of education maintained by the States," and that "the very Congress which proposed the amendment subsequently provided for segregated schools in the District of Columbia."[58]

Brown's defenders were no more confident that the justices had grounded their ruling in something more substantial than personal preference. George Meany, president of the American Federation of Labor, suggested that the decision was "a matter of simple justice." The Court, he said, had announced "a policy that is essential in a country where all people are equal and there is no place for distinction as to race, creed or color." Adding the force of expert opinion to the union chief's assessment, Professor Avery Craven of the University of Chicago contended, likewise, that the ruling "was a recognition of an evolving concept based on present day social facts and requirements rather than on historical facts." And the editors of *The Washington Evening Star* asserted that, while the desegregation ruling lends "sturdy vitality" to the old saw "that the law is what the judges say it is," "concern over a dubious assumption of power by the court . . . does not alter the fact that this decision finds much support in wisdom and fairness."[59]

The passage of time and the arguments of jurists and scholars did nothing to alter the conventional view regarding the instrumental basis of *Brown*. When he delivered the annual Holmes Lectures at Harvard Law School in 1958, Learned Hand, the august former appellate court judge of the second circuit, declined to brand as illegitimate judicial decisions that contravened the framers' intentions. "I cannot believe," he argued, "that any of us would say that the 'meaning' of an utterance is exhausted by the specific content of the utterer's mind at the moment." Hand insisted, however, that, in a democracy committed to the rule of law, it is "absolutely essential to confine the power [of judicial review] to the need that evoked it: that is, it was and always has been necessary to distinguish between the frontiers of another 'Department's' authority and the propriety of its choices within those frontiers." Although he failed to articulate a standard that would prevent the Court from "assum[ing] the role of a third legislative chamber," he nevertheless concluded that *Brown* was an example of impermissible judicial legislation. "It seems to me," he stated, "that we must assume that [the Court] did mean to reverse the 'legislative judgment' by its own appraisal." As Gerald Gunther notes, "Southern editorial writers quickly jumped on the bandwagon, cheering . . . Hand's criticism of *Brown*."[60]

Herbert Wechsler, who delivered the Holmes Lectures the following year, reinforced Hand's critique of *Brown*'s basis, although he was careful to express his sympathy with the result of the decision. "For one of my persuasion," he confessed, "the school decision . . . stirs the deepest conflict I experience in testing the thesis I propose." Wechsler also emphasized that he did not find troubling the Court's refusal to abide by the traditional materials of constitutional interpretation: "The words [of the Fourteenth Amendment] are general and leave room for expanding content as time passes and conditions change." His "problem inhere[d] strictly in the reasoning of the opinion." The Court's treatment of social fact, or the supposed harms of segregation, he believed, hardly seemed sufficient to justify the result in the present case. The social scientists and expert witnesses in the lower courts were not of one mind that segregation had the negative effects that the Court mentioned. And it was not clear whether the witnesses who acknowledged such harm compared the "position [of the black child] under separation with that under integration where the whites were hostile to his presence and found ways to make their feelings known," or whether the point of comparison was simply "an integrated school where he was happily accepted and regarded by the whites." Similarly, Wechsler wondered whether the Court denied the existence and relevance of "the benefits that [segregation] entailed," such as a "sense of security" for black children or "the absence of hostility." He warned that "courts ought to be cautious to impose a choice of values on the other branches or a state, based upon the Constitution, only when they are persuaded, on an adequate and principled analysis, that the choice is clear." Wechsler saw no principled basis for the value choice that the justices made in *Brown*.[61]

The willingness of nonsouthern jurists and scholars and of *Brown*'s defenders to concede that the decision smacked of politics rather than law made it difficult to dismiss as the sour sentiment of segregationists the emotional denunciations of the ruling voiced by the likes of Governor Talmadge and Senator Eastland. The difference between the groups was one of tone rather than substance. The conventional view that *Brown* merely reflected the liberal policy preferences of the justices became even more firmly established after academic opinion embraced a decision-making model that, likewise, portrayed Supreme Court justices as unrestrained makers of public policy.

TWO

The Attitudes of the Justices

Since the 1960s, most political scientists in the field of judicial studies, and some law professors, have accepted a strongly instrumental, or attitudinal, understanding of Supreme Court decision making. Recent scholarship lends credence to the attitudinal model—and to a strongly instrumental interpretation of *Brown*—by demonstrating that the desegregation decision was consistent with the liberalization of American racial attitudes that occurred in the middle of the twentieth century. Yet aggregate data regarding the social and political context in which the Court rendered *Brown* cannot provide definitive conclusions about the behavior of individual justices. While some information gives the impression that certain members of the Court favored desegregation, methods that scholars have devised to measure ideological values suggest, if anything, that a number of the justices may have served as counterexamples to societal trends by voting contrary to their values when they ruled against segregation.

A Strongly Instrumental View of the Court

The conventional view that *Brown* merely reflected the personal policy preferences of the justices earned academic respectability when Glendon Schubert published *The Judicial Mind* in 1965. In criticizing a legalistic understanding of judging, Schubert followed the lead of C. Herman Pritchett, who brought the force of the behavioral movement in political science—with its emphasis on empirical over normative concerns, its aspiration that the study of politics become a predictive science, and its shift of focus from formal institutions to individual acts or forms of behavior—to bear on the field of public law. "We are all sufficiently legal and political realists to repudiate the mystique of a constitutional law spun in a seamless web," Schubert declared. Yet, while acknowledging his intellectual debt to Pritchett, he also stated that, unlike his colleague, he would not dilute the force of his work with descriptions of cases "in terms of their 'facts,' the ad hoc theoretical categories employed by the justices themselves in their opinions, legal doctrines, constitutional principles, and philosophical maxims of judicial parsimony (such as *stare decisis,* or judicial activism versus restraint)." "My view of decisions," Schubert explained, "is that these are the products of sets of judicial attitudes that have been activated by particular stimuli; and from this perspective, the attitudes of the justices are of much more fundamental importance than the decisions."[1] Because of the consistency in voting that he observed for justices serving between 1946 and 1968, Schubert assumed that the policy preferences of Supreme Court justices remain stable over time.[2]

David W. Rohde and Harold J. Spaeth supported Schubert's strongly instrumental understanding of Supreme Court decision making by arguing that the institutional context in which the justices (as opposed to lower federal or state court judges) operate serves as anything but a limitation on the Court's policy-making role. The justices' lifetime tenure liberates them from having to render decisions in accordance with public opinion. Their lack of ambition for higher judicial office releases them from any obligation to conform to the values of politicians involved in staffing the federal courts. Finally, the justices' status in the judiciary also ensures that they need not follow the pronouncements of higher courts. The Court's institutional setting thus permits the justices to take advantage of the indeterminacy of law and render decisions in conformity with their personal policy preferences.[3]

In *The Supreme Court and the Attitudinal Model,* the most thorough contemporary defense of a strongly instrumental interpretation of Supreme Court decision making, Jeffrey A. Segal and Harold Spaeth provide reason to believe that the institutional context in which the Court operates has, in fact, enabled the justices to act as policy makers, and that they did so in *Brown.* In an effort to offer a "systematic picture of the policy making of the Warren, Burger, and Rehnquist Courts," Segal and Spaeth divide the decisions of each Court and the justices' voting into a number of issue areas—criminal procedure, civil rights, First Amendment, privacy, due process, unions, economic activity, judicial power, federalism, and federal taxation—and identify case outcomes, as well as the justices' votes, as liberal or conservative. In their analysis, which begins with the Warren Court in 1953 and concludes with the end of the fifth term of the Rehnquist Court, they find that "the proportion [of cases] decided liberally and conservatively varied across the three Courts,"

and that the "individual justices . . . var[ied] greatly in their support and/
or opposition to the policy areas that encompass civil rights and liberties (criminal procedure, civil rights, First Amendment, due process, and
privacy)."[4]

In view of "the fact that different courts and different judges do not
decide the same question or issue the same way, to say nothing of the fact
that appellate court decisions—particularly those of the United States
Supreme Court—typically contain dissenting votes," Segal and Spaeth
contend, it is necessary to abandon the traditional assumption "that judicial decisions are objective, dispassionate, and impartial." If "both litigants generally have precedents supporting them; both capably formulate
arguments that the balance of societal interests rests in their respective
favor; and both sides typically allege that either the plain meaning of
the Constitution and/or the intent of the framers supports its position,"
the indeterminacy of legal rules provides justices with opportunities to
decide cases on the basis of something other than law. And, since Segal
and Spaeth find "virtually no support . . . for non-attitudinal factors,
such as judicial restraint, public opinion, and interest group activity" as
alternative explanations of the Court's decisions, it is reasonable to believe
that "the Supreme Court decides disputes in light of the facts of the case
vis-à-vis the ideological attitudes and values of the justices."[5]

Considering the force of these arguments, it is perhaps not surprising
that the attitudinal model is "the most influential conception of judicial behavior in political science."[6] As Martin Shapiro observed early on,
however, data regarding the voting patterns of justices is not sufficient to
prove the validity of an attitudinal account of Supreme Court decision
making. "Although statistics may demonstrate that Justice X always votes
probusiness," he explained, attitudinalists "offer no proof that he does so
because he allows strongly probusiness sentiments to shape his decisions."
Instead, "there is a kind of basic circularity" in the attitudinal model since
"consistency in voting behavior is used to infer the attitude, and then the
attitude is used to explain the consistency." Even Schubert concedes that
his work "is full of talk about the 'attitudes' of Supreme Court justices,
but the attitudinal differences delineated and denoted obviously are hy-
pothetical rather than empirical constructs, because the data analyzed are
based on observations of judicial votes in the decisions of cases—and not
even on judicial responses to questionnaire items."[7]

Marshaling evidence of the justices' values regarding the matter of
racial equality would seem to be of some importance to an attitudinal
account of *Brown*. To suggest, as was done in the preceding chapter,

that something other than traditional legal criteria informed the justices' desegregation votes is not necessarily to say that the justices' values were operative in the decision.[8] Furthermore, the high degree of consensus that the Warren Court justices displayed in their votes on the matter of segregation was not reflected in their votes in any of the other salient issue areas that the Court addressed.[9] It is reasonable to wonder if something other than shared policy preferences contributed to this unusual instance of uniformity in the Court's decisions. In the absence of evidence supporting an attitudinal account of *Brown,* then, we cannot assume that the policy preferences of the justices provide a complete account of the decision.

Schubert's failure to act on Shapiro's admonition that attitudinalists break the circularity of their model "by seeking for information on attitudes in materials other than voting records"—and thus to provide a means by which to prove an attitudinal account of *Brown*—was due neither to indolence nor to inertia. As C. Neal Tate observes, "It is difficult to imagine what independent measure of judicial values could be used [when studying the Supreme Court]. Attitude surveys, often used to measure the values (and role perceptions) of sitting lower court judges, have their limitations when most of the justices being analyzed are dead" or, if living, are unwilling to respond.[10] Attitude surveys, however, do not represent the only means by which scholars have attempted to assess the validity of the attitudinal model or an instrumental account of *Brown.*

Brown and the Current of History

In his important study of the impact of Supreme Court decisions, Gerald N. Rosenberg challenges the conventional view that the *Brown* decision inspired meaningful civil rights legislation in the 1960s. After presenting a detailed empirical analysis of *Brown's* indirect political effects, or lack thereof, he attempts to describe the economic, political, and ideological forces supporting racial equality that were "independent of the Supreme Court and could plausibly have accounted for eventual congressional and executive branch action" on civil rights. While Rosenberg has generated enormous scholarly interest with his assessment of the Court's impact, students of the Court should also find intriguing his suggestion that the same social and political factors that might have inspired civil rights legislation—"growing civil rights pressure from the 1930s, economic changes, the Cold War, population shifts, electoral concerns, [and] the increase in mass communication"—might have accounted for

Court action as well. He observes that "even Jack Greenberg, head of the NAACP Inc. Fund, admits that by the time of *Brown* there 'was a current of history and the Court became part of it.'"[11]

Rosenberg's supposition regarding the sociopolitical forces at work in *Brown* receives strong support in the scholarship of Michael J. Klarman. Although Klarman differs from Rosenberg over the matter of *Brown*'s impact, he presents a thoroughgoing defense of the view that the most compelling explanation for the justices' behavior in the desegregation decision is one that focuses on "the deep-seated political, social, economic, and ideological forces that have rendered possible the [judicial] transformation of large areas of constitutional doctrine." By "excavating and exposing these potent, yet often intangible, background forces," he maintains, scholars will discover that *Brown* was not only "congruent with [but also] . . . dependent upon the broad sweep of historical forces."[12]

Klarman does not go so far as to suggest that background forces necessarily determine Supreme Court decisions; he characterizes judicial decision making as a complex process that "involves a combination of legal and political factors." Nevertheless, he contends "that because constitutional law is generally quite indeterminate, constitutional interpretation *almost inevitably reflects the broader social and political context of the times.*" More precisely, "in the absence of determinate law," or when law is determinate but the justices' personal preferences are strong enough to overcome legal scruples, "constitutional interpretation necessarily implicates the values of the judges, which themselves generally reflect broader social attitudes." He concedes that judges "are not perfect mirrors of public opinion"; they "occupy an elite subculture, which is characterized by greater education and relative affluence." Still, this qualification "does not negate the principal point" that "judges are part of contemporary culture, and they rarely hold views that deviate far from dominant public opinion."[13]

Because Supreme Court justices are "embedded in majoritarian culture" and thus typically "possess neither the inclination . . . nor the power" to frustrate the dominant opinions of the times in which they live, Klarman contends that students of the Court must abandon the conventional view that the justices serve a "heroic countermajoritarian function." "To risk putting the point somewhat cynically," he remarks, "the Court identifies and protects minority rights only when a majority or near majority of the community has come to deem those rights worthy of protection."[14]

Klarman believes that "the conventional assessment of the Court's countermajoritarian capacity has been distorted . . . by a single decision—*Brown*." By "rescu[ing] us from our racist past, the conventional story line runs, the Court plainly [demonstrated that it] can and does play the role of heroic defender of minority rights from majority oppression." In Klarman's view, *Brown* reinforced a regrettable tendency among scholars to wrest the Court's decisions, including *Brown,* from their political and social contexts. Not one to be accused of failing to practice what he preaches, Klarman draws on the work of Doug McAdam and other social historians to place *Brown* in the context within which the Court rendered the decision. He contends that "no adequate account of *Brown* can ignore the deep-seated political, social, economic, and ideological forces that were propelling the nation toward racial equality around mid-century."[15]

One major factor that helped to transform American attitudes on race was the Great Migration of nearly three million southern blacks into the cities of the industrialized North during the first half of the twentieth century. This process was initiated by a decline in cotton farming and an increased demand for industrial labor. The political significance of the Great Migration was enormous. Those who relocated not only gained the right to vote; they also tended to settle in the urban centers of seven electorally significant industrial states: New York, New Jersey, Pennsylvania, Ohio, California, Illinois, and Michigan. The fall of cotton also prompted a rural-to-urban migration within the South that afforded African Americans a context within which to organize politically, given the increased proximity and improved communications of city life. The movement of blacks to urban centers in both the North and South further facilitated political activity by improving their economic situation. The diversified employment opportunities that the cities afforded led gradually to the development of a sizable black middle class, which possessed the time, resources, and education necessary for meaningful political activity.[16]

The political status of southern as well as northern blacks continued to improve during the Second World War. Aside from marking the beginning of an extended period of economic expansion that benefited blacks and whites alike (although not equally), the war had an enormous impact on black attitudes. Upon returning home, large numbers of African American soldiers demanded racial equality as compensation for their sacrifices overseas. Ideological forces associated with the war complicated the lives of white Americans who were disinclined to acknowledge black demands for equality. The evil nature of a fascist regime that espoused and acted on a creed of racial supremacy forced whites to evaluate the content of their own racial attitudes, while the atrocities that were a logical consequence of Nazi racial ideology provided a strong incentive for social scientists to challenge and reject the presumption of black intellectual and moral infirmity that informed prevailing, biologically based theories of racial difference and white supremacy. For those who failed to note the contradiction between American rhetoric and racial policies, Soviet propaganda during the Cold War ensured that world opinion would provide a strong incentive for Americans to engage in self-criticism.[17]

While ideological forces associated with the Second World War and the ensuing Cold War made it hard for white Americans to ignore burgeoning demands for racial equality on the part of blacks, technological improvements in transportation and communication bound the nation together, making it much more difficult for the South to preserve social customs that deviated sharply from national norms. Southerners who traveled and spent time outside the region came to feel less committed to traditional racial mores, while shocking reports of lynchings and of the maiming of black veterans put the South on the defensive and helped to promote a national consciousness regarding civil rights.[18]

The not-so-surprising result of deep-seated material and ideological forces that supported racial equality, Klarman contends, was a rather significant change in American race relations by the time the Court rendered *Brown.* As evidence of this change, he points to a rise in the number and activity of civil rights organizations in the North in the postwar years and to an increase in registered black voters in the South (from approximately 250,000 in 1940 to over 1 million in 1952). Such developments led to, among other things, prohibitions on racial discrimination in public accommodations in the North and progress toward desegregation—in public swimming pools, department and drug stores, theaters, public libraries, and public transportation—in the border states and portions of the upper South. President Harry Truman's decision to promote civil rights in the late 1940s provided evidence at the national level of a significant change in race relations. Upon the advice of his principal domestic advisor, Clark Clifford, Truman endorsed most of the proposals made in the report of the President's Committee on Civil Rights, and he issued executive orders desegregating the military and federal civil service. The Truman Justice Department also began to investigate and prosecute lynchings and to submit *amicus* briefs on behalf of petitioners in civil rights cases.[19]

The shift in attitudes that prompted the social and political changes in American race relations, Klarman notes, was evident in opinion polls. By the time the Court rendered *Brown,* 54 percent of Americans supported the desegregation of public schools. The percentage of people favoring desegregation at the elementary and secondary school level rose to almost three quarters when the field of respondents was narrowed to college graduates. Klarman observes that even postwar polls of southerners revealed a discernible change in racial attitudes. "This shift . . . translated into more tolerant positions on specific racial policies, as the percentage of white southerners favoring integrated transportation rose from 4% to 27% [between 1944 and 1956], and the number expressing no objection to interracial residential proximity rose from 12% to 38%." While it was not true "that most white southerners had abandoned their commitment to racial segregation by the mid-twentieth century, the political, social, and economic forces [supporting racial equality] were gradually undermining the strength of that commitment."[20]

After examining the postwar racial transformation that preceded *Brown,* Klarman reiterates the point that justices "cannot help but be influenced by their personal values and the social and political contexts of their times." "The social and political context of race had changed so dramatically, as had the personal racial attitudes of the justices," he avers, "that even a relatively weak legal case [in support of the petitioners in *Brown*] could not deter [the Court] from invalidating segregation." The fact that the legal argument for *sustaining* segregation in the nation's elementary and secondary schools was so powerful "suggests that [the justices] had *very strong* personal preferences to the contrary."[21]

Although national opinion regarding segregation "was divided roughly down the middle," Klarman assumes that "most of the justices considered racial segregation . . . to be evil" because they "held culturally elite values." "On many policy issues that become constitutional disputes," he explains, "opinion correlates heavily with socioeconomic status, with elites tending to hold more liberal views on certain social issues. . . . Racial attitudes and practices were changing dramatically in postwar America. As members of the cultural elite, the justices were among the first to be influenced."[22]

Measuring the Justices' Ideological Values

THE PROBLEM OF PROOF

Klarman's effort to place *Brown* in its social and political context, although supportive of an attitudinal account of the decision, does not offer proof of such an explanation. Since individuals might serve as counterexamples to societal trends, a discussion of the forces that promoted a transformation in American race relations is not an adequate substitute for evidence of the justices' personal policy preferences. As Kevin J. McMahon observes, while "the forces of history [supporting racial equality] are undoubtedly strong, . . . we should [not] ignore individual and institutional action"; justices are not "mere pawns executing predetermined maneuvers in the march of history."[23]

Apparently conceding the point, Klarman offers evidence of the values of certain members of the Court. He expresses some confidence regarding the desegregation policy preferences of three Roosevelt appointees—William Douglas, Felix Frankfurter, and Robert Jackson. He suggests that "Douglas's vote may be the easiest to explain." Although the former Yale law professor and chairman of the Securities and Exchange Commission "had revealed no special racial sensitivity in his pre-Court years, . . . he was a quintessential northern liberal." Before the Second World War, persons of this ideological stripe "were generally more interested in economic issues than racial ones." But "by the late 1940s . . . racial egalitarianism had become a defining characteristic of theirs. By 1952, the immorality of segregation was no longer debatable for someone of Douglas's political ilk." Klarman avers that Frankfurter's credentials as a racial progressive are similarly easy to demonstrate. Indeed, "more than any other justice, [the former Harvard law professor's] personal behavior evinced egalitarian commitments. In the 1930s, he had served on the NAACP's National Legal Committee, and in 1948, he had hired the Court's first black law clerk, William Coleman." Like Frankfurter, Klarman contends, Jackson, the former solicitor general and then attorney general, "found segregation anathema." He points out that "in a 1950 letter, Jackson, who had left the Court for a year in 1945–46 to prosecute Nazis at Nuremberg, wrote to a law professor friend: 'You and I have seen the terrible consequences of racial hatred in Germany. We can have no sympathy with [the] racial conceits which underlie segregation policies.'"[24]

Klarman, however, is willing to consider the *noninstrumental* nature of the desegregation votes of three other members of the Court—Stanley Reed, Harold Burton, and Sherman Minton. He concedes that, "of all the justices, [Reed] was the most supportive of segregation, in terms of both policy and constitutionality." This fact should not be too surprising since this Roosevelt appointee from the border state of Kentucky "refused to attend a Court party [in 1947] because black messengers were invited, and in 1952, he was appalled that 'a nigra' might sit down beside his wife at a restaurant after the Court had interpreted an old civil rights statute to require the desegregation of public accommodations in the District of Columbia." Reed's desegregation vote is thus best understood as a response to "pressure to suppress [his] convictions for the good of the institution," a decision made easier because "his culturally elite status diminished the intensity of his segregationist sentiment."[25]

Klarman finds it "harder to explain" the desegregation votes of the Truman appointees, Burton, a former Republican senator from Ohio, and Minton, a former Democratic senator from Indiana. Klarman points out that "neither was as liberal as Douglas," and that "their personal histories regarding race are thin." What "little surviving evidence" there is "suggests that they shared neither Reed's support for segregation nor Frankfurter's passion for racial equality." And, "on civil liberties issues generally, they were the most conservative justices, nearly always siding with the government and celebrating judicial restraint." So, Klarman asks, "why would Burton and Minton, generally averse to civil liberties claims, have been so receptive to the civil rights claim in *Brown?*" He suggests that, since the justices "were fierce judicial Cold Warriors" in terms of their support for government loyalty and security programs, they may have found compelling "the Justice Department's brief [that] invoked the Cold War imperative as a principal justification for invalidating school segregation."[26] In short, rather than undergoing an attitudinal shift inspired by the prevailing forces regarding American race relations, Burton and Minton may have cast their desegregation votes based on the executive's plea that the Court deprive America's chief international rival of the ability to use segregation in its propaganda campaign against the United States.

Klarman reveals less confidence that he can demonstrate the motives of the three remaining justices—Earl Warren, Hugo Black, and Tom Clark. In the case of Warren, the Dwight Eisenhower nominee and former governor of California, Klarman makes no effort to point to evidence that would explain his desegregation vote. As for the Truman nominee, Clark, Klarman notes that, while the former attorney general possessed some "sympathy for segregation," he hailed from a state in the "peripheral South—. . . Texas—and thus [his] commitment to white supremacy was probably somewhat attenuated." Finally, with regard to Black, the former senator from Alabama, Klarman concedes that "one cannot know for sure" "why . . . [he] personally condemn[ed] segregation at a time when few white Alabamians his age did so." He regards "Black's ready condemnation of segregation [as] perhaps the most surprising position taken by any of the justices," given that "he was the only member of the Court from the Deep South, and he had been a Klan member." Klarman opines that the justice may have voted against expectations because he "was just idiosyncratic." Black, he observes, "certainly had a contrarian personality." In a creative attempt to portray past involvement in a racist organization as a liberalizing influence, Klarman also posits that Black may have been "so chastened upon his appointment in 1937 by public criticism of his former Klan membership that he dedicated his judicial career to rebutting it."[27]

In view of the noninstrumental arguments Klarman employs in his treatment of the desegregation votes of Justices Reed, Burton, and Minton, evidence of the instrumental nature of the votes of at least two of the three justices about whom he is least certain (viz., Warren, Clark, and Black) is required if Klarman is to demonstrate that the *Brown* decision simply reflected a national trend toward racial egalitarianism. But the southerners, Clark and Black, present a problem for Klarman's thesis, and the problem is not simply a lack of convincing evidence of instrumental motivation. In the same way that Black's membership in the Klan is difficult to explain away, geographical considerations provide reason to believe that Clark, likewise, favored segregation. While Klarman emphasizes the fact that Texas is a peripheral southern state, the western portion of which had "few blacks" and thus a "relatively thin" commitment on the part of whites to preserving segregation, he also notes that East Texas, the part of the state in which Clark resided, "resembled the Deep South; many counties had majority or near-majority black populations, and most whites were deeply invested in Jim Crow."[28] Klarman cannot even assume that membership in the cultural elite separated Clark and Black from the segregationist norms of the South; he fails to mention that, when only southerners were considered in a 1954 poll, the percentage of college-educated respondents favoring desegregation was a mere 38 percent.[29] Assuming the accuracy of Klarman's method of measuring the justices' policy preferences, in all likelihood Clark and Black as well as Reed ruled contrary to their policy preferences in *Brown*. In short, Klarman's research does not obviate the need for those who champion an attitudinal account of *Brown* to locate a method of measuring the policy preferences of justices.

PERSONAL ATTRIBUTES OF THE JUSTICES

In an effort to overcome the problem of circularity in the attitudinal model, C. Neal Tate employs a method of indirectly measuring the attitudes or policy preferences of justices that involves quantifying the personal attributes or background characteristics of the individuals whose votes are to be explained. Tate maintains that personal attributes are the "proximate causes" of both values and judicial role perceptions. Properly constructed, "attribute models could provide highly statistically satisfactory explanations of judicial behavior even though they failed to include unmeasured (and often unmeasurable) attitudinal variables which intervene between the attributes and decisions in the models."[30]

Acting on this belief, Tate developed attribute models of twenty-five postwar Supreme Court justices in an effort to account for their decisions in the areas of civil rights and liberties and economic rights. In selecting the background traits to serve as the independent variables in the study, Tate sought "as far as possible" to investigate "*all* characteristics found to be potentially important in previous research." The attributes Tate selected using this standard fell into four main categories, with the first combining "traits relat[ed] to the birth, upbringing, and education of the justices." The second "consists of the justices' career characteristics," including their appointment regions and the existence, or nonexistence, of prior judicial or prosecutorial experience. The third category "consists of measures of the justices' age and tenure," while the final one combines traits related to the justices' "partisanship," specifically party identification and appointing president.[31]

Tate reports that he obtained "quite impressive" results with his models and that a mere five independent variables—judge's party identification, appointing president, appointment region, extensiveness of judicial experience, and type of prosecutorial experience—were required to achieve predictive success in the area of civil rights and liberties. Tate concedes that his findings are "hardly conclusive . . . on the utility of attribute models in explaining the decision making of judges in general," given his small sample size. Nevertheless, he contends that his results are "suggestive"—that "the substantial explanatory powers attached to the models in this study may reflect a close causal linkage between judicial values and judicial votes."[32]

Assuming the relevance of justices' background characteristics to their votes in civil rights and civil liberties cases, Tate's results may provide indirect evidence of the influence of attitudes in Supreme Court decision making. But the question that this chapter attempts to answer is much narrower: Do the attitudes of the justices explain the results observed in the *Brown* decision? While Tate was not interested in explaining a particular decision, his indirect measures of the values of the justices who were on the Supreme Court in 1954 are useful in assessing the validity of an attitudinal account of *Brown.* His findings do not suggest that the personal policy preferences of the Warren Court justices explain the *Brown* decision. Table 1 delineates the presence in *Brown* of those background characteristics that Tate found *negatively* correlated with liberal voting in civil rights and civil liberties cases. While no justice possessed all of these attributes, all of the justices possessed at least one of them. One justice possessed four of the attributes, while three members of the Court possessed three of them, and three justices possessed two. The impression that the justices' attitudes, if operative in *Brown,* would have led to a badly fragmented Court does not change when considering only "the most significant of these [background] variables, relatively speaking, . . . [viz., Justice's] Party Identification, Truman Appointee, and Type of Prosecutorial Experience." (The final variable refers, in order of decreasing liberality, to no prosecutorial experience; prosecutors with judicial experience; and prosecutors with no judicial experience. Tate found that the final two categories were negatively correlated with liberal voting in civil rights and civil liberties cases.)[33] No justice possessed all three of the most significant attributes that were negatively correlated with liberalism, and two of the justices possessed none of them. Yet three justices possessed one of the three background characteristics while four members of the Court possessed two of them.

Greater specificity in Tate's dependent variables might reveal that at

TABLE 1 Presence in *Brown v. Board of Education* (1954) of judicial attributes negatively correlated with liberal voting in civil rights and civil liberties cases

JUSTICES IN ORDER OF APPOINTMENT	REPUBLICAN PARTY OR INDEPENDENT	TRUMAN APPOINTEE	APPOINTED FROM SOUTH OR BORDER STATE	PROSECU-TORIAL EXPERIENCE	NO PRIOR JUDICIAL EXPERIENCE
Black			X	X	
Reed			X		X
Frankfurter	X			X	X
Douglas					X
Jackson				X	X
Burton	X	X			X
Clark		X	X	X	X
Minton		X			
Warren	X			X	X

Sources: Based on Tate, "Personal Attribute Models of the Voting Behavior," 361–62, and Goldinger, ed., *The Supreme Court at Work.*

least certain of these attributes are irrelevant to *Brown*. President Truman, for instance, was relatively *liberal* on the matter of civil *rights* as opposed to civil *liberties*. He demonstrated his liberalism in this policy area primarily on racial issues rather than on matters involving women, aliens, juveniles, or indigents.[34] Narrowing the dependent variable to votes in cases involving claims to racial equality, then, might eliminate the negative correlation that Tate observed between Truman's appointees and support for civil rights. Similarly, a justice's prior prosecutorial experience would seem to have *less* relevance to his views on civil *rights* questions involving race, as opposed to civil *liberties* issues involving criminal procedure.

On the other hand, the independent variable regarding appointment region might have *greater* significance if the dependent variable is narrowed to votes on matters of racial equality. Tom Clark, although a Texan, served as attorney general during the late 1940s when the Truman administration reached out to African Americans by proposing civil rights legislation and participating as *amicus curiae* in the LDF's racial covenant cases then before the Supreme Court.[35] But it is more difficult to identify background characteristics for Stanley Reed that would offset or overcome the conservative influence of his membership in the southern establishment. For Reed, serving in the Kentucky General Assembly, managing a small town legal practice, and ultimately acting as Franklin Roosevelt's solicitor general (before the president, in the midterm elections of 1938, identified conservative southerners as a hinderance to his constitutional vision) would not mark him as an advocate, let alone a champion, of racial equality.[36] And Black's membership in the Alabama Ku Klux Klan would seem to require reference to liberalizing influences of significant moment. Such influences are not to be found in his ten-year career in the U.S. Senate when he served as a champion of the New Deal. Black remained in power by balancing the claims of two constituencies—Alabama's poor whites and the state's plantation elites—that were hostile to the goal of racial equality.[37]

Aside from these problems, Jeffrey Segal and Harold Spaeth raise objections to Tate's research that counsel against *ever* relying on attribute models as indirect measures of judicial attitudes. They note, first, that certain independent variables that often appear in attribute models (and Tate's model is no exception) are at best *surrogates* for judicial attitudes as opposed to being *causes* of them. An appointing president and a judge's party identification, for example, almost certainly do not lead a justice to embrace a particular ideology. Instead, presidents appoint certain persons to the Court *because* of their ideologies. And those persons belong to certain political parties *because* those parties in some measure reflect their attitudes. In short, while these variables may help to *predict* judicial behavior, they do little to help *explain* that behavior.[38]

Segal and Spaeth contend, more fundamentally, that one cannot rely on these models to predict, let alone to explain, judicial behavior. They note that political socialization studies suggest that the social backgrounds of individuals have only a limited to moderate relationship to their attitudes. In view of these findings, they conclude, "We would not expect models that predict behavior from social backgrounds, which is one step removed from attitudes, to perform particularly well." To support this contention, Segal and Spaeth note that, "with one exception [viz., Tate], virtually every study of [judicial] background and behavior has either failed to explain a large percentage of the variance in the decisions or explained a large percentage of variance by employing as many or more variables than cases, which makes it mathematically impossible not to explain a large percentage of the variance."[39]

RECOURSE TO NEWSPAPER EDITORIALS

Jeffrey Segal, Harold Spaeth, Lee Epstein, and Charles M. Cameron defend a more promising method of indirectly measuring the attitudes or policy preferences of Supreme Court justices. They claim to derive independent, reliable measures of the values of a large group of justices (which includes the individuals who voted in *Brown*) through content analyses of newspaper editorials that were published in the period between presidential nomination and senatorial confirmation.[40] Segal developed this method of measurement with Albert D. Cover in an earlier, less comprehensive study in which the two men conceded that "measures of *perceived* values are obviously imperfect measures of the *real* values of Supreme Court justices." But the strengths of this method of indirectly measuring the ideological values of justices, they emphasized, are that newspaper editorials have ideological content, are comparable, exist in similar form for each justice, are independent of the votes the justices cast (unlike postconfirmation newspaper editorials or opinions justices wrote while on the Supreme Court), are not rationalizations of votes already cast (as the justices' postconfirmation speeches or articles may be), and have no systemic errors, as are present in the statements nominees make during confirmation hearings.[41]

To acquire newspaper editors' assessments of the justices' ideological values in the more comprehensive study, Segal and his colleagues examined six of the nation's leading papers, three with a liberal stance (the *New York Times,* the *Washington Post,* and the *St. Louis Post-Dispatch*) and three with a more conservative outlook (the *Chicago Tribune,* the *Los Angeles Times,* and the *Wall Street Journal*). In conducting content analyses of the editorials contained therein, they coded paragraphs as liberal, moderate, conservative, or not applicable.[42] The dependent variables in the study were "the percentages of formally decided (including orally argued per curiams) civil liberties and economics cases from the start of the Vinson Court in 1946 through the end of the 1992 term in which the justices took a liberal position."[43]

Segal and his colleagues observe "that the ideological values of the Eisenhower through Bush appointees correlate strongly with votes cast in economic and civil liberties [which included civil rights] cases, [while] the results are less robust for justices appointed by Roosevelt and Truman." They note, however, that the ideological measures for William Douglas and Robert Jackson do not correspond with "broad-based impressions" of the men, and that removing these figures from the analysis, because of probable measurement error, yields results that have "strong predictive power, at least for aggregated votes in civil liberties and economic cases."[44]

Like Tate, Segal and his colleagues were not interested in explaining a particular Supreme Court decision. Nevertheless, their findings are useful for assessing an attitudinal account of *Brown.* Assuming the rough accuracy of their ideological measures, the relationships observed between values and votes may provide support for the attitudinal model of Supreme Court decision making.[45] These measures, however, do not appear to support the view that the justices' attitudes informed their votes in *Brown.* Earl Warren and his colleagues ranged along an ideological continuum as depicted in figure 1. Of the justices who participated in *Brown,* four joined the Court in the late 1930s and all, save Warren, had been appointed by 1949. In order for Segal's measures to support an attitudinal account of *Brown,* ideological designations less progressive than "liberal" that were used before the mid-twentieth century should have implied sentiment favoring school desegregation. Progressive as the Court's ideological alignment may have been, it is difficult to believe that persons whom newspaper editors would characterize in the years before *Brown* as moderate conservatives, moderates, or even moderate liberals would have possessed policy preferences favoring the desegregation of the nation's elementary and secondary schools.

Polling data from midcentury, which help to contextualize the political discourse of the time period, reinforce the view that in almost every

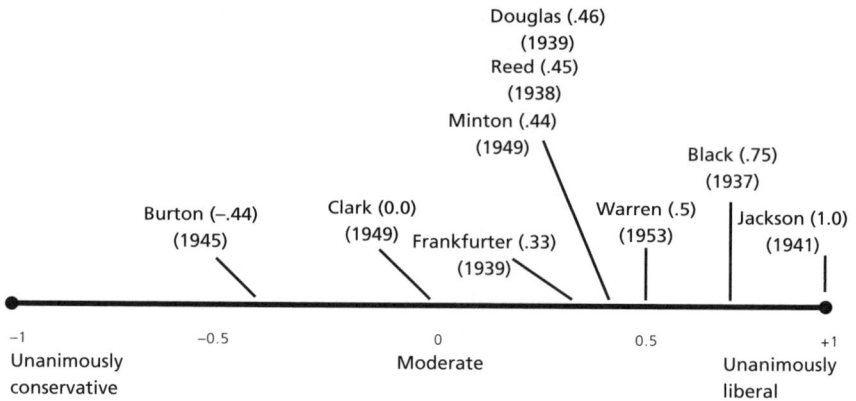

FIGURE 1. Ideological alignment and years of appointment of justices in *Brown v. Board of Education* (1954).

Source: Based on Jeffrey A. Segal et al., "Ideological Values and the Votes of U.S. Supreme Court Justices Revisited," *Journal of Politics* 57 (1995): 816.

case the ideological designations newspaper editors employed to describe the individuals who participated in *Brown* did not imply opposition to public school segregation. Polls taken in 1948, for example, suggest that even those who were described as fairly liberal were assumed to possess views on racial equality that fell short of support for public school de-segregation. A majority of Americans (69 percent) supported the view that "poll taxes should be done away with." A minority of respondents, however, indicated that the federal government "should have the right to step in and deal with the crime" of lynching (43 percent); that the federal government should go "all" or "part of the way" in "requiring employers to hire people without regard to their race, religion, color, or nationality" (42 percent); and that "Negroes . . . should not be required to occupy a separate part of a train or bus when traveling from one state to another" (49 percent).[46] In view of these figures, it is reasonable to assume that people regarded as moderately liberal might have favored some or most of these initiatives. But, given the fact that a majority did not yet support efforts by the federal government to remedy even obvious racial injustices (i.e., unlike segregation, lynching and economic discrimination were not rationalized as being in the best interests of blacks), it is questionable whether even the designation "liberal" would have implied the possession of strong anti-segregation norms.

Note that these polls did not control for the region of the respondents. But the proposition that progressive ideological designations, when used outside the South, implied a preference for school desegregation receives less than ample support from a 1948 poll that focused on President Truman's civil rights program. Controlling for region, the poll revealed that a mere 32 percent of respondents from New England and the Middle Atlantic—the part of the country that registered as most progressive—indicated that "Congress should . . . pass [Truman's civil rights] program as a whole." Forty percent of the region's respondents indicated that they had not heard of the program.[47] But even if this group of respondents had duplicated the distribution of opinion among those who indicated an awareness of Truman's initiatives, the poll would still have revealed that less than a bare majority of people in the country's most progressive region supported the enactment of a program that conspicuously avoided the recommendation of the President's Committee on Civil Rights that forms of federal assistance stipulate that recipients not segregate on the basis of race.[48]

A poll taken in 1949 provides further reason to believe that, regardless of a person's geography, individuals who were thought of as fairly liberal were assumed to have views that fell short of support for public school desegregation. In the poll, which controlled for region, 69 percent of nonsoutherners—and even 53 percent of southern respondents—thought "poll taxes should be abolished." By contrast, only 20 percent of southerners thought that the federal government should go "all" or "part of the way" in "requiring employers to hire people without regard to their race, religion, color, or nationality," while the portion of nonsoutherners who favored complete or partial federal action in this matter did not rise above 42 percent. Similarly, a mere 14 percent of southerners thought "Negroes . . . should not be required to occupy a separate part of a train or bus when traveling from one state to another," and only a slight majority of nonsoutherners—55 percent—expressed opposition to segregation in interstate transportation.[49] In short, since widespread support for policies promoting racial equality existed for only the most basic initiatives even in nonsouthern regions, only individuals regarded as extraordinarily liberal outside the South might have been thought at this time to support desegregation in the sensitive area of elementary and secondary education.

At the risk of putting too fine a point on this conclusion, it is also possible to question the intensity of feeling among Americans who expressed support for civil rights initiatives at this time, since another 1949 poll did not even list the issue of race relations among the numerous responses given to the question: "What do you think is the most important problem facing the American people today?"[50] When civil rights appeared in a 1953 poll as a response to a similar question, only 1 percent of respondents thought that the issue qualified as the nation's most pressing problem.[51] These data imply that, in common parlance at midcentury, the term "liberal" may have had little connection to the concept of racial justice.

Polling data is not necessarily an appropriate device to use to ascertain the meaning of the ideological designations in Segal's study. Newspaper editors, as part of the social elite, might not have taken general public opinion as their ideological reference point; instead, they might have regarded elite political behavior as the proper standard by which to assess a Supreme Court nominee's ideological bent. And political elites at midcentury had begun to move against racial segregation. In 1947, as noted, the President's Committee on Civil Rights went so far as to call on Congress to eliminate segregation from American life by attaching conditions to federal grants-in-aid. The following year, President Truman issued an executive order to desegregate the armed forces. In 1949, the LDF presented the Supreme Court with a direct constitutional challenge to segregation in graduate and professional education. The Truman administration's *amicus curiae* briefs placed the imprimatur of the executive branch on the LDF's arguments in these cases, as well as on an effort, independent of the LDF's litigation campaign, to challenge the constitutionality of racial segregation in interstate transportation.[52]

But this information also reveals that by the time editorials had been written on eight of the nine Supreme Court nominees who would participate in *Brown,* the President's Committee on Civil Rights was the only elite body to call for desegregation in elementary and secondary education. Even the LDF had yet to move beyond the strategy of asking judges merely to enforce the separate-but-equal principle in this especially sensitive area.[53] In view of these considerations, while an elite understanding of moderate liberalism might have implied support for the desegregation of certain aspects of American life, editors would not yet have employed anything less than the term "liberal" to refer to nominees who favored desegregation at the lowest levels of education. Even assuming unrealistically that the desegregation of elementary as opposed to graduate education was, to newspaper editors at this time, a distinction without a difference, only three justices who participated in *Brown* were appointed during the years that elites began to call for an end to racial segregation. Only two of the three—Minton and Warren—were regarded as sufficiently progressive to be listed in Segal's study as moderate liberals. (Clark was identified as a political moderate.)

Michael Klarman's observation that it was only "after the war . . . [that] civil rights headed the liberal reform agenda" has important implications for the import of the ideological designations editors assigned to justices who were not nominated in the postwar period, assuming editors took elite behavior as their ideological reference point. Before that time—when most of the justices who participated in *Brown* were nominated to the Court— *"liberals had usually had little to say about race."*[54] As a consequence, even Supreme Court nominees whom newspaper editors identified as liberals prior to the late 1940s—of which there were only two who voted in *Brown*—would not have been assumed to support desegregation in elementary and secondary schools.[55] By the same token, however, nominees who received less progressive ideological designations would not have been assumed to favor segregation. Simply put, if liberals were not even thinking seriously about race in America before midcentury, it may be that greater specificity in the measurement of Supreme Court nominees' views on racial equality was not even possible until the postwar period (although this degree of specificity was not present in newspaper editorials regarding the three postwar nominees, viz., Clark, Minton, and Warren).[56]

Consistent with these observations, the prenomination writings and speeches of the justices who joined the Court before the end of the war lack content regarding the matter of race and are thus of no use as an alternative means of inferring the justices' attitudes on desegregation. The same can be said for the writings and speeches of two of the three justices appointed in the postwar period.[57] And, with one exception, even the justices' postconfirmation communications written prior to *Brown* do not afford insight into their policy preferences regarding desegregation.[58] So, unless social scientists develop an alternative method of attitude measurement that is not restricted to living persons, an attitudinal account of *Brown* will remain a matter of conjecture rather than empirical proof.

Evidence of Ideological Drift

To say that an attitudinal account of *Brown* is unproven, it should be emphasized, is not to say that such an explanation is wrong. The upshot of this chapter's interpretation of the meaning of ideological designations used in newspaper editorials, combined with the critique of Tate's use of judicial attributes to overcome the circularity of the attitudinal model, is the preservation of an attitudinal account of the decision through the neutralization of data that appear to discount such an explanation.

Although Klarman provides evidence of a desegregation policy preference for only Justices Douglas, Frankfurter, and Jackson, attitudinalists
would contend that the burden rests with the model's critics to afford a
more compelling explanation of *Brown*. After all, Rohde and Spaeth's
contention—that the institutional context in which the Supreme Court
operates liberates the justices from the force of external constraints—is
certainly plausible. Furthermore, an attitudinal account of *Brown* seems
reasonable for at least a majority of the justices, given that the Court
rendered the decision in spite of what appeared to be insuperable legal
obstacles and in view of the evidence that Klarman marshals regarding a
postwar shift in American racial attitudes.

Recent scholarship that examines the phenomenon of ideological drift
on the Court, however, should give pause to those who believe that the
burden of proof rests entirely with those who would challenge an attitudinal interpretation of *Brown*. Lee Epstein, Andrew D. Martin, Kevin
M. Quinn, and Jeffrey Segal note that the "near-hegemonic" view that
justices' policy preferences remain stable over time is based on both "intu-
ition and empirical observation." With regard to the former, they concede
that "it seems implausible to believe that Justices would take pause to
rethink their presumably well-entrenched beliefs over matters jurisprudential." And they observe that a "wealth of behavioral data lends weight
to these intuitions," especially "the extent to which initial impressions
of the ideology of many Justices, as nominees, correlate with their subsequent voting on the Court." A "handful of quantitative studies of the
Justices' voting," however, suggest that the policy preferences of certain
justices changed significantly over the course of their careers. But these
studies "examine voting records without satisfactorily attending to the
content of the litigation they analyze," which means that "any observed
shifts in voting could be as much a result of differences in the cases as in
the Justices' underlying preferences."[59]

In order to solve the problem of variation in case content and to acquire an accurate sense of whether justices' policy preferences can change
over time, Epstein and her colleagues adopted a solution that uses "data
derived from votes cast by the Justices and a Bayesian modeling strategy."
Employing this technique, they "generated term-by-term ideal point estimates," essentially the positions that a justice's votes are assigned along
an ideological continuum in a particular area of law, "for all the Justices
appointed since the 1937 term—estimates that attend to variation in case
content." They discovered that, "of the twenty-six Justices who served on
the Court for ten or more terms since 1937, all but four exhibit ideologi-

cal drift over the course of their tenures."[60] Although this study offers no explanation for ideological drift, Epstein and Segal, along with Valerie Hoekstra and Harold Spaeth, had earlier hypothesized that justices might be "affected by members of their work (i.e., the other justices) and political (e.g., Congress, the president) milieus," or that they might respond "to [their] external environment."[61] Presumably, the latter possibility would include such stimuli as the forces that began to liberalize American attitudes toward race around the middle of the twentieth century.

While Epstein and her colleagues are primarily concerned with contributing to a more accurate understanding of Supreme Court decision making, their results also provide reason to question the assumption that a majority of the justices who voted in *Brown* were swept up in the current of history that altered American racial attitudes. Assuming that the changes observed in the justices' ideal points were the result of changes in policy preferences, eight of the justices who were on the Court in 1954 exhibited signs of ideological drift. (Since Minton did not serve on the Court for ten or more terms, Epstein and her colleagues do not comment on whether his policy preferences changed during his judicial tenure.) Five members of the Court—Reed, Frankfurter, Black, Jackson, and Burton—became "significantly more conservative" in the years following their respective first terms. For each of these justices, the ideological drift rightward occurred before 1954. Only three of the justices—Warren, Clark, and Douglas—became "significantly more liberal" during their years on the Court. Warren had turned sharply to the left by his second term (i.e., the year after *Brown*), while Clark's trend leftward occurred shortly before 1954. Douglas exhibited a more exotic pattern in that he made an early and significant shift to the right but, for most of his career, was "significantly more liberal" relative to his first year on the bench. Douglas had moved leftward shortly before *Brown*.[62]

The finding that the voting patterns of certain justices shifted significantly leftward before *Brown* does not prove that their votes in that case reflected a preference for desegregation. It suggests, however, that those who would challenge an attitudinal account of the decision should assume the burden of providing evidence of the presence of noninstrumental goals on the part of these justices. This burden is especially weighty for those who would defend a noninstrumental interpretation of Douglas's vote, since Klarman provides reason to believe that the justice would have favored desegregation. The finding that the voting patterns of five individuals shifted significantly rightward before *Brown* does not prove that most of the justices acted contrary to their policy preferences in voting for desegregation. But this finding complicates the view that we can safely assume that the forces that were beginning to liberalize American attitudes toward race in the middle of the twentieth century affected these justices in such a way as to explain their votes in *Brown*. At the very least, these results suggest that those who would defend an attitudinal understanding of the decision should search for evidence that demonstrates a desegregation policy preference on the part of each of these men. Klarman's discussion of Frankfurter's membership on the NAACP's National Legal Committee would seem to meet this burden, as would his reference to Jackson's anti-segregation statement in his letter to Charles Fairman (unless his analysis is shown to be incomplete).[63]

The most obvious primary sources regarding the justices' behavior in *Brown*—the documents relating to the justices' deliberations in the case—give further reason to doubt the completeness of an attitudinal account of the decision. These documents indicate that certain members of the Court might have voted for desegregation for reasons other than the satisfaction of a personal policy preference and that nearly all of the justices maintained the impracticality of ordering immediate compliance with a desegregation decree. In short, the justices' notes and memoranda regarding the conference deliberations in *Brown* provide reason to consider the insights of scholars who challenge the attitudinalist assumption that Supreme Court justices are unconstrained makers of policy.

THREE

Law, Anticipated Violence, and Loyalty to the Court

The strategic model of Supreme Court decision making, which scholars developed in response to perceived deficiencies in the attitudinal model, posits that justices, while primarily seekers of policy, are constrained in the pursuit of that objective by both internal and external factors. The notes of the conference deliberations in *Brown* do much to illustrate the point, contrary to the assumptions of attitudinalists, that the institutional context in which the justices operate does not necessarily free them to pursue their sincere policy preferences. Even assuming that the legal considerations to which many of the justices referred were too unconvincing to explain the votes of those who invoked the law as support,[1] and recognizing that these considerations were not strong enough to prevent the desegregation votes of those who identified the law as a barrier, the conference notes reveal that most of the members of the Court settled for delayed enforcement, and thus an approximation of their policy preferences, because they anticipated a violent reaction to a desegregation decree. The notes also suggest that certain justices voted against their policy preferences, including Stanley Reed who did so out of a sense of loyalty to the Court. The strategic model helps to explain such behavior on the part of the justices and to provide a framework for understanding the process by which they resolved their differences over the form of the Court's opinion and the matter of enforcement. The latter aspect of the history of *Brown* is worthy of explanation, given the importance of unanimity in such a sensitive case and because of the controversial nature of the social science evidence to which the Court referred as support for its desegregation rationale.

The Strategic Alternative

At the same time that Glendon Schubert was developing an attitudinal account of Supreme Court decision making, Walter F. Murphy provided an alternative model that would appear to be of special relevance to such a controversial and highly visible case as *Brown*. In *Elements of Judicial Strategy,* Murphy retained the behavioral emphasis on the individual judge and, like the attitudinalists, acknowledged the centrality of "the preferences and predilications of judges" to an accurate model of Supreme Court decision making. But he viewed justices as strategic actors whose efforts to achieve their preferences "are subject to political, legal, institutional, social, ideological, and ethical restraints."[2]

Murphy's work, although not very influential for some two decades after its publication, eventually helped to inspire the strategic or rational choice model of Supreme Court decision making. This model of judging was one manifestation of the "new institutionalist" emphasis in political science that appeared during the 1980s and served as "a challenge to the reductionist and [purely] instrumentalist conception of politics that characterized behavioralism." As a group, new institutionalists express "a renewed interest in studying how political behavior is given shape, structure, and direction by particular institutional arrangements and re-lationships." But rational choice or strategic new institutionalists retain the instrumental assumptions about judicial behavior that characterize the attitudinal model.[3]

Elaborating on this understanding of Supreme Court decision making, Lee Epstein and Jack Knight identify particular exogenous constraints—that is, factors external to the Court itself—that limit the ability of the justices to make policy: "Because [the justices] operate within the greater social and political context of the society as a whole, [they] . . . must attend to those informal rules that reflect dominant so-cietal beliefs about the rule of law in general and the role of the Supreme Court in particular—the norms of legitimacy." Judicial cognizance of social expectations regarding the rule of law are reflected in the justices' copious references in their opinions to, among other things, the plain meaning of legal language, the intentions of the framers, and, especially, past decisions of the Court. While proponents of the attitudinal model regard judicial references to legal sources merely as cover for personal policy preferences, defenders of the strategic model suggest that judicial policy making is *conditional* on the *public's willingness to accept* the Court's interpretation of legal language. In certain instances, justices may follow their perception of the public's understanding of precedent or the fram-ers' intentions rather than their own policy preferences; or they may settle for less than the full realization of their preferences in order to conform more closely to perceived public sentiment.[4]

Murphy identified an external constraint on Supreme Court policy making that also stems from the pressure of public opinion but, unlike societal norms regarding the rule of law, is extralegal in nature. Murphy opined that the justices may believe that their policy preferences are so incommensurate with cultural norms and assumptions that they risk inefficacy and perhaps even a loss of judicial prestige in rendering decisions consistent with those preferences. "Under such circumstances," he maintained, justices "might decide that it would be more moral [and productive] to compromise and aim for a lesser but possibly attainable good."[5]

Focusing on the political context in which the Supreme Court attempts to engage in policy making, Epstein and Knight contend that it is unreasonable to "expect the Court to ignore completely the external constraint imposed by the separation of powers system in constitutional cases." The justices are aware that Congress has used the power to amend the Constitution to override the Court's decisions, and that legislators have the powers to impeach justices, to curtail the Court's appellate jurisdiction, and to refuse to increase judicial salaries. Furthermore, since, as Alexander Hamilton observed, the Court has influence over neither sword nor purse, "government actors can refuse, implicitly or explicitly, to implement particular constitutional decisions, thereby decreasing the Court's ability to create efficacious policy."[6]

The factors that limit the ability of justices to convert their policy preferences into law are not simply exogenous, or external, to the Court; the justices also face endogenous constraints, that is, rules, procedures, and norms internal to the institution. Reflecting on the internal constraint that was most obvious to Chief Justice Earl Warren in *Brown,* Murphy observed, "Since [a member of the Court] shares decision-making authority with eight other judges, the first problem that a policy-oriented Justice would confront is that of obtaining at least four, and hopefully eight, additional votes for the results he wants and the kinds of opinions he thinks should be written in cases important to his objectives." As a result, justices must engage in strategic behavior with their colleagues as they attempt to shape the Court's rulings to conform to their policy preferences.[7]

In discussing the types of strategic behavior available to justices, Murphy declined to embrace a radically instrumental view of law. While he conceded that "the work of courts revolves around basically subjective value judgments," he suggested that "judges can and do weigh such factors as legal principles and precedents and well thought-out ideas of proper public policy." He added that "judges can be persuaded to change their minds about specific cases as well as about broad public policies, and [that] intellectual persuasion can play an important role in such shifts." (Presumably, Murphy believed that the parties before the Court, as well as the justices themselves, can serve as sources of legal arguments that inform a justice's vote.) Murphy noted that a justice can increase the chances that his colleagues will be receptive to his attempts to persuade them on the merits of the case by cultivating a collegial environment. The basic principle for members of the Court to follow is that "human courtesy and thoughtfulness . . . can do much to keep interpersonal relations on a plane where a meaningful exchange of ideas is possible."[8]

A justice who is unsuccessful in persuading others to accept his position is aware that his colleagues possess two major sanctions that they may employ to secure their preferences—their votes and their willingness to write separate opinions. Murphy observed that the potency of the former sanction "usually depends on the closeness of the vote." However, "there may be special situations, . . . as in the school segregation cases, [when] the general political environment in which the Court functions makes unanimity or near unanimity extraordinarily desirable." The effectiveness of a justice's willingness to write separately "depends largely on the literary and forensic skill of the particular judge." But, in a case like *Brown,* where a concurrence from any justice—to say nothing of a dissent from a southerner—risks increased social resistance, a justice need not possess special qualities for his threat to write separately to carry enormous weight. When persuasion has failed, the justices will "either turn to bargaining," with the ever-present threat of sanctions serving to encourage cooperation, "or reconcile themselves to loss of the advantages which they would accrue from compromising over the . . . points of difference." "Bargaining is most likely to occur," Murphy suggested, "when men agree on some matters, disagree on others, and still feel that further agreement would be profitable." Bargaining will involve even the most recalcitrant member of the Court when, as in *Brown,* "the general political environment requires unanimity."[9]

When bargaining fails to secure the support of justices—and when a justice is "trying to pick up additional votes or [is] trying to get a majority to agree to an institutional opinion in preference to seriatim expression of views"—a would-be policy maker still has recourse: He might "appeal to loyalty to the Court as an institution." Circumstances permitting, a policy-oriented justice might also "play on the isolation of a would-be dissenter." In short, while Murphy contended that the making of policy is of primary interest to the justices, he believed that the willingness of members of the Court to abide by an appeal to institutional loyalty demonstrates that policy making is not their exclusive goal.[10]

External Constraints (1952)

CONCERNS OVER THE RULE OF LAW

Even a cursory examination of the available conference notes from the Court's initial consideration of *Brown* in 1952 indicates that, in conformity with the tenets of the strategic model, the justices recognized the existence of exogenous constraints on their decision making. In an apparent effort to facilitate discussion of a complicated issue, the justices heeded Justice Robert Jackson's advice and avoided taking a formal vote.[11] But, of the eight justices who eventually decided the case (Chief Justice Fred Vinson died during consideration of *Brown*), most regarded social expectations concerning judicial fidelity to the rule of law as a major barrier to a desegregation ruling.[12]

In sharp contrast to the LDF's lawyers, the Kentuckian, Stanley Reed, maintained that segregation satisfied the requirement of the Fourteenth Amendment that a legislative classification have a basis in reason. He "agree[d] [that the] Constitution [is] not fixed" and that "what was due process [or equal protection] in 1860 may not be today." Yet he confessed that he could "not say [the] time [had] come when [the] 17 states [that allow or require segregation] are denying equal protection or due process." True, "there are some who want to hold [the] negro down by denying him educational equipment," who "desire [to] keep [him] a laborer" through school segregation. But he believed that "there is a reasonable body of opinion in the various states" that believes "separation of [the] races is for [the] benefit of both." As evidence of the reasonableness of segregation, he observed that, while "there has been some amalgamation of the races," "negroes have not been assimilated." Certainly, in "the deep south," Reed insisted, "separate but equal schools must be allowed." He also maintained that "the advancement of the interests of the negroes" had occurred under segregation and that "segregation is gradually disappearing." Until the day when the practice vanishes altogether, however ("in 15 or 20 years" in the border states), he believed that, under the Fourteenth Amendment, the Court had no choice but to respect the "informed views" of the state legislatures and to allow those bodies "to make up their minds on this question." Several justices recorded Reed as stating explicitly that he would vote to uphold segregation as constitutional.[13]

At the same time that Felix Frankfurter voiced sympathy for the petitioners, he, like Reed, expressed deep skepticism concerning the legal basis of a desegregation decree. While the former Harvard law professor confessed that he "never had close living relations to negroes," he was careful to note that he was "asst. counsel to [the] NAACP," and that, as a Jew, he was also a member of a minority group. Moreover, Frankfurter stated that he was "prepared today to vote that segregation in [Washington, D.C.] *does* violate [the] due process" clause of the Fifth Amendment. Referring to "the experiences of colored people [in Washington,] especially [those of William] Coleman, one of his old law clerks," he said that he found it "*intolerable* that DC would permit segregation." Yet he declared that the "D.C. *case raises different questions*" than the state cases. With regard to the state litigation, he conceded that he did not "see anything . . . in [the] Equal Protection [clause] . . . that leads me to say [we] must deal only with [the] physical" dimension of equality in public education. But, echoing the mistrust that he had expressed during oral argument toward the petitioners' use of social science evidence to demonstrate the less tangible harms of segregation as well as the unreasonableness of the practice, he said the Court could "not treat [the state cases] as sociological questions." He also believed that the evidence regarding the framers' intentions afforded little basis for declaring segregation unconstitutional. Justice William Douglas recorded Frankfurter as stating that "he has read all of [the] history [of the Fourteenth Amendment] and he can't say it meant to abolish segregation." In conclusion, Frankfurter asked, "What justifies us in saying that what *was* equal in 1868 is not equal now[?]" He confessed that he could not say that "this Court has long misread the Const[itution]" in permitting segregation, that "it's unconstitutional to treat a negro differently than a white." Unlike Reed, however, he did not suggest that he would vote to sustain the constitutionality of segregation. Instead, he found it "*highly desirable*" that the Court "put all [of] the cases down for reargument."[14]

Jackson apparently believed that the legal barriers to a desegregation ruling were even more formidable than either Reed or Frankfurter suggested. Unlike Frankfurter, he did not state that he was willing to declare segregation unconstitutional in the District of Columbia. And, unlike Reed, he did not suggest that the meaning of the Constitution is flexible. He emphasized that standard interpretations of conventional legal materials provided no support for a constitutional challenge to segregation. Approaching the matter "as a lawyer," the former country lawyer from upstate New York and attorney general for Franklin Roosevelt said he found "nothing in the text [of the Constitution] that says [segregation] is unconstitutional . . . nothing in the opinions of the courts that says [the practice is] unconstitutional . . . [and] nothing in the history of the 14th Amendment" that should move the Court to side with the petitioners. With regard to the petitioners' efforts to demonstrate that segregation both harms black children and violates the reasonableness requirement of the equal protection clause, he, in contrast to Reed, claimed no special insight into the cultural landscape of the South. He admitted that he had "never really [been] conscious of racial issues until [he] came to D.C." Like Frankfurter, he expressed skepticism toward "[Thurgood] Marshall's brief [which] starts and ends with sociology." Furthermore, he suggested, contrary to the statements of the petitioners' expert witnesses, "it will be bad for the negroes to be put into white schools." "I don't know the effect of segregation or [the] reason for it," Harold Burton recorded Jackson as saying, but "[we] can't cure this situation by putting [black and white] children together."[15]

Tom Clark spoke with more assurance about the rationale for segregation, at least in his home state of Texas. There, he said, "the problem [of maintaining racial harmony] is as acute as anywhere." Besides the complicated matter of relations between blacks and whites, "Texas also has the Mexican problem." By way of illustration, he maintained that "some negro girls get in trouble" when a "Mexican boy of 15 is in a class with a negro girl of 12."[16] Like Reed, Jackson, and, to a lesser degree, Frankfurter, Clark was suggesting that segregationist states had met the baseline requirement of the equal protection clause—that there exist a rational relationship between the trait used as the basis of a legislative classification (i.e., race) and the legislative goal (i.e., the preservation of racial harmony).

Hugo Black was equally confident that he understood the purpose of segregation. In sharp contrast to the other southerners on the Court, however, he concluded that the practice neither satisfied the reasonableness requirement of the equal protection clause nor accorded with the intentions of the framers of the Fourteenth Amendment. He told the conference that "he is compelled to belief [sic] that [the] reason for segregation is the opinion [that] the colored people are inferior." The Alabamian insisted that he did "not need books" to reach that conclusion. Southerners desire segregation "to prevent the mixture of the races," which they regard as "very dangerous [because it will] weaken the white race." Just as Black was certain that "the purpose of [segregation] law is to discriminate on account of color," he was equally convinced "that the [Civil War]

Amendments had as their basic purpose the abolition of such castes." He informed his brethren that he was inclined to "vote to end segregation."[17]

In spite of these observations, Black conceded that society's commitment to the rule of law served as something of a barrier to desegregation. He revealed, first, that he was "not sure Congress is barred by the same limitations as the states." Taking a position opposite to that of Frankfurter, he explained that Congress might be able to "legislate [to enforce segregation] where [the] states cannot [because only the latter are] bound by the 14th Amendment." Black also indicated that his conclusion that "segregation itself violate[s] [the Fourteenth] Amendment" might be rendered problematic if "the long line of [Court] decisions [regarding the practice] bars that construction of the amendment." He even recommended that if "equal and separate . . . is going to be [the] rule [of the Court] wide latitude should be given [to the] findings in state courts."[18]

In contrast to their brethren, Douglas, Burton, and Sherman Minton demonstrated little of the same concern over squaring a desegregation ruling with the rule of law. Douglas told the conference that the "cases [are] very simple for me." "I can't avoid [the] conclusion Hugo [Black] has reached in [the] State cases," he said, and indicated that the Court should render the "same [result] in [the] D.C. [controversy]." In Douglas's view, "no classification on the basis of race can be made" under either the equal protection clause of the Fourteenth Amendment or the due process clause of the Fifth.[19]

Similarly, Burton declared that, just as the "states do not have [a] choice [since] segregation violates [the] equal protection" clause of the Fourteenth Amendment, the due process clause of the "5th Amendment bars segregation" at the federal level. He believed that the Court could not rule otherwise. As the LDF's lawyers had argued, the university cases—"*Sipuel [v. Board of Regents of the University of Oklahoma* and] *Sweatt [v. Painter*—]control" in the present suits. In those cases, the Court acknowledged the relevance of the intangible aspects of education to a determination of equality and indicated that "education is more than buildings and faculties—it's a habit of mind." Consequently, "separate education is not sufficient for today[']s problems[,] [it is] not reasonable to educate [children] separately for a joint life." As evidence of the ability of whites and blacks to coexist in an integrated setting, Burton "referr[ed] to his policies as Mayor of Cleveland in putting colored nurses, etc. in white hospitals" where they earned the "respect" of those with whom they worked.[20]

Finally, Minton noted that the Court was confronted with a "body of law [that] has laid down [the] separate but equal doctrine." But, like Burton, he thought "that [principle] . . . has been whittled away" by *Sweatt* and *McLaurin v. Oklahoma State Regents for Higher Education.* "Classification on the basis of race," he asserted, is "invidious and can't be maintained." As for "Congress [having long] authorized segregation," he simply declared, "It's not legal." "Segregation is per se unconstitutional," he announced; "[I am] ready to vote [against it] now."[21]

EXTRALEGAL CONCERNS

While none of these three justices believed that societal norms regarding the rule of law presented a substantial barrier to a desegregation ruling, two of them acknowledged another external constraint on judicial policy making—the supposed inability or reluctance of affected populations to adapt to a judicial directive that requires profound changes in behavior. Minton conceded that the Court's "decree will cause trouble." But he downplayed the significance of this likelihood, stating that "the [black] race carries trouble with it"; Americans should be willing to endure such a burden, given that "the negro is oppressed and has been in bondage for years after slavery was abolished." Douglas, by contrast, observed that while "the answer [to the legal questions presented] is simple . . . the application of [the principle announced] may present great difficulties" that "will take a long time to work out." He informed his brethren that he would "not mind setting down [the] DC [case]" for reargument, although he was against using a similar strategy in the state cases. Even in the state cases, however, he counseled that the Court "not rush [its] pronouncements." Burton, likewise, indicated that "he would give plenty of time [to the segregating states] in this decree"; he "agree[d] that [desegregation] should be done in [as] easy [a] way as possible." "We can use time," he said.[22]

Nearly all of the justices who had commented on the impediment that social expectations regarding the rule of law presented to a desegregation ruling also indicated that the Court had to expect and respond to social resistance to such a decision. Apparently anticipating substantial opposition to desegregation, Frankfurter nevertheless "deprecate[d] any activities by force of law that might be used" against recalcitrant segregationists. Intimating that he believed immediate enforcement of a desegregation order would embolden the Court's opponents, he observed that "these are equity suits . . . [that] involve imagination in shaping decrees." He suggested to his brethren that they "ask counsel on reargument to address themselves to [the] problems of enforcement" and put forth "very specific questions . . . [regarding the] manner in which [a desegregation order] would be carried out."[23]

Jackson echoed Frankfurter's concerns when he stated that the Court "should perhaps give [the states] time to get rid of [segregation] and [that] he would go along on that basis." The Court, he said, should pursue "equitable remedies that can be shaped to the needs" of particular communities. Indeed, he declared that he "won't be a party to immediate" enforcement of a desegregation order.[24]

Clark, likewise, believed that the Court could help matters "if [it] can delay action." He even went so far as to state that the justices "should give lower courts the right to withhold relief in light of troubles" that attend the Court's decision. He informed the conference that "he would go along with that." In a not-so-veiled threat to dissent, however, he indicated that, should his brethren do "otherwise[,] he would say [the Court] had led the states on to think segregation is OK and . . . should let them work it out."[25]

Black spoke more forcefully than any of his colleagues about the external constraint of social intransigence toward desegregation. He warned that "there may be violence if [the] Court holds segregation unlawful." At the very least, "states would probably take evasive measures while purporting to obey" the Court's directive, and "S[outh] C[arolina] will . . . [even] go [through the] forms [of] abolishing" public education. "The courts," he reminded the conference, "would then be in the firing line for enforcement through [their use of] injunctions and contempt [citations]." Black stated that he was "driven to the issue [that segregation is unconstitutional] with [the] knowledge that it will mean trouble" and "bring drastic things." As a consequence, he, like almost all of his brethren, recommended that "there should be leeway for change" in the states.[26]

To the external, extralegal factor of anticipated social intransigence, Frankfurter and Jackson added the preferences and actions of the elected branches of the federal government. Acknowledging the importance of executive involvement for the successful implementation of a desegregation order, Frankfurter mentioned as one reason for rearguing the cases the "enormous" "social gains of having them accomplished with executive sanction." He told the conference that it is "very important that [the] D[istrict] of C[olumbia] case be set down for reargument when the new [Eisenhower] administration comes in . . . [because] it is a gain in law administration if [desegregation] comes not [simply] as a pronouncement

of coercive law [from the Court] but with the help of the new administration that has promised to change the law here in the District."[27] In a
similar vein, Jackson underscored the significance of legislative involvement for an efficacious desegregation ruling. He spoke of "work[ing mat-
ters] out so we can say segregation [is] 'bad' . . . under approval of [the]
Court + [with the] support of Congress." Jackson even alluded to the
happy possibility that asking "the Senate & House [Judiciary] Committees . . . to file briefs and [re]argue" the District of Columbia case might
get them "stirred up to [the] point [that] they may abolish [segregation]"
without judicial involvement.[28]

IMPLICATIONS

The response of attitudinalists to the justices' numerous references
to external factors in the conference notes in *Brown* is predictable.
Frankfurter's and Jackson's recorded comments regarding the supposed
constraint of the elected branches of government include no recommendations that the justices curtail or modify a desegregation order to
correspond more closely to the policy preferences of national politicians.
Rather, these justices hoped that the federal government would provide
support for, rather than resistance to, a desegregation decree, at least in
the District of Columbia. More significantly, none of the justices who
expressed concern over the possibility of social disorder or the difficulty
of demonstrating fidelity to the rule of law ultimately voted to sustain
the constitutionality of segregation. Judicial hand-wringing over the rule
of law or the public's anticipated response to a ruling, no matter how
conspicuous, does not amount to evidence of an exogenous constraint
on decision making. Finally, in view of the difficulty that the petitioners
experienced in articulating a compelling legal argument regarding the
unconstitutionality of segregation, attitudinalists would suggest that the
burden rests with those who would use legal considerations to explain
the votes of those justices who maintained that law led them to side with
the petitioners in *Brown.*

But this response to the conference notes overlooks the fact that, while
the justices voted in favor of the petitioners, they were also nearly unanimous in insisting on delayed implementation of a desegregation order.[29]
In short, even assuming the centrality of the justices' attitudes to their
votes in *Brown,* the attitudinal model cannot account for the willingness
of the justices to postpone the realization of their policy preferences in
response to anticipated resistance. By contrast, a strategic interpretation
of *Brown* posits that the justices would respond in just this way to such

external constraints in an effort at least to approximate their preference that federal and state governments abandon school segregation forthwith. As Walter Murphy observed, the justices thought it the better part of wisdom not to demand "that white America make instantly operational the kind of casteless society explicit in democratic theory and implicit in the Fourteenth Amendment."[30]

The justices' conference notes also provide reason to question the instrumental assumption that all members of the Court voted according to their personal policy preferences in *Brown*. Certainly, a justice's intimation that the respondents satisfied the reasonableness requirement of the equal protection clause, or his suggestion that the framers of the Fourteenth Amendment accepted segregation, does not necessarily indicate personal support for racial separation. Rather, such comments may merely represent an admission that legal norms presented barriers, albeit surmountable ones, to the achievement of a desegregation policy preference. Moreover, three of the four justices who voiced the strongest concerns over the rule of law—Frankfurter, Jackson, and Clark—at least intimated a willingness to support a declaration of the unconstitutionality of segregation when they expressed the desire and need for delayed implementation of a desegregation order. But it is much more difficult to reconcile the comments that Justice Reed made in conference with an instrumental interpretation of his desegregation vote. Reed gave no indication of support for a desegregation ruling under any circumstances. The fairest interpretation of his remarks as recorded in the justices' notes—especially recalling from the preceding chapter the racist comments that he made out of Court, the 1954 polling data that revealed a low level of support for desegregation among college-educated southerners, and studies of ideological drift which suggest that he had become significantly more conservative by the time the Court rendered *Brown*—is that his defense of the reasonableness of elementary and secondary school segregation betrayed not a begrudging acknowledgement that the respondents had satisfied the baseline requirement of the equal protection clause but a belief in the wisdom of the practice as a matter of public policy.

Similarly, Clark's remarks in conference regarding the relevance of segregation to the particular circumstances of Texas, and his threat to dissent if his brethren did not permit the lower courts to deny relief, render problematic any effort to characterize his vote in *Brown* as indicative of a marked preference for desegregation. Clark's remarks would seem to fit with the 1954 polling data and with the fact that he hailed from East Texas, which resembled the Deep South. Those comments led

Justice Frankfurter to think that, had the justices rendered a decision after the initial hearing, Clark would have dissented along with Chief Justice Vinson and Justices Reed and Jackson. Justice Douglas went even further, suggesting that Clark—along with Reed and Vinson—believed not only "that segregation was constitutional" but also "that the *Plessy* case was right." That Douglas drew a distinction between a belief in constitutionality and a belief in the rightness of segregation as a matter of public policy is implied by the fact that he suggested Frankfurter and Jackson believed only "that segregation in the public schools was probably constitutional."[31]

Given the outcome in *Brown,* something Clark and Reed experienced permitted them to feel less reluctant about declaring segregation unconstitutional in the nation's elementary and secondary schools. But an explanation of the desegregation votes of these men requires more than reference to the petitioners' responses to the questions that the Court posed for the rehearing of the case. The justices' conference notes provide no indication that the petitioners' arguments did anything to assuage Reed's concerns (or the concerns of his brethren, for that matter), or that the petitioners inspired a statement by Clark after the rehearing that he scorned segregation.

External Constraints (1953)

EXTRALEGAL CONCERNS

The exogenous constraint of anticipated social resistance figured prominently in the comments of the justices during reconsideration of the cases in 1953. In view of the cursory manner in which Thurgood Marshall and his colleagues had addressed the justices' questions regarding the enforcement of a desegregation order, and considering that the lawyers could not substantiate their optimistic prediction of ready compliance with such a decision, few members of the Court felt comfortable ordering an immediate end to segregation in elementary and secondary schools.

Although the new chief justice, Earl Warren, expressed clear support for desegregation (he precluded a formal vote on the cases by recommending that they "be discussed informally in view of their importance"), he provided detailed comments on the issue of social resistance to such a ruling. Presiding over the conference of the justices (from which Justice Black was absent because of an illness in his family), Warren told his new colleagues that it would be "unfortunate if we had to take precipitous

acts that would inflame [the situation] more than necessary." He counseled that "the conditions in [the] extreme South should [be] carefully
considered." He expected that the situation in Kansas and Delaware was
"not much diff[erent] from [that in his home state of] Calif[ornia]," since
each of these states had limited numbers of African Americans. But he
anticipated that, especially with regard to the Deep South, it "will take
all the wisdom of the Court to [secure desegregation] with a minimum
of emotion and strife." The justices, he said, "should abolish [segregation]
in a tolerant way" and recognize "that [the] time element is important in
the deep south."[32]

Except for Black, who was absent, Warren received support on this
point from every justice who had voiced similar concerns the preceding
year. Frankfurter averred that the Court "must not be self-righteous and
'God-Almighty' when writing" its decision, lest it provoke even greater
resistance than it could already expect. Douglas suggested that the justices
"not try to anticipate too much" in their decision, and should "recognize
[that] adjustments will have to [be made]" during enforcement of the
ruling. Jackson insisted that the Court "must go way beyond what the
[federal government] has worked [out]," in terms of grade-by-grade or
school-by-school desegregation plans, if it hopes to secure its ruling. And
he recommended against declaring segregation unconstitutional while
"leav[ing] the [issue of remedy] to another fight." "We would have to
give advice to the lower courts," he said, lest "some put all Boards of
education in jail . . . [while] others would not give negroes any relief."
Nevertheless, he predicted that "resistance would be immeasurably increased" if the justices demanded immediate compliance with the decision. Likewise, Burton indicated that he "would go a long way to agree
to put off enforcement and to give [the] District Court[s] discretion."
Finally, Clark apparently spoke with some passion about the dangers of
insisting on immediate compliance. He claimed special insight into the
issue before the Court, having "lived with" segregation and been "closer
to [the practice] than any [justice] except [Black]." Clark warned of the
"danger of violence if [the matter of remedy is] not well handled," and he
mentioned the prospect that Governor (and former U.S. Supreme Court
justice) James Byrnes of South Carolina might "just abolish [that state's]
public schools." He declared that he "does not like the system of segregation and will vote to abolish it" but insisted that "the remedy should be
carefully worked out." Specifically, he thought that "various conditions
will require different handling . . . [and] the [Court's] opinion must indicate that clearly."[33]

In contrast to his colleagues, Minton, as in 1952, did not expect that social resistance would present a significant barrier to a desegregation ruling. He even retreated from his prediction of the preceding year that a desegregation decree would inspire problems, which the Court could overcome. While conceding there "may be trouble in the offing," he now said "he doubts it" will occur. Nevertheless, following the example of his brethren, he informed the conference that "as to remedies [he was] inclined to let the District Courts have their heads in this matter." In other words, he wanted them to have ample discretion to respond to local conditions.[34]

CONCERNS OVER THE RULE OF LAW

The consistency that the justices demonstrated between 1952 and 1953 in their attentiveness to the external constraint of social resistance was also present in their individual views regarding the matter of desegregation as it related to social expectations concerning the rule of law. While the negligence of the LDF's lawyers was at least partly responsible for the Court's continued concern that social resistance worked against prompt desegregation, Thurgood Marshall and his colleagues were less culpable for the persistent belief among several of the justices that a decision in favor of the petitioners would lack a legal basis. Yet, in spite of the LDF's concerted and painstaking efforts to address the justices' questions for reargument regarding the intentions of the framers of the Fourteenth Amendment and the import of precedent, Chief Justice Warren—who was not on the Court in 1952 and thus did not respond to the LDF's initial presentation of the case—was apparently the only justice whose position on the legal basis of desegregation might have been influenced significantly by the petitioners' briefs and presentations. The positions of his colleagues remained virtually unchanged.

In determining "whether [the Court is] called upon to override the older cases and lines of reasoning," Warren first examined the view that segregation satisfies the reasonableness requirement of the Fourteenth Amendment. He told the conference that the "only way to sustain Plessy" and the "separate but equal doctrine [is to accept its] basic premise that the Negro race is inferior." "If we are to sustain seg[regation]," he insisted, "we must do it on that basis." He then declared that the "argument of [the] negro counsel [in the present cases] proves they are not inferior." Warren could "not see how segregation can be justified in this day and age." To "set one group apart from the rest & say [they are] not entitled to *exactly [the] same* treatment of all others," he continued, would also violate traditional legal norms, since the "13th, 14th, and 15th Amendments were intended to make equal those who once were slaves."[35]

Warren received the support of those justices who, during the initial consideration of the cases, had suggested that the rule of law was not a barrier to a desegregation ruling. Although Black did not attend the conference, Douglas reported that "he sent in his vote indicating that he thought that segregation in the public schools was unconstitutional." While Black was still concerned that segregation in the District of Columbia was constitutional (Douglas noted in conference that his colleague "probably" held his earlier view that the "DC [case presented] a different problem"), his reservations about the force of precedent in the state cases apparently were insufficient to overcome his conviction that the original purpose of the Fourteenth Amendment was to abolish such caste distinctions.[36]

Douglas conceded more to the segregationists' argument than he had the preceding year, noting that the "history [of the Fourteenth Amendment has] mixed light in it." But he still regarded the issue before the Court as "a simple problem." "Race and color," he said, "cannot be a constitutional standard for segregating the schools." He indicated that he "would join Warren's [position] and reasons."[37]

Burton reiterated his belief that the Court had "no choice in [the] matter but to act," and he suggested that the justices would have no difficulty "work[ing] it out on a judicial basis." "Prior to [the] 14th Amendment," he declared, the "states could do what they liked . . . [but] now they cannot." In accordance with his views of the preceding year that the decisions in the university cases supported desegregation in the present suits, he stated that the Court "can't draw a line between types of schools"; the "principle applicable to graduate school," he argued, "is applicable to primary school." "At [the] time of [the] 14th Amendment life was separate," he observed. But now racial separation in school is unreasonable and, therefore, unconstitutional because it provides "inadequate preparation for the life [of] today." He contended that the due process clause of the Fifth Amendment requires the same conclusion in the District of Columbia case.[38]

Minton, as he had in 1952, supported Burton's views regarding the force of precedent. "Plessy v. Ferguson is a weak reed today," he argued, because the *McLaurin* decision "greatly weakened" the concept of separate but equal. He added that he could not "imagine a valid distinction in *color*" that government could advance to support the reasonableness of segregation. Along with Warren, he maintained that the "only basis left [for segregation] is [a belief in the] inferiority" of blacks, a belief that time had proven to be false. "This is a different world today than [in the] 1860s," he observed. Adding a historical dimension to his analysis, courtesy of the LDF, Minton now suggested that segregation and the separate-but-equal principle conflicted with the original purpose of the Fourteenth Amendment, which "was to wipe out the badge of slavery" of racial caste distinctions. That amendment, he asserted, "says 'equal' rights not separate but equal"; the latter "is a lawyer's addition to the language." Echoing the LDF's lawyers, he contended that, in fact, the Court's "early [Fourteenth Amendment] cases indicate that these badges [of slavery] should [be] wiped out"; specifically, the "Slaughter [House] and Strauder [v. West Virginia] cases say so." He also suggested, once again, that segregation in the District of Columbia represented a "denial of due process."[39]

While the LDF's efforts during reargument may have reinforced or complemented the views that Minton, among others, possessed in 1952, the justices who had expressed concerns at that time about squaring a desegregation decision with the rule of law found these efforts singularly unconvincing. Reed, for instance, categorically rejected the view that the framers of the Fourteenth Amendment had intended to do away with all racial distinctions in the law including segregation. He believed that the evidence of intent that the justices might acquire from "contemporaneous interpretation[s]" of the amendment by "people [who] were familiar with it at firsthand" suggests that "it was valid to have separate school leg[islation]." As in 1952, Reed conceded that the Court did not necessarily have to follow this understanding of the amendment; the Constitution, he reiterated, is "dynamic" and "what was const[itutional] in Plessy might not be const[itutional] now." But he still believed that "children may be forced to separate without a violation of the equal protection clause." He forcefully rejected Warren's contention that segregationists could only put forth an unreasonable belief in racial inferiority to justify the practice. Consistent with his statements to the conference in 1952, he asserted that "segregation is not done on [the basis of a belief in racial] inferiority but on [the basis of] racial differences." Segregation, in short, "protects people against [the potentially incendiary] mixing of races." He agreed that "there is no 'inferior race'" and that state compliance with the separate-but-equal principle "has not been satisfactory." But he announced that if he were "writing on a clean slate [he] probably would say [along with the states that we] should have seg[regation]." He recommended, once again, that the Court "not move to change the law. . . . If there is to be a change Congress should do it."[40]

While Frankfurter did not implore his brethren to sustain the constitutionality of segregation, he, like Reed, retained strong doubts about the legal basis for a desegregation ruling. In terms reminiscent of his aggressive response during reargument to the petitioners' historical analysis of the Fourteenth Amendment, he told the conference that "as a pure matter of history . . . [the Amendment] did not have a purpose to abolish segregation." The "most [that] the history shows," he suggested, is "that the matter was [i]nconclusive." Here, Frankfurter drew on the work of his law clerk, Alexander Bickel, who, at the request of the justice, had "read afresh every word in the Congressional Globe bearing on what ultimately became the Fourteenth Amendment." Frankfurter had circulated the product of Bickel's efforts—a detailed, sixty-three page document—shortly before reargument. In an attached cover memorandum, he asserted that the research was, "in a word, inconclusive in the sense that the 39th Congress as an enacting body neither manifested that the Amendment outlawed segregation in the public schools or authorized legislation to that end, nor that it manifested the opposite." Although Frankfurter was willing to entertain Bickel's conclusion, a conclusion the federal government had put forth during reargument, he still found troubling "a host of legislation passed by Congress [which] presupposes that segregation is valid," as well as the "history . . . in this [C]ourt [which] indicates that *Plessy* is right."[41]

With the exception of indicating no receptivity to the idea of the inconclusiveness of the history of the Fourteenth Amendment, Jackson sounded a similar theme in his remarks to the conference. He observed, as had the petitioners, that "education at [the] time of the 14th amendment was not an issue." But he also noted that, while "[President Abraham] Lincoln [was] not quoted in the argument [before the Court,] . . . he was extremely limited in his objectives." Furthermore, he argued, "precedents and custom" support those who would maintain the constitutionality of segregation. Jackson informed his brethren that he "personally [did] not [have] a problem" with desegregation. But, reiterating his concerns of the preceding year, he said that the "problem is to make a judicial basis for a congenial political conclusion." "As a political decision," he declared, "[I] can go along with it." But he did not "know how to justify the abolition of segregation as a judicial act."[42]

Clark provided yet more evidence of the limited effectiveness of the LDF's efforts to demonstrate a legal basis for a desegregation ruling. He now confessed that, while "he [had] always thought the 14th Amend[ment] covered the matter and outlawed segregation[,] . . . the history shows different[ly.]" He regarded the fact that the "same Congress [and] same legislators" that proposed the Fourteenth Amendment also "recognized separate schools" in the District of Columbia as "almost unassailable" evidence of the historical legitimacy of segregation. After indicating that he would "go along [with a desegregation decree] as [he] said before," he insisted that the Court "can't rely on leg[islative] history" to justify such a ruling.[43]

UNRESOLVED ISSUES

Since Frankfurter, Jackson, Reed, and Clark each ultimately voted against school segregation, attitudinalists would characterize as insignificant the concerns that these men voiced after as well as before reargument over squaring a desegregation ruling with the rule of law. Indeed, Clark's comment after the rehearing that he disliked segregation, which is consistent with studies of ideological drift that identify him as one of only three justices who had become significantly more liberal by the time the Court rendered *Brown,* suggests a connection between the justice's desegregation vote and his personal policy preferences. But it is difficult to explain the abruptness of his supposed ideological transformation, given that he defended segregation in 1952, while the significant leftward shift that scholars recorded in his voting occurred around 1953.[44] The social forces that promoted a liberalization of American racial attitudes at midcentury should have inspired a more gradual change. It is even less likely that those forces affected Justice Reed in such a way as to explain his vote in *Brown.* Reed's forceful defense of segregation after as well as before the rehearing (to say nothing of his racist comments off the Court or of the increased conservatism to which studies of ideological drift point) strongly suggests that, while his legal concerns did not prevent him from voting for desegregation, an explanation of his behavior must be found in something other than his policy preferences.

Evidence that Earl Warren accommodated or responded to the legal concerns of Reed and others when he wrote the opinion for the Court would suggest not only that the chief justice's colleagues did not vote for desegregation in spite of their legal objections but also that Warren took the norm of the rule of law seriously as an external constraint on judicial policy making. Put another way, if he, like most people, viewed the actions and words of others through the lens of his own motives, such accommodations of his colleagues' stated concerns would indicate a belief on his part that something more than personal policy preferences operate in judicial decision making—that precedent or history can lead a justice to a conclusion at odds with his own preferences. Had he believed that rulings are mere reflections of justices' values, he would have regarded efforts to accommodate the legal views of colleagues who favored his policy as necessary only to prevent them from writing separately. And he would have viewed as futile attempts to respond to the legal concerns of those opposed to that policy. If Warren possessed any sense that the rule of law functioned as a constraint on judicial policy making, he would have been concerned about each of the justices who expressed reservations on this matter. He said that he understood "the desirability of achieving unanimity if possible" in a ruling likely to be so controversial.[45]

The obstacles to a united Court involved more than the legal qualms of four justices, since four of the five individuals who expressed *no* reservations regarding the rule of law still voiced concerns about social resistance to desegregation. (Recall that Frankfurter, Jackson, and Clark expressed these concerns as well.) Subsequent conference discussions on *Brown* revealed clearly that agreement on the need for delayed implementation of a desegregation ruling in no way implied consensus on the specifics of executing the order.[46]

We must continue to look to the strategic model for an explanation of the manner in which the justices resolved their differences over the rule of law and the matter of implementation since an attitudinal understanding of Supreme Court decision making explains only voting behavior.[47] While the justices' willingness to delay implementation of a desegregation order renders *Brown* a counterexample to the attitudinalist premise that justices simply vote their sincere policy preferences in cases, the existence and ultimate resolution of substantial differences among the justices over implementation and the rule of law provides another illustration of important judicial behavior for which the attitudinal model cannot account: Chief Justice Warren had good reason to believe that a desegregation decision which featured a number of opinions would present the Court with a host of problems that a unanimous ruling would help to avoid.

Internal Constraints

EFFORTS TO PROMOTE COLLEGIALITY

Earl Warren's attempt to create a collegial environment during consideration of such a volatile issue as desegregation was of considerable importance to the achievement of unanimity in *Brown*. He commenced these efforts during his first conference on the cases, when, as noted earlier, he suggested, as had Jackson the preceding year, that the justices postpone a formal vote. "Realizing that when a person once announces he has reached a conclusion it is more difficult for him to change his thinking," he later explained, "we decided that we would dispense with our usual custom of formally expressing our individual views . . . and would confine ourselves for a time to informal discussion of the briefs, the arguments made at the hearing, and of our own independent research . . . , reserving our final opinions until the discussions were concluded."[48] Presumably, Warren was relieved that he had not asked his brethren to state, and thus rigidify, their formal positions when his initial discussion of the merits of the cases proved so unconvincing to a number of his colleagues and even inspired Reed's forceful response to his suggestion that only a belief in racial inferiority could explain the existence of segregation.

Warren continued to encourage informality in subsequent conferences on the cases, and he also attempted to promote collegiality and consensus by organizing luncheon discussions with his colleagues. Although Frankfurter and Jackson declined, and Black and Douglas were only occasional participants, Reed and Burton dined with Warren some twenty times after the initial conference, and Clark and Minton attended the discussions frequently. Burton's diary entry regarding a lunch that took place five days after the conference that followed the rehearing provides some insight into this particular effort to unify the Court. "After lunch," Burton wrote, "the Chief Justice told me of his plan to try [to] direct discussion of [the] segregation cases toward the decree—as presenting . . . the best chance of unanimity in that phase."[49] Warren may have thought that the near-universal sense among the justices that desegregation required delay would facilitate further agreement on the specific form that the Court's remedy should take. He also may have thought that resolution of the issue of remedy might, in turn, lessen the concern that several members of the Court had over reconciling a desegregation order with the rule of law.

If so, a record of a conference that occurred in mid-January 1954 reveals that Warren's optimism was unwarranted. Frankfurter's conference notes suggest that agreement was limited to the general point that the Court itself could not order relief in the individual school districts. As Warren said, the justices should engage in "as little administration as [they] can." Significant differences of opinion emerged when each justice turned to the matter of the appropriate body to handle the implementation of a desegregation order. Of those who expressed an opinion on the matter, and whose views Frankfurter managed to record, Warren and Black contended that the district courts should bear the burden of providing relief. Frankfurter and Douglas, by contrast, thought the Court should consider using a special master to enforce the ruling.[50]

The justices were even more divided on the issue of the degree of specificity that the Court's directions should assume. Warren believed that the justices "ought not to turn [the district courts] loose without guidance of what paths are open to them." Black could not have disagreed more, suggesting that they ought to "let [the district courts] work it out." When Warren inquired whether Black "would . . . give them any framework," the Alabamian responded, "I don't see how you could do it." Reed, Douglas, and Frankfurter took positions between the chief justice and Black. Reed indicated that the justices should articulate "general principles," although they "must say a few things" about the content of those principles. (Subsequent events would reveal that Reed's comments did not suggest that he had come to accept desegregation.) Douglas believed that, while it was "difficult to decide anything concrete," an enforcement decree should demonstrate "generosity [and] flexibility." Frankfurter argued in a memorandum to his colleagues that "an initial decree is bound to confine itself to general terms." Echoing the presentation of Assistant Attorney General J. Lee Rankin at the rehearing, Frankfurter averred, "When the wrong is a deeply rooted state policy the court does its duty if it decrees measures that reverse the direction of the unconstitutional policy so as to uproot it *'with all deliberate speed.'*"[51]

Perhaps in response to the impasse, and reflecting his own anguish over the matter, Jackson advocated, apparently in rather forceful terms, "a reargument on [the] terms of a decree!!" This suggestion represented a departure from his earlier admonition that the Court not separate the issue of remedy from the matter of the unconstitutionality of segregation. He displayed some of the vexation that inspired his call for reargument when, in contrast to his statement at the prior conference (that the Court could not insist on immediate enforcement of its decree), he observed, "If [desegregation is a] personal right [there is] no answer to Thurgood M[arshall]" of the LDF, who said that relief must not be delayed.[52]

Clark informed the conference that he, too, was "inclined" toward reargument, while Black indicated that he had "no objection to reargument" on the matter of remedy. Black gave the conference ample reason to ask the parties for a more careful treatment of the issue. Speaking as an authority on the South, he declared that the Court "can't take too long" to enforce desegregation. "In Ala[bama]," he said, "most liberals [are] praying for delay," because "any man [there] who would [speak] in [support of a desegregation decree] would be dead politically forever." He encouraged his brethren to "let it simmer" and to "let it battle time." Allowing the matter of remedy to stew was infinitely preferable to any rash attempt at enforcement, which, he warned, would bring a "Storm over this Court."[53]

In spite of these differences among the justices, according to Warren's account, the Court achieved consensus the following month on at least the constitutional issue in *Brown*. In February, he recalled, "it was agreed that we were ready to vote. [And] on the first vote, we unanimously agreed that the 'separate but equal' doctrine had no place in public education." "At the suggestion of some of the Justices," he added, "it was thought that [the Court's opinion] should bear the signature of the Chief Justice." Warren accepted the responsibility of writing the opinion and, given "the sensitiveness of the school segregation matter and the prying for inside information that surrounded the cases," he wrote his drafts under strict conditions of secrecy. Only the chief justice's law clerks assisted him, and "any writing between [his] office and those of the other Justices [was] delivered to the Justices personally." Warren had to deliver communications to Jackson in a hospital room, where he was convalescing after a serious heart attack on March 30. "Finally, at our conference on May 15," Warren said, "we agreed to announce our opinion the following Monday, subject to the approval of Mr. Justice Jackson." The still-recuperating justice agreed to the proposed opinion and even "insisted on attending the Court that day in order to demonstrate our solidarity."[54]

SEPARATE OPINIONS

While achieving unanimity in *Brown* was a stunning accomplishment, Warren's account of the Court's path to consensus is flawed in certain respects. As Richard Kluger notes, the Court was more likely to have voted on the issue of segregation in March—not February, as Warren remembered—given that, in February, the Senate had yet to confirm Warren's appointment to the chief justiceship. (In 1974, Warren indicated to a journalist that the vote occurred in late March.)[55] More important, the justices do not appear to have been unanimous in their vote. Warren had to confront the possibility that certain of his colleagues would write separately.

At some point after reargument, Reed drafted a dissent in which he asserted, "If 'equal protection,' in fact and now, is accepted as a true touchstone by which to judge the constitutionality of segregation, the argument is finished. . . . [The clause only] give[s] each citizen an opportunity to obtain facilities substantially equal to his neighbor for himself."[56] Correspondence between Frankfurter and the Kentuckian just days after the Court announced the rulings in the segregation cases indicates that Reed persisted in his belief in the constitutionality of segregation. Frankfurter wrote to his colleague: "I am not unaware of the hard struggle this involved in the conscience of your mind and in the mind of your conscience. I am not unaware, because all I have to do is look within. As a citizen of the Republic, even more than as a colleague, I feel deep gratitude for your share in what I believe to be a great good for our nation." To which Reed responded, "While there were many considerations that pointed to a dissent, they did not add up to a balance against the Court's opinion." He thought "the factors looking toward a fair treatment for Negroes are more important than the weight of history."[57]

Frankfurter was not disingenuous in referring to his own difficulties over declaring segregation unconstitutional, as his comments in the 1952 and 1953 conferences indicated. Like Reed, he felt compelled to commit his thoughts to paper, and he wrote several drafts of a short statement in the summer and fall of 1952. Unlike his colleague, he attempted to craft a legal argument that would *support* desegregation. Appearing to challenge the reasonableness of segregation under the Fourteenth Amendment, Frankfurter declared that a judge "cannot write into our Constitution a belief as to the different stages of development of colored and non-colored peoples. . . . To attribute such a view to science, as is sometimes done, is to reject the very basis of science, namely, the process of reaching verifiable conclusions." After challenging the notion of black intellectual inferiority, he implicitly questioned the view that segregation serves to prevent racial conflict. "Experience happily shows," he suggested, "that [racial] contacts tend to mitigate antagonism and to engender mutual respect." Surprisingly, Frankfurter then asserted, "All those considerations do not dispose of the Constitutional issue that is involved." Instead, he sought to justify a desegregation ruling with the observation that the concept of equal protection "does not reflect, as a congealed summary, the social arrangements and beliefs of a particular epoch." He concluded, "The effect of changes in men's feelings for what is right and just is equally relevant in determining whether differentiation of treatment by law is a denial of 'the equal protection of the laws.'"[58]

The tone of Frankfurter's 1952 memorandum suggests that, unlike Reed, he voted to end segregation in conference in March 1953. He sent the memorandum to Warren, although, with no date of receipt on the copy in the chief justice's file, it is not clear if the document figured into Warren's thinking when he drafted the opinion for the Court. Assuming a timely delivery on Frankfurter's part, the memorandum's unfinished quality and its apparent lack of confidence in the legal basis of a desegregation ruling suggest that the document merely reinforced the impression that the chief justice would have received of his colleague at the initial consideration of the cases after reargument: Frankfurter personally favored desegregation, but he had considerable trouble reconciling such a holding with the rule of law. While Frankfurter's remarks during oral argument and in conference precluded resort to precedent or constitutional history to justify the Court's ruling, his memorandum appeared to obviate a challenge to the reasonableness of segregation. Warren's consolation was that the date and cursory nature of Frankfurter's memorandum disclosed little desire on the part of his colleague to write a concurring opinion in the school segregation cases.

Jackson's progressively elaborate drafts of a statement for the cases, by contrast, gave every indication of a willingness on his part to write separately if he found the Court's opinion unsatisfactory. Indeed, his first draft, which he wrote in early January 1954, reads much like a dissent. While he conceded in the memorandum that desegregation "is congenial to my own background and views of fair and wise public policy," he said he "candidly [had] great difficulty in finding that segregation is contrary to any law that presently exists." Moving beyond the narrow conception of constitutional meaning that he had emphasized in conference, he agreed, "as Judge [Benjamin] Cardozo reminded us, that these Constitutional generalities [of due process and equal protection] 'have a content and a significance that vary from age to age.'" But, in elaborating on the point that "the Fourteenth Amendment . . . makes provision for recognizing and giving effect to changing conditions and currents of opinion in application of its principles to an expanding and developing society," he made abundantly clear that he was speaking of *Congress's* authority, under section five of the amendment, to eradicate segregation in American society: "If Congress were to find segregation an obstacle to achieving the purposes of the Amendment and that legislation to abolish it was therefore necessary and proper, I do not suppose any Justice would doubt the Constitutionality of such an act." "It is said," he observed, "that the South has enough representation to prevent such a step." But he apparently regarded this probability as insufficient reason for the Court to act since his final sentence—that this "means nothing less than we must act because our representative system has failed"—reads more like an expression of disbelief than a clarion call to judicial activism.[59]

Jackson's subsequent two drafts, which he wrote in February and March respectively, reveal that, in relatively short order, he had developed a legal argument for declaring segregation unconstitutional. In his third draft, and in a conciliatory gesture toward those who wondered "how it is that the Constitution this morning forbids what for three-quarters of a century it has tolerated or approved," he retained his personal confession regarding the difficulty of squaring a desegregation ruling with the rule of law. After a lengthy treatment of the difficulties that would attend the enforcement of a judicial decision invalidating segregation, however, Jackson explained why the Court could no longer sustain the constitutionality of that practice. "The necessity for judicial action on this subject," he declared, "arises from the doctrine concerning it which is already on our books." Specifically, the Court is beholden to the requirement of the equal protection clause that "classifications of different groups rest upon real and not upon feigned distinctions, that the distinction have some rational relation to the subject matter for which the classification is adopted." And, echoing the petitioners, he contended that the basis of racial classifications in education—that there are "differences between the Negro and the white races, viewed as a whole, such as to warrant separate classification and discrimination"—can no longer be maintained. (He omitted the fact that segregationists also portrayed racial separation as a necessary means to avoid racial conflict.) Jackson conceded that he did not know whether the presumption regarding black intellectual inferiority was warranted in earlier times, when blacks had little opportunity to demonstrate their capacity for education or even for self-support. The spectacular progress of black Americans, however—"one of the swiftest and most dramatic advances in the annals of man"—has enabled them "to outgrow and to overcome the presumptions on which [segregation] was based." In other words, "The handicap of inheritance and environment has been too widely overcome today to warrant these earlier presumptions based on race alone. . . . Mere possession of colored blood, in whole or in part, no longer affords a reasonable basis for a classification for educational purposes and . . . each individual must be rated on his own merit."[60]

The substance of Jackson's memoranda suggests that he voted to end segregation in the March conference. But the first and second of the three drafts reveal that he was committed to the view that the Court should base its argument on the unreasonableness of separating school children on the basis of race. He expressed profound skepticism concerning the wisdom of an effort to demonstrate the harms or inherent inequality of segregation, what with the vagaries of the social science evidence upon which the petitioners based this claim. Neglecting to mention that the petitioners had also used social science evidence to demonstrate the *un-reasonableness* of segregation, Jackson said, "[Even] if all the woes of colored children would be solved by forcing them into white company, I do not think we should import into the concept of equal protection of the law these elusive psychological and subjective factors. They are not determinable with satisfactory objectivity or mensurable [*sic*] with reasonable certainty. If we adhere to objective criteria the judicial process will still be capricious enough."[61]

BARGAINING AND APPEALS TO INSTITUTIONAL LOYALTY

Jackson's secretary, Elsie Douglas, reported that, although the justice did not circulate his draft opinions to the members of the Court generally, he used them "in conference with C. J. Warren at Doctors Hospital."[62] While Warren would have regarded a dissent from Reed as a catastrophic blow to the force of a desegregation ruling, he would have viewed a concurrence in Jackson's characteristically brilliant prose as only slightly less damaging. Jackson's weakened condition reduced the likelihood that he would have the will or energy to write separately. But Warren could not and did not expect that his efforts to promote collegiality during consideration of the segregation cases would be sufficient to secure the support of Jackson or any of the other justices. With several members of the Court still expressing concerns about the form or even the existence of a legal basis for a desegregation order, and with the justices severely divided over the issue of remedy, Warren demonstrated a marked willingness to bargain with his colleagues when he composed the opinion for the Court.

Bargaining typically occurs during the circulation of opinions, when the justices indicate their preferences to an opinion writer, either by issuing bargaining statements (i.e., requests for changes) on a circulated draft or by circulating their own writings, which they hope will influence the final form of that justice's opinion. As Lee Epstein and Jack Knight observe, however, bargaining "can begin directly after conference, even before opinions begin to circulate."[63] Apparently, the bargaining in the segregation cases commenced well before Warren submitted his opinion to his colleagues since, in his uncirculated first draft, he put aside his preference regarding the appropriate method for implementing a desegregation decision. Rather than attempt to convince his brethren to provide guidance and hoist on the district courts the responsibility for executing the Court's judgment, he sought consensus by adopting Jackson's suggestion that the justices request reargument on the matter of remedy.[64]

Warren was also willing to bargain with those justices who expressed concerns about reconciling a desegregation order with the rule of law. He would not go as far as Jackson and suggest that conventional interpretations of traditional legal materials supported the constitutionality of segregation. But, with regard to the matter of constitutional history, he abandoned his (and Black's and Minton's) contention that segregation violates the intentions of the framers of the Civil War amendments. Like Frankfurter—and as a gesture to Clark, Reed, and Jackson—he entertained the possibility that academic treatments of the history of the relevant constitutional provisions provided no definitive conclusions. He mentioned that the federal government, which "was particularly objective and helpful" at oral argument, had "concluded that both the legislative history and the contemporary statements concerning the scope of the Amendment as they apply to these cases were inconclusive." In support of this view, he asserted that only the conflicting intentions of the Fourteenth Amendment's most ardent supporters and critics can be discerned with any degree of accuracy.[65]

Before submitting a draft of his opinion for the justices to examine, Warren also dropped his view that segregation violates the reasonableness requirement of the equal protection clause. Instead, he put forth only an analysis of the harms, and thus the inherent inequality, of segregation in public education. The chief justice's uncirculated first draft, however, was consistent with his remarks in conference regarding the unfounded beliefs that informed the practice. He maintained that, in the nation's capital, "as in the states which require or permit segregation, separate schools were maintained on the basis of Negro inferiority until Plessy v. Ferguson announced its rationalization of segregation." Continuing the line of reasoning that would base a declaration of unconstitutionality on the irrationality of the racial theory underpinning segregation, he declared "that anything which arbitrarily sets [a child] apart from other children and circumscribes his right to [a public] education abridges his privileges and denies him equal protection of the laws."[66]

At this point in his draft, however, Warren abandoned his discussion of the beliefs informing segregation and focused, instead, on the harms stemming from the practice: "To separate [children] from others of their age in school solely because of their color puts the mark of inferiority not only upon their status in the community but also upon their little hearts and minds in a form that is unlikely ever to be erased. We believe that it has many other divisive results not necessary to enumerate here, but which, in the aggregate make the doctrine of separate but equal inapplicable to education." Emphasizing the continuity of the present ruling with past cases, the chief justice noted "that the reasons stated for striking down segregation in the college cases apply with added force to children in the grade and high schools."[67]

In the draft opinion that Warren submitted to his colleagues on May 7, he elaborated significantly on the argument concerning the harms of segregation in public schools. He also placed greater emphasis on the consistency of the Court's desegregation order with past cases. Following the lead of the LDF's lawyers, Warren asserted, "In the first cases in this Court construing the Fourteenth Amendment, decided shortly after its adoption [viz., the *Slaughter House Cases* and *Strauder v. West Virginia*], the Court interpreted it as proscribing all state-imposed discriminations against the Negro race." He stressed that "the doctrine of 'separate but equal' did not make its appearance in this Court until 1896 in the case of *Plessy v. Ferguson,* involving not education but transportation." Since that time, the Court has not reexamined "the validity of the doctrine itself." In the present cases, however, "the question whether *Plessy v. Ferguson* should be held inapplicable to public education" is "directly presented." For "there are findings below that the Negro and white schools involved have been equalized, or are being equalized, with respect to buildings, curricula, qualifications and salaries of teachers, and other 'tangible' factors." Borrowing again from the arguments of the petitioners, as well as from the remarks of Justices Burton and Minton at the conference after reargument, Warren noted that the university cases, *Sweatt v. Painter* and *McLaurin v. Oklahoma State Regents for Higher Education,* "resorted to intangible considerations" in comparing the quality of educational institutions. As in his first draft, he declared that "such considerations apply with added force to children in grade and high schools," since segregation places a "mark of inferiority" on those children. He now supported this conclusion not only with a reference to the similar factual findings "in the Kansas case by a court which never-the-less ruled against the Negro plaintiffs" but also with a citation to the social science studies the petitioners used to demonstrate the sociological and psychological implications of school segregation. The footnote (which apparently was a contribution of Warren's law clerk, Earl Pollock) followed the chief justice's statement: "Whatever may have been the extent of psychological knowledge when *Plessy v. Ferguson* was decided, this finding is amply supported by modern authority."[68]

Warren's decision to focus on the damage that segregation caused to the personalities of black children was interesting, in part because Justices

Frankfurter and Jackson had objected strongly to the use of social science studies. The conference notes for *Brown* also indicate that none of the justices made explicit, favorable references to that rationale or to the supporting evidence. Moreover, Warren's footnote represented the Court's first explicit use of modern social science data to invalidate governmental action. Prior to *Brown,* progressive jurists had referred to social science data only to *defend* the constitutionality of—to call for *judicial deference toward*—legislative efforts to regulate an urban-industrial economy.[69] Finally, in spite of Warren's suggestion to the contrary, the respondents had demonstrated that the soundness of the studies he cited was very much open to question.

Warren's discussion of the belief in racial inferiority that he claimed informed the practice of segregation was conspicuously absent from this draft opinion. In view of Reed's strong response in conference to this understanding of segregation, the chief justice concluded that any hope of securing his colleague's vote required the removal of this portion of the opinion. Warren also understood that such references to southern life and history from a Court composed primarily of nonsoutherners would do nothing to facilitate compliance with the decision. As he said in a letter to his brethren when he distributed the draft for their comments: "The memos were prepared on the theory that the opinions should be short, readable by the lay public, non-rhetorical, unemotional and, *above all, non-accusatory.*"[70] Controversial though Warren's opinion would prove to be, the rationale on which he settled was not as incendiary as the charge that the South was engaged in institutionalized racism. And Warren's reference to the petitioners' social science evidence limited the blameworthiness of southerners by implying that the harms of segregation were not self-evident.[71] Warren also must have realized that the argument that segregation was predicated on an unreasonable belief in racial inferiority would have complicated the Court's task by undermining the rationale for segregation in *any* circumstance. By using the petitioners' social science evidence, Warren appeared to limit the Court's ruling to the context of education.[72]

Warren could not avoid addressing the unreasonableness of segregation in the District of Columbia case. Because the equal protection clause of the Fourteenth Amendment applies only against the states, he could not focus on the inherent inequality of segregation in public education at the national level. He was thus limited to examining the petitioners' claim that the federal government, in separating children on the basis of race, violated the command of the due process clause of the Fifth Amendment that a rational relationship exist between the government's objective and the means chosen to effectuate that objective. In his opinion for the Court in *Bolling v. Sharpe,* Warren accepted the petitioners' position, stating, "Segregation in public education is not reasonably related to any proper governmental objective, and thus it imposes on Negro children of the District of Columbia a burden that constitutes an arbitrary deprivation of their liberty in violation of the Due Process Clause."[73] He declined to mention, let alone evaluate, any reason that the lawyers for the government did or could have put forth to justify the practice. The chief justice even abandoned his suggestion, which he made in an early draft of his opinion, that the burden of this arbitrary deprivation "places the brand of inferiority on the minority group, saps them of their motivation to obtain an education, and thus hampers them throughout life."[74] Apparently, Warren preferred an incomplete constitutional argument to one whose thoroughness would have appeared self-righteous to Justice Reed or to southerners generally.

Warren's willingness to bargain with his brethren and his efforts to create a collegial atmosphere, although very important, were necessary rather than sufficient conditions for securing a unanimous Court in the desegregation cases. By the time Warren circulated his opinions to his colleagues on May 7, Reed, along with the other justices, suggested only minor changes to the draft for the state cases.[75] But only the actions of Reed's colleagues in this instance were testimony to the effectiveness of Warren's emendations during the opinion-writing phase. Warren secured Reed's vote not through bargaining but by emphasizing his colleague's isolation and by appealing to his institutional loyalty. Reed's law clerk, George Mickum, who was present at a meeting between Warren and the Kentuckian toward the end of the Court's consideration of the cases, recalled that the chief justice "said, 'Stan, you're all by yourself in this now. You've got to decide whether it's really the best thing for the country.'" Reed understood, Mickum added, that "[as] a Southerner, even a lone dissent by him would give a lot of people a lot of grist for making trouble. For the good of the country, he put aside his own basis for dissent."[76]

In view of Justice Jackson's position in his later memoranda on the segregation cases, Warren did not have to appeal to his institutional loyalty or patriotism to secure his vote. But, to ensure Jackson's support for the Court's opinion, the chief justice probably had to convince him of the substantial drawbacks of challenging the reasonableness of segregation. Warren may have informed his colleague of his own reasons for abandoning this legal argument, namely the resistance that Reed and southerners generally would demonstrate toward a seemingly self-righteous opinion that emphasized the racist underpinnings of segregation. Warren also may have pointed up the likelihood that such an approach would borrow enormous trouble by undermining the rationale for segregation in any setting. Richard Kluger notes that, during a conference with Jackson at Doctors Hospital on May 10, Warren rejected "one of [Jackson's] proposed additions . . . because he felt it could be interpreted as being directed toward segregation in general, not only in public education." If the unreasonableness of segregation was not the suggestion that Warren rejected in this instance, the chief justice's point nevertheless provided sufficient reason for Jackson not to insist that Warren abandon his treatment of the harms of school segregation and instead focus on the irrationality of the belief in racial inferiority that informed the practice. Making only one minor revision at Jackson's behest, Warren would obtain his colleague's support on May 17, two days after the conference at which the other justices approved the same opinion.[77]

By accounting for the willingness of the justices to accept something less than desegregation forthwith; illuminating the reasons behind Reed's, if not Clark's, decision to set aside his objections to desegregation; and providing a framework for analyzing the process by which the justices resolved their differences, the strategic model contributes substantially to our understanding of *Brown.* The model also reveals an ironic aspect of the history of that decision: The price of unanimity in such a sensitive case was the adoption of a desegregation rationale to which Jackson and Frankfurter objected because of the vagaries of social science evidence, that none of the justices demanded or even defended, and that proved to be controversial even with scholars who were sympathetic to the Court's holding.

Although Warren's opinion for the Court affords little insight into *Brown*'s actual basis, strategic model proponents might argue that this chapter erred in failing to examine critically the attitudinal assumption regarding the irrelevance of the justices' copious legal references in conference and in their draft opinions. In view of the enormous difficulty the petitioners had in articulating a legal argument for the unconstitutionality of segregation, however, the justices' conference comments and legal memoranda present certain challenges for further insight into *Brown*'s basis. Few would be convinced by a justice's reference to a weak legal argument, especially if, as with Douglas, there is reason to believe that the justice had a personal policy preference for desegregation. On the other hand, the explanatory value of legal considerations might be persuasive if a justice invoked a compelling legal argument, especially if evidence suggests that the justice did *not* possess desegregation policy preferences.

As the next chapter reveals, there is sufficient documentation to place several members of the Court into the latter category. But the strategic model cannot account for the behavior of at least certain of these individuals. Since that model is instrumental in nature, its proponents would contend that sincere legal behavior, while possible, is infrequent and limited to discrete instances. For certain members of the Court, however, *Brown* indicated an acceptance of a judicial mission designed to compensate for the problematic nature of American racial politics. In short, a complete account of the *Brown* decision requires consideration of the insights of scholars who suggest that noninstrumental behavior on the part of Supreme Court justices extends beyond the limited instances that strategic model proponents are willing to acknowledge.

FOUR

A Sense of the Court's Mission

In sharp contrast to instrumental models of judging, which emphasize the significance of personal policy preferences in Supreme Court decision making, the constitutive variant of the new institutionalism posits that justices are socialized to consider cues for normatively appropriate judicial behavior from relevant legal actors and institutions. The petitioners' legal argument in *Brown*—that under the Fifth and Fourteenth Amendments the Court's role or mission in racial discrimination cases is to afford considerable protection to minorities, rather than to defer to the decisions of legislators—was an example of such a cue. Documentary evidence reveals that Chief Justice Earl Warren and Justices Hugo Black and Robert Jackson found compelling the historical argument that supported this sense of the Court's mission—that segregation was predicated not upon a desire to promote racial harmony (as the respondents would have it) but upon a belief in the inferiority of blacks. Efforts to portray the justices' comments regarding this matter as cover for desegregation policy preferences are complicated not only by the power of the petitioners' argument for abandoning judicial deference but also by evidence that suggests Hugo Black, the former member of the Ku Klux Klan, was not the only justice whose racial views were less than progressive.

The Constitutive Alternative

At the same time that certain scholars rediscovered Walter F. Murphy's *Elements of Judicial Strategy*, which they used to develop the strategic model of Supreme Court decision making, other political scientists reacted against the instrumentalism that informed both attitudinal and strategic interpretations of judicial behavior. The work of James G. March and Johan P. Olsen was of particular interest to the latter group of new institutionalists. March and Olsen accept the renewed emphasis on institutions that the rational choice or strategic form of the new institutionalism brought to bear on the behavioral approach to politics. But they champion, instead, a constitutive understanding of institutions. In their words, they support a "new institutionalism [that] insists on a more autonomous role for political institutions" or regards such institutions as "political actors in their own right." Whereas the strategic version of the new institutionalism "makes political outcomes a function of three primary factors"—"the distribution of preferences (interests) among political actors, the distribution of resources (powers), and the constraints imposed by the rules of the game (constitutions)"—a constitutive understanding of institutions "argues that preferences and meanings develop in politics, as in the rest of life, through a combination of education, indoctrination, and experience." Put another way, in the strategic model, "political actors consult personal preferences and subjective expectations, then select actions that are as consistent as possible with those preferences and expectations." In a constitutive model, by contrast, "political actors associate certain actions with certain situations by rules of appropriateness. What is appropriate for a particular person in a particular situation is defined by the political and social system and transmitted through socialization." While "self-interest undoubtedly permeates politics, action is often based more on discovering the normatively appropriate behavior than on calculating the return expected from alternative choices. As a result, political behavior . . . can be described in terms of duties, obligations, roles, and rules."[1]

Taking up the call for the development of a constitutive understanding of political institutions, Rogers M. Smith examines the relevance of the observations of March and Olsen to the study of public law. Instrumental models of decision making, he suggests, inaccurately portray judging as "a tedious, crassly self-interested, and rather ineffectual game among programmed players." A more realistic conception of Supreme Court decision making acknowledges the role that legal institutions perform as independent forces in that process. "They . . . have a kind of life of their own," he argues. "They influence the self-conception of those who occupy roles defined by them in ways that can give those persons distinctively 'institutional' perspectives." "The role of institutions," in short, "goes well beyond providing the rules governing decision-making situations in the manner [that the strategic model] stresses. It influences the relative resources and the senses of purpose and principle that political actors possess. And sometimes, at least, those purposes and principles may be better described as conceptions of duty or inherently meaningful action than as egoistic preferences."[2]

The comments of Smith, March, and Olsen reveal that the constitutive variant of the new institutionalism posits a broad, abstract conception of institutions. While acknowledging the relevance to political analysis of tangible structures of authority and resources that relate in some way to the state, constitutive model proponents emphasize the significance of informal norms or habits of thought. Central to this abstract understanding of institutions, Howard Gillman notes, is the concept of mission—"an identifiable purpose or a shared normative goal that, at a particular historical moment in a particular context, becomes routinized within an identifiable corporate form as the result of the efforts of certain groups of people." "With respect to Supreme Court politics," Gillman and Cornell W. Clayton contend, "this means that the justices' behavior might be motivated not only by a calculation about prevailing opportunities and risks but also by a sense of duty or obligation about their responsibilities to the law and the Constitution and by a commitment to act as judges rather than as legislators or executives."[3]

This sense of duty or mission, Ronald Kahn elaborates, is acquired through reference in constitutional controversies to a judicial philosophy that acknowledges both "polity and rights principles." Justices, in other words, discover that normatively appropriate behavior requires that decisions regarding constitutional rights (i.e., "entitlements for individual citizens from agencies or other parts of the political system") be informed by polity principles, that is, a developed theory of democratic governance, which implies a particular "attitude—critical or trusting—toward legislative and interest group politics." The development and "work[ing] out [of] polity and rights principles," Kahn avers, occur not in isolation but in "a dialogue with what Owen Fiss has called 'the interpretive community'" of scholars, jurists, and legal actors.[4]

This noninstrumental variant of the new institutionalism necessarily relies on an historical-interpretive methodology. Since constitutive model proponents are interested in discovering the goals or purposes that motivate justices, they are compelled to ascertain the institutional history or mission of the Court that informs those goals. As Stephen Skowronek explains, if institutions actually "prescribe actions, construct motives, and assert legitimacy," then "the analysis of institutional action will . . . be driven to a consideration of origins, toward an understanding of official behavior in terms of original purposes." For the constitutive effect that office holders, including judges, experience is the means by which "institutions perpetuate the objectives or purposes instilled in them at their founding; that is what lies at the heart of their staying power."[5]

The historical dimension of this version of new institutionalist analysis is not limited to a search for the founders' original purposes in constructing the federal judiciary. As Smith concedes, political institutions "are themselves created by past human political decisions that were in some measure discretionary, and to some degree they are alterable by future ones." Gillman and Clayton add "that, over time, as institutions interact with other features of the political system and attempt to cope with a changing society, they might transform themselves and develop new norms, traditions, and functions." Such potentially significant changes in institutional mission are a consequence of members of the Court acting not in a strategic effort to actualize personal policy preferences but out of a sense of institutional maintenance or stewardship. "As with any institution," Gillman explains, "those who are affiliated with the Court should be expected to deliberate about protecting their institution's legitimacy." While justices may believe in certain situations that institutional maintenance simply involves working for a united Court or avoiding intensely controversial issues, they may determine on other occasions that the task requires them to adapt "their institution's mission to changing contexts and the actions of other institutions." Only by adopting an historical perspective can scholars remain apprised of the current institutional mission or purpose that informs judicial behavior.[6]

The historical focus of the constitutive model of Supreme Court decision making, in turn, requires new institutionalist scholars to engage in interpretive analyses of the actions of relevant judicial figures. We can acquire a sense of the Court's institutional mission during a certain period of time only by examining conference notes, memoranda, draft opinions, and memoirs with a view to reconstructing the justices' states of mind. Furthermore, we can ascertain the degree to which a particular individual internalized that, or an earlier, understanding of the Court's role only by attempting explanations of his judicial performances that focus on the meanings he ascribed to his behavior. In short, interpretivist analyses enable us to determine whether "the justices view the Supreme Court as promoting specific goals or performing specific functions in the political system," and whether "they feel a sense of personal or professional responsibility to act in ways that facilitate the accomplishment of its distinctive mission." If such evidence exists, "then (reiterating Smith's point) we can say that the *idea* of the Court influenced 'the self-conception of those who occupy roles defined by them in ways that give those persons distinctively "institutional" perspectives,' including a sense of duty that is designed to filter out the influence of those nonjudicial interests and preferences that are inconsistent with sustaining institutional functions (i.e., the overt use of judicial power to advance partisan goals)."[7]

By acknowledging judge-initiated change in the mission of the Court, constitutive model proponents cannot be accused of positing a conception of institutions that is "too full of reification and anthropomorphism to be plausible." Constitutive model proponents also acknowledge "the existence and importance of genuine judicial discretion in decision making—the phenomenon that is traditionally at the heart of public law analyses, whatever their methodological differences"—by portraying institutional influence not as a force that dictates results in particular controversies but as something that shapes or guides the decisions of justices.[8]

Yet, by acknowledging the influence of judicial choice or discretion to avoid the charge of implausibility, defenders of the constitutive model become vulnerable to a more basic criticism—that their view of Supreme Court decision making lacks conceptual and analytical clarity and thus has little explanatory value. By noting the relative autonomy of judicial behavior from legal institutions (i.e., that institutions guide rather than determine judicial actions), defenders of a constitutive understanding of Supreme Court decision making have difficulty ascertaining the degree to which those structures serve as a cause of judicial behavior. More fundamentally, because they adopt an abstract notion of legal institutions and acknowledge the openness of these institutions to judge-initiated change, they have difficulty defending the view that such cognitive structures of supposedly relative permanence qualify as institutions in any meaningful sense.[9]

Problematic as the concern over the meaningfulness of an abstract and mutable notion of institutions might be for the constitutive model in certain contexts, the circumstances of the *Brown* decision reveal that this problem is not necessarily the undoing of this version of the new institutionalism. For it is possible to identify a concrete source for a sense of judicial mission that was under consideration in *Brown*. The extended debate between the parties in that case over the matter of judicial deference to legislative judgment was, at base, a dialogue over the Court's appropriate role or mission in cases involving claims of racial discrimination. In challenging the view of the respondents' lawyers that state officials were entitled to deference on questions involving the reasonableness and alleged harms of segregation, the LDF sought on behalf of the petitioners to affect the justices' polity principles—their perception of the nature of American society and politics—and, by extension, to alter their understanding of the Court's role. The petitioners' contention and their historical defense of the view that segregation laws were an integral part of a long-standing effort in the South to subjugate African Americans invited the justices to regard American racial politics as hierarchical, albeit, amenable to—and in need of—judicial redress.

Constitutional Dialogues

THE NATURE OF AMERICAN RACIAL POLITICS

Recall that John Davis, in defending the legislative motives behind and maintaining the reasonableness of school segregation, had contended at the hearings that the burden of proof belonged properly with those who would challenge the policies of democratically elected officials. Insisting that it was "not racism" that inspired racial segregation, he implored the justices to "recognize that for sixty centuries and more humanity has been discussing questions of race and race tension, not racism." "Confident of its good faith and intention to produce equality for all of its children of whatever race or color," he continued, the state of South Carolina "is convinced that the happiness, the progress and the welfare of these children is best promoted in segregated schools, and it thinks it a thousand pities that by this controversy there should be urged the return to an experiment which gives no more promise of success today than when it was written into their Constitution during [Reconstruction]."[10]

T. Justin Moore, who spoke after Davis, brought his colleague's argument to its logical conclusion. With Davis having defended the motives of southern officials as well as the reasonableness of segregated schooling, Moore argued that "this case presents a matter . . . for judicial restraint if there ever was a case presented." Professing a belief in the relative superiority of state legislatures to federal judicial machinery in the making of educational policy, he informed the Court that "the size, the history of this problem before the Court here, makes it clear that the solution should be left with the legislatures."[11]

As noted in chapter 1, the petitioners' brief for the rehearing attacked the argument for judicial deference by expanding on the efforts of Spottswood Robinson and Louis Redding at oral argument the preceding year to demonstrate the baselessness of the public order rationale for segregation laws. The brief suggested that "the history of segregation laws reveals that their main purpose was to organize the community upon the basis of a superior white and an inferior Negro caste." Indeed, "segregation in its operation and effect has meant inequality consistent only with the belief that the people segregated are inferior and not worthy, or capable, of enjoying the facilities set apart for the dominant group," a belief "taken from slavery."[12]

Drawing on the arguments of the historians John Hope Franklin and C. Vann Woodward, among others, the petitioners' brief averred that "segregation originated as a part of an effort to build a social order in which the Negro would be placed in a status as close as possible to that he had held before the Civil War." This effort began with the notorious Black Codes of the 1860s, which prevented the economic ascendance of newly liberated slaves. With former slaves attempting to enter the workforce as farmers and artisans, poor whites of the South "became firm advocates of the Negro's subjugation to insure their own economic well being." "To the [plantation] aristocracy, too, the Negro's subjugation was an economic advantage." "This group found that they could build a new economic structure based upon a depressed labor market of poor whites and Negroes." The large planters thus "sought to regain their economic and political pre-eminence by rebuilding the pre-war social structure on the philosophy of the Negro's inferiority" and through legal limitations on black mobility and property ownership.[13]

The racial hostility that informed the Black Codes was held in check during Reconstruction. But this regrettable characteristic of southern politics reappeared after the Compromise of 1877 and withdrawal of federal forces from the South. Subsequently, the "militant irreconcilables" who "held fast to the notion of the Negro's preordained inferiority returned to power in state after state." The petitioners' brief regarded as "significant [the fact] that one of the first measures adopted was to require segregated schools on a permanent basis in disregard of the Fourteenth Amendment." These laws ensured the "separate, inferior" education of blacks, while the adoption of electoral devices, such as the poll tax and the white primary, served "to destroy the political power of the Negro so that he could never seriously challenge the order that was being established."[14]

Lest anyone doubt that segregation reflected the oppressive designs of southern whites, the petitioners referred to the rhetoric of "racist spokesmen" of the nineteenth century, such as Ben Tillman of South Carolina, who, "with unabashed boldness, set forth views regarding the Negro's unassimilability and uneducability even more pernicious than those held by the old South." The petitioners also noted that "politicians [were not] alone in uttering such views about the Negro. Drawing on the theory of evolution as expressed by Darwin and the theory of progress developed by Spencer, persons of scholarly pretension speeded the work of justifying an inferior status for the Negro." The claims of the lawyers for the respondents in the present cases notwithstanding, "such was the real philosophy behind the late 19th Century segregation laws—an essential part of the whole racist complex." "Controlling economic and political interests in the South were convinced that the Negro's subjugation was essential to their survival," and the concept of racial inferiority served to justify measures that drove "Negroes . . . from participation in political affairs" and to excuse "a veritable maze of Jim Crow laws [that] had been erected to 'keep the Negro in his place' (of inferiority)."[15]

By placing segregation in the broader context of southern racial history, the petitioners provided the justices with ample reason to assume the unconstitutionality of this and any form of racial discrimination. But the brief emphasized that the Court itself had recently recognized the oppressive designs of racial majorities and, as a result, had articulated the need for the judiciary to assume a guardianship role over racial minorities. The petitioners reminded the justices that *Hirabayashi v. United States* "characterized racial distinctions as 'odious to a free people,'" while "*Korematsu v. United States . . .* viewed racial restrictions as 'immediately suspect.'" True, "the restrictions placed upon persons of Japanese origin on the West Coast were sustained in . . . [these cases] as emergency war measures taken by the national government in a dire national peril of the gravest nature." Yet, "in upholding these [curfew and internment] orders, the Court made some of the most sweeping condemnations of governmentally imposed racial and color distinctions ever announced by our judiciary." And, if "Congressional action grounded upon color [is unconstitutional] except in so far as it may have temporary justification to meet an overwhelming national emergency," then "the power of states is even more rigidly circumscribed" under the equal protection clause of the Fourteenth Amendment. "For there is grave doubt that their acts can be sustained under the exception made in . . . *Korematsu* with respect to the national government."[16]

At oral argument, the LDF's lawyers reiterated the legal brief's statement of judicial mission. In the rehearing of the federal case, *Bolling v. Sharpe,* James Nabrit and George Hayes reminded the justices that the Court had already recognized the validity of the assumption that oppressive motives typically inform racial distinctions in law, and that legislators are thus undeserving of judicial deference when they discriminate on that basis. Hayes concluded his presentation to the justices with a ringing declaration: "We say to this Court that under whatever angle the situation is looked at in the District of Columbia, . . . that this Court . . . cannot say to a waiting world that we sanction segregation in the District of Columbia for no other reason than because of the fact that the skin of the person is dark. That, this Court has said, is suspect; that, you have said, is void; that, you have said, should not be sanctioned; that, we believe, must be your decision." And Nabrit suggested that "the Court has had a remarkable record in dealing with the exertions of power by the federal government on its citizens where it was [based] solely on race or color, and, if I am correct, the only instance where the Court has permitted that to be done since *Dred Scott* has been in the case where war was involved, and implied power essential to effectuate the war power."[17]

THE NATURE OF CONSTITUTIONAL INTERPRETATION

Important as the analysis of the nature of racial politics was to the petitioners' understanding of the Court's role in racial discrimination cases, the justices would not have embraced this sense of judicial mission had they merely conceded that segregation was part of an effort to subjugate African Americans. The petitioners' sense of the Court's role in such cases depended upon a particular—and novel—understanding of constitutional meaning: that the terms of the Fourteenth Amendment are living in the sense that they empower judges to expand constitutional rights as circumstances require.[18] The justices could not have placed the burden of proof on segregationist states, as the petitioners' conception of the Court's mission required, if the justices felt compelled to restrict the use of judicial review to those examples of unconstitutional governmental conduct that the framers of the Fourteenth Amendment had in mind. As noted in chapter 1, the petitioners conceded that they lacked evidence that the framers of the Fourteenth Amendment sought to prohibit school segregation. And the respondents presented considerable evidence that the framers accepted segregated schools.

The petitioners sought to overcome this legal obstacle by arguing that the framers of the Fourteenth Amendment did not intend for judges to be limited to the framers' particular examples of unconstitutional conduct. But the respondents informed the justices that many of those in the Thirty-Ninth Congress who spoke in favor of the amendment stated that the measure merely would secure the protections of the Civil Rights Act of 1866. Furthermore, Justice Felix Frankfurter aided the respondents when he observed that Congress would not have had to propose that the Fifteenth Amendment protect suffrage from racial discrimination if the framers of the Fourteenth Amendment had intended for the meaning of the concept of equal protection of the laws to evolve.

As an alternative to the argument that the framers intended for the terms of the Fourteenth Amendment to be living or open-ended, the petitioners contended that *the Court* had embraced the notion of a living Constitution as applied to individual rights. They observed that, in the university desegregation cases, the Court clearly adopted a flexible notion of constitutional meaning, one that had important implications for the present controversy. The petitioners conceded the respondents' point that "*Sweatt v. Painter* and *McLaurin v. Oklahoma State Regents* were not in terms rejections of the separate but equal doctrine." Nevertheless, they insisted that "their application in effect destroyed the practice of segregation with respect to state graduate and professional schools." *Sweatt* acknowledged the professional detriment that black law students experience in being separated from future judges and lawyers drawn from "the state's dominant racial group." And, in *McLaurin,* "the racial distinctions imposed in an effort to comply with the state's segregation laws were held to impair and inhibit [the] ability to study, to exchange views with other students and, in general, to learn one's profession."[19]

Chief Justice Earl Warren

WARREN'S VIEW OF THE COURT'S ROLE

Earl Warren's mature reflections on the process of judging provide reason to believe that the arguments of the LDF and of defenders of the constitutive model of Supreme Court decision making help to explain his performance in *Brown.* In the first chapter of his memoirs, Warren spoke of a distinction between the political and judicial processes:

> In my more than fifty years of public service, I have been exposed to both processes, the political and the judicial, and to the interrelationship between the two, until I have what I believe is a clear concept of each in the administration of justice. In those official positions I have held, I have tried to carry this distinction in mind, and to honor both sides as essential ingredients of our governmental system. One is not born with such a concept, nor is it acquired overnight. It is an evolving thing that stems from one's experiences in life and from interpretations he or she gives them, particularly when the paths of the two processes cross.[20]

He explained that, "through [the judicial process], and particularly in the Supreme Court, the basic ingredient of decision is principle." If a "principle is sound and constitutional," he continued, the Court's role is to accord it, "not . . . begrudgingly or piecemeal or to special groups only, but to everyone in its entirety whenever it is brought into play." Were judges, instead, to mimic the political process—where "progress [can] be made and most often [is] made by compromising and taking half a loaf where a whole loaf [cannot] be obtained"—"minority groups, the poor, the uneducated, and the otherwise underprivileged" would suffer an unacceptable deprivation of constitutional guarantees that are "the birthright of every American." A failure to appreciate the Court's responsibility under the Constitution and the uncompromising manner in which the justices must enforce constitutional principle, he believed, "was responsible for the outburst of emotion in some quarters when *Brown v. Board of Education* was decided." While Warren understood that many Americans would not be convinced, he insisted that, in *Brown* and other controversial decisions during his tenure, he "was acting from conscience in accordance with [his] view of the judicial process."[21]

Warren failed to reconcile his acceptance of the gradual enforcement of desegregation with his belief that the Court must not compromise constitutional principles. But this omission does not nullify the point that his discussion of the process of judicial decision making and of the role of the Court is redolent of the arguments of the LDF and of proponents of the constitutive model of Supreme Court decision making. Like the latter, Warren declined to portray judicial decisions simply as expressions of judges' attitudes or values. Furthermore, he apparently believed that the institutional context in which the Supreme Court operates does more than simply structure or impede a justice's ability to act on his personal policy preferences. Warren's comments suggest that legal institutions, while they do not provide definitive answers to particular legal controversies, in some way constitute or guide judicial behavior.

As for the impact of legal institutions on Warren's thinking, his remark that judges should view constitutional provisions as matters of principle (as opposed to references to the framers' specific examples of unconstitutional governmental conduct) echoed the petitioners' position in *Brown* regarding the nature of constitutional interpretation. Warren's comments regarding the Court's mission in constitutional controversies were also strongly reminiscent of the petitioners' arguments. As he said almost a decade before he reflected in his memoirs on the distinction between the political and judicial processes, "The essential function of the Supreme Court in our democracy is to act as the final arbiter of minority rights, and the Fourteenth Amendment is a basic repository of those rights. By remaining a responsive forum of last resort for Negroes and other minority interests, the Court can assure that the spirit of the Fourteenth Amendment will become a tangible reality of American life."[22]

The similarity between Warren's reflections and the petitioners' statements regarding constitutional interpretation and the Court's mission, of course, is insufficient to prove the relevance of the constitutive model to the *Brown* decision. As instrumentalists would hasten to point out, the petitioners may simply have afforded Warren legal cover to enact his personal policy preferences in that case. Such an account of Warren's desegregation vote is rendered problematic, however, by the import of his prenomination writings and speeches. These documents reveal that the new chief justice did not possess desegregation policy preferences when he joined the Court in 1953.

WARREN AND RACIAL POLITICS

When Warren later reflected on this part of his judicial career, he suggested that the result in *Brown* was consistent with his own values. "As the wartime governor of California," he explained, "I had integrated the National Guard shortly after its return from the War." Warren also noted that he "appointed some Negroes as judges" and "saw to it that Negroes and all minority groups shared in the employment benefits of [California's] Civil Service of sixty thousand employees." Warren might have added that, as governor, he proposed to the state legislature (albeit unsuccessfully) the establishment of a Fair Employment Practices Commission. During his years as the chief executive of his state, he also spoke out occasionally on national racial matters. He criticized the New Deal coalition—which he characterized as a combination of "corrupt city machines" and extreme leftist politicians from the Northeast, cobbled together with "the conservative Democrats of the South" for "the sake of expediency"—for its cynical approach to the issue of racial justice. He noted that, in order to preserve this fragile political alliance, the "conglomerate New Deal machine" "preaches political and economic equality to the Negroes of the North and West, where they already have such rights under Republican state administrations, and practices the opposite doctrine in the southern and border states."[23]

Yet neither these statements nor the policies Warren championed as governor necessarily implied support for what was a more controversial policy in the 1940s and 1950s—desegregation in the nation's elementary and secondary schools. For example, when Warren gave the keynote address at the 1944 Republican National Convention, he suggested that New Deal bureaucrats "are using every device and excuse to insinuate themselves into control over the public schools of our states." The Republican party, he declared, "will strengthen our great public school system, keep it under the control of state and local government, where it is responsive to the people, and prepare it to play a stronger part in the life of the Republic."[24] Warren's comments regarding an intrusive federal bureaucracy are surprising only because such hyperbole contrasted sharply with his accurate assessment of the ties that bound the New Deal coalition; his stated distrust of federal involvement in public schooling is easily reconciled with his other statements and policies on racial equality. It is necessary, however, to examine his behavior as a national political figure in order to determine if his support for local control of schools merely reflected the parochial perspective of a California politician or, alternatively, was the result of a considered belief that racial equality did not require the repudiation of the separate-but-equal principle in education.

Although the Republican party's formal position on civil rights featured only modest proposals (specifically, anti-lynching, anti–poll tax, and fair employment practices legislation) during the years that Warren had national visibility as a state politician, he should have felt free—and he had a number of reasons—to champion stronger measures. Republican (as opposed to Democratic) party unity did not depend on inattentiveness toward the issue of racial equality. Furthermore, the electoral power of 1.7 million African Americans who had migrated from the South to northern, urban centers during the early to mid-1940s became apparent after the midterm elections of 1946 (which resulted in a Republican Congress in part because African Americans punished the Democratic party for its tepid approach to civil rights) and the presidential election of 1948 (in which Harry Truman prevailed in part by actively courting black voters). That Republicans could have any success by appealing to southern whites was not known until Dwight Eisenhower won the electoral votes of four border states and four southern states in the presidential election in 1952. Prior to that time, the South, historically opposed to the party of the North, had voted overwhelmingly Democratic in national elections.[25]

The possibility appears slim that Warren would have steadfastly avoided expressing a desegregation policy preference in a strategic bid to appease southern senators who were in a position to block his nomination to the Supreme Court. Warren had no realistic hope of an appointment until Eisenhower spoke with him about filling a vacancy on the Court. Eisenhower recalled that it was "a few months prior to the death of Chief Justice Vinson" in September 1953 that he discussed with Governor Warren "the possibility of appointing him to the Supreme Court."[26] Implicitly challenging Eisenhower's recollection of events, one of Warren's biographers contends that the political rivals spoke about a possible Court appointment a little over a year before the election.[27] Presumably, then, Warren's judicial ambitions would not have affected his public statements on segregation until, at the earliest, September 1952.

Moving from domestic to international considerations, the fact that segregation was one of the main themes in the Soviet Union's propaganda campaign against the United States in the 1940s provided a strong incentive for Warren to promote desegregation. A particularly embarrassing instance of Soviet criticism occurred in 1947 after the NAACP filed a petition (entitled "An Appeal to the World") at the United Nations in which it protested American racial injustice. The petition, which received extensive media coverage in this country and around the world, asserted, "It is not Russia that threatens the United States so much as Mississippi; not Stalin and Molotov but Bilbo and Rankin; internal injustice done to one's brothers is far more dangerous than the aggression of strangers from abroad." Exploiting the opportunity, the Soviet Union proposed that the United Nations investigate the NAACP's charges.[28]

If Warren favored desegregation, he likely would have referred to these domestic and international considerations to convince Republicans to liberalize their stance on civil rights, especially since he was more than willing to adopt positions at odds with his party when he served as governor of California. As G. Edward White observes, "The core of the Republican party platform from 1946 to 1952 . . . was partisan opposition to the New Deal, the Fair Deal, and the philosophy of affirmative participation by the federal government in social and economic affairs." Warren, however, "had sought, as governor, to tax oil companies, regulate the medical profession, and increase public control of utilities. And he had been the opposite of a party loyalist in his campaigning, his appointments, his staffing, and the conduct of his offices."[29]

Prior to agreeing (begrudgingly) to become Thomas Dewey's running mate in the 1948 presidential election, when he was too restricted in his supporting role to give voice to his own positions on issues of national importance, Governor Warren was a presidential aspirant himself.[30] The dark horse candidate for the Republican nomination did not abandon his commitment to active government in an effort to curry favor with party regulars. One month before the 1948 Republican national convention, he defended economic liberalism as a means for Republicans to recapture the White House. Should Republicans fail to recognize the need to broaden the social security program or address such concerns as impoverished schools, substandard housing, and inadequate medical care, he argued, "America [will] lack the strength to raise living standards here at home and fulfill at the same time the world obligations which we have assumed in recent years." Warren continued this line of argument when he sought the Republican presidential nomination for the second time. He admonished those members of his party who "call these things Socialism" to recognize the difference "between socialism and social progress."[31]

Warren's iconoclasm on economic matters contrasted sharply with his conventionalism on the issue of racial equality. He did respond affirmatively in 1948 when asked if "there should be a clear-cut civil rights plank in the Republican platform." He said that he favored "plain simple language, for instance 'We shall insist upon having the same law for all men.'" Warren's formal public statements, however, reveal that he did not regard desegregation as essential to the fulfillment of that promise of racial equality. In a speech that he gave in the year before the Republican convention but some six months after he first entertained the idea of becoming a presidential candidate, Warren contended that economic justice, while important in its own right, was an essential component of the effort to win the Cold War. He declared that the United States is "the object of propaganda designed to make it appear that democracy lacks character, lacks efficiency and a genuine desire to meet the needs of common men and women." "Our only defense against this demagoguery," he maintained, is to make our government "more responsive to . . . the needs of all."[32] Warren, however, declined to emphasize the need to respond as well to racial injustice in spite of the fact that, less than a week before he gave this speech, the NAACP had filed its petition at the United Nations.

If Warren's failure to mention the need for racial justice was a consequence of his having too little time to recognize the significance of the NAACP's action, he had no excuse for failing explicitly to attack segregation in a speech he gave the following year. Speaking to the Anti-Defamation League of B'nai B'rith, he suggested that "many people in all parts of the world think of the United States when they read [the] language" of the United Nations' charter, which makes reference to "'the equal rights of men and women, and of nations, large and small.'" He argued further that, "because their eyes are upon us, it is all the more important that our example of living in America measures up to the language of our own constitution, and of the charter of the United Nations." "Intolerance of any kind," he declared, "is violative of these principles." Rather than segue into an attack on segregation, however, he merely counseled that Americans "must . . . believe that by marshalling the better elements of human nature against prejudice and intolerance, we can repress and subdue them through education, through kindly example and through the great force of enlightened public opinion." This platitude, which might have served to introduce a discussion of the educative impact of desegregation, merely inspired more uncontroversial generalizations.[33]

Warren was only slightly less platitudinous when, in 1951, shortly before he sought the Republican presidential nomination for a second time, he spoke to the national convention of the National Education Association. He informed his audience that "education will never be sound until th[e] principle of equalization is recognized and practiced, both in the states and nationally." Rather than call for an end to school segregation, however, he defined equalization to mean "adequate education for all our children without regard to whether they live in a rich or a poor district." If Warren favored desegregation, it is ironic that he did not regard this speech as an ideal opportunity to make public his belief. In addition to speaking of equality as it pertained to education, he also returned to the danger that inadequate governmental action presented to the American effort to prevail in the Cold War. Americans, he declared, must "demonstrate to an observing and critical world that our governmental and economic systems can work hand in hand in the elimination of poverty, suffering and degradation."[34] In view of the use that Soviet propagandists were making of a particularly visible form of degradation—the practice of segregation—Warren's failure to address the matter appears rather telling.

During his run for the Republican nomination in 1952, Warren claimed that he was "for a sweeping civil rights program, beginning with a fair employment practices act." As in 1948, he said he "insist[ed] upon one law for all men." It is unlikely, however, that these statements were expressions of support for desegregation. Warren had a wonderful opportunity—but declined—to encourage such a policy change when, in February of that year, he gave the Lincoln Day Address to the Middlesex Club of Boston. He began his talk by suggesting that such events "make it possible for [Republicans] to . . . determine whether we are following the principles of Lincoln or are merely using his hallowed name as a trademark of the Party." Warren argued that, were Abraham Lincoln alive, he would show concern not only for the threat of communism but also for the fact "that some of the inequalities of his day still existed and that the freedom of opportunity he strove for was not yet a reality." Rather than suggest that desegregation represented a return to the Republican party's founding principles and the fulfillment of Lincoln's promise of racial equality, however, Warren merely restated his belief that Republicans had to adapt their economic policies to fit contemporary circumstances.[35]

In view of Warren's consistent refusal to promote desegregation when he was a presidential aspirant—even though he had strong political incentives and few, if any, disincentives to do so—it is reasonable to conclude that the modest support for civil rights he demonstrated as governor of California, and his adoption of the Republican party's moderate civil rights stance during his 1952 bid for the party's nomination, revealed the limits of his understanding of racial equality, as opposed to serving as the foundation of a more expansive policy. In a 1952 interview with *U.S. News and World Report,* the presidential hopeful combined a strong endorsement of a fair employment practices commission with a restatement of his conviction, which he had articulated before becoming a national political figure, that public schools should remain free of federal oversight. He emphasized that his belief in the need for federal aid to education was contingent on the "Federal Government put[ting] *no controls of any kind on education which is a state function and a state problem.*" "Whenever it is possible," he elaborated, "I want to diffuse . . . administrative authority and put it in the states or even in local governments to the extent of their jurisdictions." In short, John O'Donnell, a conservative columnist for the New York *Daily News,* had good reason to hope and expect that Eisenhower's nominee for the chief justiceship would uphold racial segregation, and the editors of *The Nation* and the *New Republic* had cause to express doubt that Warren would amount to much of a defender of civil rights.[36]

WARREN AND THE INTERNMENT OF JAPANESE-CALIFORNIANS

Warren's performance as attorney general of California in the early 1940s calls into question the sincerity or depth of even his mild commitment to racial equality. As other scholars have demonstrated, Warren was a central figure in the events that led to the tragic and unjustifiable internment in 1942 of some 120,000 individuals of Japanese ancestry, most of whom were American citizens. Moreover, he did not hesitate to employ racial stereotypes or manipulate evidence to accomplish this objective.[37]

In attempting to explain Warren's desegregation vote, it is possible to argue that his attitudes toward West Coast Asians had no bearing on his view of segregation in the South, since he may have held differing views of the relevant racial groups. But some scholars of the *Brown* decision who focus on his role in the internment of Japanese-Californians do not view his racism toward Asians as a complicating factor that can, at best, be neutralized in this manner. Rather, they argue that his support for internment is the key to understanding his call for racial equality in *Brown*. Warren came to acknowledge that racism informed his actions in the early 1940s, the argument runs, and his critical self-awareness sensitized him to the claims of the petitioners in the desegregation controversy.[38]

The suggestion that Warren's attitudes regarding the plight of Japanese-Californians changed, however, founders on the fact that he declined for many years to acknowledge that internment was unjustified, let alone that his motives were racist. Eight years after *Brown*, he wrote an article in which he defended the Supreme Court's decision that sustained the constitutionality of the internment policy. *Korematsu v. United States*,[39] he argued, "demonstrate[s] dramatically that there are some circumstances in which the Court will, in effect, conclude that it is simply not in a position to reject descriptions by the Executive of the degree of military necessity." "Where the circumstances are such that the Court must accept uncritically the Government's description of the magnitude of the military need, actions may be permitted that restrict individual liberty in a grievous manner."[40]

Ultimately, in his posthumously published memoirs, Warren lamented his part in the internment effort. Still, he refused to acknowledge the influence of racism on his behavior toward Japanese-Californians. "I have always believed," he wrote, "that I had no prejudice against the Japanese as such except that directly spawned by Pearl Harbor and its aftermath."[41]

In view of Warren's steadfast refusal to acknowledge his racial motivation in calling for internment, Sumi Cho suggests a seemingly more compelling explanation of Warren's performance in the desegregation controversy. She proffers that Warren sought in *Brown* not to act on newly acquired values that resulted from self-critical analysis but to "to clear his name"—to demonstrate "that his obligation to bar Japanese Californians from returning to California was not 'an appeal to race hatred,' but 'an appeal for safety.'"[42] In short, Cho would have her readers consider the possibility that Warren voted strategically to end segregation in a bid to disguise the reprehensible nature of his wartime behavior.

Cho's thesis, however, is predicated on the tenuous assumption that, in the early 1950s, Warren felt more pressure to justify Japanese internment than to sustain the constitutionality of segregation in elementary and secondary education. Since the Court rendered *Brown* less than a decade after the unconditional surrender of Japan, Warren could not have felt much external pressure to absolve himself of the harm done to Japanese-Californians. Few people, and Warren was not among them, regarded internment as an injustice. Even Cho notes that former internees had to wait until the late 1980s before the federal government offered them a formal apology and reparations.[43] And, since *Brown* occurred over a decade before Congress would pass substantive civil rights legislation (indeed, neither political party even defended a progressive vision of racial equality in the early 1950s), Warren could not have believed that the costs associated with a ruling against segregation would be nominal.[44] As the preceding chapter demonstrates, the justices, including Warren, anticipated the enormous social resistance that would meet a desegregation decree. In short, the racial injustice that Warren helped to perpetrate in 1942 inspired within him neither a commitment to the principle of racial equality nor a sense that he had to prove the purity of his wartime motives, and thus serves only to complicate an explanation of his behavior in *Brown*.

THE CONSTITUTIVE EFFECT OF THE DIALOGUE BEFORE THE COURT

While it does not appear that Warren came to the Court with a policy preference for desegregation, that his involvement in the mistreatment of Japanese-Californians sensitized him to the plight of African Americans, or that he sought to use the desegregation decision to justify the internment of Japanese-Californians, there is evidence that he was guided in *Brown* by the statement of judicial mission that the petitioners defended and upon which he elaborated in his memoirs. As noted in chapter 1, neither Warren nor his brethren questioned the respondents' lawyers about their view that segregation benefited blacks as well as whites. But the chief justice signaled his acceptance of the argument that informed the petitioners' sense of the Court's mission when he stated in conference and in his draft opinions that segregation existed only because of a continuing belief among southerners in the inferiority of blacks. Indeed, the educative or constitutive effect of the dialogue before the Court was evidenced clearly when Warren said to his brethren: "The *more I read [and] hear [and] think, the more I come to conclude* that the basis of the principle of seg[regation and] sep[arate] but equal rests upon a concept of the inherent inferiority of the colored race."[45] Recall that he also mentioned in conference that the performances of the petitioners' lawyers revealed the groundlessness of the concept of racial inferiority.[46]

An alternative interpretation of Warren's recognition of the connection between segregation and the concept of racial inferiority—that his comment disclosed a newly acquired desegregation policy preference that the petitioners' statement of judicial mission merely served to rationalize—is difficult to maintain. Having recourse to studies of ideological drift, it is possible to argue that Warren's remark anticipated and helps to explain a significant leftward shift in his voting and (the studies maintain) his values, which occurred in just his second year on the Court.[47] But, even setting aside the problem that most instrumentalists would have with the idea that persuasion can cause sudden, significant shifts in value preferences (to say nothing of the concept of ideological drift itself), Warren's statement in conference necessarily implies that he accepted the full critique of democratic institutions that informed the idea that the Court must serve a corrective function in American racial politics. Warren, in other words, embraced not just a position on a particular policy matter but a set of polity principles or critical arguments about democratic government that served to guide his decision making in future cases across a range of issues. The petitioners' academic criticism of the conventional view that segregation was an essential component of a long-standing, good-faith effort to promote racial harmony was compelling only because the petitioners' brief situated the practice within the broader context of southern racial history. (The televised images of violence that exposed the brutality of the racist system of which segregation was a part would come well after *Brown,* when civil rights marches and protests threatened southern racial mores.)[48] The oppressive nature of segregation was made evident to Warren because the brief demonstrated that the pronouncements of Ben Tillman and other Jim Crow apologists were not the isolated declamations of racist outliers. Rather, he learned that segregation was a contemporary manifestation of a theory of racial inferiority that informed southern society and politics and that could be traced back to the Black Codes and, ultimately, the institution of slavery.

Warren sacrificed his observations regarding the oppressive nature of segregation in order to preserve unanimity and out of a desire not to offend the segregationist South. But the reference in *Bolling v. Sharpe* to the Japanese curfew and internment cases was testimony to his acceptance of the petitioners' understanding of the Court's mission, which their critique of American racial politics inspired. Echoing the petitioners, he presented *Hirabayashi* and *Korematsu* as evidence that the Court itself had already acknowledged the hierarchical nature of race relations and, as a result, assumed the unconstitutionality of laws that discriminate on that basis. In his words, "Classifications based solely upon race must be scrutinized with particular care, since they are contrary to our traditions and hence constitutionally suspect."[49] While an explanation for the Court's placement of the burden of proof in race cases seemed even more important in a decision that, unlike *Hirabayashi* or *Korematsu, invalidated* governmental action, Warren concluded that incompleteness in this context was anything but a vice.

As Warren's reference to *Korematsu* suggests, the petitioners had presented an argument to the Court that was particularly appealing to the former attorney general of California. Not only had they convinced him that segregation was part of a long-standing effort to subjugate African Americans and that the Court's duty or mission was to prevent such injustices, they had also provided him with an argument that reconciled the Court's new role in protecting civil rights with his belief in the legitimacy of the internment of Japanese-Californians. Only a dire emergency on the order of the security threat that followed the bombing of Pearl Harbor, he was told (and he now believed), justified judicial passivity in the face of racially discriminatory policies.[50] Warren necessarily rejected the respondents' narrow reading of the *Korematsu* precedent—that heightened scrutiny applies *only* to instances in which government detains or imprisons persons because of their race.

It would be a mistake to conclude that the petitioners' arguments in the desegregation controversy were entirely responsible for the sense of mission that informed Warren's voting behavior in racial discrimination cases during his tenure on the Supreme Court. The detailed quality of his writings and speeches on the hierarchical nature of American race relations, and the surety with which he expressed the attendant view of the Court's role in confronting racial oppression, were traceable as much to, among other factors, the brutality of the southern response to civil rights protests in the 1960s as to the arguments of the lawyers in *Brown* and *Bolling.*[51] As Warren observed in 1968, "The Negro's peaceful demonstrations against a segregated society in the South . . . awakened the Nation's conscience to the realities of racial injustice."[52] After witnessing these events, Americans would no longer accept southern protestations that segregation reflected consideration of the welfare of blacks. But, rather than mark Warren's first exposure to the oppressive nature of segregation, the violence that occurred in the decade following *Brown* merely reinforced what the petitioners in the desegregation controversy had already led him to believe about that institution and racial politics generally.

The constitutive effect that the dialogue before the Court had on Warren necessarily went beyond the matter of the Court's mission and extended to the nature of constitutional interpretation. As noted, Warren could not have placed the burden of proof on segregationists, as his sense of the Court's mission required, unless he was free to disregard the historical evidence that the framers of the Fourteenth Amendment accepted the practice. Warren indicated his rejection of the respondents' narrow model of constitutional interpretation and his acceptance of the petitioners' alternative view when he stated in conference that the Civil War amendments were intended to equalize the status of former slaves. His statement implied that the framers did not seek to limit the meaning of the Fourteenth Amendment's provisions to the specific examples of racial equality that they had in mind. In the interest of preserving unanimity, Warren abandoned this vulnerable point and, instead, declared the inconclusiveness of the history of the Fourteenth Amendment. But his willingness to determine the constitutionality of segregation in light of present circumstances, *in spite of* the supposed indeterminacy of constitutional history, demonstrated his commitment to the petitioners' concept of a living Constitution. As he stated in the year following *Brown,* the Constitution is "a living, growing, dynamic organism of freedom for ourselves and for those who are to follow us." On another occasion that same year, he said he admired the document for its demonstrated "capacity for adaptation to the most challenging new conditions." Leaving no doubt that he believed the open texture of the Constitution extended to rights as well as powers, he contended, "If these rights are real, they need constant and imaginative application to new situations."[53]

In support of the approach to constitutional interpretation that the Court adopted in *Brown,* Warren advanced the petitioners' interpretation of case law. He presented the university desegregation cases as statements of the relevance of intangible considerations to determinations of educational equality. Warren juxtaposed this uncontroversial point with a footnote reference to the petitioners' social science evidence regarding the psychological damage that segregation causes in order to identify intangible considerations that explained the holding that segregated schools at the elementary and secondary school levels are inherently unequal. Warren's footnote was controversial not only because it represented the Court's first use of modern social science data to invalidate governmental action; in spite of Warren's suggestion to the contrary, the respondents had also demonstrated that the validity of the studies that he cited was very much open to question.

Even setting aside the strategic considerations that informed his decision to focus on the psychological harms of segregation, Warren's reference to the petitioners' social science evidence is understandable (although no less novel) considering that, under the suspect classification doctrine, which was implicit in his conception of the Court's mission and to which he referred in the federal desegregation case, *government* assumes the burden of proving the empirical assumptions informing its policies.[54] More specifically, the petitioners in the desegregation controversy needed only to make a reasonable argument regarding the harmfulness of segregation in order to require the defendants to prove that racial conflict was likely in integrated elementary and secondary schools and that segregation represented the only means to address the problem. The oppressive purpose that informed segregation laws when southern legislatures first passed them in the nineteenth century, Warren might have explained, justified the Court's demand that states prove that contemporary rationales for the practice are not simply cover for continued racial persecution. Warren's desire to write a nonaccusatory opinion, however, precluded him from elaborating on the assumptions underpinning the suspect classification doctrine and thus from explaining that the Court accepted only the reasonableness, as opposed to the validity, of the social science evidence of the petitioners.

The impact that the petitioners' arguments in *Brown* had on Warren's approach to constitutional interpretation, as well as on his understanding of the Court's mission, demonstrates that the complexity of the constitutive model—its acknowledgment of the influence of judicial discretion—does not necessarily sacrifice the explanatory value of the model's institutional focus. Warren's performance illustrates well what Rogers Smith terms "the dialectical interplay of meaningful decisions and structural constraints." With regard to the former, the chief justice's discretionary choices in *Brown,* and his consistent support for African American petitioners in subsequent racial discrimination cases, confirm "the possibility that [a justice's] actions themselves may not prove epiphenomenal to any combination of background structures, and that they may have unexpected significance for later events." On the other hand, the demonstrated link between the constitutional dialogue before the Court and Warren's sense of mission and his view of constitutional interpretation makes his "choices explicable in terms of relatively constant structural factors." Warren's assessment and internalization of the petitioners' arguments, in short, reveals the folly of assuming along with the instrumentalists "that all can be explained in terms of individual or group calculations."[55]

Justices Black and Jackson

"COURTS STAND AS HAVENS OF REFUGE"

Defenders of the constitutive variant of the new institutionalism might look to the desegregation votes of certain of Warren's brethren for further evidence of the explanatory power of this understanding of Supreme Court decision making. The vote of the Alabamian Hugo Black is worth investigating from such a noninstrumental perspective, given the evidence that suggests that he, like Warren, did not harbor desegregation policy preferences. Indeed, the task of providing an account of the desegregation vote of a justice who had been a member of the Ku Klux Klan is a challenge for instrumentalists and noninstrumentalists alike. This chore is complicated by the fact that Black's public papers do not contain probative information specifically relating to *Brown*.[56]

An explanation of Black's desegregation vote should begin with the observation that this erstwhile member of the Klan possessed a hierarchical view of society and politics. As a young attorney, Black chose sides in a political landscape that was sharply divided between Alabama's working classes and the state's plantation and industrial elites. Serving as an advocate almost exclusively for labor, he represented the United Mine Workers of Birmingham in a number of cases, was the regularly retained lawyer of the Local Carpenters' Union, and, for several years, represented the Brotherhood of Railroad Trainmen in all of their business. Black also demonstrated his commitment to labor through his hostility toward convict leasing, a system that exploited prisoners and depressed the wages of workers. He served as president of the Anti-Convict Lease Association, and his contributions in this role were instrumental in persuading the Alabama legislature to abolish the system.[57]

Black made his most significant efforts to aid Alabama's working classes as a U.S. senator. As a candidate for national office, he made no secret of his allegiances. "I am not now, and have never been a railroad, power company, or corporation lawyer," he declared. "They have never shaped my ideals, fashioned my political creed, nor helped in my aspirations for public office." Rather, he emphasized that he had "represented the injured and broken, the widows and orphans of men killed beneath the wheels of trains or buried in the falls of rock down in the mines of coal and iron."[58] After winning the Senate seat, Black came into open conflict with Alabama's propertied classes. As the Senate sponsor of the Fair Labor Standards Act (FLSA), which included requirements of minimum wages, maximum hours, and the abolition of child labor, he was accused of being complicit in northern efforts to sabotage southern industry. The FLSA was not an isolated instance of agreement between Black and President Franklin Roosevelt on appropriate means for achieving economic reform. Among southern senators who were part of a fragile New Deal coalition that included northern labor, none ranked higher than Black (near 80 percent) in terms of voting with nonsouthern Democrats in support of New Deal agricultural and labor policies.[59]

In spite of his sensitivity to the plight of the economically underprivileged, Black demonstrated that, at this time, racial oppression was not a form of hierarchy that figured into his politics. Senator Black fought against federal anti-lynching legislation and he questioned whether blacks should be permitted to vote. He claimed that an anti-lynching law would have the unfortunate effect of dividing blacks and whites who had been living together peaceably. Congress, he insisted, should recognize a truth that was not respected during Reconstruction—"that even though a province should be conquered, a wise conqueror [should leave] its local habits, customs, and manners untouched." Black had referred to the principle of "local control" in an earlier debate over a bipartisan bill authorizing a Federal Emergency Relief Board to allocate $375 million to Depression-weary Americans. Although he agreed that "we should have more federal assistance," he insisted that the people of Alabama would not "surrender to a Federal bureau in Washington their right to determine their own social habits and social customs; to regulate the schools in their states; [or] to regulate the administration of charity within their States." The ostensible reason for his stance was that Alabamians "have intelligence enough and honesty enough to determine for themselves how they will administer charity." But, as Richard Franklin Bensel observes, "Southern congressmen [at this time] were often reluctant to support the creation of a strong central state which could subsidize regional development because a powerful federal government could also restructure race relations."[60]

Although the policies a political figure promotes are not necessarily a reflection of his personal preferences, the evidence suggests that Black's defense of southern racial mores was something more than strategic in nature. Black did, in fact, make his statements in support of local control after certain events (in particular, a precipitous decline in Alabama's Klan membership) left him politically vulnerable and thus less inclined to challenge the policy preferences of Alabama's plantation and industrial elites. But, of course, racial conservatism was central to the ideology of Black's supporters in the Klan, as well as to the thinking of his political adversaries. Black claimed that expediential considerations informed his decision to join the Klan, specifically that he tried many cases before juries composed largely of Klansmen. Also, "the Alabama Klan was about the only organization that could provide help for an aspiring politician cut off from the campaign treasure chests of the 'Big Mules.'" As evidence of his equanimity regarding race, Black recalled that in his fight against convict leasing he took the case of Willie Morton, "a colored prisoner . . . [who] had been held over some time beyond his term of imprisonment."[61]

But the frequency and ease with which Black exploited racial enmity demonstrate that membership in the Klan did not compromise his moral convictions. Black was neither averse to appealing explicitly to racial and religious prejudice before juries when doing so benefited his clients nor uncomfortable or circumspect in the use of racist code and rhetoric. Mark Silverstein provides perhaps the fairest assessment of Black's racial views:

> For every indication of fairness to blacks, there is in [Black's] early career more than a suggestion of unconscious or unreflective racism in his actions. Regardless of subsequent explanations, membership in the Klan was a politically wise move, which did not seriously compromise his racial views. Black was not a violent man, and the floggings and terrorism of the Klan were out of character for him; nonetheless, the Klan often spoke the language of populism, invoking the image of the common man against centralized wealth and power. This ideal appealed to Black as well as to his constituency, and the fact that racism was a significant element of that appeal did not seriously trouble him.[62]

In spite of the racism that Black demonstrated before joining the Court, his performance in *Chambers v. Florida* indicated that, fourteen years prior to *Brown,* he had come to recognize the need to protect African Americans from one of the more obvious tools of racial oppression. *Chambers* involved a due process challenge to the manner in which Florida policemen secured confessions to the brutal murder of an elderly white man. The officers had arrested the suspects—four young black males—without warrant and had subjected them to five days of questioning. In his opinion for a unanimous Court, Black noted the racial context of the case—that the "cross questioning of these ignorant young colored tenant farmers by state officers and other white citizens . . . [occurred] in a fourth floor jail room, where as prisoners they were without friends, advisers or counselors, and under circumstances calculated to break the strongest nerves and the stoutest resistance." Displaying his hierarchical view of society and politics, he observed, "They who have suffered most from secret and dictatorial proceedings have almost always been the poor, the ignorant, the numerically weak, the friendless, and the powerless." But Black now added a racial dimension to his thinking: "Tyrannical governments had immemorially utilized dictatorial criminal procedure and punishment to make scapegoats of the weak, or of helpless political, religious, or racial minorities and those who differed, who would not conform and who resisted tyranny." His view of the Court's role followed from these observations. "Under our constitutional system," he contended, "courts stand against any winds that blow as havens of refuge for those who might otherwise suffer because they are helpless, weak, outnumbered, or because they are non-conforming victims of prejudice and public excitement." Black declared that the Court had "no higher duty, no more solemn responsibility" than to maintain "this constitutional shield deliberately planned and inscribed for the benefit of every human being subject to our Constitution—of whatever race, creed or persuasion."[63]

Black's racist background presents a problem for those who would characterize his statements in *Chambers* regarding a judicial mission to protect vulnerable—including racial—minorities as cover for his personal policy preferences. Black made these statements a mere three years after he joined the Court and well before the end of the Second World War (i.e., before the events associated with that conflict contributed to a liberalization of American racial attitudes). That the Kentuckian Stanley Reed joined Black's opinion helps to make the Alabamian's position less of a mystery. But accounting for the fact that a former Klansman authored such a forceful statement of the Court's role in race cases would seem to require more than the observation that Black was not the only southerner on the Court to recognize the injustice of coerced confessions.

Perhaps the most promising alternative explanation for Black's newfound concern for racial minorities (alternative to a noninstrumental account that emphasizes the significance of his sense of the Court's mission) is the hypothesis that Michael J. Klarman posits in order to account for both Black's desegregation vote in *Brown* and his *Chambers* opinion— that the justice might have sought to respond to public criticism of his Klan membership by demonstrating his capacity to treat blacks fairly.[64] If this was Black's purpose in *Chambers,* he achieved a good deal of success since his opinion for the Court earned him accolades from prominent black figures. Black was told that "the Negro race has been waiting for men like you on the bench for many year[s]," and that "Negroes all over the nation would [like to] recall every single word of derision heaped upon you and smother you with the glory of their praise."[65]

Yet the positive response that Black received for his *Chambers* opinion diminishes the force of Klarman's explanation for the justice's performance in *Brown.* Since *Chambers* did much to establish Black's reputation for fairness, he would have felt less of a need to use *Brown* for the same purpose. And, while Reed's willingness to join Black's opinion in *Chambers* helps to make Black's position in that case less mysterious, the Kentuckian's conference comments in *Brown* (in which he forcefully defended segregation) reveal that we cannot extrapolate from the Alabamian's performance in *Chambers* to explain his desegregation vote fourteen years later. It is curious that a former Klansman did not draw a similar distinction between coerced confessions and racial segregation.

While the Court decided *Brown* fourteen years after *Chambers*—in the postwar period when American (in particular, elite) attitudes toward race had begun to liberalize—recall from chapter 2 that the available evidence does not suggest that the forces that promoted racial egalitarianism at midcentury affected Black's personal policy preferences. A poll taken in 1954 revealed that only 38 percent of educated southerners supported desegregation. And scholars who study ideological drift contend that Black had become significantly more conservative after his first year on the bench and before the Court decided *Brown.*

In view of these considerations, scholars need to examine noninstrumental explanations for Black's desegregation vote. Black's statement in conference regarding the intentions of the framers of the Fourteenth Amendment, however, does not seem to provide much insight into his performance in *Brown.* Given the force of the arguments in support of the historical legitimacy of segregation, which the lawyers for the school boards presented at the initial hearing and, especially, the rehearing, Black's adoption of the LDF's contention that the Civil War amendments had as their purpose the abolition of all policies supporting racial castes, including segregation, qualifies more as a rationalization than a rationale for his desegregation vote.

Other portions of the petitioners' argument in *Brown,* however, appear to have had a constitutive impact on Black, although not identical to the impact that Chief Justice Warren experienced. In his comments in the 1952 conference, Black echoed the message that the petitioners conveyed to the Court regarding the nature of segregation—that the practice was part of an effort to maintain white supremacy rather than to preserve public order for the good of blacks and whites alike. Recall that Black informed his brethren that segregation was based on a belief in the inferiority of blacks and an attendant desire to preserve the purity of the white race by preventing racial intermixture.[66] He declared that he did not need books to reach this conclusion. He apparently did not need the arguments of the petitioners, either, to understand that segregation reflected a fear of race mixing. At the initial hearing, Spottswood Robinson and Louis Redding briefly addressed the point that segregation laws "were intended [to] and did indeed accomplish the disability of the Negro."[67] And, as noted, the petitioners' brief for the rehearing provided a detailed treatment of that same point, as well as the idea that segregation was grounded in a belief in the inherent inferiority of blacks. But the petitioners did not discuss at either of the hearings the degree to which a dread of miscegenation was part of the ideology of segregation.[68] In short, the petitioners reminded the former Klansman about a collection of racist ideas with which he was all too familiar.

While the petitioners in *Brown* did not deepen Black's understanding of the nature of segregation, they did an effective job of informing this justice, in particular, of the legal implications of the insight that segregation was part of a system of racial oppression. They reminded Black, who had authored the majority opinion in *Korematsu v. United States*, of what he had said in that case—that racial classifications are "immediately suspect." Black had stated that the Court would "subject . . . to the most rigid scrutiny" "*all* legal restrictions which curtail the civil rights of a single racial group." He had also insisted that "pressing public necessity," such as the prevention of sabotage or espionage during war, "may sometimes justify the existence of such restrictions; *racial antagonism never can.*"[69] In view of such expansive language, Black would have been hard pressed to accept the narrow interpretation of the Japanese internment case that the respondents in the District of Columbia desegregation case offered—that strict scrutiny is appropriate only in instances in which government detains persons because of their race. Rather than inquire at oral argument about the alternative interpretations of *Korematsu*'s scope, Black asked whether strict scrutiny "applies with reference to the Fourteenth Amendment which was passed under different circumstances and for entirely different purposes" than the Fifth Amendment (which was at issue in *Korematsu*). Although George Hayes answered that strict scrutiny would be warranted under the Fourteenth Amendment, he neglected to support his assertion with the point that the petitioners emphasized in their brief for the rehearing—that "the power of states is even more rigidly circumscribed" under the Fourteenth Amendment than the federal government is under the Fifth, since the Court has viewed the former (a post–Civil War amendment) "as a broad prohibition against state enforcement of differentiations and discrimination based upon race or color."[70]

As in *Korematsu*, Black had available to him in *Brown* an argument that he could have used to rationalize a ruling against the petitioners (even though the government would not have met the burden of demonstrating that the racial classification was necessary to accomplish the ostensible public purpose). Unlike Justice Reed, however, Black proved unreceptive to the contention that school segregation was necessary to avoid racial conflict. As an erstwhile member of an organization that made little effort to disguise the racial enmity that informed its policy positions, Black was compelled to concede that segregation reinforced white supremacy.[71] He agreed with the petitioners that such racism cannot be reconciled with the concept of equal protection, especially in view of his own statement in *Korematsu* that policies based on racial antagonism cannot survive strict judicial scrutiny. Black, in other words, did not have to be a racial progressive to vote for desegregation; he needed only to be honest enough to admit that siding with the petitioners in *Brown* was the consequence of a proper application of *Korematsu*'s strict scrutiny standard. His position in *Brown* was also a logical extension of his *Chambers* opinion, which identified African Americans as a group historically vulnerable to prejudice. And his positions in both of these cases were logical extensions of the hierarchical view of society and politics that informed his thinking prior to his appointment to the Court. That Black felt more strongly about the sense of judicial mission that he articulated in *Chambers* than he did about the racial views that he set aside in that case and in *Brown* was suggested when his second wife recalled, "He could never read aloud from his [*Chambers*] opinion without tears streaming down his face."[72]

The high rate of liberal voting that Black demonstrated in civil rights cases (72.2 percent in 277 cases for the years 1953 to 1971) suggests that he continued to have a strong sense that the Court's mission is to serve as a corrective for American racial politics. That Black's liberal voting rate was lower than that of Chief Justice Warren (82.8 percent in 221 cases for the years 1953 to 1969) demonstrates that a shared sense of mission does not imply identical views regarding the proper application of that mission in the circumstances of individual cases.[73]

"TO SEE THIS THING DECIDED WISELY RATHER THAN TO SEE EITHER SIDE WIN"

In view of Michael Klarman's contention that Robert Jackson "found segregation anathema," an explanation of the justice's desegregation vote seems less likely to benefit from the insights of a noninstrumental understanding of Supreme Court decision making.[74] But Jackson's preferences regarding segregation were more complicated than Klarman suggests. As the former chief prosecutor for the United States at the Nuremberg War Crimes Trial, Jackson knew of what he spoke when, in a letter that he wrote to Charles Fairman while the Court was considering the university desegregation cases, he remarked upon "the terrible consequences of racial hatred in Germany." Jackson followed that statement with the observation (on which Klarman focuses) that he had "no sympathy with [the] racial conceits which underlie segregation policies." But other portions of Jackson's letter reveal that he was not an ardent desegregationist. He confessed that he was "almost embarrassed to be in doubts about a matter on which nearly everyone here seems . . . to be fully convinced." These doubts were due in part to his views regarding the limits of judicial power—to the conviction "that widely held beliefs and attitudes, even if mistaken, are real factors in law and statecraft and a state of mind may be as real a hazard as a mountain range or a river boundary." But he also suggested that his confusion regarding segregation was a consequence of his "background," specifically his unfamiliarity with the problem of race in America. Jackson recalled that he "was brought up in a community where no serious racial problems or tensions existed." After noting that he "first encountered real racial consciousness and antagonism in Washington, D.C.," he declared (in a statement that one cannot imagine him directing at the victims of Nazi oppression): "I am amazed and disappointed at the depth and bitterness of the feeling among the Negroes." Making no allowance for the nature of the cause, and failing to identify the persons he had in mind, Jackson suggested an equivalence between the strongest voices for and against segregation: "The stupidity and recklessness of extremists on both sides is such that they seem ready to precipitate any kind of conflict. So I find a good deal of demagoguery and hypocrisy on both sides of this issue."[75]

It is not surprising, then, that Jackson declared his "real concern . . . [was] to *see this thing decided wisely rather than to see either side win.*" And, since Jackson revealed that he was neither a defender of segregation nor an avid reformer—that the strength of his policy preference was insufficient to convince him of the proper course of action—his allusions to the importance of the rule of law when considering "the function of the Court in the matter" should not be dismissed as mere rhetoric. He proclaimed that he "really did, and still do[es] believe the doctrine on which the Roosevelt fight against the old Court was based—in part that it had expanded the Fourteenth Amendment to take an unjustified judicial control over social and economic affairs." Recalling that the New Dealers "insisted that a majority out of nine appointed life-tenure men should not settle such issues," he lamented that "a good many who were associated in that fight now abandon that position but think the Court should decide such questions provided it will decide their way."[76]

When the justices shifted their attention to elementary school segregation, Jackson acted on the themes that he articulated in his letter to Fairman. Recall that, in conference, he informed his colleagues of his naïveté regarding the problem of race; told his brethren that he did not object to desegregation but suggested that integrating classrooms will not be all to the good for black children; and restated his belief in the importance of the rule of law, insisting that the Court find a legal basis for its decision. When Jackson put his thoughts to paper in memoranda for *Brown,* he made the same points. In particular, he reiterated that the justices "can not oversimplify this decision to be a mere expression of our personal opinion that school segregation is unwise or evil. We have not been chosen as legislators but as judges."[77]

In considering whether Jackson's memoranda provide a basis for a noninstrumentalist interpretation of his desegregation vote, note, first, that the justice penned three draft opinions in approximately two months, with the space allotted to the rationale for invalidating segregation increasing from no pages (out of thirteen) in the first version, to two pages (out of fifteen) in the second, and finally to six pages (out of twenty-three) in the final draft.[78] Also, a heart attack Jackson suffered shortly after completing the third draft put an end to any plans he may have had to continue refining his argument. But even the presumably incomplete argument of the final draft, which devoted more space to the barriers to desegregation than to the legal rationale for declaring segregation unconstitutional, is sufficient to shift the burden of proof to those who would explain Jackson's vote entirely in instrumental terms. As noted in chapter 3, Jackson based his opinion on the petitioners' argument that segregation violated the reasonableness requirement of the concept of equal protection because the practice necessarily implied an untenable belief in racial inferiority. In contrast to Warren's controversial point that school segregation caused psychological harm to black children, Jackson's borrowed rationale accorded with the dominant opinions of the scientific community. As Klarman writes, "By 1940, few respectable scientists espoused biological explanations for observable differences in the behavior of racial groups." Furthermore, "this shift in scientific paradigms was filtering down to popular opinion, assisted by widespread revulsion against Nazism."[79] By arguing that segregation was based on insupportable racist assumptions and implying that the practice was unacceptable in any setting, Jackson's rationale was politically infeasible. But this consideration suggests that the rationale was *not* fatally flawed as a means to justify judicial action. Furthermore, given Jackson's value preferences, we can assume that he believed in the empirical validity of his argument.

In view of the force, if not the feasibility, of Jackson's legal argument, it appears unlikely that the justice intended the portions of his opinion devoted to matters other than the specific rationale for invalidating segregation to serve merely as gratuitous discussions of problems confronting the Court. Rather, these sections of his third draft opinion are more properly viewed in strategic terms. In his ten-page examination of the history, case law, and custom supporting segregation, Jackson made the telling observation that "it would retard acceptance of this decision if the Northern majority of this Court should make a Pharisaic and self-righteous approach to this issue or were inconsiderate of the conditions which have brought about and continued this custom or should permit a needlessly ruthless decree to be promulgated." Similarly, in his seven-page treatment of the limitations of judicial efforts to engage in social reform, Jackson declared, "The Court can strike down legislation which supports educational segregation, but any constructive policy for abolishing it must come from Congress." Of course, Jackson's law clerk was correct to inform his superior that "it is one thing to have and express many doubts about a difficult decision," but "it is another to state them at such length and in such precedence over your affirmative views that the result you reach is swallowed up in them."[80] Yet Jackson, like Warren, recognized the importance of a nonaccusatory opinion. Prescient in his observation that *Brown* would be stillborn without the support of Congress, he also understood the compelling need to craft an opinion that would induce a legislative response.[81]

While the strategic model of Supreme Court decision making explains Jackson's efforts to respond to perceived impediments to a desegregation ruling (as well as his decision to abandon his opinion in the interest of unanimity), the constitutive model appears relevant to his vote in *Brown*. The justice's successive draft opinions reveal a deliberate consideration of the relative worth of the various arguments made before the Court and his selection of a rationale that satisfied his requirement that a compelling legal argument accompany a desegregation order. In his first two drafts, Jackson declared his opposition to the petitioners' effort to "read into the concept of equal protection the shadowy and changing doctrines relating to mental and emotional reactions" and identified as problematic the argument that segregation is "offensive to the best contemporary opinion here and damaging to our prestige abroad." He conceded that "the past few years have witnessed a profound change in the responsible and rational public opinion toward segregation" as a result of "the post mortem upon the Nazi regime in Europe." But he characterized the transformation of American racial attitudes and the Cold War implications of segregation as "arguments of policy," which were irrelevant to the constitutional issue before the justices. In sharp contrast, Jackson determined that the petitioners' arguments concerning the irrationality of the segregationists' belief in racial inferiority were relevant to a doctrine "which is already on our books," namely the equal protection requirement that a rational relationship exist between a law's purpose and the means selected to effectuate that purpose.[82]

In order for Jackson to conclude that this doctrine justified judicial action, he also had to accept the petitioners' view that the living Constitution concept contained therein—the idea that "Constitutional generalities 'have a content and a significance that vary from age to age'"—empowered the Court, as well as Congress, to take note of contemporary factors that ran contrary to the notion of racial inferiority. Jackson went from stating in his first draft "that a complete and undoubted power to deal with this subject exists in a branch of the government co-ordinate with our own and one which is chosen by political methods," to declaring in his final draft "that present-day conditions *require us* to strike from our books the doctrine of separate-but-equal facilities and to hold invalid provisions of state constitutions or statutes which classify persons for separate treatment in matters of education based solely on possession of colored blood."[83]

Jackson abandoned his separate opinion in part because of his poor health. Most likely, Warren also convinced him of the need to adopt a less powerful rationale in order to avoid the anticipated reaction that southerners would have to a legal argument that identified segregation as racist and unacceptable in any context. That Jackson died too soon to determine the degree to which he thought the Court had a mission to serve a corrective function in American racial politics is not reason to disregard the constitutive impact of the petitioners' legal argument in *Brown*.[84] In view of the relative weakness of Jackson's denunciation of segregation as against the strength of the legal argument that he borrowed from the petitioners (to say nothing of studies of ideological drift, which suggest that the justice had become considerably more conservative before the Court rendered *Brown*), it is difficult to characterize his draft revisions merely in instrumental terms—as evidence of a search for an acceptable argument to serve as window dressing for a predetermined conclusion.[85] His failure to address the other rationale for segregation—that racial separation preserves racial harmony—might still tempt us to conclude that his writing betrayed a value choice in search of legal cover. But Jackson had not completed his draft revisions when a heart attack felled him, and, as Warren and Black realized, the petitioners provided ample evidence to doubt the claim that segregation was intended to and did, in fact, promote racial accord.

The explanatory power of the constitutive variant of the new institutionalism, as it pertains to *Brown,* is not limited to an explanation of the votes of Warren, Black, and Jackson. Recent studies of the *Brown* decision, which partly reflect or draw on the insights of the constitutive model of Supreme Court decision making, are especially powerful in that they, like the argument in this chapter, manage to avoid the confusion which might issue from a decision-making model that embraces an abstract notion of legal institutions and acknowledges the openness of these institutions to judge-initiated change. By illuminating the constitutional relevance of the Court's connections to elements within the broader political system or regime, this scholarship more accurately belongs to a "political regimes" approach to Supreme Court decision making.

FIVE

The Relevance of Foreign Affairs

The sensitive nature of the issue litigated in *Brown* suggests that the petitioners' argument regarding the link between school segregation and white supremacy was not the only powerful desegregation message the Court considered. Individuals who champion a "political regimes" model of Supreme Court decision making—an approach that combines a non-instrumental sensibility with the understanding that the Court is one point in a pattern of institutional relationships that constitute a political regime—provide reason to believe the justices also looked to the executive branch for cues regarding normatively appropriate judicial behavior in *Brown.* This perspective is reflected in recent scholarship that emphasizes the significance of the federal government's participation as *amicus curiae,* in particular the Truman administration's extended treatment of the Cold War implications of segregation. In support of the argument that *Brown* was intended to preclude the Soviet Union from exploiting racial segregation in its propaganda campaign against the United States, there is evidence that the Cold War represented an additional factor in the desegregation votes of Justices William Douglas, Stanley Reed, Robert Jackson, and Felix Frankfurter. But the justices who proved most receptive to the foreign policy implications of segregation were those who had been appointed by the administration that brought these considerations to the Court's attention—Harold Burton, Sherman Minton, and especially Tom Clark.

A "Political Regimes" Approach

Cornell W. Clayton and David A. May, two scholars who recently emphasized the need for an "alternative way" to conceptualize Supreme Court decision making, point up the weaknesses of each of the variants of the new institutionalism. Defenders of the strategic model, they contend, fail to see "that justices tend to make decisions on the basis of what they believe to be the most authentic understanding of 'the law' and the appropriate mission or role of the Court, not on the basis of their personal policy preferences alone." By contrast, those who champion the constitutive model invite conceptual and analytical confusion by adopting "an overly porous conception of institutions." In other words, "Removing the distinction between ideas and formal institutions (between dependent and independent variables) makes it difficult to investigate empirically how institutions shape ideas and patterns of belief, or how ideas may in turn shape institutions."[1]

In order to avoid these drawbacks, Clayton and May "suggest the advantages of adopting an institutionalism that holds a constitutive conception of politics but retains a more traditional conception of political institutions." More specifically, the approach to Supreme Court decision making that they champion "owes much to Rogers Smith's brand of interpretive institutionalism but also to the work of judicial scholars who have engaged in 'political systems' analysis or a so-called 'political jurisprudence.'" Scholars whose work falls under the rubric "political jurisprudence" draw in significant measure on the insights of Martin Shapiro (who coined the term) and Robert A. Dahl.[2] Dahl and Shapiro sought to understand the Court by illuminating its power relationships in the broader American political system.[3]

Clayton and May note that constitutive model proponents criticize scholars who adopt a "political jurisprudence" perspective (and portray "the role of the Court, and hence the cumulative impact of its decisions, . . . [as] dependent on such things as party realignments or the alignment and interrelation between powerful social forces and groups") for replicating the error of the strategic model. These political jurisprudents (and, by implication, the original exponents of "political jurisprudence," Dahl and Shapiro) are reproved for relying "upon the premise that within certain institutionalized constraints judicial decisions reflected the instrumental politics of self-interest or preference maximization." In contrast to the instrumentalism of "political jurisprudence," Clayton contends that "the Court has tended to view the law as a constitutive political process in which the relative positions and substantive views of other political actors are not just barriers to the promotion of particular preferences but are themselves the basis of appropriate legal outcomes."[4]

Since "the Court is engaged in a constitutive dialogue with other branches and political actors over the meaning of law," Clayton argues, "any understanding of judicial decision-making as responsive to legal institutions would require attention to the pattern of institutional relationships within the existing political regime." In other words, scholars should combine a traditional legal focus (on "judicial doctrines, precedents, statutes, etc.") with analyses of "political system relationships . . . that political systems scholars emphasized," including "the views of law held by interest groups and electoral coalitions, found in such things as party platforms, public speeches, and debates around judicial appointments, and the *amicus* briefs filed by the Solicitor General, members of Congress or interest groups." Clayton and May suggest that, by viewing "judicial choices not as discrete acts but as embedded within the broader political system or political regime that gives individual institutional components their meaning," a "political regimes" approach to Supreme Court decision making acknowledges the noninstrumental "desire [of justices] to give a professionally principled interpretation of law or an authentically held view about the appropriate mission of courts," while employing "definitions of institutions and institutional structures with enough specificity so as to make empirical investigation of their influence on attitudes and ideas possible."[5]

Recent scholarship on *Brown* that reflects a "political regimes" approach to Supreme Court decision making emphasizes the significance of the *amicus curiae* brief that the Truman administration filed in that case in 1952. This focus is understandable because of both the substance of these documents and the "special and unique relationship" that exists between the Court and the solicitor general (and the attorney general and Department of Justice, more generally). As Rebecca Mae Salokar observes, "the solicitor general is the ideal 'Repeat Player'"—a frequent participant in cases before the Court who, in addition to being free of the financial constraints that face most litigants, "enjoys advance intelligence, expertise, access to specialists throughout the Department of Justice, and opportunities to develop facilitative informal relations with institutional incumbents." These factors help the solicitor general to maintain "a high degree of credibility before the Court." A commonality of perspective between the Court and the chief courtroom officer of the federal government also exists, a perspective that stems from the practical matter of the president's involvement in choosing both the solicitor general and the justices before whom that individual practices and from a shared concern with the interpretation and execution of law. A final factor that connects the Court and the solicitor general is the fact that the justices, having control over neither sword nor purse, must rely on the executive to enforce their decisions. In view of this consideration, "the Court must be cautious and supportive of the executive" lest "repeated decisions by the Court against the executive's power . . . result in conflict and antagonism between the branches to the extent that even the legitimacy of the Court may be called into question."[6]

The factors that suggest the Court's receptiveness to the position of the executive in cases in which the United States is a party are also present when the government files *amicus curiae* briefs on behalf of litigants before the Court. In this situation, the solicitor general does not have a direct interest to protect or an agency to represent but still seeks to provide the justices with information or guidance regarding the case's implications for broader legal developments.[7] As Steven Puro observes, *amicus* briefs are "an important way for the executive to communicate his desires to the Court," since he "can indicate his willingness to support the Court's decision and explain [his] policy on statutory or constitutional questions." "Frequently [as with the reargument of *Brown*] the Court will ask for the Solicitor General's opinion in an *amicus* brief if he does not come forward himself; in part, this invitation can be viewed as an attempt to ascertain if the executive or federal government as a whole has a real stake in the outcome of a case." Such "information becomes even more significant in cases concerning major political issues" such as desegregation, since "the executive's position helps the Court to assess the difficulties of policy implementation or the degree of compliance that will be given to [the justices'] decision." The government's *amicus* briefs can also "indicate the inability or unwillingness of other governmental institutions to deal with pressing political problems. In this way the U.S. as *amicus* may be urging the Court, as the last hope for 'out' groups, to espouse socially unpopular views it would be politically risky for the executive to adopt. In this way, such 'unpopular' or 'progressive' views are transformed into public policy but the onus of having made the decisions rests on the Court and not upon the executive."[8]

In addition to the factors already mentioned that suggest the Court's receptiveness to the position of the executive as *amicus curiae,* Clayton provides another consideration that suggests most of the justices involved in *Brown* were inclined to support the federal government's position. "The New Deal," he observes, "forged a practical political alliance between the federal judiciary and the executive branch." In other words, the New Deal marked a turning point in American constitutional history as judicial fidelity to the founders' notion of a national government with limited powers over economic development gave way to judicial acceptance of the modern notion of a living Constitution, at least with respect to the *powers* of government. Franklin Roosevelt's instrumental role in convincing Congress and the Supreme Court to accept the legitimacy of an activist national state, combined with his performance as commander in chief during the Second World War, ensured that defenders of the living Constitution concept recognized the importance of presidential policy formulation. In view of these considerations, Clayton believes it is significant that "Roosevelt and Truman appointed the next thirteen Justices to the Supreme Court"—eight of whom participated in *Brown*—since "all embraced the New Deal jurisprudence that political liberalism could best be advanced by judicial deference to presidential policy direction."[9]

A Cold War Imperative

The factors that suggest judicial receptiveness to the position of the executive as *amicus curiae* should lead students of *Brown* to consider the scholarship of Mary L. Dudziak, who, borrowing from the insights of Derrick A. Bell, Jr., believes that the desegregation decision was a "Cold War imperative." Put another way, Dudziak maintains that, at the prompting of executive officials, the justices intended *Brown* to serve a crucial symbolic function during a time when the Soviet Union effectively exploited the existence of racial injustice in the United States in its propaganda campaign against its chief international rival. As Dudziak notes, "By 1949, according to the U.S. Embassy in Moscow, 'the "Negro question" [was] one of the principal Soviet propaganda themes regarding the United States.'" Dudziak regards as telling the fact that the *Brown* decision appeared during a time when the federal government adopted a *restrictive* approach toward civil *liberties*. At the same time that federal officials sought to crush subversive activities within the United States, she explains, they "realized that their ability to sell democracy to the Third World was seriously hampered by continuing racial injustice at home. Accordingly, efforts to *promote* civil *rights* within the United States were [viewed as] consistent with, and important to, the more central U.S. mission of fighting world communism."[10]

The postwar establishment of the United Nations substantially aided Soviet efforts to challenge America's commitment to racial equality. Although the United States was instrumental in the creation of the United Nations, the organization's human rights orientation made it an appropriate forum for African Americans to alert the international community to their plight. The Subcommission on the Prevention of Discrimination and Protection of Minorities, which the United Nations established at the behest of the Soviet Union, presented the greatest challenge to U.S. officials. As noted in chapter 4, the NAACP filed a petition in October 1947 protesting the treatment of blacks in the United States. After declaring that southern racial politics was more of a danger to the nation than the Soviet Union, the petition emphasized that "the disfranchisement of the American Negro makes the functioning of all democracy in the nation difficult; and as democracy fails to function in the leading democracy in the world, it fails the world." Four years later, the Civil Rights Congress (CRC) would likewise use the United Nations as a forum for drawing international attention to the problem of racial injustice in America. Invoking the Genocide Convention, which the United Nation's General Assembly had adopted in 1948, the CRC's petition charged that the United States had committed genocide against black Americans.[11]

President Harry Truman's Committee on Civil Rights expressed concern regarding the international attention given to the problem of racial injustice in the United States. The committee's final report stated, "We cannot escape the fact that our civil rights record has been an issue in world politics." In an effort "to prove our democracy an empty fraud, and our nation a consistent oppressor of underprivileged people," nations with "competing philosophies" had emphasized and misrepresented America's problems. The report warned that "the United States is not so strong, the final triumph of the democratic ideal is not so inevitable that we can ignore what the world thinks of us or our record."[12]

Dudziak opines that concern about the impact of racial discrimination on American foreign policy during the Cold War led the Truman administration to consider a pro–civil rights posture as one means to contain communism. This approach was evidenced primarily in the administration's involvement in desegregation litigation. While Truman's speeches and legislative initiatives on behalf of racial equality "would help him achieve the [domestic] political mileage he needed in the area of civil rights," Dudziak avers, legislative proposals that would die in committee at the hands of powerful southern congressmen "were not likely to dampen international criticism." In other words, "some actual change in American racial policies was needed to silence foreign critics," and "in the late 1940s and early 1950s that change would not come from Congress. It might, however, come from the courts."[13]

Dudziak maintains that the connection between the Truman administration's foreign policy concerns and its involvement in desegregation litigation is readily apparent. Most obviously, the *amicus curiae* brief that the administration filed for the initial hearing of *Brown* contended, in significant measure, that foreign policy considerations revealed desegregation to be in the national interest. Elaborating on a theme that the administration had articulated in earlier cases involving restrictive covenants, dining car segregation in interstate transportation, and desegregation in higher education, the document emphasized the critical importance of desegregation in Washington, D.C.: "Foreign officials and visitors naturally judge this country and our people by their experiences and observations in the nation's capital; and the treatment of colored persons here is taken as the measure of our attitude toward minorities generally." The continued existence of segregation "furnishes grist for the Communist propaganda mills, and it raises doubts among friendly nations as to the intensity of our devotion to the democratic faith."[14]

Conceding that foreign policy concerns alone did not explain the Truman administration's call for desegregation at the bar of the Court, Dudziak observes, "Concern about racial injustice and political motivations also played a part." Nevertheless, she points up the fact that "the Justice Department devoted a considerable amount of space to these arguments, and stressed to the Supreme Court that a decision upholding segregation would have demonstrable, negative effects on international relations." She also notes that "the NAACP made the same point, although briefly, when [*Brown*] was reargued." Thurgood Marshall and his colleagues "stressed that the 'Survival of our country in the present international situation is inevitably tied to resolution of this domestic issue.'"[15]

Dudziak acknowledges that, on the strength of her evidence, she cannot claim definitively "that the Cold War imperative determined the way members of the Court cast their votes in *Brown*." But, with considerable justification, she contends that the mere absence of "explicit Cold War rhetoric" in Earl Warren's opinion for the Court does not negate this possibility. After all, "it would have been . . . somewhat impolitic of the Court to suggest that the decision was motivated not by a dispassionate reading of the Constitution, but rather by a concern about how others viewed the morality of the American form of government." Dudziak suggests that "archival research on Supreme Court Justices might disclose specific ways in which members of the Court were influenced by Cold War ideology." But, she contends, even without such evidence, "the Supreme Court, in any given historical period, is necessarily influenced by the intellectual history of its times. . . . During the late 1940s and early 1950s, a period of substantial progress in the area of minority rights by the Court, Cold War ideology informed the broader discourse on civil rights in important and powerful ways." These arguments were so powerful that it "is unlikely that [they] did not inform the Court in a manner similar to that in which they informed executive branch actions during this period."[16]

In Dudziak's view, at least two justices revealed a concern with the international implications of the controversy over segregation. "Justice William O. Douglas, in particular, addressed the impact of race discrimination on American prestige abroad in his writings" before the Court rendered *Brown.* He "found that in India. . . . 'The treatment of colored peoples by other nations is an important consideration in the warmth of [that country's] relations to the outside world.'" And he recalled being told on a trip to Pakistan that the Soviet Union would emerge victorious in the battle for Asia in part because the United States was not regarded as a champion of social justice. Dudziak contends that "Chief Justice Earl Warren saw things the same way" as Douglas. In the month following *Brown,* Warren gave a speech in which he said "that the American conception of justice 'separates us from many other political systems of the world.'" Later, in a speech to the American Bar Association, he declared "that ' . . . the extent to which we maintain the spirit of our Constitution with its Bill of Rights . . . will in the long run do more to make it both secure and the object of adulation than the number of hydrogen bombs we stockpile.'"[17]

An Additional Goal

His references to foreign affairs notwithstanding, Earl Warren does not appear to corroborate the view that *Brown* was an executive-inspired Cold War imperative. Warren was certainly in need of instruction on the relevance of the segregation controversy to the Cold War. Recall that, as a presidential aspirant and during a time when the Soviet Union was using segregation in its anti-American propaganda, he did not pressure his party to expand its position on civil rights to include desegregation. Warren declined to do so even though he had strong political incentives and few disincentives to champion this reform. At the same time, he had no reservations about counseling Republicans that economic liberalism was an essential component of the effort to win the Cold War, as well as a means for the party to recapture the White House. But the suggestion that the Truman administration's brief, with its elaborate treatment of the Cold War implications of a desegregation ruling, may have had a constitutive impact on the new chief justice is complicated by an article Warren wrote in the year following *Brown.* Focusing on "the struggle between Communism and freedom," he commented, "As long as the U.S. leads the forces of freedom in the world's great ideological struggle, our institutions will remain under a global spotlight, and what we do will speak much louder than what we say." When he moved to concrete prescriptions, however, he emphasized only the importance of ensuring equal access to procedural justice and of judicial enforcement of the provisions of the Bill of Rights. Surprisingly, Warren made no mention of the significance of desegregation to the Cold War even though he sought to emphasize the contribution of judicial protection of constitutional rights to American foreign policy.[18] For that matter, Warren made no mention of desegregation in the speeches from which Dudziak quotes. In view of the evidence marshaled in the preceding chapter, which revealed that Warren did not possess desegregation policy preferences when he joined the Court, it is necessary to consider noninstrumental explanations for his behavior in *Brown.* But Warren's consistent failure to link desegregation to the Cold War places the burden of proof on those who would argue that foreign policy considerations coincided with his marked sense of the Court's mission to prevent racial injustice, and contributed to his vote in *Brown* and his strong support for civil rights after 1954.[19]

The Cold War thesis seems to be of limited utility in explaining Douglas's desegregation vote as well. Like Warren, Douglas was very protective of petitioners in First Amendment cases, the context in which the Court examined challenges to the government's anticommunist efforts. Douglas's extraordinarily high level of support for civil rights petitioners in the years following *Brown* also seems more in keeping with Michael J. Klarman's instrumental interpretation of his desegregation vote than with the Cold War thesis, since significantly less vigilance on the part of the justices was required in order to frustrate the Soviet Union's propaganda campaign against the United States.[20] Indeed, the point of Dudziak's effort to link *Brown* and civil rights law generally to American foreign policy during the 1950s is to lend credence to Derrick Bell's "interest convergence" principle—that "the interest of blacks in achieving racial equality will be accommodated only when it converges with the interests of whites." According to this principle, the Cold War imperative ensured only symbolic gestures that would blunt Soviet criticism as opposed to thoroughgoing and meaningful progress toward racial equality. "With *Brown* and Little Rock," Dudziak explains, "formal equality could protect the image of American constitutionalism even if the reforms supported by the federal government would not lead to meaningful social change in the communities affected."[21]

Nevertheless, the fact that, prior to *Brown,* Douglas commented on the foreign policy implications of racial discrimination advises against dismissing Cold War considerations as a contributing factor to his performance in that case. Douglas's desegregation vote may serve to illustrate the point that judicial behavior patterns are often consistent with multiple goal orientations.[22] Although it is impossible to determine with any precision the relative influence of the goals that appear consistent with Douglas's behavior, each of those objectives may be relevant to an explanation of his particular vote in *Brown.*

A skeptic of the Cold War thesis might suggest that, if foreign policy considerations were operative in the justices' minds when they decided *Brown,* it is difficult to explain the absence of direct evidence to that effect. As even Dudziak concedes, there are no explicit references to the matter in the available conference notes.[23] It is tempting to argue that the justices devoted their formal deliberations to the task of finding an acceptable legal argument for a Cold War imperative, and that they reserved discussions of the foreign policy implications of desegregation for other, more informal contexts. But, as chapter 3 demonstrates, the members of the Court did not limit themselves to legal arguments in conference; the available notes are replete with references to the potential for violence, an issue that had no bearing on the legal validity of the petitioner's constitutional claims. While it is not surprising that the justices discussed the potential negative consequences of a desegregation ruling, it is reasonable to ask why the strongest proponents of such a decision failed to meet these extralegal concerns, or even the legal concerns of others, with observations regarding the decision's likely positive impact in the international realm.

It is difficult to believe, however—given the special relationship that exists between the Court and the solicitor general, the frequency with which the executive informed the Court of the foreign policy implications of segregation, and the seriousness of this issue—that the justices found Cold War matters irrelevant to *Brown.* The recollections of John D. Fassett, who served as one of Justice Reed's law clerks during the Supreme Court's 1953 term, lend credence to the Cold War thesis. Fassett remembered one conversation with Reed in which he mentioned to the justice "the importance of a decision rejecting segregation to our country's position in the community of nations." While Fassett could "not recall the Justice's exact words," he believed that "the substance of his reply was that he had been *hearing considerable [talk] on that subject and it was causing him much thought* although it should be irrelevant."[24]

One indication that Cold War considerations *were* relevant to Reed's desegregation vote—that his recognition of the need for unanimity in *Brown* may not have been the only noninstrumental factor that prompted him to set aside his stated preference for segregation—is the discrepancy between his approaches to civil rights and civil liberties claims. Indeed, in contrast to Douglas and Warren, Reed exhibited voting behavior that suggests that the Cold War was central to his thinking. Although Reed voted against school segregation, he supported civil rights petitioners only 35.5 percent of the time in 31 cases from 1953 until his retirement in 1957.[25] While his anemic support for civil rights may have reflected a mere desire to frustrate the Soviet Union's anti-American propaganda, his First Amendment decisions revealed great deference toward the anticommunist measures of government.[26]

Robert Jackson was apparently involved in the conversation regarding segregation and the Cold War to which Fassett referred. In the memoranda that he drafted in *Brown,* Jackson observed that segregation "is said to be offensive to the best contemporary opinion here and damaging to our prestige abroad." Like Reed, he indicated that such "arguments of policy" are irrelevant to the matter of the constitutionality of the practice.[27] Unfortunately, Jackson's death six months after the *Brown* ruling means scholars cannot examine further trends in his decisions to determine whether he viewed these policy concerns as constitutionally relevant. Scholars can, however, take note of his receptiveness to the government's position when communists challenged security measures under the First Amendment prior to *Brown.*[28] If not probable, it was certainly possible that Jackson's powerful, LDF-inspired legal argument—that the irrationality of segregation rendered the practice unconstitutional—freed him not only to pursue his moderate desegregation policy preference but also to act on the executive's foreign policy concerns.

Felix Frankfurter's comment in conference—that it was "intolerable that DC would permit segregation"—could be considered an indirect reference to the Cold War implications of a desegregation decision.[29] Frankfurter's level of support for civil rights petitioners from 1953 until his retirement in 1962, although rather modest (55.7 percent in 88 cases), was higher than that of Reed.[30] The probability that the former member of the NAACP's National Legal Committee had a stronger commitment to the concept of equality may explain this difference. In his First Amendment decisions, however, Frankfurter, like Reed and Jackson, was not much of an impediment to the government's anticommunist efforts.[31] In short, there is reason to believe that the Cold War, like Frankfurter's desegregation policy preference, helped him to set aside the legal scruples that he expressed in conference in *Brown.*

The Truman Justices: Clark, Burton, and Minton

While Justices Douglas, Reed, Frankfurter, and perhaps Jackson (if not Warren) offer some support to the Cold War thesis, the most promising avenue to investigate the relevance of foreign policy considerations to the *Brown* decision involves the justices who were appointed by the administration that advanced the Cold War argument before the Court—Burton, Minton, and Clark. Recall that, in conference after the initial hearing in *Brown,* Clark defended segregation. But, consistent with studies of ideological drift, which suggest that he became more liberal shortly before the Court rendered the decision, he expressed a dislike for and his intention to vote against the practice after the Court reheard the case in 1953. Archival research that goes beyond the justices' conference notes, however, reveals not a shift in Clark's personal policy preferences so much as a consistent tension in his thought, one that Cold War considerations resolved in favor of school desegregation.

It is highly relevant that Clark served as attorney general from 1945 to 1949, a period during which the Truman administration's response to the Cold War combined a restrictive approach to civil liberties with a more liberal understanding of civil rights. Clark was the nation's chief legal officer when, on March 22, 1947, Truman signed Executive Order No. 9835, which initiated loyalty investigations for all persons entering employment in the offices and agencies of the federal executive branch. As Dudziak notes, these investigations led to the summary dismissal of ten State Department officials for their alleged involvement with an unspecified foreign government. In December 1947, Attorney General Clark demonstrated that he was anything but a passive observer in these efforts when he issued a list of radical organizations that the government and private employers used as a measure of disloyalty.[32]

That same year, Clark was made painfully aware of the need for the administration to adopt a more progressive approach to the matter of civil *rights* after the NAACP filed its petition regarding the mistreatment of American blacks at the United Nations. As Attorney General Clark told the National Association of Attorneys General: "I was humiliated, as I know you must have been, to realize that in our America there could be the slightest foundation for such a petition. *And that the association could conclude that amongst all of our honorable institutions there was no tribunal to which such a petition could be presented with hope of redress.*" Spelling out the international implications of the NAACP's petition, Clark intoned, "No act of accidental injustice, let alone those of calculation, will go unobserved by our enemies. Lip-service to our ideals will be seen for the mockery that it is."[33]

Clark's tenure as attorney general extended through the beginning of the administration's involvement in civil rights litigation. Clark's name appeared on the government's brief in *Shelley v. Kraemer,* the first of the postwar civil rights cases in which the United States participated as *amicus curiae,* and the first time before the Supreme Court that the government broadly condemned all forms of racial discrimination.[34] In that brief, the government elaborated on the foreign policy implications of racial discrimination (which, in this case, took the form of racially restrictive covenants) by quoting from a 1946 letter that Acting Secretary of State Dean Acheson had written to the chair of the Fair Employment Practices Committee. Acheson argued, "The existence of discrimination against minority groups in this country has an adverse effect upon our relations with other countries. We are reminded over and over by some foreign newspapers and spokesmen, that our treatment of various minorities leaves much to be desired. . . . Frequently we find it next to impossible to formulate a satisfactory answer to our critics in other countries."[35]

Philip Elman, who served in the solicitor general's office at the time, recalled that Tom Clark "probably" chose to file a brief in *Shelley* "after checking with Truman" and after receiving "a formal memorandum [from Elman] recommending that the United States file an *amicus* brief" in the case. After noting how unusual it was for the attorney general's name to appear on *amicus* briefs to the Supreme Court, Elman said that he "put Tom Clark's name on [the document] because [he] wanted this brief . . . to be as authoritative a statement of the position of the United States as possible." While Elman did not say whether Clark gave his permission to have his name on the brief, Dudziak suggests that "it is unlikely that such a departure from Justice Department policy involving the use of his name in such a high-profile case would have happened without his knowledge. The fact that the filing of the brief was an innovation in Department policy reinforces the likelihood that Clark knew about and approved the fact that his name was being placed on the brief." What is more, Clark and Solicitor General Philip Perlman "were so pleased with the *Shelley* brief that they published it as a book."[36]

Soon after he joined the Court in 1949, Clark was on the receiving end of Truman administration arguments delineating the connection between racial discrimination and foreign affairs. In that year, the Justice Department first became involved in cases challenging school segregation, one of which revolved around the most prestigious law school in Clark's home state of Texas. In its *amicus* brief for the university desegregation cases, *Sweatt v. Painter* and *McLaurin v. Oklahoma State Regents for Higher Education,* the government emphasized the relevance of the Cold War to the controversy.[37] "The Court is here asked to place the seal of constitutional approval upon an undisguised species of racial discrimination," the brief opined. "If the imprimatur of constitutionality should be put on such a denial of equality, one would expect the foes of democracy to exploit such an action for their own purposes. The ideals embodied in our Bill of Rights would be ridiculed as empty words, devoid of any real substance. . . . It is in the context of a world in which freedom and equality must become living realities, if the democratic way of life is to survive, that the issues in these cases should be viewed."[38]

In a draft version of a conference memorandum that he wrote for *Sweatt* and *McLaurin,* Clark provided a sense of the complicated nature of his view of segregation, if not of the degree to which Cold War considerations influenced his statements regarding the practice. He began the memo with the suggestion that his "convictions, based in part upon [his] experience in Texas, might be helpful to the Court." Revealing that the anti-segregation remark he made in conference after the rehearing of *Brown* was not the first time that he expressed his discomfort with the practice, Clark stated, "We need no modern psychologist to tell us that 'enforced separation of the two races [*does*] stamp the colored race with a badge of inferiority,' contrary to *Plessy v. Ferguson.* My question, then, is 'how' to reverse, not 'whether,' or 'why.'" He emphasized that he "[did] not suggest . . . that [the justices] write an opinion reaffirming *Plessy* as to all but graduate schools." Indeed, he declared that he "would not sign an opinion which approved *Plessy.*"[39]

While Clark stated that he did not want the Court to reaffirm *Plessy,* he also indicated that he was "in accord with the suggestion that [the Court] limit [its] opinion to graduate schools." He conceded that "in terms of social equality . . . segregated grammar schools may instill racism in young minds at a time and in a manner more destructive of society's fabric than segregated colleges and graduate schools ever will." Clark insisted, however, that the Court's "concern in these cases is not with social equality, but with educational equality." While education understood "broadly" means "infinitely more than acquiring a specific skill—in engineering, medicine, language, law," he "submit[ted] that we must treat 'education' in its normal, more narrow connotation and concern ourselves here with but one question: is the segregated Negro's opportunity to acquire specific skills 'equal' to that afforded the white?" In Clark's view, "It is entirely possible that Negroes in segregated grammar schools, learning arithmetic and spelling would receive skills in those elementary subjects equivalent to those of white students, providing that the quality of texts, physical facilities and instructors is 'equal.'" By contrast, "It is obvious that the same cannot be said of graduate schools." Apparently unaware—or unwilling to acknowledge—that his primary reason for declaring graduate school segregation unconstitutional applied as well to elementary and secondary school segregation, Clark contended that black students "should not be compelled to defer until their formal education has ended the association with whites against whom they must compete and whose professional views they often must understand in order adequately to accomplish their professional tasks."[40] He reiterated that he "would not approve *Plessy* in any manner," but he also emphasized his indecisiveness on the issue of the constitutionality of segregation at the lower levels of education. After asking rhetorically, "How will I vote when the swimming pool and grammar school cases arise?" he answered, "I do not know; that is irrelevant. Should they arise tomorrow I would vote to deny certiorari or dismiss the appeal, so that we would not be compelled to decide the issues."[41]

Clark's reluctance to jeopardize elementary school segregation was evident in the significantly revised version of the memorandum that he circulated to his colleagues. In that document, he retained the discussion of his belief that, unlike segregated graduate institutions, segregated grammar schools could be equal. But, apparently recognizing that certain of his supporting arguments served to undercut this distinction, he dropped altogether his observation that segregation stamps blacks with a badge of inferiority. He also toned down considerably his comment regarding the role of school segregation in perpetuating racism. He now wrote, "Limitation to graduate schools ignores, of course, the influence of segregation upon children's minds when they are four or five years old." Finally, Clark softened his statement regarding the educational importance of association with whites, writing that "acquaintance is important in the professions and segregation prevents it, thus depriving the Negro of many state-wide opportunities."[42]

The care that Clark took to distinguish between levels of education stemmed in part from the same fear of social disorder that he and most of his brethren expressed in conference in *Brown*. He was willing to say that expectations of riots were groundless only with reference to state-supported institutions of higher learning in the South.[43] Clark's stated concern that desegregation might inspire violence would not necessarily reveal a preference for segregation, especially in view of the anti-segregation comments in his draft memorandum for the university cases. But Clark's other comments after the initial hearing in *Brown* reveal that he was not an ardent desegregationist. Rather, the fairest interpretation of the available evidence is that he had mixed feelings about the practice and that his distaste for segregation may have been gounded in the Cold War considerations that he voiced as attorney general. As demonstrated in chapter 3, Clark apparently did not repeat any of his concerns regarding the negative effects of segregation when he was actually faced with deciding the constitutionality of its use in elementary schools. Instead, he chose to focus on the importance of segregation to the maintenance of racial harmony in his home state. Clark's comments led Justice Douglas to believe that his colleague thought segregation was both constitutional and sound as a matter of public policy.

Nonetheless, when the Court considered *Brown,* Clark did not combine his discussion of the need for school segregation in Texas with a restatement of his desire to avoid deciding the constitutionality of the practice. (The Court still could have accomplished this goal by, among other methods, dismissing the petition as having been improvidently granted.) But in a manner consistent with Dudziak's Cold War thesis—and inconsistent with an instrumental interpretation of his vote—he sought to acquire the symbolic advantage that a desegregation decree would afford while essentially preserving segregation by threatening to dissent if the Court did not permit the lower courts to deny relief. In short, after the initial hearing in *Brown*—after considering the government's insistence that elementary and secondary school segregation, like segregation in housing and higher education, severely damaged the reputation of the United States in its competition with the Soviet Union—Clark was compelled to abandon his desire to avoid deciding the constitutionality of the practice at issue but not his conviction that segregation served a necessary function in the South.

In conference after the rehearing of *Brown,* Clark expressed his dislike for segregation and appeared to be more flexible on the matter of enforcement. But his insistence that courts be sensitive to local conditions did not mark a significant departure from his earlier threat to support the states if lower court judges were not permitted to deny relief. Clark could afford to moderate his language because his colleagues agreed that the implementation of a desegregation ruling would have to be delayed and because the Eisenhower administration gave considerable comfort to segregationists when it provided its interpretation of the Truman administration's argument that desegregation should occur "with deliberate speed." The government noted in its *amicus* brief that the petitioners could argue that the individual nature of constitutional rights required the immediate enforcement of a desegregation decree. However, the brief continued, "It is one thing to direct immediate relief where a single individual seeks vindication of his constitutional rights in the relatively narrow area of professional and graduate school education, and an entirely different matter to follow the same course in the broad area of public school education affecting thousands of children, teachers, and schools." The government opined that "the time required for eliminating school segregation in any particular community will depend on numerous factors which neither this Court nor counsel can now evaluate." But, "as the responsible authorities in charge of the public schools," the brief stated—echoing John Davis's admonition on behalf of the school board in the South Carolina case—"the *defendants*" "would be in the best position to develop a program most suited to local conditions and needs, and to indicate the length of time required to put it into effect."[44]

Clark could not have regretted the withdrawal of his threat to dissent in *Brown.* After the Court rendered the decision and ordered a rehearing on the matter of enforcement, the Eisenhower administration continued to defend an approach to desegregation that emphasized the need to be sensitive to the concerns of segregationist states. In conference, Clark and his brethren continued to agree on the importance of delaying the implementation of a desegregation decree.[45] In the Court's 1955 enforcement order, Chief Justice Warren achieved unanimity by adopting language that proved acceptable to justices with a range of views regarding the degree to which desegregation should be postponed. The aspects of the opinion that appealed to Clark were the same features that pleased southern officials—the opinion placed responsibility for devising desegregation plans in local school authorities (subject to supervision by federal district court judges) and set no specific date for desegregation to occur.⁴⁶ Subsequent events were gratifying to those, like Clark, who were concerned primarily with the Cold War implications of segregation and sought the symbolic advantage of a desegregation ruling. The Court's enforcement order inspired almost no change in the racial composition of southern schools during the years between *Brown* and the passage of civil rights legislation in the mid-1960s.⁴⁷

Aside from Clark's participation in the government's anticommunist efforts before he joined the Court, his statement as attorney general that America's enemies would benefit if blacks had no faith in the nation's courts, and his insistence after the initial hearing in *Brown* that segregation served an important function in Texas and that lower courts should have the power to deny relief, the relevance of the Cold War thesis to Clark's desegregation vote is indicated by the fact that his performance in *Brown* was part of a broader voting pattern that suggested a marked concern with the need to meet the communist threat. Clark's votes in the areas of civil rights and civil liberties reflected the Truman administration's Cold War–inspired efforts to expand the former while restricting the latter. From 1953 until his retirement in 1967, Clark voted in favor of civil rights petitioners 57.3 percent of the time but was willing to support First Amendment claims in only 34.6 percent of cases. As noted in table 2, only Justice Minton exhibited a greater differential in his votes in these areas of constitutional law after 1953; none of the other seven justices involved in *Brown* came close to matching the differential that Clark's voting exhibited. And, while Minton, Burton, and

TABLE 2 Percentage of liberal votes by justices involved in *Brown v. Board of Education* (1954), 1953 through 1975 terms (number of cases)

	CIVIL RIGHTS CASES	FIRST AMENDMENT CASES	DIFFERENCE
Minton	37.9 (29)	14.3 (14)	23.6
Clark	57.3 (185)	34.6 (136)	22.7
Reed	35.5 (31)	20.0 (15)	15.5
Jackson	62.5 (8)	50.0 (4)	12.5
Burton	42.1 (57)	32.4 (37)	9.7
Frankfurter	55.7 (88)	49.4 (79)	6.3
Warren	82.8 (221)	79.9 (159)	2.9
Douglas	92.7 (397)	96.8 (249)	−4.1
Black	72.2 (277)	87.0 (192)	−14.8

Source: Based on Epstein and Mershon, "Measuring Political Preferences," 287.

Reed demonstrated even less support for First Amendment claims than did Clark, case analysis reveals that Clark hardly could have been more deferential toward the government's anticommunist efforts. He voted in favor of punishment for advocacy of the overthrow of government by force, punishment for membership in an organization advocating the violent overthrow of government, and compelled registration of "communist controlled" groups.[48] He also supported loyalty oaths and employment restrictions on those advocating or belonging to organizations advocating violent overthrow of government,[49] and legislative investigations into "un-American activities" and "subversive persons."[50]

As indicated, there is evidence to suggest that Harold Burton and Sherman Minton were also concerned in *Brown* with preventing the Soviet Union from using segregation as a propaganda weapon. While neither Burton nor Minton boasted Clark's strong connection to the Truman administration, each man was a friend of the president as well as a Truman appointee to the Supreme Court.[51] As table 2 reveals, each justice also exhibited a voting pattern that reflected the administration's Cold War stances on civil rights and First Amendment rights. While the 9.7 percent differential between Burton's liberal votes in these areas of constitutional law did not rival that of Minton (23.6 percent) or Clark (22.7 percent), he, like Minton, was extraordinarily deferential toward the government in First Amendment cases. As Michael Klarman observes, the "enthusiasm [of Burton and Minton] for judicial restraint was most evident in cases challenging government loyalty and security programs, where they almost never found a constitutional violation."[52] Furthermore, neither of these justices (or Clark) could have been accused of radicalism in the area of civil rights. Burton's liberal voting record in civil rights cases (42.1%) was significantly more conservative than Clark's modest performance (57.3 percent) and not much more progressive than that of Minton (37.9 percent). By comparison, Reed, who candidly supported segregation, voted in favor of civil rights petitioners in 35.5 percent of cases, while Hugo Black, Warren, and Douglas supported civil rights 72.2, 82.8, and 92.7 percent of the time, respectively. In short, the Truman appointees were vulnerable to the liberal criticism that they supported civil rights only to the degree necessary to frustrate Soviet criticism of the United States.

Unfortunately, neither Burton nor Minton left a documentary record that reveals the degree to which desegregation policy preferences might have contributed to their shared belief that neither precedent nor constitutional history presented a barrier to desegregation. An instrumental explanation of Burton's desegregation vote might note that, as a Republican state legislator, mayor of Cleveland, and U.S. senator, he made overtures to Ohio's black voters. For example, he supported the anti–poll tax amendment as well as legislation that would have created a permanent Fair Employment Practices Commission. Burton, however, refused to sign a petition protesting the treatment of blacks during the Detroit Race Riot of 1943, and he declined the request of Walter White, secretary of the NAACP, to help black youths by supporting the National Youth Administration and the Civilian Conservation Corps. In short, like Earl Warren before he joined the Court, "Burton behaved like a moderate, but politically astute, Republican" on race relations issues.[53] Remember that, during the Court's deliberations in *Brown,* he challenged the reasonableness of segregation, given his conviction that the practice failed to prepare students of differing racial backgrounds to live and work together. But in view of studies of ideological drift, which suggest that Burton became significantly more conservative in the years following his first term on the Court in 1945, the burden of proof belongs with those who would look to the forces at midcentury that liberalized American attitudes toward race, as opposed to the LDF's discussion of the unreasonableness of segregation, in order to explain the justice's comments. It is an equally difficult task to determine the relative weight that Burton accorded the matter of the unreasonableness of segregation versus Cold War considerations, which appear to have influenced his broader voting behavior.

Regarding the possibility of explaining Minton's desegregation vote in instrumental terms, it is important to note that he clashed with the Ku Klux Klan when he campaigned for a congressional seat in Indiana, and that he supported anti-lynching legislation when he was in the U.S. Senate.[54] That Minton quarreled with the Klan, however, does not necessarily mean he favored desegregation. Segregation was not a campaign issue in Indiana, and, in that state, the Klan was allied with the Republican party. Similarly, Minton's opposition to racial violence does not necessarily imply hostility to the less controversial practice of segregation. True, Minton stated during the conference deliberations in *Brown* that African Americans continued to be oppressed after slavery was abolished, and, like Warren, Black, and Jackson, he maintained that segregation was based on the principle of racial inferiority. In the absence of compelling information regarding his values, however, it is impossible to determine whether his statements were a reflection of the forces that liberalized American racial attitudes at midcentury or were evidence of the constitutive impact of the LDF's historical analysis of segregation. With regard to the former possibility, there is no evidence that his attitudes became more progressive while he was on the Court, since studies of ideological drift examine only justices who served on the bench for at least ten years.[55] Regardless of whether it was the forces of liberalism or the arguments of the petitioners in *Brown* that informed Minton's comments, it is difficult to believe that either factor contributed more to his desegregation vote than did the Cold War. Again, Minton exhibited the largest differential in liberal voting percentages in civil rights as against First Amendment controversies. And his voting behavior in the former category rivaled the conservatism of Justice Reed, while he had no peer among his more conservative brethren when it came to supporting the government against a First Amendment challenge.

As the examples of Minton, Burton, and Clark illustrate, the amount and quality of evidence that is available leads to varying levels of certainty regarding the pertinence of foreign policy considerations to the desegregation votes of each of the justices. Nevertheless, the explanatory power of the noninstrumental Cold War thesis is impressive, given the number of justices for whom there is some evidence of its primary or secondary relevance. In view of the justices' recognition of the interconnectedness of the elements of the political regime within which they operated and their receptiveness to the executive's policy concerns, any thorough explanation of *Brown* must also consider the work of scholars who, like Dudziak, believe in the relevance of institutions to Supreme Court decision making, but focus instead on the justices' attentiveness to *domestic* political considerations.

SIX

Domestic Political Considerations

The relevance of the domestic policy concerns of the executive to the *Brown* decision cannot simply be traced to the statements of either of the administrations that participated as *amicus curiae*. The Eisenhower administration sent the Court anything but a clear message regarding its position on desegregation, and the Truman administration's support for civil rights must be reconciled with the fact that, like African Americans, southern conservatives were an important element of the New Deal coalition. "Political regimes" scholarship, which portrays *Brown* as a logical consequence of Franklin Roosevelt's attempt to use civil rights to remove the impediment that southern conservatives presented to his progressive constitutional vision of an empowered national executive, affords a more promising argument. But such scholarship is incomplete in that it does not adequately address the point that, after the presidential election of 1952, the New Dealers on the Court realized Democrats could no longer assume that southern conservatives were captives of the party. With regard to the puzzle of the New Dealers' willingness to vote for desegregation in spite of the likelihood that doing so would contribute to the loss of a Democratic majority, the evidence does not support the contention that the justices believed politicians on both sides of the issue had asked the Court to resolve the dispute over segregation because it threatened to destabilize partisan arrangements. Instead, it is necessary to consider the fact that the New Dealers recognized social and political forces that were altering race relations in the South. The justices' comments regarding these developments—as well as their votes on federalism and the rights of minorities and labor—are consistent with the argument linking *Brown* to Roosevelt's constitutional vision. These behaviors suggested a hope that the growth of progressive forces in the region would eventually offset the loss of southern conservatives to the Republican party.

Brown and the Eisenhower Administration

In 1957, Robert A. Dahl provided an influential analysis of Supreme Court decision making and an interesting interpretation of the *Brown* decision. Dahl emphasized that the justices work in an institutional context that conditions or restricts the Court's ability to function as "a national policy-maker." The Supreme Court, he argued, "is inevitably a part of the dominant national alliance," save "for short-lived transitional periods when the old alliance is disintegrating and the new one is struggling to take control of political institutions." Since "presidents are not famous for appointing justices hostile to their own views on public policy nor could they expect to secure confirmation of a man whose stance on key questions was flagrantly at odds with that of the dominant majority in the Senate," it is logical to assume that "the policy views dominant on the Court are never for long out of line with the policy views among the lawmaking majorities of the United States." In those instances in which the policy views of the justices and politicians do not coincide, the Court jeopardizes its institutional prestige "if it flagrantly opposes the major policies of the dominant alliance." "Such a course of action . . . is [thus] one in which the Court will not normally be tempted to engage."[1]

While Dahl focused on demonstrating the infrequency with which the Court overturned *federal* legislation (in order to challenge the conventional view that the Court "stands in some special way as a protection of minorities against tyranny by majorities"), he sought an explanation for the *Brown* decision in a supposed affinity between the Court and the contemporary governing coalition on the matter of civil rights. "There are times," he suggested, "when the coalition is unstable with respect to certain key policies" and the Court, "at very great risk to its legitimacy powers, . . . can intervene . . . and may even succeed in establishing policy." In such cases, however, the Court "probably . . . can succeed only if its action conforms to and reinforces a widespread set of explicit or implicit norms held by the political leadership; norms which are not strong enough or are not distributed in such a way as to insure the existence of an effective lawmaking majority but are, nonetheless, sufficiently powerful to prevent any successful attack on the legitimacy powers of the Court." Without elaborating on the leadership elements that he thought relevant, he opined that "this is probably the explanation for the relatively successful work of the Court in enlarging the freedom of Negroes to vote during the past three decades and in its famous school integration decisions."[2]

Dahl's explanation of *Brown* compels consideration of the most obvious leadership element of the dominant national alliance at the time of the *Brown* decision—the legal arm of the executive branch. Regarding the administration that argued as *amicus curiae* in the year that the Court rendered *Brown,* it would be a mistake to conclude that the justices understood Dwight Eisenhower's posture as a clear indication of political support for desegregation, or, to use Dahl's terminology, that the justices thought desegregation reflected the clear policy preferences of the leaders of at least one branch of the dominant national alliance.[3] In all probability, the justices did not regard the Eisenhower administration's *Court-requested* participation in oral argument during the rehearing of *Brown* as conclusive evidence that the administration possessed a widespread set of norms, implicit or explicit, favorable to desegregation in the nation's elementary and secondary schools. Rather, the totality of circumstances and events preceding and surrounding the administration's involvement in oral argument sent conflicting signals to the justices. They would have understood that support for desegregation varied within the administration and that executive officials who ostensibly sought to end school segregation may have been making insincere overtures to black voters.

The justices would have interpreted the Eisenhower administration's involvement in the desegregation controversy through the lens of the presidential election of 1952 and the newly elected president's racial policies. During the campaign, Eisenhower indicated that he supported the Truman administration's effort to desegregate the military; he even suggested that greater success in this endeavor was likely to be had with a former general as president. He also described discrimination against nonwhite foreign visitors in the nation's capital as "a humiliation to This nation," declared that he intended to consider blacks for cabinet positions, and characterized the poll tax as "a blemish upon our American ideal of political equality." But Eisenhower refused to support a "compulsory" federal fair employment agency, stating that employment problems "are not best handled by punitive or compulsory federal law." And, with regard to the specific matter of school segregation, he indicated that he had not thought carefully about the details of the practice, let alone whether it should be abandoned.[4] In short, Eisenhower's behavior as a candidate conformed with the Republican party's effort to court southern whites by emphasizing state initiative, while recognizing the growing importance of black voters by paying homage to the notion of racial equality. This strategy was made evident in the party's civil rights plank, which "condemn[ed] bigots who inject class, racial and religious prejudice into public and political matters," but also declared that "it is the primary responsibility of each state to order and control its own domestic institutions, and this power, reserved to the states, is essential to the maintenance of our Federal Republic."[5]

The strategy proved successful as Eisenhower's victories in four border states and four southern states contributed substantially to his electoral vote total (90 of 442 electoral votes). These results were surprising since the South, for historical and cultural reasons, had voted overwhelmingly Democratic in previous presidential elections. Eisenhower's success in cracking the edifice of what had been the solidly Democratic South helped to bring about the Democratic party's most significant defeat in any national election since the 1920s. Adlai Stevenson, who received 73 percent of the black vote, managed to tally only 17 percent of the electoral vote.[6]

In view of these results, it is not surprising that the new president's civil rights policies, which the justices witnessed in the year before they rendered *Brown,* were not especially threatening to southern racial mores. Even though Eisenhower had promised greater success in bringing racial equality to the armed forces, he "was content to confine his administration's military desegregation activities to the quiet continuation of policies established by the Truman administration and the service branches." With regard to the District of Columbia, the press concluded "that [the president] had judged any compulsory civil rights program [there] or elsewhere to be 'beyond the realm of practical possibility for a long time to come.'" Eisenhower's placement of blacks in his administration in the year before *Brown* was limited to lower-level positions in the Departments of Justice and Agriculture. And, in spite of the import of his campaign comments on the poll tax, "the new President and his advisors demonstrated little interest in seeking federal protections for black voting rights" in the two years prior to *Brown.* Eisenhower did create a Committee on Government Contracts, which administration spokesmen described as an educational forum on fair employment. But the administration's representatives emphasized that the committee would never become a federal fair employment agency given to using coercive tactics against employers.[7]

Information regarding the administration's decision to participate in the desegregation controversy, to which at least certain members of the Court were privy, reinforced the impression that the administration's approach to civil rights may have been calculated to be strong on form rather than substance. The justices learned that the impetus for federal involvement in the reargument of *Brown* apparently came not from President Eisenhower or even his attorney general but from holdovers from the Truman administration. Philip Elman, Felix Frankfurter's former law clerk, who served as an assistant in the solicitor general's office in both the Truman and Eisenhower administrations, remained in touch with the notoriously garrulous justice during the *Brown* proceedings. Elman recalled that the Court's reargument order, with its invitation to the attorney general to take part in oral argument, "brought misery to [Eisenhower's] Department of Justice." "The new people in the Eisenhower administration had been waiting on the sidelines for the Court to decide," Elman explained. "They had had nothing to do with the cases, they had never taken a position on the issue, they didn't want to get involved, and here the Supreme Court was asking the Attorney General of the United States to file a brief and present oral argument." In a meeting that Attorney General Herbert Brownell called "to discuss what to do in view of [the Court's reargument] order," Assistant Attorney General J. Lee Rankin, Robert C. Stern, who had served as first assistant to the solicitor general under Harry Truman and was acting solicitor general at the time, and Elman "were the only ones . . . who recommended that the government accept the Court's invitation."[8]

Elman credited Brownell and Rankin "for the Eisenhower administration's decision to participate," and he was "sure that Brownell had talked to Eisenhower" about the plan. But Elman said that "the feeling we all had at the time was that Eisenhower would not be sympathetic to the idea, because he was known to believe that public education was something for the states, the federal government should stay out of it, and this problem was the Court's and not his as President." As evidence of Eisenhower's discomfort with desegregation, Elman noted that the instructions Rankin received "from Brownell, who presumably had cleared them with Eisenhower," were simply to answer the Court's questions in the reargument order and not to volunteer a position on the unconstitutionality of segregation during oral argument. Rankin was told, "If you're asked, and only if you're asked, then you say, 'We adhere to the position previously taken by the United States.'" Elman also alleged that Eisenhower administration officials removed from his draft of the government's brief a statement regarding the unconstitutionality of and need to overrule *Plessy v. Ferguson.*[9]

It is unlikely that Elman's account of events was self-serving, since President Eisenhower informed his first appointee to the Supreme Court,

Chief Justice Earl Warren, of his discomfort with desegregation. Indeed, Eisenhower gave Warren reason to suspect that the leader of the dominant national alliance harbored a covert racism, as opposed to a weakly held set of desegregation norms as Dahl would have it. Warren recalled that, while the Court was considering *Brown,* the president used the occasion of a White House dinner to tell him that southerners "are not bad people. All they are concerned about is to see that their sweet little girls are not required to sit in school alongside some big overgrown Negroes."[10]

In view of the circumstances preceding and surrounding the Eisenhower administration's participation in the desegregation controversy, the justices would have required considerable evidence in order to conclude that senior officials in the Justice Department, to say nothing of President Eisenhower himself, clearly supported school desegregation. A reference that the government's brief was "supplemental" to the Truman administration's document, which had argued that *Plessy v. Ferguson* should be overturned, would not have been sufficient to remove doubts as to the strength of the government's commitment to desegregation.[11] Assistant Attorney General Rankin's statement during oral argument that the government "adhere[s] to the views expressed in the original [1952] brief of the Department" would not have clarified matters either. Indeed, Rankin made this statement only after Justice William Douglas indicated that he sought "to clear up . . . confusion in [his] mind" regarding the government's position in the case.[12]

The government's recommendations regarding the matter of enforcement only heightened such confusion. The Eisenhower administration helped the justices achieve consensus on the question of constitutionality by endorsing the Truman administration's compromise on implementation. As Cornell W. Clayton observes, the Truman administration "suggested that district courts be given a 'reasonable period of time' to implement the decision: in other words, 'with all deliberate speed.'" This proposal "offered the Court a way out of a sticky remedial dilemma"— how "to rule segregation unconstitutional" without "requiring immediate integration," which many of the justices regarded "as an open invitation to mass noncompliance."[13] But the Eisenhower administration's opposition to desegregation forthwith merely reinforced the impression that its civil rights policies were insincere. As noted in chapter 5, the administration echoed John Davis's argument on behalf of the school board in the South Carolina case, contending in its brief that the *defendants* were in the best position to determine the amount of time that would be required to comply with a desegregation order.

To say that the Eisenhower administration did not provide a clear statement of support for desegregation in *Brown* is not to suggest that the administration marched in lockstep with segregationists. Some scholars even challenge the conventional view that Attorney General Brownell was primarily responsible for federal efforts made on behalf of racial equality during Eisenhower's two terms of office; the president, the argument runs, employed a "hidden-hand" strategy in the realm of civil rights.[14] Yet, even if the president and his attorney general favored civil rights, it is difficult to conclude that in 1953 the justices felt confident that a desegregation decision would have corresponded with the policy preferences of either of these men. It was as reasonable for the justices to think that the leaders of the Eisenhower administration would have been comfortable with a ruling *against* the petitioners in *Brown* as to conclude that the administration favored school desegregation, albeit something other than desegregation forthwith. At best, the justices might have anticipated that the executive branch would not offer resistance to a desegregation order. But this point, important though it is in helping to explain *Brown,* is not relevant to the justices' reasons for voting against segregation.

Brown and the New Deal Coalition

THE SIGNIFICANCE OF BLACK VOTERS (AND SOUTHERN CONSERVATIVES)

Martin Shapiro offers a seemingly more convincing explanation of *Brown*'s connection to the politics of that era. Echoing Dahl (and David B. Truman's influential study, *The Governmental Process*), Shapiro suggests that judicial scholars should investigate the constraints that the Court's power relationships in the broader political system impose upon the justices. He places special emphasis on the Court's connections to various client groups or constituencies.[15] Adopting this perspective, Shapiro argues, one can see that the activism inhering in the "preferred position" doctrine, which informed the Warren Court's decisions on such issues as the freedoms of speech and press and the rights of racial and religious minorities,[16] "served as a gigantic umbrella and blueprint for transferring Supreme Court political services from Republican to Democratic clienteles." Shapiro thus views *Brown* as an instance of judicial solicitousness toward certain elements of the broad "New Deal . . . coalition of union members, the poor, Negroes, and liberal intellectuals." The reality that "the Court at its activist peak in the 1950s and 1960s, and even into the 1970s, is actually the history of a political institution working out the implications of the victory of the New Deal coalition," Shapiro opines, "has been obscured by the fact that it was a 'Republican' Court, the Warren Court," which was acting on behalf of the elements of that coalition. The truth of the matter is that "after 1937 the Court was controlled by Roosevelt [and Truman] appointees."[17]

Setting aside the question of whether or not the Warren Court's rulings on free speech and reapportionment merely served as tribute to the New Deal coalition, Shapiro's attempt to characterize *Brown* and its progeny in this manner is worth investigating, given the developments in the first half of the twentieth century—especially the Great Migration of several million southern blacks into the cities of the industrialized North—that forced the Truman administration to take more seriously the demands of African Americans.[18] As noted in chapter 2, the political significance of the Great Migration stemmed in part from the fact that "the move was more than a simple migration and change in folkways; for blacks, it was a move, almost literally, from no voting to voting." Black immigrants from the South also tended to settle in the urban centers of seven industrial states—New York, New Jersey, Pennsylvania, Ohio, California, Illinois, and Michigan. As their populations expanded, these states—and their black residents—gained national political prominence.[19]

Democrats became painfully aware of the need to secure the votes of the North's recent arrivals when, as a result in part of Democratic negligence regarding civil rights, the midterm elections of 1946 ushered in a Republican Congress. Republicans managed to win 57 of 138 House seats and 7 of 8 Senate seats that nonsouthern Democrats with liberal legislative records had held previously. In a 1947 memorandum to President Truman, Clark Clifford, the president's special counsel, outlined a strategy to ensure that the loss of the Congress the preceding year would not be followed by the loss of the White House in 1948. In particular, after suggesting that blacks might hold "the balance of power in presidential contests" because of their concentration "in the pivotal, large and closely contested electoral states such as New York, Illinois, Pennsylvania, Ohio, and Michigan," Clifford warned, "Under the tutelage of Walter White, of the National Association for the Advancement of Colored People, and other intelligent, educated and sophisticated leaders, the Negro voter has become a cynical, hardboiled trader." As a consequence of "the rising dominance of the Southern conservatives in the Democratic councils of the Congress and of the Party," "he is just about convinced today that he can better his present economic lot by swinging his vote in a solid bloc to the Republicans." Whereupon Clifford counseled Truman, "It would appear to be sound strategy to have the President go as far as he possibly could go in recommending measures to protect the rights of minority groups. This course of action would obviously cause difficulty with our Southern friends but that is the lesser of two evils." Clifford reassured the president that "the South can be considered safely Democratic" given its historic antipathy to the Republican party.[20]

This memorandum led Truman to consider carefully the recommendations of the President's Committee on Civil Rights, which were published the month before Clifford wrote to the president. Truman had established that body some three months after he discussed the problem of lynching with the National Emergency Committee against Mob Violence and one month after the Democrats lost their congressional majority in the midterm elections of 1946. The committee went so far as to call for "the elimination of segregation, based on race, color, creed, or national origin, from American life." And, to make this goal a fact rather than mere aspiration, the committee championed "the conditioning by Congress of all federal grants-in-aid and other forms of federal assistance to public or private agencies for any purpose on the absence of discrimination and segregation based on race, color, creed, or national origin."[21]

Following the publication of the committee's report, the Truman Justice Department submitted to the Supreme Court an *amicus curiae* brief regarding the case *Shelley v. Kraemer*.[22] In that document, the government challenged the constitutionality of racially restrictive covenants. And some nine months before the November election, Truman proposed in a message to Congress that it establish a civil rights division in the Department of Justice, afford federal protection against lynching, provide more adequate protection of the right to vote, create a Fair Employment Practice Commission, and prohibit discrimination in interstate transportation facilities. Following the election and Democratic victories in Congress and the White House, Truman would submit his proposals as actual bills. In July 1948, the president issued two executive orders pertaining to civil rights. The first established a Fair Employment Board to serve as a final review body for appeals from the decisions of departmental heads regarding discrimination complaints. The second created the President's Committee on Equality of Treatment and Opportunity in the Armed Forces, which Truman charged with resolving the problems of discrimination and segregation in the military.[23]

Truman's efforts to attract black voters proved successful in the 1948 election, as he received nearly 70 percent of the votes of African Ameri-

cans in 27 major cities and communities. The president's good fortune
in this regard was critical to his victory over Thomas Dewey, given that
Truman carried California, Illinois, and Ohio by a total of fewer than
60,000 votes. Had the results shifted slightly in these three states, the
electoral vote—and the White House—would have gone to Dewey.[24]

Note, however, that in attempting to appeal to African Americans,
Truman stopped short of embracing the proposal of the Committee on
Civil Rights that federal grants-in-aid and other forms of federal assistance stipulate that recipients not segregate on the basis of race. Instead,
the president's anti-segregation initiatives, except for military desegregation, would take the form of *amicus* briefs to the Supreme Court. The
year following Truman's electoral victory, the Department of Justice submitted briefs in cases involving segregation in interstate transportation
and higher education. In its brief regarding the former, the government
contended for the first time that *Plessy v. Ferguson* should be overturned.
Three years later, the administration submitted its brief in *Brown* challenging the constitutionality of racial segregation in elementary and secondary schools.[25]

The relative timidity that Truman exhibited in his legislative initiatives reflected an acknowledgment of political reality. To elaborate on a
point to which Clifford alluded in his memorandum to the president,
one-party politics and restricted voting in the South ensured reelection of
conservative southern legislators who, in turn, benefited from a seniority
system that placed them in powerful positions in both houses of Congress. But those very congressmen—who doomed the president's civil
rights bills even though Truman put forth no desegregation initiatives—
were responsive to an important element of the Democratic coalition.
The South's plantation and industrial elites and the working classes of
the industrialized North, which shared an antipathy for northern capital,
were the main components of the New Deal coalition that Franklin Roosevelt established in 1933. (Southerners also favored New Deal measures
that ameliorated the impact of the Depression on southern agriculture.)
Northern workers bridled at the antilabor posture of northern industry,
while southern economic elites resented their subordinate position in a
national economy in which they served primarily to provide raw materials to the market-oriented industries of the North. "For the life of the
New Deal coalition," Richard Franklin Bensel observes, "one of the underpinnings of Democratic party unity was the exclusion of the southern
periphery from most provisions of federal labor law." But the "*principal* compromise among the policy positions assumed by the New Deal

alliance . . . centered on race. . . . Under this arrangement the northern wing implicitly tolerated southern racism as the price of participation in a majority coalition."[26] Notwithstanding the importance of Shapiro's insight regarding the relevance of black voters to *Brown,* then, no account of the decision is complete if it fails to explain why the New Dealers on the Court would have issued a ruling so harmful to the southern element of the New Deal coalition.

FDR'S CONSTITUTIONAL VISION (AND ITS UNINTENDED CONSEQUENCES)

Recognizing the need to explain the willingness of the New Deal justices to render a decision that cut across the coalition of Democratic voters, Kevin J. McMahon illuminates the significance of an undeveloped point in Shapiro's research—that "President Roosevelt was attempting to purge [conservative southern whites] from the party at the very time the preferred position doctrine was being announced by the court."[27] Adopting a "political regimes" (and, therefore, a noninstrumental) perspective, McMahon contends that *Brown* was not intended simply to reward black voters; rather, the decision was supposed to help the executive branch *alter the nature* of the Democratic party. He avers that *Brown* was the culmination of "a drive" that the Roosevelt administration initiated in the mid-1930s "to undermine southern democracy and end the worst abuses of southern white supremacy."[28]

McMahon concedes that caution was "a virtual creed" of the early New Deal, especially where reform affected the South. Given the importance of southern Democrats to the New Deal coalition, African Americans were often excluded from legislation. McMahon contends, however, that the scholarly propensity to believe the contemporary political commitment to racial equality began not with Roosevelt but with the Truman administration stems from a failure to appreciate Roosevelt's constitutional vision ("his image of an ideal institutional order") and its connection to individual, including civil, rights. Roosevelt believed that for governmental policies to meet national needs in an interdependent, urban-industrial society, political parties would have to cede leadership to the national executive. And, in order "to create a new legal order that challenged the traditional localized structure of the American party system," "the executive branch would have to wrest control over the traditional channels of political participation to open them up to the previously disfranchised" and to "newly activated groups supporting the New Deal," especially unionized workers.[29]

Roosevelt concluded in his second term that one of the primary obstacles to the achievement of his constitutional vision was "a form of democracy below the Mason-Dixon line that consistently sent representatives to Congress who were more conservative than [he] . . . thought appropriate." The southern component of the New Deal coalition—an oligarchy of plantation and industrial interests that presided over a political landscape where a minority of adults, and almost no blacks, voted—was not "particularly enamored with the [labor-friendly] policies of the New Deal" or with the notion of a powerful national government with authority concentrated in the executive. As a result, this oligarchy "consistently limited the progressiveness of the president's program and of the Democratic Party."[30]

Initially, Roosevelt sought to overcome this obstacle to his constitutional vision by attempting to purge recalcitrant southern congressmen during the primaries for the 1938 midterm elections. After this effort failed, the president came to recognize the significance of an event that had occurred four years earlier: In response to an effort on the part of the Democratic National Committee to court blacks in an unprecedented manner, "'a majority of Afro-American voters went Democratic [for the first time],' helping to elect a decidedly progressive Congress." Roosevelt determined that a properly formulated civil rights program would help him to achieve his constitutional ambitions. A legislative effort to secure civil rights, he understood, would negatively affect his relations with southern conservatives and would perish in committee. But an indirect approach that utilized judicial institutions to secure the rights of African Americans, he hoped, would be less visible and, therefore, less controversial, even though the program would eventually "destabilize southern politics" and remove the major impediment that the region's elites presented to his notion of an empowered national executive. As evidence of Roosevelt's commitment to civil rights, McMahon refers to the creation of a Civil Rights Section within the Justice Department, which "became a center for testing creative legal theories" to challenge "the white primary, the poll tax, lynching, and police brutality, four pillars of political repression in the segregated South."[31]

In order for the Justice Department's efforts on behalf of civil rights to succeed (so that the influence of African Americans could help alter the balance of power in southern and, ultimately, national politics), the Roosevelt administration had to ensure that the Supreme Court accepted the president's constitutional vision. A judiciary that favored states' rights over national power would not defer to the executive's position in cases involving civil rights. Among the efforts the president made to enlist the aid of the Supreme Court, his use of the appointment power was most relevant to the *Brown* decision.[32] "Significantly," McMahon observes, during the four-year period when he made eight of his Supreme Court appointments, "the president was in open conflict with those conservative members of his own party who disdained his policies that concentrated powers in the executive branch and committed the federal government to a rights-expanding agenda." It should not be surprising, then, that of his nine nominees, five of whom participated in *Brown,* "eight were unquestionable progressives." "In an effort to secure his institutional ambitions," McMahon explains, "FDR chose individuals for the Court he thought would cooperate with the executive branch—justices who would help him install his constitutional vision." With regard to the nominees' willingness to secure this vision by altering the complexion of southern politics, McMahon concedes that "there is no clear evidence that FDR nominated jurists with a specific desire to advance African American rights." Nevertheless, the Roosevelt "nominees' adherence to rights-centered liberalism, combined with their devotion to defer to the executive branch," increased the chances that the government's arguments on behalf of civil rights would be well received.[33]

The attractiveness of McMahon's analysis stems from his recognition of the need to explain "why . . . a court dominated by justices appointed by two Democratic presidents—and approved with the overwhelming support of southern senators—issue[d] a ruling so harmful to southern democracy."[34] By arguing that *Brown* was part of the logical unfolding of events following Roosevelt's initiation of a judicial policy designed to remove the obstacle that conservative southern Democrats presented to his constitutional vision of an empowered national executive, McMahon would seem to fill a large gap in Martin Shapiro's account of the decision.

The problem with this explanation, however, is that it underestimates the impact on the justices of the unanticipated consequences of Roosevelt's efforts to turn the Democratic party into a national organization that championed working-class and minority interests for the more fundamental purpose of reordering the distribution of power between levels and among branches of government. (Interestingly, McMahon acknowledges the dramatic nature of these consequences.) Roosevelt and Truman assumed that, for historical and cultural reasons, southerners were captives of the Democratic party.[35] Before the Court rendered *Brown,* however, it had become clear that this assumption was flawed; indeed, events had revealed that pursuit of a civil rights agenda risked the destruction of the New Deal coalition and the relegation of the Democratic party to minority status.

The failure of President Truman's effort to limit conflict with southern Democrats while reaching out to black voters was apparent even before Congress rejected his civil rights bills. The civil rights plank in the Democratic party platform of 1948, which merely praised Truman's modest efforts on behalf of racial equality (and the inclusion of which the president declined to support in an effort to preserve party unity), inspired the Dixiecrat Revolt. This third party movement, which championed the cause of states' rights over the party's stance on civil rights, was limited in scope. Still, Governor J. Strom Thurmond of South Carolina, the States' Rights Democratic (Dixiecrat) party candidate for president in 1948, managed to carry Alabama, Mississippi, Louisiana, and his own state for a total of thirty-nine electoral votes. In short, while the Dixiecrats failed in their effort to throw the presidential election into the House of Representatives, they succeeded in proving as unfounded Clark Clifford's assurance to Truman that the South would remain solidly Democratic in spite of efforts to liberalize the party's position on race.[36]

The presidential election of 1952, in which Eisenhower appealed to and won a significant portion of the southern white vote, informed Democrats that the willingness of southern conservatives to bolt the party in 1948 over the issue of civil rights was not an historical aberration. This election also revealed that one unfortunate consequence of intraparty division over civil rights was the very thing that Clifford thought the party could avoid by appealing to black voters—the loss of the White House to Republican control. The fact that Adlai Stevenson received an even higher proportion of the black vote than Truman did in 1948 (73 percent and 69 percent, respectively) illustrated for Democrats the relative importance of southern whites to the New Deal coalition.[37]

Progressive Democrats could not hope, at least in the short term, that an increase in southern black voters would compensate for the loss of the resources and votes of southern whites. Partly as a result of the Supreme Court's invalidation of the white primary in 1944, the registration of African Americans in the South had increased from around 3 to 20 percent by 1952. Some 80 percent of African Americans remained unregistered, however, and many counties with black majorities in the Deep South were able to disenfranchise blacks altogether through poll taxes, literacy tests, fraud, and intimidation. African Americans could not look to Washington to protect them from such behavior, since the political considerations that discouraged politicians from offering civil rights

proposals also discouraged executive officials from prosecuting southerners who interfered with black voting. And, even if these officials had been
willing to risk alienating the region's conservative Democrats, such pros-
ecutions would have failed since white jurors were strongly disinclined to
convict individuals who acted in support of southern racial mores. It is
not surprising, then, that Justice Department officials usually chose not
to prosecute assaults on or even murders of black voters.[38]

In view of these considerations, the New Deal justices in *Brown* would
not have thought that, in ruling against segregation in the especially sensitive area of elementary and secondary education, they were simply altering the nature of the New Deal coalition. Rather, the justices would have
anticipated that a desegregation decree would inspire calls for civil rights
legislation exceeding Truman's efforts on behalf of African Americans,
legislation that would lead to intraparty, sectional conflicts even more
profound than those witnessed in 1948 and 1952. The reasonableness of
these assumptions was demonstrated in the mid-1960s when the issue of
civil rights destroyed the odd political alliance that had united the Democratic party since the Depression. As Bensel notes, "The 89th Congress
(1965–66) marked the end of New Deal coalition effectiveness" because
"the enactment of major civil rights legislation [by that body] . . . destabi-
lized the political hegemony of the plantation elite within the South and
signaled a more or less explicit campaign to turn the Democratic party
into a truly national working-class organization."[39]

McMahon acknowledges that "a Roosevelt-influenced Court mission
wound up structuring the judicial activism that eventually tore his New
Deal electoral alliance asunder." But, in view of the strong possibility that
the New Deal justices anticipated that their civil rights decisions would
contribute to this unfortunate event, McMahon must accompany his
ironical observation with a more elaborate discussion of the justices' goals
in *Brown.* He does point up the fact that the justices' conference deliberations revealed "a clear concern about pushing the South too hard or too
fast on race." He also notes that "*Brown,* which unequivocally outlawed
segregation in the schools, was followed by an implementation decision
(*Brown II*) that was largely a victory for the South." But the justices
would not have assumed that attentiveness to southern concerns in a desegregation order would be sufficient to halt the southern abandonment
of the Democratic party, which had begun over matters less controversial
than elementary and secondary school desegregation. It is only marginally
more helpful to suggest that "any concern the Roosevelt and Truman appointees . . . might have had about the ramifications of their decision on

the Democratic Party would have been partially erased when they agreed to join a decision written by a prominent Republican."[40] It is highly unlikely that the justices' concerns about their blameworthiness for the damage that would be done to the party approximated their concerns about the damage itself.

Unless the New Deal justices thought that an immediate increase in the numbers of black voters would be sufficient to offset current and anticipated losses in the numbers and resources of southern conservatives (as noted, black voter registration in the South had stalled at around 20 percent in 1952), they would have assumed that, by ordering desegregation, they risked hastening the end of the Democratic party's dominance and thus *sacrificing* the fulfillment of Roosevelt's constitutional vision. And, even if the justices believed that the achievement of a powerful national executive was inevitable, they were likely to have thought that, by continuing to abet the dismemberment of the New Deal coalition through the pursuit of civil rights, the authority of the presidency would be wielded for Republican rather than Democratic ends. In short, McMahon appears vulnerable to the charge that he levels at Martin Shapiro—that he "fails to show convincingly why the Court would have agreed to reach decisions . . . that ultimately tore the New Deal coalition asunder."[41]

These observations do not imply that McMahon's analysis, even without additional supporting considerations, is of little use in accounting for *Brown.* At the very least, he does much to explain the significance of civil rights cases that preceded the desegregation ruling. Although the Court's decision in 1954 to employ the living Constitution concept to strike at the separate-but-equal principle was a watershed event in American constitutional history, certain of these earlier cases were essential components of the legal edifice that the Court offered as a justification for *Brown.* These cases were grounded in the sense of judicial mission that the Roosevelt administration helped to construct with its judicial policy. In McMahon's words, "[Roosevelt's] nominees' adherence to rights-centered liberalism combined with their devotion to defer to the executive branch ensured that the NAACP would find fertile ground to lay its antisegregation precedential seeds, seeds that would one day—nourished in part by the Justice Department—sprout into *Brown v. Board.*"[42]

But the Roosevelt justices' early civil rights decisions indicated that this sense of mission—one that proposed that the Court play a special role in protecting minority rights—did not emerge fully formed with the appropriate judicial response made evident for all civil rights controversies.[43] And, as the conference deliberations in *Brown* demonstrated, the passage of time did not remove the justices' doubts regarding the proper course of action to take in individual civil rights cases. Most likely, the 1952 presidential contest, which revealed to the New Dealers on the Court just how important southern conservatives were to at least an approximation of New Deal liberalism, added significantly to their level of indecision when they were confronted with the issue of elementary and secondary school segregation.

The insight regarding the fragile nature of the New Deal coalition has significant implications for the story of the basis of the *Brown* decision: The strong possibility that the justices anticipated that a desegregation ruling would redound to the detriment of the Democratic party complicates *every* account of *Brown* discussed thus far. It must be explained why the New Dealers on the Court voted to end racial segregation at the lower levels of education—whether to help the United States respond to Soviet propaganda, carry out an institutional mission that required the Court to respond to instances of racial oppression, demonstrate loyalty to the Court, or pursue a desegregation policy preference—if they understood that receipt of the benefits of such a ruling risked the loss of the Democratic party's majority status and with it the enactment of progressive social and economic legislation generally.

A REQUEST TO RESOLVE A POLITICAL STALEMATE?

Although *Brown* is not the focus of Mark A. Graber's important study of "legislative deference to the judiciary," he provides a possible explanation for the willingness of the New Deal justices to vote for desegregation in spite of the fact that many southerners responded to efforts to expand civil rights by abandoning the Democratic party. Using a "political regimes" perspective, Graber presents *Brown* as an example of the point that the Supreme Court can function as a national policy maker when "prominent elected officials consciously invite the judiciary to resolve those political controversies that they cannot or would rather not address." In these situations, the justices "help maintain the national party system by removing from the political agenda issues that are disruptive to existing partisan alignments and by resolving those matters in a way that is consistent with the preferences of elites in both the dominant majority and minority coalitions."[44]

With regard to the divisive issue of race, Graber argues, the executive's request that the Court resolve the conflict was contained in the *amicus* briefs that the Truman and Eisenhower administrations submitted in *Brown*. Although the overtures emanating from Congress were not apparent, Graber believes that they were nevertheless telling. He contends that the very individuals who forced Truman to pursue racial equality through judicial rather than legislative means—"Southern Democrats who were unwilling to vote for civil rights proposals"—"proved willing to confirm federal justices who were known to be strong proponents of racial equality." At the time of the *Brown* decision, then, it was clear to the justices that "the political leaders and presidential wings of both national parties wanted to eradicate segregation practices." In ruling against the interests of the segregationist South, the Court sought to aid moderate Democrats and Republicans who hoped to remove from the nation's political agenda an issue that was both a threat to the stability of the Democratic party and a potential source of conflict between a Republican president and congressional Democrats from the South.[45]

Assuming the validity of Graber's political assessment, and accepting his measure of success for judicial policy making undertaken in response to the encouragement of politicians, *Brown* actually serves to demonstrate the likelihood of *failure* when the Court attempts to moderate the conflict that a crosscutting issue inspires within American politics. As noted in chapter 1, the South did not accept the Court's authority to invalidate racial segregation in the nation's elementary and secondary schools. More important, this chapter discusses the profound political consequences of *Brown*'s intensification of the battle over civil rights.[46] Graber's time frame (1936 to 1960) stops short of the period when Congress finally acted to implement *Brown* and, in so doing, destroyed the New Deal coalition that had united the Democratic party.[47]

Brown's failure in this regard, however, in no way disproves Graber's account of the decision. The validity of his thesis depends not on the success or failure of the Court's effort but on the accuracy of the contention that the justices ruled against segregation because they *thought* politicians had enlisted their aid. The attractiveness of Graber's argument is that it appears to explain why the New Deal justices would have voted for desegregation in spite of the demonstrated willingness of some southern congressmen to abandon the Democratic party over civil rights. Graber would contend that the justices concluded that a desegregation ruling would not lead to the disintegration of the New Deal coalition because they thought southern congressmen had signaled a desire to use the Court as political cover when the justices ruled against the school boards.

But, in contrast to the other historical examples Graber uses to illustrate his thesis, it is difficult to characterize *Brown* as an instance in which a desire to resolve a crosscutting political issue on behalf, and at the request, of elected officials motivated the justices.[48] Only the Truman administration sent a clear message to the Court regarding desegregation. As noted, the circumstances surrounding the Eisenhower administration's participation in *Brown* would have led the justices to think that support for desegregation within the executive branch was not uniform and that executive officials who ostensibly sought to end school segregation may have been making insincere overtures to black voters.

It is even less likely that the justices believed congressmen—southerners, in particular—were seeking the Court's help in resolving the segregation controversy, or that southern legislators were willing to abide by anything other than a ruling in favor of the practice. It is difficult to identify federal judicial nominees whose approval by southern senators would have convinced the justices that they had received an invitation to engage in political brokering in such a sensitive policy area. While several Eisenhower appointees to the lower federal courts made "major contributions to the movement for racial integration," the administration placed all of these individuals on the bench *after* the *Brown* decision.[49] And none of the nominees to the Supreme Court who were named before *Brown* by either of the administrations that participated in the case as *amicus curiae* could have been considered "strong proponents of racial equality," especially if that phrase implies likely support for desegregation in elementary education. Recall that Earl Warren had stated publicly as a national political figure (on more than one occasion) that he favored localism in matters of education. Harold Burton and Sherman Minton had so little experience with racial matters before joining the Court that southern senators could not have viewed them as anything other than unknown quantities. Tom Clark was associated with the Truman administration's early efforts to reach out to African Americans. But his record, as well as his Texas background, stopped short of communicating an unambiguous personal commitment to racial equality. Even assuming unrealistically that the justices regarded the voting records of southern senators on Supreme Court nominees as uncharacteristically progressive, the validity of Graber's thesis still requires the members of the Court to have been ignorant of a distinct possibility: that the senators were willing to support such nominees only because the efficacy of liberal civil rights rulings would depend on the passage of enforcement legislation. These congressmen not only had the power to filibuster proposals to end segregation; as noted, they also held important posts during the 1950s, which essentially guaranteed that civil rights bills would not even be reported out of committee.

The notes from the Court's conference deliberations in *Brown* reinforce the point that the justices did not believe they were responding to congressional requests for aid in resolving the controversy over segregation. These documents provide no evidence (save for Robert Jackson's expressions of hope regarding the District of Columbia) that the justices anticipated support from Congress. On the contrary, they spoke at length about the profound opposition that a desegregation ruling would encounter. Presumably, the justices expected that such social resistance would preclude southern congressmen from declaring that they had no choice but to support the Court's order. And, since these congressmen had the power to derail civil rights legislation, the justices could not have anticipated adequate support from anti-segregationist legislators, the only members of Congress that the justices had any reason to believe would ask the Court to resolve the segregation controversy.

In the same way that the justices could not have believed reasonably that congressmen were requesting the Court's aid in removing this issue from the political landscape, they also had little reason to think that the existence of segregation was a problem in that it threatened to destabilize existing political arrangements. Even assuming unrealistically that the justices would not have anticipated that a desegregation ruling might hasten the collapse of the fragile New Deal coalition, Graber does not refer to evidence that would have led the justices to believe that the *failure* to render a desegregation ruling would rupture this important partisan alliance. He concedes that the issues *Brown* raised "did not immediately threaten to disrupt existing political cleavages." Yet he goes on to say that, "with rare exception, legislative deference to the judiciary has taken place concerning those issues that the major parties are, by their nature, not well structured to debate. In particular, the Court has . . . played a major role when sectional disputes have arisen that crosscut national party alignments, as we have seen when slavery (*and civil rights*) pitted North against the South."[50] The problem with this argument is that there was no indication that the matter of segregation would rupture the New Deal coalition if the Court did not intervene to invalidate the practice. While many southern Democrats had already demonstrated a willingness to leave the party over the issue of civil rights, northern liberals did not threaten to do likewise in the event that the party failed to support desegregation measures.

Forecasting (and Attempting to Influence) the Future

If the justices could not have thought that politicians (other than members of the Truman administration) were asking them to resolve the desegregation controversy, it is necessary to search for an alternate explanation for the willingness of the New Dealers to contribute to the dismemberment of the coalition that gave the Democratic party a controlling majority in Congress. The beginnings of such an explanation are contained in the justices' comments regarding trends they perceived in southern race relations.[51] These comments point to, although they do not prove, the relevance to *Brown* of Franklin Roosevelt's constitutional vision, specifically his desire to empower the national executive in part through the expansion of civil rights in the South.

Beginning with the Truman justices, Minton observed in conference that "segregation is on its way out in Indiana" and that "this is a different world today."[52] In a draft of the memorandum that he wrote for the university desegregation cases, Justice Clark declared, "Nowhere are the forces of progress in the South more apparent than in our colleges and graduate schools." Among other things, he noted that, for over a decade, some Texas colleges "have been permitting or sponsoring Negro speakers before white student groups," while "white students have been going in deputations to Negro communities, organizations, and churches." He suggested that "the only protests have come from the parents and others of an older generation; non-participating students have been for the most part indifferent; the others are simply amused."[53]

Several of Roosevelt's appointees also commented on changes in southern race relations. In conference, Stanley Reed noted "the constant progress in this field and in the advancement of the interests of negroes." He went on to suggest that "segregation is gradually disappearing."[54] Similarly, Justice Frankfurter made reference in his unpublished, separate opinion in *Brown* to "the great changes in the relations between white and colored people since the first World War." "The policy of segregation," he continued, "has in the short period of thirty years undergone great modification. The results of this tendency afford no ground for complacency to those who view segregation with a hostile eye. But it is fair to say that the pace of progress has surprised even those most eager in its promotion." Four years prior to *Brown,* Justice Jackson noted in correspondence that he had "seen a good deal of progress in the recognition of Negro rights in the South in the last few years." Jackson returned to this point in the draft opinions that he wrote for *Brown.* He remarked on "a profound change in the responsible and rational public opinion toward segregation and all related problems" that was inspired in part by a revulsion against Nazism. He added, "Economic, social, and political consideration[s] seem to mark [segregation] for certain and early, if gradual extinction. Whatever we may say the law is today, I have no doubt that within a generation segregation will be outlawed."[55]

The significance of the economic, social, and political forces to which Jackson referred, and which informed the justices' musings regarding change in the South, had been illuminated in the work of two eminent scholars, V. O. Key, Jr., and Gunnar Myrdal. In his comprehensive study of southern politics, which appeared five years before *Brown* and on which the petitioners drew in their brief for the rehearing (albeit not specifically for his view of the future of southern politics), Key stated, "Not only is there diversity within the South; the region is also changing." While conceding that the South's "rate of evolution may seem glacial," he insisted that "fundamental shifts in the conditions underlying its politics are taking place. All these changes drive toward a political system more completely in accord with the national ideas of constitutional morality."[56] Myrdal revealed similar optimism in *An American Dilemma*—a monumental study of race in America that was published ten years before *Brown,* which the petitioners referenced in the appendix to their brief for the initial hearing and in their brief for the rehearing (although not specifically for Myrdal's predictions regarding the future of the South), and which the Court cited in its opinion in *Brown.* Like Key, Myrdal observed that, "superficially viewed, the situation [in the South] looks static and stable." He was quick to point out, however, that "this is . . . an illusion. Great changes are working underneath the visible surface, and a dynamic situation full of possibilities is maturing." Indeed, "not since Reconstruction has there been more reason to anticipate fundamental changes in American race relations, changes which will involve a development toward the American ideals" of "the essential dignity of the individual human being, of the fundamental equality of all men, and of certain inalienable rights to freedom, justice, and a fair opportunity."[57]

When Myrdal and Key explained the changes that they observed in the South, they corroborated Franklin Roosevelt's sense of the connection between civil rights and progressive politics. Myrdal contended that events had conspired to make "the Southern conservative position on [denying] the Negro [the] franchise . . . politically untenable for any length of time." He suggested that the "general political atmosphere of the nation"—especially the widespread realization that "America, for its international prestige, power, and future security, needs to demonstrate to the world that American Negroes can be satisfactorily integrated into its democracy"—had placed enormous pressure on the South to abandon the poll tax and other devices that it used to prevent blacks from voting. Myrdal anticipated that, once African Americans entered southern politics in greater numbers, they "will . . . be in favor of a political party which stands for social reform [as well as] civic equality." For "Negroes, in both the higher and the lower strata, seem to understand pretty well that a liberal attitude in questions of economic relief and social reform is generally connected with a more equalitarian attitude in racial matters." Key underscored Myrdal's point when he observed, "If the Negro is gradually assimilated into political life, . . . southern liberalism will undoubtedly be mightily strengthened, for the Negro, recent experience indicates, allies himself with liberal factions whenever they exist."[58]

Myrdal and Key contended that the relationship between civil rights and progressive politics was mutually reinforcing. Key noted that the economic landscape of the South had been divided historically between independent yeoman, whose traditional attachment to the Democratic party coincided with a generally liberal perspective (evidenced in the Populist revolt of the late nineteenth century), and plantation elites, who exercised decisive power in regional Democratic politics and who were ideologically conservative. While the yeomen "had no love for the Negro," they had "a less direct concern over the maintenance of white rule" than the large planters, who "operate[d] an economic and social system based upon subordinate, black labor." With the coming of industry to the region, Key maintained, the planters "found new allies in the growing industrial and financial classes," while the agrarian liberalism of the yeomen was "re-enforced by the growing unions of the cities." Key elaborated on the significance of the latter development for the expansion of civil rights: "The growth of urban labor already has had considerable effect and will undoubtedly have further consequences. In all the recent movements for the abolition of the poll tax and for the mitigation of other suffrage restrictions labor unions have played a prominent role."[59]

Myrdal bolstered Key's point, although he acknowledged that, because of racial discrimination, the "past experiences [of blacks] with trade unions have been none too good in most cases." While conceding that "the labor vote might be primarily interested in freeing the poor whites from the poll tax in the South and, generally, in defeating the conservative hold over Southern politics," he believed that certain considerations "offer some hope" that unions would come to practice and promote racial equality. First, "the labor market and its organization will in all probability be subject to more government control, and the national administration will be forced to attempt to defend a place for the Negro in the labor market against exclusionistic and segregational practices by unions."

Second, organized labor would eventually realize that, "if it wants to become strong, [it] must be based on a still largely absent, but gradually developing, labor class solidarity, which must be all-inclusive." With regard to the *promotion* of racial equality by organized labor, Myrdal observed, "It is not desirable from a tactical standpoint . . . that labor tolerate discrimination against the Negro, at least as far as legislation and national policy are concerned. This is so because labor must seek support in the industrial South from the Negro, where the Negro constitutes an important element in the industrial population."[60]

Over time, Myrdal and Key believed, the reciprocal relationship that exists between civil rights and progressive politics would establish the conditions for a significant realignment of political forces in the South. Having given "reasons to anticipate both that the Negro and the labor bloc will exert increasing political power, and that liberalism generally will become stronger in both the South and in the North," Myrdal was "inclined to envisage such a reorganization of the two-party system that one of the two parties carrying on the tradition of the New Deal becomes a liberal reform party, while the other remains a conservative party." Suggesting that "the Dixiecratic movement may turn out to have been the dying gasp of the Old South," Key predicted similarly that a "continuing growth of industry [and unions] and a continued leftward veering of the Democratic party nationally would place a greater and greater strain on the Democratic loyalties of rising southern big business." "The potentialities in national politics of a South freed from the restraint of the Negro and of the one-party system are extremely great," he declared; the "underlying liberal drive [that] permeates southern politics," and which had been held in check in part by one-party rule, "is not to be underestimated."[61]

This analysis of the changes in the South helps us to understand the justices' willingness to contribute to the demise of the New Deal coalition with a desegregation ruling. As noted, Myrdal and Key corroborated Franklin Roosevelt's belief that the expansion of civil rights was related to the promotion of progressive politics. Unlike Roosevelt, however, Myrdal and Key recognized that the South would not remain safely Democratic if the party pursued a liberal agenda. As the trend toward equality progressed in the South, the issue of race would continue to contribute to divisions within the Democratic party because African Americans would support progressive political goals. Myrdal and Key anticipated that southern conservatives would eventually abandon the Democratic party, as it provided greater support to working-class interests. But they thought that African Americans and unions—the constituencies that Roosevelt viewed as central to the accomplishment of his constitutional vision of an empowered national executive—would develop into formidable political forces in the region.

While optimism regarding the advance of southern liberalism implies a lessening of the need on the part of New Deal liberals to placate southern conservatives, it still raises the question why the New Dealers on the Court were not averse to ruling against segregation. In view of the supposed fluidity of the southern political situation, the wisest course of action would seem to have been the avoidance of the issue altogether. Doing nothing under these circumstances would have prevented any short-term damage to the Democratic party (as occurred in the presidential election of 1952), while the justices waited for the trend toward racial egalitarianism to remove the barrier that the segregationist South presented to Roosevelt's constitutional ambitions.

As Myrdal and Key emphasized, however, the trend toward liberalism in the South was not inexorable. In Key's words, "It is not to be supposed that . . . fundamental trends automatically bring political change. They only create conditions favorable to change that must be wrought by men and women disposed to take advantage of the opportunity to accelerate the inevitable." Myrdal concurred when he said, "Man is a free agent, and there are no inevitabilities." Regrettably, "the great majority of Southern conservative white people do not see the handwriting on the wall." Rather, "they live . . . in the pathetic illusion that the matter is settled," "not car[ing] to have any constructive policies to meet the trends." Myrdal also suggested that, in spite of promising signs in the region, southern liberalism *"gets its power from outside the South."* After acknowledging the salutary impact of, among other things, "the New Deal in the South," "the agitation for . . . an abolition of the poll tax by Congress," and "a whole set of Supreme Court decisions," he called on Americans who expect their country to live up to its ideals "to do something big and do it soon."[62]

This is not to suggest that the New Deal justices' desegregation votes were in part direct responses to academic entreaties that the Court act to encourage southern liberalism. It is reasonable to believe, however, that the justices were familiar with academic arguments about trends in the South, or, at the very least, that the New Dealers' comments regarding such changes revealed that they possessed similar thoughts and hopes about the future of liberalism in the region. As noted, the petitioners drew the justices' attention to Key in their brief for the rehearing and to Myrdal in both the appendix to their brief for the initial hearing and their brief for the rehearing. (The Court's inclusion of Myrdal in the eleventh footnote in *Brown* is worthy of special note.) Frankfurter, in particular, was familiar with Myrdal's work, given that he had become friends with the Swedish economist during his visits to the United States, and that "Myrdal had carried on long discussions about the race problem with the Supreme Court justice."[63] The New Deal justices also had before them an example of southern liberalism in the person of Hugo Black, the former advocate for the working classes of Alabama. Even if the justices had not read the portions of Myrdal's and Key's studies that were devoted to the careers of Senator Black and other progressive southern politicians, they nevertheless understood that their colleague represented an element of the South that sought considerably more for the region than the conservative politics of old.[64]

The voting patterns of the New Dealers on the Court also were consistent with efforts to support the development of progressivism in the South. Table 3 provides summaries of the seven justices' voting behavior in five areas relevant to the matter: civil rights, unions, economics, federal taxation, and federalism. In the first two categories, liberal voting involves, respectively, support for women and minorities and "pro-union votes against both individuals and the government." Liberal voting in the area of economic activity "represents pro-government votes against challenges to its regulatory authority and pro-competition, anti-business, pro-liability, pro-injured person, and pro-bankruptcy votes." A liberal vote in federal taxation cases supports the national government over taxpayers, while liberal voting in the area of federalism supports national supremacy against claims of states' rights.[65] Since southern conservatives demonstrated hostility not only to civil rights and labor but also to Roosevelt's "wealth tax, the NRA, the AAA, business regulations, and 'arbitrary little [federal] bureaucrats,'" they would have found troubling the voting records of the New Dealers who were on the Court at midcentury.[66] The justices leaned in a liberal direction in twenty-nine of the thirty-five cells listed in table 3. In sixteen of those twenty-nine cells, the justices voted in a liberal direction over two-thirds of the time. Only one justice—Jackson—leaned in a conservative direction in more than one area. Since Jackson died in 1954, however, it is impossible to know whether the direction of his voting represented a trend in any of these areas (except, perhaps, economics).[67]

In addition to supporting interests that were antagonistic to southern conservatism, the New Deal justices sought in their rulings to facilitate the cooperation between African Americans and organized labor to which,

TABLE 3 Percentage of liberal votes by New Deal (Democratic or independent) justices involved in *Brown v. Board of Education* (1954), 1953 through 1975 terms (number of cases)

JUSTICES IN ORDER OF APPOINTMENT	CIVIL RIGHTS	UNIONS	ECONOMICS	FEDERAL TAXATION	FEDERALISM	AVG. % OF LIBERAL VOTING
Black (Dem.)	**72.2**	**76.3**	**84.2**	**84.9**	64.9	**76.5**
	(277)	(135)	(467)	(126)	(111)	
Reed (Dem.)	35.5	**81.8**	52.2	**75.0**	52.6	59.4
	(31)	(22)	(99)	(24)	(19)	
Frankfurter (Indep.)	55.7	53.1	38.6	**75.7**	60.4	56.7
	(88)	(64)	(241)	(70)	(53)	
Douglas (Dem.)	**92.7**	64.9	**86.3**	38.6	**69.0**	**70.3**
	(397)	(168)	(568)	(140)	(129)	
Jackson (Dem.)	62.5	**66.7**	42.9	33.3	**75.0**	56.1
	(8)	(6)	(28)	(3)	(4)	
Clark (Dem.)	57.3	**69.3**	**74.6**	**78.0**	54.5	**66.7**
	(185)	(114)	(389)	(109)	(88)	
Minton (Dem.)	37.9	60.0	66.3	**85.7**	58.8	61.7
	(29)	(20)	(86)	(21)	(17)	

Bold numbers = liberal direction over two-thirds of the time.

Source: Based on Epstein and Mershon, "Measuring Political Preferences," 287.

in Myrdal's view, these interests were predisposed and which Franklin Roosevelt realized was necessary for the advancement of southern liberalism. The fact that progressives had long associated union autonomy with the goal of industrial democracy complicated this task. That the value of union autonomy presented an obstacle to the advancement of civil rights was demonstrated in the early to mid-1940s, when the Fair Employment Practices Commission, which had no authority to correct the injustices it discovered, published findings that labor unions were engaging in racial discrimination. At this time, "the Roosevelt and Truman Courts, in an intriguing series of statutory interpretation cases, took up the project of negotiating the reconciliation of a layered reformist commitment to labor rights and civil rights."[68]

While the justices' voting patterns suggest a faith in southern liberalism (which helps to explain why they were willing to vote for desegregation in spite of the threat that doing so posed to the New Deal coalition) and are consistent with Franklin Roosevelt's constitutional vision, it is well beyond the scope of this (or, probably, any) study to prove that the votes in so many cases across a number of issues reflected this noninstrumental political purpose. Aside from the sheer difficulty, if not impossibility, of locating evidence that connects the justices' votes with Roosevelt's constitutional aspirations, noninstrumentalists must also consider the possibility that the constitutional views and concerns of subsequent administrations contribute to an explanation of the justices' decisions.[69]

But the burden of proof does not rest entirely with those who would defend a noninstrumental understanding of the justices' voting patterns. While Jeffrey A. Segal and his colleagues observe a strong correlation between their indirect measures of the New Dealers' ideological values (which they obtained through content analyses of newspaper editorials) and the justices' votes in economic and civil liberties cases, it is not apparent that these ideological measures adequately explain the levels of liberal voting in the specific areas presented in table 3.[70] Setting Jackson aside (because he died shortly after *Brown* and because of the probable measurement error that Segal notes for the justice), instrumentalists can claim consistency between the ideological measures and voting patterns for Douglas and Clark. While Segal notes a probable measurement error for Douglas's ideological designation (viz., moderate liberal) and identifies Clark as a political moderate who did not even lean toward the liberal side of the continuum, chapter 2 refers to studies of ideological drift which indicate that each justice became considerably more liberal in the years following their respective first terms on the Court and that these shifts occurred before *Brown*. Instrumentalists might also claim that Minton's voting record was what one would expect from a justice whose ideological measure was closer to moderate than to liberal. But, if this is the case, it is difficult to believe that ideology adequately explains the voting records of Reed and Frankfurter; these justices, whose ideological measures and voting patterns in the relevant areas are similar to those of Minton, became significantly more conservative prior to *Brown*. (Minton was not on the Court long enough for scholars to ascertain whether he exhibited an ideological shift.) Finally, while Black was the only justice among the New Dealers (other than Jackson) whose ideological designation was closer to liberal than to moderate, scholars of ideological drift contend that he, like Reed and Frankfurter, became considerably more conservative before *Brown*. While it is possible to use the concept of ideological drift to provide an instrumental interpretation of Clark's voting pattern, Black's rightward ideological shift precludes such an interpretation for his votes, especially considering that he exhibited the most liberal voting pattern of all of the New Dealers.

Instrumentalists could still challenge the view that the *Brown* decision, in particular, was a consequence of a judicial policy that Roosevelt initiated in order to remove the obstacle that southern conservatism presented to his constitutional vision of an empowered national executive. Kevin McMahon's thesis is vulnerable since he presents no compelling documentary evidence that individual justices consciously sought to accomplish this objective in this one case. Justice Jackson's statement in correspondence that he wrote regarding the university desegregation cases—that "some want to see the Administration's hand strengthened politically"—might have been a reference to colleagues who were aware of and sought to use segregation to advance the executive's constitutional imperatives.[71] But such an indeterminate phrase does not constitute convincing proof of McMahon's argument. The chances are slim that more explicit statements from the New Deal justices regarding *Brown's* relevance to Roosevelt's constitutional vision will ever surface. After all, ostensibly neutral justices who viewed the segregation controversy through the lens of a president's constitutional aspirations would have been strongly disinclined to leave documentation to that effect.

A rigorous standard of proof, however, should extend to instrumental accounts of *Brown* as well. The justices who voted in that case might have served as counterexamples to social and political forces that operated on the Court at midcentury. But this observation applies whether the forces under consideration are those that were moving national opinion toward an acceptance of racial equality (and recall that the research on ideological drift suggests that five of the justices had actually become considerably more conservative by the time the Court rendered *Brown*) or those that prodded the New Deal justices to promote Roosevelt's constitutional vision. As the evidence reveals, several members of the Court, and probably a majority, voted against segregation not to pursue personal policy preferences but to promote one or more noninstrumental goals. In the same way that instrumentalists might contend that there nevertheless remains good reason to believe that instrumental and noninstrumental goals coincided in the desegregation votes of some members of the Court, while personal policy preferences were the primary influence in the votes of other justices, McMahon is equally justified in insisting that any complete account of *Brown* requires attention to the role that the New Deal justices played in Roosevelt's effort "to liberalize his party and disrupt the conservative tendencies of southern politics, each in the pursuit of a reformulated electoral coalition and his reconstructive constitutional vision."[72] The justices, however, believed that they had contributed to the realization of this goal not merely by taking a progressive stance in an intraparty dispute (as McMahon would have it) but by helping to alter significantly the partisan landscape of the South.

It must also be emphasized that the New Deal justices' aspirations in *Brown* were broader than the eventual achievement of Roosevelt's constitutional vision. Not only does the evidence suggest as much, but the belief that a desegregation decision secured additional aims—whether the satisfaction of a personal policy preference, the demonstration of institutional loyalty, the fulfillment of an institutional mission to protect racial minorities against white supremacy, or the satisfaction of a Cold War imperative—also reconciled the New Deal justices to the regrettable damage, however temporary, they thought such a ruling might inflict on the Democratic party. And the same consideration that enabled the justices to pursue Roosevelt's constitutional vision—the expectation that the growth of southern liberalism would offset the loss of southern conservatives to the Republican party—allowed them to pursue these additional goals. For the prospect of relegating the Democratic party permanently to minority status, and thus destroying the possibility of achieving other progressive goals, would have been deeply unattractive to a New Deal justice, whether his purpose in *Brown* was noninstrumental in nature or the instrumental goal of satisfying a policy preference.

Interestingly, the justices' predictions regarding the future of southern liberalism turned out to be overly optimistic. As Earl and Merle Black noted near the end of Ronald Reagan's second term as president, not only had conservatism "become the dominant ideological force in southern Republican parties" but "Democratic victories in statewide contests [could] no longer be taken for granted." They argued further, with considerable prescience, that "presidential Republicanism in the South [had] advanced so far that the party [could] be expected to carry most, if not all, of the region's states in presidential politics in the foreseeable future."[73] The fact that the growth of progressive forces in the South was insufficiently robust to offset Republican gains, however, does not negate the point that the New Deal justices' hopefulness regarding the transformation of the region tipped the decision-making scale in *Brown* in favor of desegregation.

Conclusion

In his discussion of the relevance of the new institutionalism to the field of public law, Rogers M. Smith leavens his defense of a constitutive understanding of Supreme Court decision making with an acknowledgement of the contributions of alternative methodologies. While he maintains that defenders of instrumental accounts of decision making "should agree that the impact of structures of ideas forms a part of their enterprise," he also insists that scholars who favor noninstrumental explanations must, where possible, respect demands for empirical rigor by becoming "more aware of the need to connect their claims with measured patterns in actual decision making." In an effort to promote a "sense of common endeavor" among students of the Supreme Court, Smith expresses the hope "that both quantitative and qualitative public-law scholars might consider exploring further how we might realize this suggested recasting of their work in terms of a common focus on the interplay of specified structures and decisions."[1]

So long as judicial scholars ignore Smith's ecumenical plea and focus, instead, on determining which theory of Supreme Court decision making is "doing the most work," the prospects for significant cooperation among institutionalists, to say nothing of attitudinalists and noninstrumentalists, do not seem especially bright.[2] If, however, the task at hand is to explain the votes of nine justices in one Supreme Court ruling, then methodological diversity is a necessity. As this book demonstrates, the most convincing account of the *Brown* decision is one that employs the insights of numerous approaches to Supreme Court decision making. While the task of tracking and summarizing the explanatory factors relevant to *Brown* is daunting, the increased accuracy achieved through reference to multiple perspectives—and the important normative concerns about American democracy that these empirical findings raise—compensate for the inelegance that necessarily attends abandoning the quest for a single explanation of the decision.

A Multifaceted Approach

Attentiveness to the insights of multiple models of Supreme Court decision making alerts students of *Brown* to the fact that numerous and varied forces at midcentury supported desegregation. The justices learned of the executive's positions regarding the threat that segregation posed to America's reputation during the Cold War and the impediment that the southern conservative element of the New Deal coalition presented to a progressive interpretation of the Constitution. Several institutional considerations—including the manner in which Supreme Court justices are appointed, the solicitor general's status as a repeat player, and the Court's dependence on the executive for the enforcement of its rulings—suggest that the justices were receptive to the executive's concerns in the case. The petitioners' powerful critique of the southern contention that segregation was an institution designed to benefit blacks and whites alike complemented the executive's arguments. The petitioners' historical analysis of the nature of segregation informed their legal argument that the Court should regard as its mission the protection of minorities from racial oppression. Finally, justices who had reservations, legal or otherwise, about ruling against school segregation felt considerable pressure, implicit or explicit, to vote against the practice in the interest of institutional loyalty.

In spite of these considerations, attitudinalists would insist that, in the absence of evidence linking individual justices to institutional accounts of *Brown,* scholars should regard as irrelevant factors other than the policy preferences of the members of the Court. For the institutional factors that promote the independence of the Supreme Court enabled the justices to vote in accordance with their personal values, and, as members of the cultural elite, they likely possessed progressive racial views. The Court rendered *Brown* after political, economic, and social forces—including the migration of millions of African Americans to the urban centers of politically significant northern states, the empowerment of blacks through improved economic circumstances, and the ideological impact of this nation's involvement in the fight against fascism during the Second World War—had served to liberalize American racial attitudes. While only half of the population at midcentury regarded desegregation as an essential component of the concept of racial equality, a majority of cultural elites favored the abandonment of Jim Crow.

Critics of an attitudinal understanding of Supreme Court decision making, however, would respond that justices are not mere pawns in the march of history; individual members of the Court may have been counterexamples to national opinion trends in 1954. Indeed, studies of ideological drift suggest that five of the justices—Hugo Black, Stanley Reed, Felix Frankfurter, Robert Jackson, and Harold Burton—had become significantly more conservative in the years following their respective first terms, and that, for each man, the shift rightward had occurred prior to *Brown.* Thus, the argument runs, institutionalists are not the only participants in the debate over *Brown*'s basis who should assume the burden of proving their claims; attitudinalists should also seek to offer evidence that demonstrates the strongly instrumental nature of the justices' individual votes.

In assuming the burden of providing evidence of the factors that informed the justices' desegregation votes, this study demonstrates both the importance of methodological diversity and the necessity of moving beyond instrumental assumptions regarding judicial behavior. Contemporary polling data that revealed that educated southerners largely favored segregation; Reed's policy defense of segregation in conference, and his racist comments off the bench; Black's erstwhile membership in the Ku Klux Klan, and his willingness to exploit racial enmity as a lawyer and politician; and Earl Warren's politically unnecessary insensitivity to the issue of racial equality as a presidential aspirant (in particular, his explicit statements that public schools should remain free of federal oversight) place the burden of proof on those who would explain the desegregation votes of these three men by reference to their personal policy preferences. Documentation reveals that, in accordance with a constitutive approach to Supreme Court decision making, Warren found compelling the petitioners' argument that segregation was part of a long-standing effort in the South to subjugate blacks, and that he accepted the corresponding view that the Court's mission is to rectify such failings of democratic government. Black's conference statements likewise echoed the petitioners' arguments, although the justice confessed that he did not need to be educated about the connection between segregation and white supremacy. But the petitioners did inform Black of the incommensurability between the nature of segregation and his statement in *Korematsu v. United States* that policies based on racial antagonism cannot survive strict judicial scrutiny. In sharp contrast to Warren and Black, Justice Reed strongly

defended the constitutionality of segregation by insisting that the institution benefited blacks as well as whites. As both strategic and constitutive model proponents would explain, however, Reed nevertheless felt
compelled to vote with his brethren (as a result of Warren's efforts, in
particular) so as not to dilute the force of the Court's ruling.

Although evidence suggests that the racial attitudes of Tom Clark and
Robert Jackson were more complicated than those of their colleagues,
noninstrumental considerations are nevertheless pertinent to their performances in *Brown*. Attitudinalists would emphasize that Clark mentioned
in conference after the rehearing of *Brown* that he disliked segregation,
that Clark discussed the negative effects of segregation in the draft of a
memorandum that he wrote for the university desegregation cases, and
that Jackson stated in correspondence regarding the same cases that he
had no sympathy with the racial conceits of segregation. Other considerations, however, suggest that the justices' discomfort with segregation
existed in tension with less progressive sentiments: Clark edited out most
of his critique of segregation from the final version of the memo that he
sent to his colleagues in the university cases; Clark chose not to discuss
the negative effects of segregation in conference when the Court was
considering *Brown,* providing instead a policy defense of the practice;
Clark threatened to dissent if district judges in elementary desegregation cases were not given the power to deny relief; and Jackson expressed
surprise at the bitterness of African Americans, suggesting in conference
and in his memoranda in *Brown* that desegregation would not be an un-
mitigated benefit for black children. Like Warren and Black, Jackson was
moved to vote with the petitioners in *Brown* on the basis of the dialogue
before the Court regarding the nature of segregation. Jackson's progressively elaborate draft opinions borrowed heavily from the petitioners'
powerful argument that the unconstitutionality of segregation stemmed
in part from the unreasonableness of the assumption of racial inferiority
on which the practice was based. Clark overcame his reluctance to declare
segregation unconstitutional for reasons that proponents of a "political
regimes" approach to Supreme Court decision making illuminate: Harry
Truman's former attorney general, who was deeply involved in the administration's efforts to expand civil rights while limiting civil liberties in an
effort to prevail in the Cold War, was uniquely situated to take to heart
the executive's contention that the preservation of America's international
reputation required a ruling against elementary and secondary school segregation. Clark's statement as attorney general after the NAACP protested
American racism at the United Nations—that the enemies of the United

States would profit if blacks did not believe they could receive redress from American courts—was especially relevant to his desegregation vote.

The writings and personal histories of Justices Harold Burton and Sherman Minton do not illuminate their attitudes toward segregation. While the forces at midcentury that liberalized American racial attitudes may have affected the desegregation votes of these men, evidence indicates that the LDF's discussion of the nature of segregation and the executive's Cold War concerns may have influenced them as well. During the conference deliberations in *Brown,* each justice echoed the LDF's legal critique of segregation. And, like Clark, Burton and Minton were appointees of President Truman and exhibited voting patterns that reflected the administration's Cold War posture toward civil rights and civil liberties. Indeed, the difference in liberal voting percentages in civil rights and First Amendment cases for Minton exceeded even the differential that Clark registered. While Minton was not on the Court long enough for scholars to measure evidence of ideological drift, the increased conservatism that Burton exhibited in studies of this phenomenon should give pause to those who would view his performance in *Brown* primarily, or even secondarily, in instrumental terms.

Attitudinalists can claim with a fair degree of certainty that Justices William Douglas and Felix Frankfurter voted in *Brown* in a manner consistent with their personal policy preferences. The commitment to racial egalitarianism that Frankfurter demonstrated prior to joining the Court provides good reason to believe, in spite of studies of ideological drift that suggest that he had become more conservative, that he felt no *personal* constraints when he supported the equal protection claims of the petitioners in *Brown.* While neither Douglas's correspondence nor his prenomination behavior revealed a similar commitment to racial equality, the extraordinary liberalism that he displayed before his Supreme Court appointment suggests that, when political elites finally began to address the matter of race in the postwar period (after Douglas was on the Court), he, like most liberals, developed an animus toward segregation.

Yet there is evidence to suggest that instrumental and noninstrumental goals coincided in the desegregation votes of Douglas and Frankfurter. Douglas's writings prior to *Brown*—in which he discussed the impact of racial discrimination on America's international prestige—indicate that he, like Clark and probably Minton and Burton, may have responded to the executive's Cold War concerns when asked to decide the constitutionality of school segregation. Frankfurter—and Reed and Jackson as well—made brief comments that recognized, if they did not acknowledge

the constitutional relevance of, the international implications of segregation. These three men also exhibited voting patterns in civil rights and
First Amendment cases that may have reflected a concern with the Cold
War. In short, Douglas and Frankfurter (and Reed and Jackson) illustrate
the point that "patterns of [judicial] behavior often are consistent with
multiple goal orientations."[3]

We cannot rule out the possibility that the desegregation votes of
Douglas, Frankfurter, and the other New Dealers on the Court also reflected President Franklin Roosevelt's constitutional ambitions, specifically his effort to restructure the Democratic party by expanding the
influence of racial minorities and labor unions at the expense of southern
conservatives for the more fundamental purpose of reordering the distribution of power between levels and among branches of government.
The seven New Deal justices had been appointed either by Roosevelt, at a
time when he was engaged in very public battles with southern conservatives, or by Truman, who expanded considerably upon his predecessor's
efforts to promote civil rights. Also, the justices' comments concerning
increased liberalism in the South, and their voting patterns regarding the
issues of national economic powers, federal taxation, national supremacy,
civil rights, and the rights of organized labor, may have reflected a desire
to promote progressive political forces in that region. The development
of southern liberalism would have helped to compensate for an unanticipated consequence of Roosevelt's and Truman's political maneuvers,
which was apparent by 1952—the demonstrated willingness of southern conservatives to abandon the Democratic party over the matter of
civil rights.

But this book emphasizes the importance of evidence that connects
the individual justices to larger forces, and there is no documentation that
conclusively links the New Dealers' desegregation votes to Roosevelt's
constitutional vision. Instrumentalists might suggest that, on balance, the
evidence supports the proposition that personal policy preferences were
the primary influence on the desegregation votes of the former NAACP
advisor, Frankfurter, and of Douglas as well. Douglas's strongly liberal
voting pattern contrasted sharply with the votes of those justices who
adopted the Truman administration's Cold War posture toward civil
rights and civil liberties.

Yet, even if we accept an instrumental interpretation of the desegregation votes of these justices, it is still necessary to move beyond the attitudinal model in order to understand the process by which Chief Justice
Warren, in writing the Court's opinion in *Brown,* addressed the concerns

that Frankfurter and Jackson, among others, expressed regarding the rule of law. The strategic model provides a framework for analyzing Warren's successful efforts to secure a unanimous decision through bargain and compromise. These efforts were remarkable, given that Frankfurter and Jackson matched Reed and Clark in terms of the intensity of their views on the barrier that law presented to desegregation. Furthermore, agreement among the justices on the importance of avoiding violence by delaying the implementation of a desegregation order (which is further evidence of strategic behavior in *Brown*) did not translate into agreement on the specifics of the decree. The illumination of the manner in which Warren overcame these formidable obstacles is an important part of any comprehensive account of *Brown* since, as the chief justice understood, a divided ruling or a ruling that appeared self-righteous would have made the Court's difficult task even more complicated. It is one of the more ironic aspects of the history of the desegregation decision that Warren's strategic calculations led him to abandon a powerful rationale based on an understanding of the oppressive nature of segregation, a view of the practice that the public would eventually adopt in response to televised images of the violence that segregationists directed at peaceful civil rights protestors in the decade after *Brown*.[4] Instead, he offered a rationale to which Frankfurter and Jackson objected because of the vagaries of social science evidence, that none of the justices demanded or even defended, and that proved controversial even with scholars who were sympathetic to desegregation.

While the strategic model affords insights essential to a complete understanding of *Brown,* the willingness of Chief Justice Warren and certain of his brethren to bargain and compromise over the Court's opinion and to allow for delayed enforcement of a desegregation order serves as a counterexample to a central assumption of this approach to Supreme Court decision making—that judicial "calculations over what colleagues will do," and responsiveness to "the preferences of other key political actors, including members of the elected branches of government and the American people," are usually done for instrumental reasons.[5] To reiterate a major theme of this book, among the institutional approaches to Supreme Court decision making that must be consulted in order to explain *Brown, noninstrumental* perspectives are especially relevant. As this study reveals, noninstrumental approaches cannot be regarded as irrelevant for any of the nine justices, they serve as probable explanations for Minton and Burton, and considerable evidence suggests that they are central to accurate accounts of the desegregation votes of Reed, Warren, Black, Jackson, and Clark.

As indicated, the quantity and quality of evidence varies with regard to the policy preferences of the justices and the bases of their desegregation votes. Such evidence also requires interpretation. As Mark A. Graber contends, "The extent to which any judicial decision was motivated by legal [noninstrumental] or strategic [instrumental] factors, at bottom, depends on contestable theories about what constitutes good legal and strategic practice."[6] Some interpretations, however, are more contestable than others. Instrumentalists might view Jackson's performance in *Brown* as a sophisticated attempt to achieve his policy preferences (in spite of evidence that suggests he was not an avid reformer of race relations), as opposed to a good faith effort to interpret the equal protection clause (in spite of the strength of the legal argument that he employed in his memoranda in the case). Instrumentalists might also regard Clark's anti-segregation statements in his draft memorandum for the university cases as sufficient to explain his desegregation vote in *Brown*. But such an interpretation requires us to explain away or ignore a good deal of documentation that points to a less than robust commitment to racial equality and a marked concern with the Cold War. In view of the available evidence regarding both value preferences and voting influences in *Brown* for Reed, Warren, and Black, it becomes even more difficult to characterize the desegregation votes of these men largely in instrumental terms.

What is incontestable is that multiple models of Supreme Court decision making must be consulted in order fully to explain *Brown*. A multifaceted approach to the decision is essential because, as this study demonstrates, different factors predominated in the desegregation votes of individual justices, and multiple factors interacted in the minds of the members of the Court. Although this is a case study—of a landmark decision, at that—other Supreme Court rulings are similar to *Brown* in terms of the multiplicity and interactivity of relevant decision-making factors. As Graber observes, "All judicial choices have legal, strategic, and attitudinal components." Echoing Rogers Smith's call for a shared scholarly focus on the interplay of variables in Supreme Court decision making, Graber adds, "Whatever areas of law scholars consider, the most fruitful investigations will explore the ways in which legal, strategic, and attitudinal factors interact when justices make decisions, and not engage in fruitless contests to determine which single factor explains the most."[7] A study focused on one ruling is of limited utility to those who would formulate theories concerning the interactions of instrumental and noninstrumental factors in various areas of law, draw distinctions between landmark decisions and cases that receive less public scrutiny or praise, and trace out the dynamic relations between instrumental and noninstrumental factors in cases over extended periods of time.[8] But this study's relatively narrow findings take on added significance when we move beyond the task of description and consider the normative implications of the factors that operated in *Brown.*

A Relevance to Contemporary Normative Concerns

In the same article in which he combines a defense of a constitutive understanding of Supreme Court decision making with a call for the development of a sense of common endeavor among scholars of differing methodological backgrounds, Rogers Smith laments that, in "the absence of any theoretical structure that could draw on normative concerns to define an appropriate agenda," empirical work on the Court has "splintered and sometimes faltered" by becoming irrelevant to current controversies in public law. The advantage of a constitutive approach to decision making, in addition to promoting greater accuracy in descriptive studies of the Court, is the establishment of a connection between empirical research and contemporary normative debates. As Smith explains, "It is their attention to the role of ideas and their assumption of the potential meaningfulness of political decisions that make [constitutive] approaches well suited to speak to normative as well as empirical concerns." Specifically, the "descriptions of the influence of enduring structures of legal ideas" contained in the works of scholars who recognize the noninstrumental nature of judging "should enable public-law scholars to argue more powerfully about the values U.S. law has really embodied historically, about the ways those values have shaped, and been shaped by, political conflicts, and about the results they have furthered or forestalled." "Many current normative arguments," he suggests, "would be greatly altered by such increased historical awareness."[9]

The example of the *Brown* decision illustrates well Smith's observation that information regarding the ideas that inform Supreme Court rulings can significantly impact normative debates. But, rather than afford a corrective to empirical scholarship that has no connection to contemporary normative concerns, the normative contribution of noninstrumental accounts of *Brown* is the provision of *alternative* ethical positions to those associated with certain studies that ascribe instrumental goals to the justices' desegregation votes. The ethical controversy concerns the legitimacy of the Warren Court's decisions, which, beginning with *Brown,* developed into a distinctive constitutional jurisprudence, one characterized by an unprecedented expansion of both civil liberties and civil rights and that has been under assault from conservative intellectuals, politicians, and judges for over four decades.[10]

"JUDICIAL ACTIVISM WITH A VENGEANCE"

Earl Warren's strategic (although noninstrumental) decision to base his opinion in *Brown* on controversial social science evidence regarding the psychological harms of school segregation—as opposed to declaring that segregation was a manifestation of white supremacy—contributed to instrumental (specifically attitudinal) interpretations of the constitutional jurisprudence of the Warren Court. Such interpretations of the Court's jurisprudence entailed distinctive normative implications in the writings of certain conservative legal scholars. Consider the scholarship of Alexander M. Bickel.[11] As Justice Frankfurter's law clerk, Bickel wrote a memorandum regarding the history of the intentions of the framers of the Fourteenth Amendment. In 1955, he published a version of that document in an effort to defend *Brown* against criticism that the decision did not accord with the framers' intentions.[12] In relatively short order, however, Bickel came to view the jurisprudence of the Warren Court as unreasonable; he became "the leading member of a group of scholarly critics who repeatedly denounced the Warren Court's activism, including the *Brown* decision."[13] Bickel lamented that "*Brown v. Board of Education* was the beginning" of an explicitly value-based constitutional jurisprudence that instituted sweeping changes in the law regarding such sensitive issues as reapportionment and the rights of the accused. Elaborating on the motives that supposedly informed these decisions, Bickel opined, "The justices of the Warren Court thus ventured to identify a goal. It was necessarily a grand one—if we had to give it a single name, that name, as Professor [Philip B.] Kurland has suggested, would be the Egalitarian Society."[14]

Returning the compliment, Kurland borrowed Bickel's statement— that "*Brown v. Board of Education* was the beginning"—for the title of an article examining the Court's school desegregation decisions in the twenty-five years following *Brown*. Kurland found troubling the Warren Court's shift in 1968 "from desegregation to integration," that is, from requiring the removal of segregation laws to demanding racially mixed schools, "as the compelled standard," since this change led the Burger Court to adopt "desegregation through racial balance accomplished by busing." Elaborating on the nature and origin of the constitutional jurisprudence that informed the implementation decisions of the Warren and Burger Courts, Kurland declared, "[*Brown*] was the beginning of many things, not the least of which was the self-licensing of the Court to recreate the equal protection clause in its own image." "In *Brown*," he continued, "the Court abandoned the search for the framers' intent . . . and chose instead to write a Constitution for our times." Kurland conceded that "distortion of 'original meaning' was not a novelty even before *Brown*." He insisted, however, that *Brown* "was the beginning of the expansive neo-natural law syndrome that allows the Justices to act not merely as interpreters of the Constitution, but as its creators."[15]

In another critique of the Court's desegregation decisions, Gary L. McDowell clarified the not-so-subtle message conveyed in the writings of Bickel and Kurland—that the jurisprudence of the Warren Court has no legitimate basis. Like Bickel and Kurland, McDowell identified *Brown* as the source of the Court's value-based decision making. Given that Chief Justice Warren relied on social science evidence to demonstrate the harms of segregation, McDowell contended that the import of the Court's opinion "was inescapable: all blacks, solely on the basis of their race, had suffered alike, whether they knew it or not. The individual plaintiff in these equity proceedings had been replaced by an aggrieved social class." "Seeking to assuage the effects of [the] past wrongs" perpetrated on that class, the Court eventually "move[d] to make decisions with respect to such matters as immediate integration of schools." McDowell emphasized that these developments represented a radical departure from the traditional conception of equity, which was "originally and historically a power addressed toward individuals," and which only permitted remedial decrees that "took the form of prohibiting actions deemed unconstitutional." The Court's "new notion of equity [was] made possible only by a new and widely accepted judicial view of the Constitution itself." Beginning with *Brown*, the decisions of the Warren Court reflected the view "that the Constitution is not bound by any particular political theory, is not permanent and fixed, but is instead free to move amoeba-like through history." By substituting "the idea of a 'living Constitution'" for the framers' understanding of that document, McDowell lamented, the Court became involved in the "making [of] policy choices," in the "exercis[e] [of] its own will." In so doing—by practicing "judicial activism with a vengeance"—the Court was guilty of "constitutional usurpation," of assuming a power that the Constitution denies to it.[16]

Writing more recently—at a time when conservative Republican efforts to alter the composition of the federal courts had borne fruit—Robert Bork marks a turning point in the conservative attack on the jurisprudence of the Warren Court.[17] The effort to impugn the jurisprudential integrity of the decision identified as the genesis of the Warren Court's constitutional usurpations had ceased to be a mere conservative lament and now functioned as the foundation of a realistic call for change. Bork underscores his agreement with the near-universal understanding that "*Brown* was a great and [morally] correct decision." But he contends that the Court's "very weak opinion" in that case "caused an enormous amount of trouble in the law." By declaring the history of the Fourteenth Amendment inconclusive, the justices indicated that they thought they had to depart "from the original understanding in order to do the socially desirable thing." Bork suggests that "much of the rest of the Warren Court's history may be explained by the lesson it learned from its success in *Brown*"; the justices became convinced of the necessity of a constitutional jurisprudence disconnected from the intentions of the framers, and they developed confidence in the rectitude of their non-originalist decision making across a range of issue areas. This confidence "led to some of the law's most blatantly illegitimate decisions," since the Court, as it did in *Brown,* merely substituted its "own view of morality"—an "ultra-liberal politics"—for that of the framers.[18]

Bork finds this history of the Warren Court's jurisprudence "massively ironic," because he believes that "the result in *Brown* is consistent with, indeed, is compelled by, the original understanding of the fourteenth amendment's equal protection clause." He concedes that "those who ratified the amendment did not think it outlawed segregated education or segregation in any aspect of life." But he contends that "the [originalist's] search is not for a subjective intention"; rather, this method of constitutional interpretation involves the discovery of the "public understanding" that prevailed when the constitutional provision at issue was ratified. With regard to the equal protection clause, "the text itself demonstrates that . . . *equality under law* was the primary goal." When *Brown* reached the Court, "it had been apparent for some time that segregation rarely if ever produced equality. . . . Since equality and segregation were mutually inconsistent, though the ratifiers did not understand that, both could not be honored." "Had the *Brown* opinion been written this way," Bork opines, "its result would have been rooted in the original understanding" and "the Court might not have been encouraged to embark on more adventures in policymaking, which is what it thought it had done in *Brown*."[19]

The obvious problem with Bork's argument is that, by regarding the equal protection clause as an abstract principle that enables judges to consider changed circumstances, his characterization of originalism appears no different from the living Constitution concept that informed the jurisprudence of the Warren Court.[20] But while Bork, among others, fails in his effort to square desegregation with originalism, his characterization of Warren's opinion in *Brown* as a manifestation of a liberal preference for an egalitarian society—a preference made possible by the judicially created notion of a living Constitution—provides a powerful indictment of the foundation of the Warren Court's constitutional revolution.[21] By characterizing *Brown* and its progeny as crassly instrumental rulings, Warren Court critics were and are able to scold the Court for "endeavoring to formulate public policies for which it lacks not only the institutional capacity but, more important, the constitutional legitimacy."[22] At the same time, they avoid having to answer the difficult questions that a constitutive account of Warren's desegregation vote raises, questions stemming from a critique of a political process that failed to prevent the subjugation of a racial minority through law. Indeed, the instrumental characterization of *Brown* enabled Bickel to charge that the Warren Court justices failed to understand that "the idea of [social] progress," which includes an appropriate understanding of minority rights, "is common property." Similarly, McDowell suggested that the justices should have "consider[ed] that the best interests of aggrieved social classes may be better served by preservation of the institutional equilibrium of an emphatically limited Constitution, dedicated to the rule of law, than by the transient opinions of judges, however noble their consciences or senses of 'moral duty' may appear, at a given moment, to be." An instrumental interpretation of *Brown* permits Bork to go so far as to charge that defenders of the Warren Court, who support constitutional decision making that is not grounded in the framers' intentions, "prefer an authoritarian regime with which [they] agree to a democracy with which [they] do not."[23] Bork's failure to specify that the ostensible danger associated with unrestrained judicial review is not authoritarianism but an *insufficient* regard for governmental power should not detract from the force of his (and Bickel's and Kurland's and McDowell's) basic claim: Beginning with *Brown,* the Warren Court engaged in non-originalist—and baldly instrumental—decision making, the illegitimacy of which was a function of the contempt that liberal justices displayed for constitutionally sanctioned democratic rule.

A JURISPRUDENCE OF POLITY AND RIGHTS PRINCIPLES

While no form of originalism manages entirely to preclude exercises of judicial discretion, this method of constitutional interpretation delivers what its defenders promise, namely significant limitations on judging.[24]

As Dennis Goldford observes, "The central point running through all originalist writings is that the Constitution is supposed to provide limits on government through the fixity of its meaning." In that spirit, and contrary to those who defend the notion of a living Constitution, originalists insist "that interpreters should be bound by the writers' and ratifiers' understanding of the constitutional text. . . . The original understanding of the constitutional text in the writing-and-ratifying generation always trumps any different understanding of that text in succeeding generations." While such limits on judging frustrate originalist efforts to justify *Brown,* they provide an effective means for challenging the legitimacy of the Warren Court's constitutional decisions. "In the absence of an originalist anchor," the argument runs (as seen in the writings of Bork and McDowell), "the Court will (1) trespass into the legitimate policy-making domains of the political branches of government and (2) have no constitutional compass but the personal values of the justices who happen to sit on the Court at any given time."[25]

As this study reveals, however, the infusion of the justices' personal policy preferences into the abstract language of the Constitution is not the only alternative to an originalist constitutional jurisprudence. Rather than act on a preference for desegregation in *Brown,* Warren, Black, and Jackson "engage[ed] in a process that consider[ed] past [legal] principles and their application in the world outside the Court." Their behavior demonstrated Ronald Kahn's point that, "when social constructions in past landmark cases are no longer tenable," such as the benign understanding of segregation that informed the holding in *Plessy v. Ferguson,* "landmark cases are ripe for serious modification, if not outright overturning." Likewise, Clark and, probably, Burton and Minton, in responding to the foreign policy concerns of the executive, failed to illustrate an explanatory link between judicial policy preferences and Supreme Court decisions. Clark and especially Jackson also revealed in conference (and, in Jackson's case, in memoranda) that they felt a strong obligation to reconcile the Court's decision with the rule of law. In short, *Brown* demonstrated the concept of the relative autonomy of Supreme Court decision making from personal preference. This phenomenon is a consequence of, among other factors, a judicially perceived "mandate to protect individuals from the tyranny of the state and the majority," and "the requirement [transmitted through judicial socialization] that judges craft their legal rulings according to a 'legal grammar' in which some forms of argument (historical, textual, structural, prudential, and doctrinal) are considered legitimate and others (whim, personal policy preference) are not."[26]

Such noninstrumental interpretations of the justices' desegregation votes complicate the efforts of conservative scholars to dismiss the jurisprudence of the Warren Court because these findings compel us to confront some discomfiting questions about the nature of American politics. Consider once again the scholarship of Ronald Kahn. Unlike the Warren Court's conservative critics, Kahn "argue[s] for a constitutive interpretation of doctrinal change and Supreme Court decisionmaking" during this period of the Court's history. Limiting his focus to the issue of equal protection but going beyond *Brown* and its progeny, he does not view the Warren Court justices as constitutional policy makers; rather, he regards them as judges who engaged in a dialogue with an interpretive community of scholars, jurists, and legal actors over the meaning and application of polity and rights principles. Kahn contends that "in the Warren Court era there was a mismatch between the view of polity held by the Court [i.e., the justices' assumptions regarding the nature of American politics] and that held by the nation and most of the interpretive community." Legal scholars embraced the pluralist assumptions of the political theorists Robert A. Dahl and David B. Truman, who maintained and emphasized the significance of such social and political factors as individual involvement in multiple group memberships, the dispersion of resources throughout society, and the responsiveness of politicians to various client groups including racial minorities. By contrast, the Warren Court "rejected the apologetic pluralism of the day and placed within its jurisprudence a more critical view of the American polity." While mainstream legal thinkers counseled that judges demonstrate marked deference to choices that issue from a political system that is ostensibly open and fair, the justices "argu[ed] that the *failure* of pluralism required that courts enter the political thicket in race and other areas."[27]

Kahn notes that scholars who embrace instrumental assumptions about Supreme Court decision making believe that the uniqueness of the Warren Court was its unprecedented "concern with ethical or rights values, particularly the value of equality, rather than polity principles." These individuals claim that "polity principles, that is, the institutional concerns of the Warren Court, were for the most part irrelevant to its jurisprudence." A richer, noninstrumental understanding of judicial behavior, however, reveals that "the genius of the Warren Court was *not* that it created rights." Rather, in rejecting the pluralism of Dahl and Truman, the Court anticipated the powerful critical pluralist interpretations of American politics that would be "represented [in the late 1960s] in the scholarship of Grant McConnell and Theodore Lowi."[28]

Kahn's critics might contend that his theory of decision making posits an unrealistically heroic role for legal and political scholars, since Supreme Court justices, although members of an elite group, may not have the ability (or interest) to develop sufficient expertise to qualify as competent political theorists. As this book demonstrates, however, there are instances in which the justices cannot help but encounter and participate in substantive discussions about the nature of American politics. This case study reveals the problematic nature of instrumental explanations for the chief justice and some of his brethren in one of the Warren Court's—in fact, the Supreme Court's—most celebrated rulings. Furthermore, in focusing on the dialogue before the Court in *Brown* and by marshaling evidence of Chief Justice Warren's receptiveness to the arguments of the petitioners regarding the oppressive nature of segregation, and thus the need for judicial action in racial discrimination controversies, this book identifies a specific source for the sense of mission that informed Warren's liberal voting record in the area of civil rights.[29] In short, by satisfying a rigorous standard of proof, this study lends credence to Kahn's contention that "a close look at the *Brown* decision . . . suggests that polity principles," that is, a critique of American racial politics, "not just a concern for equality, informed Warren Court constitutional choices."[30] Put another way, this book reveals that baldly instrumental rulings were not an inevitable consequence of the Warren Court's non-originalist decision making. If there is any validity to the contention put forth by Bickel, Kurland, McDowell, and Bork that *Brown* was the origin of the constitutional jurisprudence of the Warren Court, then this narrow case study has the ironic effect of demonstrating that a noninstrumental approach to decision making contributes much to an understanding of a period in the history of the Court during which that institution revolutionized constitutional law across a range of issue areas.

Even if we adopt a more limited view of *Brown*'s significance—that the decision's impact did not extend beyond the area of racial equality—this book's, and Kahn's, constitutive interpretation of Warren's behavior in the case lends weight to the normative considerations that flow from his serious and sympathetic critique of American democracy. The fact that Warren exhibited a deep sense of civic obligation, as opposed to a crass desire to pursue his own self-interest or personal policy preferences, should lead scholars to consider seriously his assessment of the shortcomings of American racial politics. Similarly, such an interpretation of the chief justice's goals suggests that a fair valuation of the Court's racial equality rulings should not be limited to observations regarding the judiciary's institutional deficiencies, which may appear when the Court acts on a broad interpretation of its equitable powers.[31] Scholars should also consider the possibility that Warren's critical analysis of democratic government was superficial. While "the Warren Court's critical view of polity did significantly counter political and social inequality," Kahn explains, "it did not make manifest the effects of deep social, gender, and economic inequality" or "grapple with more complex views of informal discrimination and inequality." Instead, "equal protection doctrine in the Warren Court era centered on inequalities of access to the political system by blacks—denial of the right to vote and to have that vote count the same as any other vote, denial of equal access to schools, courts, and bureaucracies, and other forms of invidious discrimination"—and "was [thus] not far outside the pluralist view of polity that dominated the scholarship of the 1950s to 1960s."[32]

Conservative legal scholars might still maintain the illegitimacy of critical inquiries of these sorts by suggesting that the jurisprudential significance of the ruling that initiated the Warren Court era is tied not only to the issue of whether the justices engaged in instrumental decision making but also to the fact that the Court's opinion in *Brown* was non-originalist—that it established a precedent that contravened the constitutional separation of powers. As Earl Maltz contends, "The most plausible defense of originalism rests on a single axiom: The framers of the Constitution had legitimate authority to make political decisions that would bind future governmental decisionmakers until superseded by judgments made through the [amendment] process specified in the Constitution itself." Or, as Bork declares, "In truth, only the approach of original understanding meets the criteria that any theory of constitutional adjudication must meet in order to possess democratic legitimacy."[33]

But this seems a peculiar objection to raise with regard to *Brown* in view of the basis for the universal sense that, to borrow Bork's words, "*Brown* was a great and correct decision."[34] *Brown*'s iconic status is a consequence of a widespread view that, despite its weak and uninspiring rationale, the decision was the initial thrust in a righteous attack on the evils of white supremacy.[35] (As this book demonstrates, this interpretation of the decision's significance accords with the rationale that informed the desegregation votes of Warren, Black, and Jackson, but which the chief justice left out of the Court's opinion so as not to alienate the South and certain of his colleagues.) The ugliness of the southern response to peaceful civil rights protests in the years following *Brown* alerted Americans to the brutal nature of segregation and thus to the rightness of *Brown*'s result. J. Harvie Wilkinson articulates the contemporary understanding of *Brown*'s contribution to American political culture when he suggests that the decision was "one of those last, great actions whose moral logic seemed so uncomplex and irrefutable" because the "opposition seemed so thoroughly extreme, rooted as it was in notions of racial hegemony and the constitutional premises of John C. Calhoun."[36] In view of this understanding, it is difficult to accede to challenges to the democratic legitimacy of *Brown*. For, if we as a nation respect and admire that de-cision (and, it should be emphasized, we also respect and admire the civil rights workers who suffered on behalf of racial equality) for having reminded us of "the better angels of our nature," then it appears that *we have come to accept and appreciate* the critique of American racial politics contained therein.[37]

To press the point of appropriate critical inquiries, the history of *Brown*'s basis might also inspire us to consider normative analyses of equal protection doctrine that go beyond the matter of whether the judi-ciary should embrace a deeper critical pluralism. In view of the de facto resegregation of American schools and the attendant concentration of poverty in nonwhite institutions, which scholars documented during the 1990s,[38] the analysis presented here should lead reformers to revisit an argument even more discomfiting than Gerald N. Rosenberg's contention that evidence of judicial inefficacy suggests "courts may serve an ideologi-cal function of luring movements for social reform to an institution that is structurally constrained from serving their needs, providing only an il-lusion of change." Rosenberg holds out hope by suggesting that reformers should reroute racial equality claims toward "substantive political battles, where success is possible, [and away from] harmless legal ones where it is not."[39] But considering the possibility that the Cold War concerns of Justice Clark and some of his colleagues were representative of the goals of government officials generally, and thus informed the civil rights poli-cies of the preceding century, the prospects for reform through the nor-mal course of interest group politics seem as nominal as the chances for judge-initiated change under Rosenberg's analysis. In the same way that this book corroborates the thesis that *Brown* was a Cold War imperative, at least for certain members of the Court, the gradual decline in inter-est among politicians in promoting racial equality in the nation's public schools or elsewhere—a lessening of concern that coincided with the attainment of formal equality in the law in the mid-1960s, the increased emphasis given to the Vietnam War as a means to prevail in the Cold War, and, ultimately, the collapse of the Soviet Union in 1991[40]—lends credence to Derrick A. Bell, Jr.'s broader "interest convergence" principle: that American government promotes racial equality only to the degree that doing so benefits whites.[41]

To accept Bell's "interest convergence" principle is to conclude that progress toward fulfilling *Brown*'s promise of educational equality is deeply problematic, not that it is impossible. Developments since the tragedy of 9/11, especially the U.S. government's use of torture against terrorism suspects, may have created circumstances conducive to a convergence of interests among whites and nonwhites. In view of the damage that this policy has done to America's international reputation, it would seem that one of the most effective ways to convince our sympathetic critics (a large proportion of whom are nonwhite) of the seriousness of our commitment to the protection of rights is to demonstrate a meaningful commitment to racial equality at home.

Assuming that expectations for a convergence of racial interests are not far-fetched, would-be reformers should understand that mutual recognition of the need for a renewed commitment to racial equality is no guarantee of cooperation, let alone meaningful reform. Even those individuals whose reformist credentials are unimpeachable differ, sometimes sharply, over the means required to ensure educational equality. Consider Bell's suggestion in 1980 (even before the publication of statistics regarding the resegregation of public education) that equality implies "real educational effectiveness," which may involve not only "the improvement of presently desegregated schools" but also "the creation or preservation of model black schools" where "black children, parents, and teachers can utilize the real cultural strengths of the black community to overcome the many barriers to educational achievement." Bell recognized that most of his colleagues would view his proposal as a "step backward toward the *Plessy* 'separate but equal' era," since the respondents in *Brown* made similar arguments regarding the psychological benefits that segregated settings provide to black children. But, in view of the fact that poverty cuts across racial categories, Bell's critics would be wise to heed his admonition that "programs which concentrate solely on achieving a racial balance" do not necessarily confer equal educational benefits. Bell also provided the most promising avenue for resolving the differences among reformers, and for ensuring that legal changes actually fulfill the promise of *Brown,* when he counseled, "Criticism, as we in the movement for minority rights have every reason to learn, is a synonym for neither cowardice nor capitulation. It may instead bring awareness, always the first step toward overcoming still another barrier in the struggle for racial equality."[42]

NOTES

ABBREVIATIONS

EWP   Earl Warren Papers, Library of Congress.
FFP—Harvard   Felix Frankfurter Papers—Harvard Law School Library.
HHBP   Harold H. Burton Papers, Library of Congress.
HLBP   Hugo L. Black Papers, Library of Congress.
NAACP Papers   National Association for the Advancement of Colored People
                    Papers, Library of Congress.
RHJP   Robert H. Jackson Papers, Library of Congress.
TCCP   Tom C. Clark Papers, University of Texas at Austin, Tarlton Law
                    Library.
WODP   William O. Douglas Papers, Library of Congress.

INTRODUCTION

1. 347 U.S. 483 (1954). The three cases consolidated with *Brown* came from South Carolina (*Briggs v. Elliott*), Virginia (*Davis v. County School Board of Prince Edward County*), and Delaware (*Gebhart v. Belton*). These cases were the result of a long-standing litigation campaign that was itself part of a larger effort on behalf of African Americans by the National Association for the Advancement of Colored People. Ross, *J. E. Spingarn and the Rise of the NAACP,* 160; Kellogg, *NAACP,* 35, 266–71; Tushnet, *The NAACP's Legal Strategy,* 10, 34.

2. 163 U.S. 537 (1896). In *Plessy,* the Supreme Court sustained the constitutionality of a Louisiana statute that required railroads to provide equal-but-separate accommodations to whites and blacks, and forbade persons from occupying rail cars other than those to which their race had been assigned. The Court held that the law, like similar laws establishing separate schools for white and black children, did not violate the equal protection clause of the Fourteenth Amendment. Rather than imply the inferiority of blacks, the Court argued, the law was simply a reasonable exercise of the state's police power to preserve public peace and good order.

3. 347 U.S. 483, 489 (1954). See also Klarman, "An Interpretive History of Modern Equal Protection," 252 n.180.

4. Hockett, "The Battle over *Brown*'s Legitimacy," 31–34. For the sake of clarity, this book refers to the African Americans who challenged school segregation but lost in the lower courts as petitioners (as opposed to appellants), and to the school boards

that defended the practice and won in the lower courts as respondents (as opposed to appellees). The terms are reversed for the parties in the Delaware case, *Gebhart v. Belton*. The Delaware Court of Chancery, while declining to declare school segregation unconstitutional, nevertheless found the facilities at Clayton High School superior to those of the black school and ordered the school board to admit the child of Ethel Belton to the white school. Thus, the school board petitioned the Supreme Court to hear its appeal. For the sake of simplicity, the chapter narratives of this book elide this exception.

5. 347 U.S. 483, 494–95 (1954). Thurgood Marshall became Special Counsel to the NAACP Legal Defense and Educational Fund (LDF) in 1939. He would lead the direct challenge to segregation that culminated in *Brown* after he concluded that the equalization suits that his predecessor, Charles Houston, had pursued at the graduate and professional school level would never result in desegregated schools. Tushnet, *The NAACP's Legal Strategy,* 36, 73, 81–88, 100, 109–10, 114–15; Ware, "*Hocutt,*" 230–31; Kluger, *Simple Justice,* 1:232–33, 276, 366–70, 396–434; Houston, "Educational Inequalities Must Go!"; Houston, "Cracking Closed University Doors"; Marshall, "An Evaluation of Recent Efforts to Achieve Racial Integration in Education," 318–19.

6. Rosen, *The Supreme Court and Social Science,* x–xi, 38–196; Hockett, "The Battle over *Brown's* Legitimacy," 34–37.

7. 347 U.S. 497, 500 (1954).

8. Perry, *The Constitution, the Courts, and Human Rights,* 1; Bork, *The Tempting of America,* 75; Horwitz, *The Warren Court,* 15.

9. Wilkinson, *From* Brown *to* Bakke, 6, 39 (emphasis added). For a listing of sources that testify to *Brown's* greatness, see Klarman, "*Brown,* Racial Change, and the Civil Rights Movement," 8 n.2. For a sense of the lack of regard that contemporary scholars have for Warren's opinion in *Brown,* see Balkin, ed., *What Brown v. Board of Education Should Have Said.*

10. Black, "The Lawfulness of the Segregation Decisions," 429–30. See also Hockett, "The Battle over *Brown's* Legitimacy," 37–49.

11. For general discussions of the rulings of the Warren Court, see Powe, *The Warren Court and American Politics,* and Kelly, Harbison, and Belz, *The American Constitution,* 593–662.

12. *Green v. County School Board of New Kent County,* 391 U.S. 430 (1968).

13. See, especially, Kluger, *Simple Justice,* and Tushnet, *The NAACP's Legal Strategy.*

14. Kluger, *Simple Justice,* 2:737–897; Tushnet, "What Really Happened in *Brown*"; Schwartz, *Super Chief,* 72–127; Hutchinson, "Unanimity and Desegregation."

15. See, respectively, Dahl, "Decision-Making in a Democracy," 293–94, and Shapiro, "The Supreme Court," 179–95.

16. See, respectively, Dudziak, "Desegregation as a Cold War Imperative"; Clayton, *The Politics of Justice,* 125–31; Graber, "The Nonmajoritarian Difficulty," 61–73; and McMahon, *Reconsidering Roosevelt on Race.*

17. Segal and Spaeth, *The Supreme Court and the Attitudinal Model,* 237; Klarman, *From Jim Crow to Civil Rights,* 1–7, 171–343.

18. "Ruling to Figure in '54 Campaign," *New York Times,* 18 May 1954, Late City edition; "Experts Approve Timetable on Bias," *New York Times,* 18 May 1954, Late City edition.

19. See, e.g., Bickel, *The Supreme Court and the Idea of Progress;* Kurland, "'*Brown v. Board of Education* Was the Beginning'"; and McDowell, *Equity and the Constitution.*

20. Caldeira and Wright, "Lobbying for Justice."

21. Bork, *The Tempting of America,* 72–78.

22. Smith, "Political Jurisprudence," 107 (quoted); Graber, "Legal, Strategic or Legal Strategy."

23. The insights of Glendon Schubert inform the attitudinal model. See Schubert, *The Judicial Mind,* and Segal and Spaeth, *The Supreme Court and the Attitudinal Model,* 67–68.

24. The insights of Walter Murphy inform the strategic model. See Murphy, *Elements of Judicial Strategy,* and Epstein and Knight, *The Choices Justices Make,* xi–xiii.

25. The insights of James March, Johan Olsen, and Rogers Smith inform the constitutive model. See March and Olsen, "The New Institutionalism"; Smith, "Political Jurisprudence," 90–96; Gillman, *The Constitution Besieged;* Kahn, *The Supreme Court and Constitutional Theory;* Keck, *The Most Activist Supreme Court in History;* Keck, "Party, Policy, or Duty"; and Whittington, "Congress before the *Lochner* Court."

26. The "political regimes" approach draws on the constitutive sensibility that informs the work of Rogers Smith, and the "political jurisprudence" of Robert Dahl and Martin Shapiro. See Smith, "Political Jurisprudence"; Dahl, "Decision-Making in a Democracy"; Shapiro, "Political Jurisprudence"; Clayton and May, "A Political Regimes Approach," 242; Gillman, "How Political Parties Can Use the Courts"; Whittington, "'Interpose Your Friendly Hand'"; and Whittington, *Political Foundations of Judicial Supremacy.*

27. See, e.g., Jackson, *The Struggle for Judicial Supremacy;* Black, *A Constitutional Faith;* and Frankfurter, *Mr. Justice Holmes and the Supreme Court.*

28. Klarman, *From Jim Crow to Civil Rights,* 1–7, 171–343.

29. Dudziak, "Desegregation as a Cold War Imperative"; Dudziak, *Cold War Civil Rights,* 79–114. The Supreme Court did not invite the Truman administration to participate in oral argument in 1952. After ordering that the case be reargued, the Court invited the Eisenhower administration to submit a new brief and participate in oral argument. Kluger, *Simple Justice,* 1:347–48; 2:779, 821–24, 948–52.

30. See Dahl, "Decision-Making in a Democracy," 293–94; Shapiro, "The Supreme Court," 179–95; and Clayton, *The Politics of Justice,* 125–31.

31. McMahon, *Reconsidering Roosevelt on Race.*

32. Graber, "The Nonmajoritarian Difficulty," 61–73.

1. BARRIERS TO DESEGREGATION

1. See, e.g., Black, *A Constitutional Faith;* Frankfurter, *Mr. Justice Holmes and the Supreme Court;* Jackson, *The Struggle for Judicial Supremacy;* and Robert H. Jackson to Charles Fairman, 13 March 1950, 2, RHJP, Box 12. For a discussion of the period in the Court's history during which the justices shifted from considering challenges to the constitutionality of governmental efforts to regulate the economy to considering challenges to the constitutionality of governmental efforts to regulate non-proprietarian rights, see McCloskey, *The Modern Supreme Court,* 129–56, and *The American Supreme Court,* 101–219.

2. 163 U.S. 537 (1896).

3. 275 U.S. 78, 82 (quoting the Mississippi Constitution), 85–86 (1927).

4. Brief for Appellants, *Brown v. Board of Education of Topeka,* 1952, 10–12 (12 quoted; emphasis added), NAACP Papers, Box II-B-138. In *McLaurin v. Oklahoma State Regents for Higher Education,* 339 U.S. 637, 641 (1950), the Court ruled that the segregation of a black student *within* an all-white graduate institution "impair[s] and inhibit[s] [that student's] ability to study, to engage in discussions and exchange views with other students, and, in general, to learn his profession." And, in a companion case, *Sweatt v. Painter,* 339 U.S. 629, 634 (1950), the justices, in denying the comparability of Texas's segregated law schools, took note of "qualities which are incapable of objective measurement but which make for greatness in a law school." These qualities include the "reputation of the faculty, experience of the administration, position and influence of the alumni, standing in the community, [and] traditions and prestige."

5. Friedman, ed., *Argument,* 32; Brief for Appellees, *Brown v. Board of Education of Topeka,* 1952, 22, 23 (quoting *Plessy v. Ferguson*), 24, NAACP Papers, Box II-B-138.

6. Brief for Appellees, *Brown v. Board of Education of Topeka,* 1952, 25, 26 (quoting *Sweatt v. Painter*), 27–28, NAACP Papers, Box II-B-138.

7. Friedman, ed., *Argument,* 72.

8. Nowak, Rotunda, and Young, *Constitutional Law,* 525.

9. Appellants' Statement as to Jurisdiction, *Brown v. Board of Education of Topeka,* 1951, 12–13, NAACP Papers, Box II-B-138; Appendix to Appellants' Briefs, *Brown v. Board of Education of Topeka, Briggs v. Elliott,* and *Davis v. County School Board of Prince Edward County,* 1952, 12, NAACP Papers, Box II-B-138.

10. Appendix to Appellants' Briefs, *Brown v. Board of Education of Topeka, Briggs v. Elliott,* and *Davis v. County School Board of Prince Edward County,* 1952, 13–16, NAACP Papers, Box II-B-138.

11. Brief for Appellants, *Brown v. Board of Education of Topeka,* 1952, 5, 10, NAACP Papers, Box II-B-138; Appendix to Appellants' Briefs, *Brown v. Board of Education of Topeka, Briggs v. Elliott,* and *Davis v. County School Board of Prince Edward County,* 1952, 10, NAACP Papers, Box II-B-138.

12. Friedman, ed., *Argument,* 90–91.

13. Newby, *Challenge to the Court,* 37–38 (quoting respondents' brief).

14. Friedman, ed., *Argument,* 58–59; Kluger, *Simple Justice,* 2:689 (quoting respondents' brief).

15. Newby, *Challenge to the Court,* 37–38 (quoting respondents' brief); Kluger, *Simple Justice,* 2:689–90.

16. Friedman, ed., *Argument,* 59–60, 93.

17. Ibid., 61.

18. 320 U.S. 81 (1943). In *Hirabayashi,* the Court, despite noting that racial distinctions are "odious to a free people," upheld wartime curfews restricting the movement of Japanese-Californians on the West Coast.

19. 323 U.S. 214 (1944). In *Korematsu,* the Court, despite noting that racial restrictions are "immediately suspect," upheld the federal government's wartime relocation and internment of West Coast Japanese-Californians to inland detention centers. Speaking for the Court, Justice Hugo Black said, "It should be noted, to begin with, that all legal restrictions which curtail the civil rights of a single racial group are immediately suspect. This is not to say that all such restrictions are unconstitutional. It is to say that courts

must subject them to the most rigid scrutiny. Pressing public necessity may sometimes justify the existence of such restrictions; racial antagonism never can." Ibid., 216.

20. Friedman, ed., *Argument,* 114, 116–17, 120–21, 284 (116–17, 120 quoted). See also Appellants' Statement as to Jurisdiction, *Brown v. Board of Education of Topeka,* 1951, 12, NAACP Papers, Box II-B-138; Brief for Appellants, *Brown v. Board of Education of Topeka,* 1952, 7, NAACP Papers, Box II-B-138; and Brief for Appellants, *Brown v. Board of Education of Topeka, Briggs v. Elliott, Davis v. County School Board of Prince Edward County,* and for Respondents in *Gebhart v. Belton* on Reargument, 1953, 22–24, NAACP Papers, Box II-B-142.

21. Friedman, ed., *Argument,* 100–101, 162–63.

22. Ibid., 85, 89, 97, 133–34, 141.

23. Ibid., 66–68, 92–93, 115 (quoted), 120–21.

24. Ibid., 63–64, 172–73 (quoted).

25. Ibid., 34. See also Hockett, *New Deal Justice,* 67–140.

26. Kluger, *Simple Justice,* 2:689 (quoting respondents' brief); Friedman, ed., *Argument,* 55.

27. In its order for the rehearing, *Brown v. Board of Education of Topeka,* 345 U.S. 972 (1953), the Court announced five questions that would serve as the focus of discussion:

1. What evidence is there that the Congress which submitted and the State legislatures and conventions which ratified the Fourteenth Amendment contemplated or did not contemplate, understood or did not understand, that it would abolish segregation in public schools?
2. If neither the Congress in submitting nor the States in ratifying the Fourteenth Amendment understood that compliance with it would require the immediate abolition of segregation in public schools, was it nevertheless the understanding of the framers of the Amendment
    (a) that future Congresses might, in the exercise of their power under section 5 of the Amendment, abolish such segregation, or
    (b) that it would be within the judicial power, in light of future conditions, to construe the Amendment as abolishing such segregation of its own force?
3. On the assumption that the answers to questions 2 (a) and (b) do not dispose of the issue, is it within the judicial power, in construing the Amendment, to abolish segregation in public schools?
4. Assuming it is decided that segregation in public schools violates the Fourteenth Amendment
    (a) would a decree necessarily follow providing that, within the limits set by normal geographic school districting, Negro children should forthwith be admitted to schools of their choice, or
    (b) may this Court, in the exercise of its equity powers, permit an effective gradual adjustment to be brought about from existing systems to a system not based on color distinctions?
5. On the assumption on which questions 4 (a) and (b) are based, and assuming further that this Court will exercise its equity powers to the end described in question 4 (b),
    (a) should this Court formulate detailed decrees in these cases;
    (b) if so, what specific issues should the decrees reach;

(c) should this Court appoint a special master to hear evidence with a view to recommending specific terms for such decrees;

(d) should this Court remand to the courts of first instance with directions to frame decrees in these cases, and if so what general directions should the decrees of this Court include and what procedures should the courts of first instance follow in arriving at the specific terms of more detailed decrees?

Felix Frankfurter was in large measure responsible for formulating these questions. See Frankfurter, Memorandum for the Conference, Re: The Segregation Cases, 27 May 1953, FFP—Harvard, Part II, Reel 4; and Frankfurter, Memorandum for the Conference, Re: The Segregation Cases, 4 June 1953, EWP, Box 570.

28. Kluger, *Simple Justice,* 2:829–43.

29. In short, the petitioners implicitly conceded that they could not provide compelling evidence to support their position as it pertained to the first question in the Court's reargument order. See note 27, above.

30. Brief for Appellants, *Brown v. Board of Education of Topeka, Briggs v. Elliott, Davis v. County School Board of Prince Edward County,* and for Respondents in *Gebhart v. Belton* on Reargument, 1953, 120 (quoted), 123–24, NAACP Papers, Box II-B-142.

31. In short, the petitioners sought to provide evidence that supported their position as it pertained to question 2(b) of the Court's reargument order. See note 27, above.

32. Brief for Appellants, *Brown v. Board of Education of Topeka, Briggs v. Elliott, Davis v. County School Board of Prince Edward County,* and for Respondents in *Gebhart v. Belton* on Reargument, 1953, 18 (quoted), 120, NAACP Papers, Box II-B-142.

33. Gillman, "The Collapse of Constitutional Originalism."

34. Brief for Appellants, *Brown v. Board of Education of Topeka, Briggs v. Elliott, Davis v. County School Board of Prince Edward County,* and for Respondents in *Gebhart v. Belton* on Reargument, 1953, 119, 93, 68, NAACP Papers, Box II-B-142.

35. Ibid., 17–18, 91, 104–6, 114–19 (17–18, 91 quoted).

36. Ibid., 19, 139–82 (19, 142–43, 158 quoted).

37. Friedman, ed., *Argument,* 212.

38. Ibid., 212–13.

39. Ibid., 207–11.

40. Ibid., 237–38.

41. Ibid., 240–52.

42. Put another way, the justices had to answer in the affirmative the third question that they had put to the parties in the reargument order. See note 27, above.

43. Brief for Appellants, *Brown v. Board of Education of Topeka, Briggs v. Elliott, Davis v. County School Board of Prince Edward County,* and for Respondents in *Gebhart v. Belton* on Reargument, 1953, 35, 32, 33, 35–36, NAACP Papers, Box II-B-142.

44. Ibid., 27–30, 48–50.

45. Ibid., 22–24, 50–65. In chapter 4, I elaborate on the petitioners' historical argument regarding the motives that informed segregation laws.

46. Friedman, ed., *Argument,* 214–15.

47. Ibid., 198; Brief for Appellants, *Brown v. Board of Education of Topeka, Briggs v. Elliott, Davis v. County School Board of Prince Edward County,* and for Respondents in *Gebhart v. Belton* on Reargument, 1953, 33 (quoting *Slaughter House Cases* and *Strauder v. West Virginia;* petitioners' emphasis removed and mine added), NAACP

Papers, Box II-B-142. See also *Slaughter House Cases,* 83 U.S. 36, 81 (1873), and *Strauder v. West Virginia,* 100 U.S. 303, 307–8 (1880).

48. Friedman, ed., *Argument,* 201–4.

49. Ibid., 215.

50. Ibid., 215–16, 227–30, 227. For cases in which Justices Holmes and Brandeis called for heightened judicial scrutiny of governmental infringement of the freedoms of speech and press, see *Abrams v. United States,* 250 U.S. 616 (1919); *Gitlow v. New York,* 268 U.S. 652 (1925); and *Whitney v. California,* 274 U.S. 357 (1927).

51. See note 27, above.

52. Brief for Appellants, *Brown v. Board of Education of Topeka, Briggs v. Elliott, Davis v. County School Board of Prince Edward County,* and for Respondents in *Gebhart v. Belton* on Reargument, 1953, 190–97 (194 quoted), NAACP Papers, Box II-B-142.

53. Friedman, ed., *Argument,* 252–58 (253 quoted). See also Brief for the United States as Amicus Curiae, *Brown v. Board of Education of Topeka, Briggs v. Elliott, Davis v. County School Board of Prince Edward County, Bolling v. Sharpe,* and *Gebhart v. Belton,* 1952, in Kurland and Casper, eds., *Landmark Briefs and Arguments,* 49:142–47; and Supplemental Brief for the United States on Reargument, *Brown v. Board of Education of Topeka, Briggs v. Elliott, Davis v. County School Board of Prince Edward County, Bolling v. Sharpe,* and *Gebhart v. Belton,* 1953, in ibid., 49:1018–53.

54. See note 27, above.

55. Friedman, ed., *Argument,* 216.

56. Kluger, *Simple Justice,* 2:856–57, 922. The reargument of the desegregation controversy was concluded on December 9, 1953, and the Supreme Court announced its decision in *Brown* on May 17, 1954.

57. "Reaction of South," *New York Times,* 18 May 1954, Late City edition; "Ruling to Figure in '54 Campaign," *New York Times,* 18 May 1954, Late City edition.

58. Congressional Record, Senate, vol. 102, part 4, p. 4515, 12 March 1956. See also Fairman, "Foreword: The Attack on the Segregation Cases," and Keck, *The Most Activist Supreme Court in History,* 50–51.

59. "A.F.L. Chief Hails Court," *New York Times,* 18 May 1954, Late City edition; "Historians Laud Court's Decision," *New York Times,* 18 May 1954, Late City edition; "Editorial Excerpts from the Nation's Press on Segregation Ruling," *New York Times,* 18 May 1954, Late City edition.

60. Hand, *The Bill of Rights,* 18–19, 29–30, 54–55; Gunther, *Learned Hand,* 649–55 (655 quoted).

61. Wechsler, "Toward Neutral Principles of Constitutional Law," 31–34, 25. For other contemporaneous responses to the Court's use of social science evidence, see Ball, "Lawyers and Social Scientists"; Garfinkel, "Social Science Evidence"; and Van den Haag, "Social Science Testimony." See also Horwitz, *The Transformation of American Law,* 258–68; Keck, *The Most Activist Supreme Court in History,* 57–58; and Hockett, "The Battle over *Brown*'s Legitimacy," 34–36.

2. THE ATTITUDES OF THE JUSTICES

1. Schubert, *The Judicial Mind,* 3–21 (8, 10 quoted). See also Pritchett, *The Roosevelt Court;* Clayton, "The Supreme Court and Political Jurisprudence," 22–24; Segal and Spaeth, *The Supreme Court and the Attitudinal Model,* 64–69; and Somit and Tanenhaus,

The Development of Political Science, 173–94. Schubert and Pritchett follow the lead of Oliver Wendell Holmes, Jr., Roscoe Pound, and the Legal Realists. See Holmes, *The Common Law,* 5; Holmes, "The Path of the Law," 465–68; Pound, "Mechanical Jurisprudence"; Pound, "The Scope and Purpose of Sociological Jurisprudence"; Llewellyn, "Some Realism about Realism"; Frank, *Law and the Modern Mind;* and Purcell, *The Crisis of Democratic Theory,* 74–94, 159–78.

2. Schubert, *The Judicial Mind Revisited,* 159.

3. Rohde and Spaeth, *Supreme Court Decision Making,* 72–74. See also Clayton, "The Supreme Court and Political Jurisprudence," 24; Maltzman, Spriggs, and Wahlbeck, "Strategy and Judicial Choice," 45; Segal and Spaeth, *The Supreme Court and the Attitudinal Model,* 69–72, 237–41; and Segal and Spaeth, *The Supreme Court and the Attitudinal Model Revisited,* 92–96.

4. Segal and Spaeth, *The Supreme Court and the Attitudinal Model,* 242–43, 255.

5. Ibid., 17–18, 64–66, 255, 65.

6. Baum, *The Puzzle of Judicial Behavior,* 25.

7. Shapiro, *Law and Politics in the Supreme Court,* 14; Schubert, *The Judicial Mind Revisited,* xi–xii.

8. Most of this book is devoted to demonstrating that instrumental decision making is not the only alternative to judicial decision making based strictly on law.

9. See Segal and Spaeth, *The Supreme Court and the Attitudinal Model,* 246–47.

10. Shapiro, *Law and Politics in the Supreme Court,* 14; Tate, "Personal Attribute Models of the Voting Behavior," 365.

11. Rosenberg, *The Hollow Hope,* 107–69 (157, 169 quoted). For responses to Rosenberg's findings regarding the impact of the Supreme Court, see a number of the contributions in Schultz, ed., *Leveraging the Law.*

12. Klarman, "Rethinking the Civil Rights and Civil Liberties Revolutions," 6–7, 32, 7. For Klarman's discussion of the impact of *Brown,* see Klarman, "*Brown,* Racial Change, and the Civil Rights Movement," 85–149, and Klarman, *From Jim Crow to Civil Rights,* 385–442.

13. Klarman, *From Jim Crow to Civil Rights,* 5–6 (quoted; emphasis added), 446–47.

14. Klarman, "Rethinking the Civil Rights and Civil Liberties Revolutions," 16 n.72, 16, 2, 17–18. The idea that the Court is not a countermajoritarian institution did not originate with Klarman. See Dahl, "Decision-Making in a Democracy."

15. Klarman, "Rethinking the Civil Rights and Civil Liberties Revolutions," 19; Klarman, "Civil Rights Law," 456.

16. Klarman, *From Jim Crow to Civil Rights,* 100, 105–12; Klarman, "Rethinking the Civil Rights and Civil Liberties Revolutions," 33–34; Klarman, "*Brown,* Racial Change, and the Civil Rights Movement," 30–31, 56–57, 60–61, 64–65; McAdam, *Political Process and the Development of Black Insurgency,* 77–80, 94–98.

17. Klarman, "*Brown,* Racial Change, and the Civil Rights Movement," 16–18, 20–21, 23–29, 70–71; Klarman, "Rethinking the Civil Rights and Civil Liberties Revolutions," 34; Klarman, *From Jim Crow to Civil Rights,* 113, 188; Dudziak, "Desegregation as a Cold War Imperative," 72–73.

18. Klarman, "Rethinking the Civil Rights and Civil Liberties Revolutions," 34;

Klarman, "*Brown*, Racial Change, and the Civil Rights Movement," 50; Klarman, *From Jim Crow to Civil Rights*, 176–77, 185.

19. Klarman, "*Brown* at 50," 1620–21; Klarman, "*Brown*, Racial Change, and the Civil Rights Movement," 34–35; Klarman, "Rethinking the Civil Rights and Civil Liberties Revolutions," 33; Klarman, *From Jim Crow to Civil Rights*, 185–90.

20. Klarman, "Rethinking the Civil Rights and Civil Liberties Revolutions," 8; Klarman, *From Jim Crow to Civil Rights*, 309; Gallup, *The Gallup Poll*, 2:1250; Klarman, "*Brown*, Racial Change, and the Civil Rights Movement," 71 (quoted).

21. Klarman, *From Jim Crow to Civil Rights*, 308 (quoted; emphasis added), 448–49; Klarman, "*Brown* at 50," 1619.

22. Klarman, *From Jim Crow to Civil Rights*, 308, 447, 452, 309.

23. McMahon, *Reconsidering Roosevelt on Race*, 205.

24. Klarman, *From Jim Crow to Civil Rights*, 299, 304. See also Murphy, *Wild Bill*, 72–175; Parrish, *Felix Frankfurter and His Times*; Urofsky, *Felix Frankfurter*, 1–44; Hockett, *New Deal Justice*, 141–68; Hockett, "Justice Robert H. Jackson, the Supreme Court, and the Nuremberg Trial"; and Robert H. Jackson to Charles Fairman, 13 March 1950, RHJP, Box 12. In chapter 4, I challenge Klarman's selective reading of Jackson's letter to Fairman.

25. Klarman, *From Jim Crow to Civil Rights*, 294, 300, 302, 310. See also Klarman, "Civil Rights Law," 444.

26. Klarman, *From Jim Crow to Civil Rights*, 299. See also Segal and Spaeth, *The Supreme Court and the Attitudinal Model*, 246–47, 252; Gugin and St. Clair, *Sherman Minton*; and Berry, *Stability, Security, and Continuity*.

27. Klarman, *From Jim Crow to Civil Rights*, 195, 298–99. See also Abraham, *Justices and Presidents*, 211–13.

28. Klarman, *From Jim Crow to Civil Rights*, 297.

29. Gallup, *The Gallup Poll*, 2:1250. The poll did not distinguish between southern and border states.

30. Tate, "Personal Attribute Models of the Voting Behavior," 363–65. See also Tate and Handberg, "Time Binding and Theory Building"; Baum, *The Puzzle of Judicial Behavior*, 25–26; and Segal and Spaeth, *The Supreme Court and the Attitudinal Model*, 231. For a discussion of the concept of judicial role orientation—that is, the idea that a justice's conception of the judicial role can serve as an intervening variable between his values or policy preferences and his votes in the cases before him—see Pritchett, *Civil Liberties and the Vinson Court*, 14–17, 186–92; Gibson, "Judges' Role Orientations, Attitudes, and Decisions"; and Gibson, "The Role Concept in Judicial Research."

31. Tate, "Personal Attribute Models of the Voting Behavior," 358–60 (emphasis in original). Tate explains that "limitations on available, comparable decision data restrict[ed] this analysis to the 25 justices serving on the Supreme Court from the beginning of the 1946–47 term to the end of the 1977–78 term." And, with regard to the decisions examined, he notes that "over two-thirds of all decisions rendered since 1946 have been unambiguously classifiable" as either civil rights and civil liberties cases or economic rights cases. By contrast, "no other issue accounted for as much as one-sixth of all decisions." Ibid., 356.

32. Ibid., 363, 366. In contrast to much previous work that used justices' background characteristics to explain voting behavior, Tate explains, his "research paid more

attention to identifying and including significant measurable attributes relating to the justices' birth and socialization, career, age and tenure, and partisanship." As important, the study "paid close attention to the operationalization of indicators for the attributes included." For example, "multiple indicators of important attributes were constructed and tested for their predictive efficacy and statistical stability." Ibid., 361, 363.

33. Ibid., 362 (italics omitted).

34. For discussions of President Truman's approach to civil rights, see Billington, "Civil Rights, President Truman, and the South"; Berman, *The Politics of Civil Rights in the Truman Administration;* Martin, *Civil Rights and the Crisis of Liberalism,* 65–91; and McCoy and Reutten, *Quest and Response.* For treatments of Truman's approach to civil liberties, see Longaker, *The Presidency and Individual Liberties,* and Westin and Hayden, "Presidents and Civil Liberties."

35. Nieman, *Promises to Keep,* 141.

36. McMahon, *Reconsidering Roosevelt on Race,* 120–27; Fassett, *New Deal Justice,* 17–19, 22–31, 82–206.

37. Hockett, *New Deal Justice,* 67–94.

38. Segal and Spaeth, *The Supreme Court and the Attitudinal Model,* 232.

39. Ibid., 233, 232. The specific counterexample to which Segal and Spaeth refer is Tate and Handberg, "Time Building and Theory Building." Tate begins his earlier study of personal attribute models by acknowledging Sheldon Goldman's and Austin Sarat's critique of efforts to use attribute models to explain judicial behavior. But Tate presents his research as evidence that attribute models are not doomed to fail. Tate, "Personal Attribute Models of the Voting Behavior," 355. See also Goldman and Sarat, eds., *American Court Systems,* 374.

40. Segal et al., "Ideological Values and the Votes of U.S. Supreme Court Justices Revisited." The justices selected for study include the seven Roosevelt and four Truman nominees (whose service extended beyond the start of the Vinson Court) through the two George H. W. Bush appointees.

41. Segal and Cover, "Ideological Values and the Votes of U.S. Supreme Court Justices," 559–61 (emphasis added). Segal and Cover add, "In a world more attuned to the needs of researchers, Supreme Court justices would annually complete attitude questionnaires on each issue the Court would consider during the year. Neither this nor a single questionnaire completed at each justice's appointment are likely to happen soon. We must turn instead to indirect methods of measuring the ideological values of justices. Some form of content analysis is needed." Ibid., 560. See also Segal et al., "Ideological Values and the Votes of U.S. Supreme Court Justices Revisited," 812–13.

42. Liberal statements included those ascribing support for the rights of defendants in criminal cases, women and racial minorities in equality cases, and the individual against the government in privacy and First Amendment cases. Conservative statements were those with an opposite direction in each of these issue areas. General mentions of a nominee's liberalism, progressivism, or identification with the Democratic party, Franklin Roosevelt, or the New Deal were coded as liberal, while identifications with conservatism or the Republican party were coded as conservative. Moderate statements included those that explicitly ascribe moderation to the nominees, or those that ascribe both liberal and conservative values. Segal et al., "Ideological Values and the Votes of U.S. Supreme Court Justices Revisited," 813–15.

See also Segal and Cover, "Ideological Values and the Votes of U.S. Supreme Court Justices," 559.

43. Segal and his colleagues define the civil liberties category as "cases involving criminal procedure, civil rights, First Amendment, due process, attorneys, and privacy." In this category, they identify liberal decisions as those "that favor the criminally ac-cused, the civil liberties/rights claimant, indigents, and Native Americans, and that are against the government in due process and privacy litigation." They define the economic category as cases involving "labor unions, commercial business activity (plus litigation involving injured people or things), employee actions vis-à-vis employers, zoning regula-tions, and governmental regulation of corruption other than that involving campaign spending." Here, liberal decisions include "pro-union votes against both individuals and the government, progovernment votes against challenges to its regulatory authority, and also procompetition, antibusiness, proliability, proinjured person, and probankrupt votes." Segal, et al., "Ideological Values and the Votes of U.S. Supreme Court Justices Revisited," 815.

44. Ibid., 812, 815–23 (812, 815, 822 quoted).

45. Cornell Clayton questions Segal's measurement technique itself when he ob-serves, "Newspaper accounts are an indirect measure of attitudes. More importantly, newspaper accounts of a prospective justice's views usually rely upon past voting records in lower courts or the nominee's self-professed agreement or disagreement with past Court decisions. Thus, the problem of circularity has not been removed." Clayton, "The Supreme Court and Political Jurisprudence," 39–40 n.3.

46. Gallup, *The Gallup Poll,* 2:782–83.

47. Ibid., 782.

48. Berman, *The Politics of Civil Rights in the Truman Administration,* 41–78, 83–84, 157–58; McCoy and Reutten, *Quest and Response,* 87–91, 99–100, 178–80.

49. Gallup, *The Gallup Poll,* 2:810. This poll did not contain a question regarding lynching.

50. The responses that the poll listed were preventing war, keeping out of war (16 percent); unemployment (12 percent); high cost of living (11 percent); foreign pol-icy problems, Russia, China, feeding Europe, etc. (11 percent); high cost of govern-ment, government waste and inefficiency (9 percent); communistic trend (7 percent); labor-management problems (6 percent); housing (5 percent); recession (5 percent); others, no opinion (18%). Ibid., 857.

51. Ibid., 1118.

52. Berman, *The Politics of Civil Rights in the Truman Administration,* 41–78, 116–18, 172–73; McCoy and Reutten, *Quest and Response,* 79–95, 129–30, 218–20; Tush-net, *The NAACP's Legal Strategy,* 125–32; Kluger, *Simple Justice,* 1:326–37, 347–48.

53. Tushnet, *The NAACP's Legal Strategy,* 82–137.

54. Klarman, *From Jim Crow to Civil Rights,* 173–96 (190 quoted; emphasis added).

55. Newspaper editorials identified Robert Jackson and Hugo Black as liberals. But Segal and his colleagues concede that "Jackson's score . . . is more liberal than antici-pated." Segal et al., "Ideological Values and the Votes of U.S. Supreme Court Justices Revisited," 817.

56. Segal and his colleagues note that, while their study of newspaper editorials regarding Supreme Court nominees "identified as liberal support for equal protection,

First Amendment freedoms, and procedural rights for the accused criminals," "such mentions were few and far between" in the 1930s and 1940s. "The only citations to civil rights issues came in the *St. Louis Post-Dispatch,* which noted Clark's opposition to civil rights . . . , and the *Chicago Tribune,* which mentioned the Ku Klux Klan's support for Black. . . . The sole citations to First Amendment freedoms accompanied a discussion of Minton's introduction of the 'Press Gag Bill of 1938' (the *Los Angeles Times* . . .) and Rutledge's support for religious freedom (the *St. Louis Post-Dispatch* . . .)." "Editorials," Segal and his colleagues explain, "tended to focus on the pressing problems of the day, most of which were economic in nature." Ibid., 814–15.

57. See chapter 4, below, where I suggest that Earl Warren's failure to attack segregation in a number of speeches that he gave as a national political figure provides strong reason to doubt that he favored desegregation when he participated in *Brown.*

58. Robert Jackson was the exception. See this chapter, above, and chapter 4, below.

59. Epstein et al., "Ideological Drift among Supreme Court Justices," 1489–90, 1494–95. See also Ulmer, "The Longitudinal Behavior of Hugo Lafayette Black," and Epstein et al., "Do Political Preferences Change?"

60. Epstein et al., "Ideological Drift among Supreme Court Justices," 1503–4. The preference measurement method that Epstein and her colleagues use is described in Martin and Quinn, "Dynamic Ideal Point Estimation." A discussion of this method is beyond the scope of this book (and the competence of the author).

61. Epstein et al., "Do Political Preferences Change?" 816.

62. Epstein et al., "On the Peril of Drawing Inferences," 174–76 (quoted); Epstein et al., "Ideological Drift among Supreme Court Justices," 1504–16.

63. See chapter 4, below.

3. LAW, ANTICIPATED VIOLENCE, AND LOYALTY TO THE COURT

1. In the next chapter, I examine the possibility of sincere legal behavior with regard to Chief Justice Warren and Justices Black and Jackson.

2. Murphy, *Elements of Judicial Strategy,* 1, 12. See also Clayton, "The Supreme Court and Political Jurisprudence," 23–24, and Epstein and Knight, "Walter F. Murphy."

3. Clayton, "The Supreme Court and Political Jurisprudence," 24, 30–31 (quoted); Gillman and Clayton, "Beyond Judicial Attitudes," 5 (quoted); Epstein and Knight, *The Choices Justices Make,* xiii; Maltzman, Spriggs, and Wahlbeck, "Strategy and Judicial Choice." For a discussion of the constitutive variant of the new institutionalism, see chapter 4, below.

4. Epstein and Knight, *The Choices Justices Make,* 157–58, 163–77 (157 quoted). Cf. Segal and Spaeth, *The Supreme Court and the Attitudinal Model Revisited,* 97–110, 312–56.

5. Murphy, *Elements of Judicial Strategy,* 20, 183, 187 (187 quoted). See also Epstein and Knight, *The Choices Justices Make,* 45.

6. Epstein and Knight, *The Choices Justices Make,* 138–45 (141, 144 quoted). See also Murphy, *Elements of Judicial Strategy,* 123–75, and Hamilton, Jay, and Madison, *The Federalist,* 504 (Essay #78).

7. Murphy, *Elements of Judicial Strategy,* 37. Other endogenous constraints on Supreme Court policy making include the Court's norms and policies relating to agenda

setting and opinion assignment. Maltzman, Spriggs, and Wahlbeck, "Strategy and Judicial Choice," 51–57.

8. Murphy, *Elements of Judicial Strategy,* 43–54 (43–44, 49 quoted).

9. Ibid., 46, 54–68 (54, 56, 46 quoted).

10. Ibid., 46. As Howard Gillman notes, such behavior is "not properly viewed as strategic in the sense of personal preference maximizing" since it "more closely resembles altruism than selfishness." Gillman, "The Court as an Idea," 81.

11. Burton, Bench Memorandum Book on Segregation Cases, Conference Notes, 13 December 1952, HHBP, Box 337; Clark, Conference Notes, n.d., TCCP, Box A27; Kluger, *Simple Justice,* 2:769.

12. Chief Justice Vinson expressed both legal and extralegal concerns over a desegregation ruling. Burton, Bench Memorandum Book on Segregation Cases, Conference Notes, 13 December 1952, HHBP, Box 337; Jackson, Conference Notes, 12 [*sic*] December 1952, RHJP, Box 184; Douglas, Conference Notes, 13 December 1952, WODP, Box 1150. Justice Douglas kept separate conference note sheets for the state and federal desegregation cases. Since the notes for both groups of cases are found in the same box, and the total number of typed pages is so few, I refer in my references only to Douglas's "conference notes." Also, considerable overlap exists in the substance of the justices' conference notes. For the reader's convenience, I have identified only the immediate sources of the quotations.

13. Jackson, Conference Notes, 12 [*sic*] December 1952, RHJP, Box 184 (quoted first, third, and fifth); Burton, Bench Memorandum Book on Segregation Cases, Conference Notes, 13 December 1952, HHBP, Box 337 (quoted second, fourth, and seventh); Douglas, Conference Notes, 13 December 1952, WODP, Box 1150 (quoted sixth, and ninth through fourteenth); Clark, Conference Notes, n.d., TCCP, Box A27 (quoted eighth). In 1952, the order in which the justices spoke in conference was as follows: Vinson, Black, Reed, Frankfurter, Douglas, Jackson, Burton, Clark, Minton. In 1953, the justices spoke in the same order, except that Warren replaced Vinson and Black was absent. In my treatment of the conference discussions, I alter the order of the justices in order to emphasize the constraints that the justices acknowledged.

14. Burton, Bench Memorandum Book on Segregation Cases, Conference Notes, 13 December 1952, HHBP, Box 337 (quoted first, second, seventh, tenth [emphasis in original], and eleventh); Clark, Conference Notes, n.d., TCCP, Box A27 (quoted third [emphasis in original], fifth [emphasis in original], sixth [emphasis in original], and thirteenth [emphasis in original]); Douglas, Conference Notes, 13 December 1952, WODP, Box 1150 (quoted fourth, ninth, twelfth, and fourteenth); Jackson, Conference Notes, 12 [*sic*] December 1952, RHJP, Box 184 (quoted eighth).

15. Clark, Conference Notes, n.d., TCCP, Box A27 (quoted first and fourth); Douglas, Conference Notes, 13 December 1952, WODP, Box 1150 (quoted second and fifth); Burton, Bench Memorandum Book on Segregation Cases, Conference Notes, 13 December 1952, HHBP, Box 337 (quoted third and sixth).

16. Douglas, Conference Notes, 13 December 1952, WODP, Box 1150. Justice Burton recorded Clark as stating that the "problem [is] serious with Mexicans." Burton, Bench Memorandum Book on Segregation Cases, Conference Notes, 13 December 1952, HHBP, Box 337. Justice Jackson wrote that Clark said the "Mexican problem [is]

more serious for more retarded." Jackson, Conference Notes, 12 [*sic*] December 1952, RHJP, Box 184.

17. Douglas, Conference Notes, 13 December 1952, WODP, Box 1150 (quoted first and third); Jackson, Conference Notes, 12 [*sic*] December 1952, RHJP, Box 184 (quoted second and seventh); Burton, Bench Memorandum Book on Segregation Cases, Conference Notes, 13 December 1952, HHBP, Box 337 (quoted fourth); Clark, Conference Notes, n.d., TCCP, Box A27 (quoted fifth and sixth).

18. Douglas, Conference Notes, 13 December 1952, WODP, Box 1150 (quoted first, second, and fourth); Jackson, Conference Notes, 12 [*sic*] December 1952, RHJP, Box 184 (quoted third); Clark, Conference Notes, n.d., TCCP, Box A27 (quoted fifth). Later, Justice Black denied that he had indicated in conference that there were any circumstances under which he would have sustained segregation. Kluger, *Simple Justice,* 2:752–53. The notes of Justices Jackson, Burton, Clark, and Douglas, however, suggest that Black at least viewed precedent as an obstacle to desegregation. And the notes of Jackson, Burton, and Clark suggest that Black called for deference to state court findings if the Court retained the separate-but-equal doctrine.

19. Clark, Conference Notes, n.d., TCCP, Box A27; Douglas, Conference Notes, 13 December 1952, WODP, Box 1150.

20. Jackson, Conference Notes, 12 [*sic*] December 1952, RHJP, Box 184 (quoted first through third); Douglas, Conference Notes, 13 December 1952, WODP, Box 1150 (quoted fourth through seventh). Assuming the accuracy of the conference notes, Burton misspoke when he identified *Sipuel v. Board of Regents of the University of Oklahoma,* 332 U.S. 631 (1948), as a precedent for the view that intangible factors are relevant to a determination of equality in education. In *Sipuel,* the Court merely held that a state had to provide a qualified black law school applicant with an equal legal education in a state institution. (Ada Sipuel had been denied admission to Oklahoma's *only* public law school.) By contrast, in *Sweatt v. Painter,* 339 U.S. 629 (1950), the obvious superiority of the faculty, student body, library, alumni, and reputation of the University of Texas Law School was central to the Court's ruling that the legal education the state afforded blacks at a separate institution was unequal. Burton probably meant to refer to *McLaurin v. Oklahoma State Regents for Higher Education,* 339 U.S. 637 (1950), which the Court announced along with *Sweatt.* In *McLaurin,* the Court ruled that the state, in segregating a black graduate student *within* an ostensibly white university, impaired that student's ability to learn and thus provided him with an unequal education.

21. Douglas, Conference Notes, 13 December 1952, WODP, Box 1150; Burton, Bench Memorandum Book on Segregation Cases, Conference Notes, 13 December 1952, HHBP, Box 337.

22. Douglas, Conference Notes, 13 December 1952, WODP, Box 1150 (quoted first through fourth, and eighth); Burton, Bench Memorandum Book on Segregation Cases, Conference Notes, 13 December 1952, HHBP, Box 337 (quoted fifth); Clark, Conference Notes, n.d., TCCP, Box A27 (quoted sixth, seventh, and tenth); Jackson, Conference Notes, 12 [*sic*] December 1952, RHJP, Box 184 (quoted ninth).

23. Clark, Conference Notes, n.d., TCCP, Box A27 (quoted first and fourth); Douglas, Conference Notes, 13 December 1952, WODP, Box 1150 (quoted second and third).

24. Douglas, Conference Notes, 13 December 1952, WODP, Box 1150; Burton, Bench Memorandum Book on Segregation Cases, Conference Notes, 13 December 1952, HHBP, Box 337.

25. Douglas, Conference Notes, 13 December 1952, WODP, Box 1150. Justice Burton recorded Clark as stating, "We have led the states on." Burton, Bench Memorandum Book on Segregation Cases, Conference Notes, 13 December 1952, HHBP, Box 337. Justice Jackson wrote that Clark said, "[We] have led [the] states on to believe separate but equal [is] ok." Jackson, Conference Notes, 12 [*sic*] December 1952, RHJP, Box 184.

26. Douglas, Conference Notes, 13 December 1952, WODP, Box 1150 (quoted first, second, and fourth); Jackson, Conference Notes, 12 [*sic*] December 1952, RHJP, Box 184 (quoted third); Burton, Bench Memorandum Book on Segregation Cases, Conference Notes, 13 December 1952, HHBP, Box 337 (quoted fifth and seventh); Clark, Conference Notes, n.d., TCCP, Box A27 (quoted sixth).

27. Clark, Conference Notes, n.d., TCCP, Box A27; Douglas, Conference Notes, 13 December 1952, WODP, Box 1150. Frankfurter apparently made his comment regarding the Eisenhower administration before consulting with his former law clerk, Philip Elman, who worked in the solicitor general's office at the time the Court was considering *Brown.* See chapter 6, below.

28. Clark, Conference Notes, n.d., TCCP, Box A27; Douglas, Conference Notes, 13 December 1952, WODP, Box 1150; Burton, Bench Memorandum Book on Segregation Cases, Conference Notes, 13 December 1952, HHBP, Box 337.

29. This sentiment was reflected in *Brown v. Board of Education of Topeka,* 349 U.S. 294, 301 (1955), where, after a hearing devoted to the matter of enforcement, the Supreme Court remanded the segregation cases "to the District Courts to take such proceedings and enter such orders and decrees consistent with this opinion as are necessary and proper to admit to public schools on a racially nondiscriminatory basis with all deliberate speed the parties to these cases." See also Kluger, *Simple Justice,* 2:902–43.

30. Murphy, *Elements of Judicial Strategy,* 204.

31. Felix Frankfurter to Stanley Reed, 20 May 1954, FFP—Harvard, Part II, Reel 4; Douglas, Memorandum for the File in re Segregation Cases, 17 May 1954, WODP, Box 1149 (quoted).

32. Douglas, Conference Notes, 12 December 1953, WODP, Box 1150 (quoted first and seventh); Burton, Bench Memorandum Book on Segregation Cases, Conference Notes, 12 December 1953, HHBP, Box 337 (quoted second through sixth). See also Douglas, Memorandum for the File in re Segregation Cases, 17 May 1954, WODP, Box 1149.

33. Burton, Bench Memorandum Book on Segregation Cases, Conference Notes, 12 December 1953, HHBP, Box 337 (quoted first through fifth, eighth, and tenth through thirteenth); Douglas, Conference Notes, 12 December 1953, WODP, Box 1150 (quoted sixth, seventh, ninth, and fourteenth through sixteenth). The federal government's grade-by-grade and school-by-school desegregation plans are discussed in the Brief for the United States as Amicus Curiae, *Brown v. Board of Education of Topeka, Shawnee County, Kansas, Briggs v. Elliott, Davis v. County School Board of Prince Edward County, Virginia, Bolling v. Sharpe,* and *Gebhart v. Belton,* 1952, in Kurland and Casper, eds., *Landmark Briefs and Arguments,* 49:145–46.

34. Douglas, Conference Notes, 12 December 1953, WODP, Box 1150; Burton, Bench Memorandum Book on Segregation Cases, Conference Notes, 12 December 1953, HHBP, Box 337.

35. Burton, Bench Memorandum Book on Segregation Cases, Conference Notes, 12 December 1953, HHBP, Box 337 (quoted first, fourth, fifth, and eighth [emphasis in original]); Douglas, Conference Notes, 12 December 1953, WODP, Box 1150 (quoted second, third, sixth, seventh, and ninth).

36. Douglas, Memorandum for the File in re Segregation Cases, 17 May 1954, WODP, Box 1149; Burton, Bench Memorandum Book on Segregation Cases, Conference Notes, 12 December 1953, HHBP, Box 337.

37. Burton, Bench Memorandum Book on Segregation Cases, Conference Notes, 12 December 1953, HHBP, Box 337 (quoted first and fifth); Douglas, Conference Notes, 12 December 1953, WODP, Box 1150 (quoted second through fourth).

38. Douglas, Conference Notes, 12 December 1953, WODP, Box 1150.

39. Burton, Bench Memorandum Book on Segregation Cases, Conference Notes, 12 December 1953, HHBP, Box 337 (quoted first, third [emphasis in original], fourth, fifth, ninth, and tenth); Douglas, Conference Notes, 12 December 1953, WODP, Box 1150 (quoted second, sixth through eighth, and eleventh).

40. Burton, Bench Memorandum Book on Segregation Cases, Conference Notes, 12 December 1953, HHBP, Box 337 (quoted first through fifth, and ninth through eleventh); Douglas, Conference Notes, 12 December 1953, WODP, Box 1150 (quoted sixth through eighth, and twelfth).

41. Burton, Bench Memorandum Book on Segregation Cases, Conference Notes, 12 December 1953, HHBP, Box 337 (quoted first); Douglas, Conference Notes, 12 December 1953, WODP, Box 1150 (quoted second, third, sixth, and seventh); Felix Frankfurter, Memorandum for the Conference, 18 May 1954, RHJP, Box 184 (quoted fourth); Frankfurter, Memorandum for the Conference, 3 December 1953, EWP, Box 571 (quoted fifth). A copy of Bickel's study of the history of the Fourteenth Amendment is in RHJP, Box 184. The document was eventually published as Bickel, "The Original Understanding and the Segregation Decision." For a critique of the substance of Bickel's study, see Tushnet, "What Really Happened in *Brown*," 1919. For the federal government's treatment of the history of the Fourteenth Amendment, see Friedman, ed., *Argument*, 240–52, and Supplemental Brief for the United States on Reargument, *Brown v. Board of Education of Topeka, Kansas, Briggs v. Elliott, Davis v. County School Board of Prince Edward County, Virginia, Bolling v. Sharpe*, and *Gebhart v. Belton*, 1953, in Kurland and Casper, eds., *Landmark Briefs and Arguments*, 49:853–1017.

42. Douglas, Conference Notes, 12 December 1953, WODP, Box 1150 (quoted first and third); Burton, Bench Memorandum Book on Segregation Cases, Conference Notes, 12 December 1953, HHBP, Box 337 (quoted second, and fourth through eighth).

43. Douglas, Conference Notes, 12 December 1953, WODP, Box 1150; Burton, Bench Memorandum Book on Segregation Cases, Conference Notes, 12 December 1953, HHBP, Box 337. Clark's suggestion that, until the reargument of *Brown*, he had always thought the Fourteenth Amendment prohibited segregation conflicts with a statement that he made in 1950: "So far as I have been able to study the historical materials, nothing really conclusive is shown for or against segregated education by statements in Congress, the legislatures or the press at the time the Amendment was adopted."

Memorandum to the Conference from Mr. Justice Clark, *McLaurin v. Oklahoma State Regents for Higher Education* and *Sweatt v. Painter,* April 1950, 2, TCCP, Box A2. Mark Tushnet suggests that Clark believed the history of the Fourteenth Amendment *supported* desegregation. Tushnet, "What Really Happened in *Brown,*" 1913–14. Tushnet reaches this conclusion by overlooking Clark's clear statements to the contrary recorded in the conference notes of both Douglas and Burton.

44. See Epstein et al., "On the Peril of Drawing Inferences," 174. I provide a detailed treatment of Justice Clark's desegregation vote in chapter 5.

45. Warren, *Memoirs,* 285.

46. See this chapter, below.

47. See Segal and Spaeth, *The Supreme Court and the Attitudinal Model Revisited,* 96–97, and Epstein and Knight, *The Choices Justices Make,* xii n.b, 57 n.a.

48. Warren, *Memoirs,* 285.

49. Ulmer, "Earl Warren and the Brown Decision," 699; Schwartz, *Super Chief,* 90; Hutchinson, "Unanimity and Desegregation," 40 (quoting Burton).

50. Frankfurter, Conference Notes, 16 January 1954, FFP—Harvard, Part II, Reel 4 (quoted); Frankfurter, Memorandum to Conference, 15 January 1954, EWP, Box 571. "A 'master' is one standing to another in such a relation that he not only controls the results of the work of that other but also may direct the manner in which such work shall be done"; a *special* master is "a master appointed to act as the representative of the court in some particular act or transaction, as to make a sale of property under a decree." *Black's Law Dictionary,* 5th ed., s.v. "master."

51. Frankfurter, Conference Notes, 16 January 1954, FFP—Harvard, Part II, Reel 4; Frankfurter, Memorandum to Conference, 15 January 1954, EWP, Box 571 (emphasis added).

52. Frankfurter, Conference Notes, 16 January 1954, FFP—Harvard, Part II, Reel 4.

53. Ibid.

54. Warren, *Memoirs,* 2, 285–86.

55. Kluger, *Simple Justice,* 2:877.

56. Fassett, "Mr. Justice Reed and *Brown,*" 57–58 (quoting Reed).

57. Felix Frankfurter to Stanley Reed, 20 May 1954, FFP—Harvard, Part II, Reel 4; Stanley Reed to Felix Frankfurter, 21 May 1954, FFP—Harvard, Part II, Reel 4.

58. Frankfurter, Memorandum, Written during the Summer, 1952 and Revised in September 26, 1952 by F.F., EWP, Box 571.

59. Jackson, Untitled Memorandum, 6 January 1954, 3, 5, 12, 13, 14, RHJP, Box 184. I examine Jackson's draft opinions in more detail in the next chapter.

60. Memorandum by Mr. Justice Jackson, 15 March 1954, 5, 18, 19, 20, 21, RHJP, Box 184.

61. Memorandum by Mr. Justice Jackson, 15 February 1954, 11–12, RHJP, Box 184. See also Jackson, Untitled Memorandum, 6 January 1954, 9–11, RHJP, Box 184.

62. E.D., Note on the Segregation Cases, n.d., RHJP, Box 184.

63. Epstein and Knight, *The Choices Justices Make,* 65–79 (65 quoted).

64. Warren, Memorandum, n.d., 7, EWP, Box 571.

65. Ibid., 2–4.

66. Ibid., 5, 6. See also Warren, Handwritten Draft, n.d., EWP, Box 571.

67. Warren, Memorandum, n.d., 7, EWP, Box 571.

68. Warren, Memorandum, 7 May 1954, 3–4, 6, 7, EWP, Box 571. The first reference to "modern authority" supporting the Court's conclusion regarding the psychological harms of segregation appears in Earl Pollock, Draft Opinion for the Chief Justice, 3–4 May 1954, 9, EWP, Box 571.

69. Rosen, *The Supreme Court and Social Science,* x–xi, 38–196.

70. Warren, To the Members of the Court, 7 May 1954, EWP, Box 571 (emphasis added). In short, Charles Black correctly hypothesized in 1960 that the justices did not place "principal reliance [in *Brown*] . . . on the formally 'scientific' authorities, which are relegated to a footnote." Rather, they understood that segregation "is perceptibly a means of ghettoizing the imputedly inferior race" but were "reluctan[t] to go into the distasteful details of the southern caste system." Black, "The Lawfulness of the Segregation Decisions," 430 n.25. See also Wechsler, "Toward Neutral Principles of Constitutional Law," 33.

71. Hockett, "Justice Robert H. Jackson and Segregation," 62.

72. If southerners assumed that the holding in *Brown* was limited to education, they soon realized they were mistaken. In a series of *per curiam* decisions, the Court extended the desegregation requirement to many other contexts: *Mayor of Baltimore v. Dawson,* 350 U.S. 877 (1955) (public recreation); *Holmes v. City of Atlanta,* 350 U.S. 879 (1955) (municipal golf courses); *Gayle v. Browder,* 352 U.S. 903 (1956) (buses); *State Athletic Commission v. Dorsey,* 359 U.S. 533 (1959) (athletic contests); *Turner v. Memphis,* 369 U.S. 350 (1962) (airport restaurants); *Johnson v. Virginia,* 373 U.S. 61 (1963) (courtroom seating); *Schiro v. Bynum,* 375 U.S. 395 (1964) (auditoriums); *Lee v. Washington,* 390 U.S. 333 (1968) (jails).

73. 347 U.S. 497, 500 (1954). See also Friedman, ed., *Argument,* 111, 127, 142, 282, 306.

74. Warren, Memorandum on the District of Columbia Case, n.d., 3, HHBP, Box 263.

75. For the justices' suggested revisions of Warren's draft opinion in the state segregation cases, see Warren, Memorandum on the State Cases, Retyped 5/12/54, EWP, Box 571. See also Schwartz, *Super Chief,* 97–98.

76. Kluger, *Simple Justice,* 2:882 (quoting Mickum).

77. Ibid., 881 (quoted); Warren, *Memoirs,* 286.

4. A SENSE OF THE COURT'S MISSION

1. March and Olsen, "The New Institutionalism," 738, 739, 741, 744. See also Murphy, *Elements of Judicial Strategy*; Clayton, "The Supreme Court and Political Jurisprudence," 30; Smith, "Political Jurisprudence," 90–91; Whittington, "Once More Unto the Breach," 613–16; March and Olsen, *Rediscovering Institutions;* and Ross, "The Many Lives of Institutionalism in American Social Science," 121.

2. Smith, "Political Jurisprudence," 96, 95. See also Clayton, "The Supreme Court and Political Jurisprudence," 30–31.

3. Clayton, "The Supreme Court and Political Jurisprudence," 32; Smith, "Political Jurisprudence," 91; Gillman, "The Court as an Idea," 79 (quoted); Gillman and Clayton, "Beyond Judicial Attitudes," 5 (quoted); Skowronek, "Order and Change," 94. The constitutive variant of the new institutionalism—which is noninstrumental—should not be confused with the concept of judicial role orientation, i.e., the idea that a justice's

conception of the judicial role can serve as an intervening variable between his values or policy preferences and his votes in the cases before him. C. Herman Pritchett developed the concept of role orientation within the context of an *instrumental* understanding of judicial behavior. See Pritchett, *Civil Liberties and the Vinson Court,* 14–17, 186–92. See also Gibson, "Judges' Role Orientations, Attitudes, and Decisions," and "The Role Concept in Judicial Research." In contrast to Pritchett, constitutive model proponents also stress the significance of the process by which justices are socialized—as members of our political culture, as law students, and as members of the bench—and thus suggest that we can speak meaningfully (at certain times, anyway) about a *shared* sense of appropriate judicial behavior that operates with some degree of *consistency.* See, e.g., Gillman, *The Constitution Besieged;* Kahn, *The Supreme Court and Constitutional Theory;* Keck, *The Most Activist Supreme Court in History;* Keck, "Party, Policy, or Duty"; and Whittington, "Congress before the *Lochner* Court."

4. Kahn, *The Supreme Court and Constitutional Theory,* 3–7, 18–22 (20–22, 4 quoted).

5. Clayton, "The Supreme Court and Political Jurisprudence," 22, 32; Skowronek, "Order and Change," 94 (quoted).

6. Smith, "Political Jurisprudence," 95; Gillman and Clayton, "Beyond Judicial Attitudes," 6–7; Gillman, "The Court as an Idea," 81. See also McCloskey, *The Modern Supreme Court,* 155, where he says, "One reason it is so difficult to define the Court's role in America is that the role has an inconsiderate habit of changing."

7. Gillman, "The Court as an Idea," 70, 78–81 (quoted; emphasis added); Gillman and Clayton, "Beyond Judicial Attitudes," 6; Clayton, "The Supreme Court and Political Jurisprudence," 27, 32.

8. Smith, "Political Jurisprudence," 100 (quoted); Clayton, "The Supreme Court and Political Jurisprudence," 26.

9. Smith, "Political Jurisprudence," 100–101; Clayton, "The Supreme Court and Political Jurisprudence," 33–34.

10. Friedman, ed., *Argument,* 215–16 (quoted), 270, 297. See also Amsterdam, "Telling Stories and Stories about Them," 15–17, 18–19, 21, 26, 29, 31.

11. Friedman, ed., *Argument,* 227 (quoted), 294.

12. Brief for Appellants in *Brown v. Board of Education of Topeka, Briggs v. Elliott, Davis v. County School Board of Prince Edward County,* and for Respondents in *Gebhart v. Belton* on Reargument, 1953, 50, NAACP Papers, Box II-B-142. See also Woodward, *The Strange Career of Jim Crow.*

13. Brief for Appellants in *Brown v. Board of Education of Topeka, Briggs v. Elliott, Davis v. County School Board of Prince Edward County,* and for Respondents in *Gebhart v. Belton* on Reargument, 1953, 50, 53–54, NAACP Papers, Box II-B-142.

14. Ibid., 56–57, 64, 58.

15. Ibid., 59–61, 63.

16. Ibid., 22–24.

17. Friedman, ed., *Argument,* 278–79, 284. See also Amsterdam, "Thurgood Marshall's Image of the Blue-Eyed Child in *Brown,*" 232–36, and "Telling Stories and Stories about Them," 17–18, 20, 26–27, 29, 31, 35.

18. While the notion of a living Constitution as applied to governmental *powers* had been an accepted part of American jurisprudence since at least the end of the New Deal,

no jurisprudential consensus had developed that judges should regard individual *rights* in a similar manner. Gillman, "The Collapse of Constitutional Originalism."

19. Brief for Appellants in *Brown v. Board of Education of Topeka, Briggs v. Elliott, Davis v. County School Board of Prince Edward County,* and for Respondents in *Gebhart v. Belton* on Reargument, 1953, 48–50, NAACP Papers, Box II-B-142.

20. Warren, *Memoirs,* 6–7.

21. Ibid. See also Warren, Notre Dame Law School Civil Rights Lectures, 16–17, 40–43.

22. Warren, "Fourteenth Amendment: Retrospect and Prospect," Fourteenth Amendment Centennial Convocation, New York University School of Law, 4 October 1968, 29, EWP, Box 825.

23. Warren, *Memoirs,* 4 (quoted); White, *Earl Warren,* 154, 162; Radio Address by Governor Earl Warren, Republican Campaign, 3 November 1944, 3–4 (quoted), EWP, Box 787; Address by Governor Earl Warren, Dewey-Bricker Campaign, Rockford, Illinois, 3 October 1944, 3, EWP, Box 787.

24. Keynote Address of Governor Earl Warren, Republican National Convention, Chicago, Illinois, 26 June 1944, 10, 12, EWP, Box 787.

25. Kluger, *Simple Justice,* 2:840; Interview with Governor Earl Warren, *U.S. News and World Report,* 7 April 1952, 24–25, EWP, Box 788; Bensel, *Sectionalism and American Political Development,* 233, 371–73, 403–5; Rosenberg, *The Hollow Hope,* 160; Goldfield, *Black, White, and Southern,* 53–55; McAdam, *Political Process and the Development of Black Insurgency,* 77–82; Burk, *The Eisenhower Administration and Black Civil Rights,* 3–20; Berman, *The Politics of Civil Rights in the Truman Administration,* 41–145, 157–78, 209–10, 230–31; McCoy and Reutten, *Quest and Response,* 317, 330–31; Key, *Southern Politics in State and Nation,* 10, 329–44. In 1952, Eisenhower won the electoral votes of the border states of Delaware, Maryland, Missouri, and Oklahoma, and the southern states of Florida, Texas, Tennessee, and Virginia. Only in 1928 did the Republican party achieve comparable electoral success in the South. In that election, however, the voters of Florida, North Carolina, Virginia, Tennessee, and Texas responded negatively to the Democratic candidate Al Smith; specifically they objected to his religion (Catholic) and his opposition to prohibition. Key, *Southern Politics in State and Nation,* 318.

26. Eisenhower, *Mandate for Change,* 226–29 (228 quoted); Abraham, *Justices and Presidents,* 252.

27. Pollack, *Earl Warren,* 146.

28. Dudziak, "Desegregation as a Cold War Imperative," 80–98 (95 quoting NAACP's petition); Dudziak, *Cold War Civil Rights,* 26–46.

29. White, *Earl Warren,* 132–33 (quoted); Pollack, *Earl Warren,* 97, 117, 131, 141.

30. Warren, *Memoirs,* 238–48; Pollack, *Earl Warren,* 109–15; White, *Earl Warren,* 133–35. As the Republican vice presidential candidate, Warren defended his party's civil rights record vis-à-vis that of the Democratic party. See Speech of Governor Warren, Madison, Wisconsin, 7 October 1948, 8–9, EWP, Box 787, and Speech of Governor Earl Warren, Central Park, Turlock, California, 29 October 1948, 3–5, EWP, Box 787.

31. Cray, *Chief Justice,* 183–87 (186 quoting Warren); Address of Governor Earl Warren, California Republican State Central Committee, San Diego, California, 16 November 1951, 8, EWP, Box 788. See also Address of Governor Earl Warren, Annual

Dinner of the New York Republican County Committee, Waldorf Astoria, 8 April 1952, 4, EWP, Box 787.

32. Interview with Governor Earl Warren, Broadcast of "Headlines Edition," 16 June 1948, 2, EWP, Box 787; Address by Governor Earl Warren, Joint Interim Committee on Constitutional Revision and Its Advisory Committees, Santa Barbara, California, 29 October 1947, 8, EWP, Box 789. Warren entertained the thought of running for the presidency as early as May 1947. Cray, *Chief Justice,* 184.

33. Address of Governor Earl Warren, Anti-Defamation League of B'nai B'rith, Los Angeles, California, 6 May 1948, 1–3, EWP, Box 790.

34. Address of Governor Earl Warren, 89th Annual Meeting of the National Education Association, San Francisco, California, 2 July 1951, 2, 4, EWP, Box 790.

35. Kluger, *Simple Justice,* 2:840 (quoting Warren); Address by Governor Earl Warren, Middlesex Club Lincoln Day Dinner, Boston, Massachusetts, 12 February 1952, 2–4, 6–7, EWP, Box 788. See also Address by Governor Earl Warren, Lincoln Day Dinner, Alameda County Republican Central Committee, 12 February 1950, EWP, Box 788.

36. White, *Earl Warren,* 153; Kluger, *Simple Justice,* 2:840; Berman, *The Politics of Civil Rights in the Truman Administration,* 209–10; Interview with Governor Earl Warren, *U.S. News and World Report,* 7 April 1952, 5–6, 8, 13, 15, EWP, Box 788 (5–6 quoted; emphasis added); Pollack, *Earl Warren,* 160–61; Press Release, Warren for President, Sacramento, California, 27 May 1952, EWP, Box 788. Cf. Kahn, "Shattering the Myth about President Eisenhower's Supreme Court Appointments," 47–50.

37. Cray, *Chief Justice,* 112–123, 157–158; Katcher, *Earl Warren,* 137–151; White, *Earl Warren,* 56–58, 67–77; Weaver, *Warren,* 105–14; Cho, "Redeeming Whiteness," 93–98, 107; Warren, "War-Time Martial Rule in California," 195; Japanese Problem, Excerpt from Speech by Earl Warren to the Newspapers Publishers Association, January 1944, EWP, Box 789.

38. See, e.g., White, *Earl Warren,* 368–69; McWilliams, "The Education of Earl Warren"; and Horwitz, *The Warren Court,* 24.

39. 323 U.S. 214 (1944).

40. Warren, "The Bill of Rights and the Military," 192, 193.

41. Warren, *Memoirs,* 149.

42. Cho, "Redeeming Whiteness," 130.

43. Ibid., 132.

44. Rosenberg, *The Hollow Hope,* 46–47.

45. Burton, Bench Memorandum Book on Segregation Cases, Conference Notes, 12 December 1953, HHBP, Box 337 (emphasis added). Justice Frankfurter recorded Warren as saying, "The more I *hear [and] read [and] think, the more I come to conclude* [that the] basis of s[eparate] + e[qual] rests upon [a] concept of [the] inferiority of [the] colored race." Frankfurter, Conference Notes, December 1953, FFP—Harvard, Part II, Reel 4 (emphasis added). Warren also may have been influenced by a similar analysis of the nature of segregation contained in Myrdal, *An American Dilemma,* 573–705. Warren cited Myrdal in his opinion for the Court in *Brown. Brown v. Board of Education of Topeka,* 347 U.S. 483, 495 n.11 (1954).

46. See also Warren, "Fourteenth Amendment: Retrospect and Prospect," Fourteenth Amendment Centennial Convocation, New York University School of Law,

4 October 1968, 26, EWP, Box 825; and Address by Chief Justice Earl Warren, Retired, 30th Anniversary Institute Luncheon of the NAACP Legal Defense and Educational Fund, 15 May 1970, EWP, Box 829.

47. See Epstein et al., "Ideological Drift among Supreme Court Justices," 1504–10, 1521–26, and Epstein et al., "On the Peril of Drawing Inferences," 174–78.

48. Nieman, *Promises to Keep,* 148–88; Franklin and Moss, *From Slavery to Freedom,* 492–531.

49. 347 U.S. 497, 499 (1954).

50. Warren did not vote for desegregation, as Sumi Cho suggests, because he sought to demonstrate to the public that a valid concern for national security (as opposed to racism) informed his involvement in the internment of Japanese-Californians in 1942. As noted earlier in this chapter, Warren would not have felt the need to use *Brown* to justify his actions in this context less than a decade after the Second World War. Rather, the LDF's lawyers understood that the only person Warren felt any need to convince that the internment was consistent with *Brown* was himself.

51. See, e.g., Warren, Notre Dame Law School Civil Rights Lectures, 16–40; Warren, "'All Men Are Created Equal'"; Warren, "Fourteenth Amendment: Retrospect and Prospect," Fourteenth Amendment Centennial Convocation, New York University School of Law, 4 October 1968, 19–20, 24, 26, EWP, Box 825; and Address by Chief Justice Earl Warren, Retired, "The Struggle to Be Equal Will Never End," Washington Urban League, 17 May 1972, 10, EWP, Box 833.

52. Warren, "Fourteenth Amendment: Retrospect and Prospect," Fourteenth Amendment Centennial Convocation, New York University School of Law, 4 October 1968, 26, EWP, Box 825.

53. Response by Chief Justice Earl Warren to an Address by the President of the United States, American Bar Association John Marshall Bicentennial Ceremonies, Philadelphia, Pennsylvania, 24 August 1955, 2, EWP, Box 796; Warren, "The Law and the Future," 6, 11.

54. Murphy, Fleming, and Harris, *American Constitutional Interpretation,* 750.

55. Smith, "Political Jurisprudence," 103. Warren supported plaintiffs in 221 civil rights cases 82.8 percent of the time for the years 1953 to 1969. Epstein and Mershon, "Measuring Political Preferences," 287.

56. I examined the Papers of Hugo L. Black (Library of Congress, Manuscript Division, Washington, D.C.) when researching *New Deal Justice,* 67–140, as well as this book.

57. Key, *Southern Politics in State and Nation,* 36–57; Rogers, *The One-Gallused Rebellion,* 335; Hackney, *Populism to Progressivism in Alabama,* 333; Black and Black, *Mr. Justice and Mrs. Black,* 31; Wyatt-Brown, "Ethical Background of Hugo Black's Career," 919; Hamilton, *Hugo Black,* 33; Hockett, *New Deal Justice,* 77–80.

58. Hockett, *New Deal Justice,* 81 (quoting Black).

59. Hamilton, *Hugo Black,* 267; Frank, *Mr. Justice Black,* 88–94; Key, *Southern Politics in State and Nation,* 365–67.

60. Berman, "Hugo Black, Southerner," 39, 41 (quoting Black); *Congressional Record,* 72nd Cong., 1st sess., 16 February 1932, 1–3 (quoted); Bensel, *Sectionalism and American Political Development,* 149–51, 256 (quoted).

61. Hockett, *New Deal Justice*, 83–86; Wyatt-Brown, "Ethical Background of Hugo Black's Career," 922–23 (quoted); Black and Black, *Mr. Justice and Mrs. Black*, 35 (quoted), 70; Shannon, "Hugo La Fayette Black as United States Senator," 124.

62. Thornton, "Hugo Black and the Golden Age," 902; Berman, "Hugo Black, Southerner," 39; Berman, "Hugo L. Black: The Early Years," 112–15; Silverstein, *Constitutional Faiths*, 102–3 (quoted).

63. 309 U.S. 227, 238–39, 236, 241 (1940). Although *Chambers v. Florida* was unanimous, Justice Frank Murphy took no part in the consideration or decision of the case.

64. Klarman, *From Jim Crow to Civil Rights*, 298–99.

65. Ball and Cooper, *Of Power and Right*, 163 (quoting the director of the Division of Negro Affairs of the National Youth Administration and the president of the Fort Worth branch of the NAACP); Yarbrough, *Mr. Justice Black and His Critics*, 84.

66. See also Black, "Justice Black and the Bill of Rights," 941.

67. Friedman, ed., *Argument*, 100–101 (quoted), 162–63.

68. In fact, George Hayes was evasive in his response when Justice Frankfurter inquired whether the petitioners' legal analysis identified laws against miscegenation as unconstitutional. Ibid., 116–17. Gunnar Myrdal discussed the connection between segregation and a fear of miscegenation. Myrdal, *An American Dilemma*, 586–92. The LDF cited Myrdal in its briefs in *Brown*, albeit not specifically his discussion of segregation and miscegenation. Appendix to Appellants' Briefs, *Brown v. Board of Education of Topeka, Briggs v. Elliott*, and *Davis v. County School Board of Prince Edward County*, 1952, 3, 8, NAACP Papers, Box II-B-138; Brief for Appellants, *Brown v. Board of Education of Topeka, Briggs v. Elliott, Davis v. County School Board of Prince Edward County*; and for Respondents in *Gebhart v. Belton* on Reargument, 1953, 202–3, NAACP Papers, Box II-B-142.

69. 323 U.S. 214, 216 (1944) (emphasis added).

70. Friedman, ed., *Argument*, 117–18; Brief for Appellants, *Brown v. Board of Education of Topeka, Briggs v. Elliott, Davis v. County School Board of Prince Edward County*, and for Respondents in *Gebhart v. Belton* on Reargument, 1953, 24, NAACP Papers, Box II-B-142.

71. Woodward, *The Strange Career of Jim Crow*, 115; Franklin and Moss, *From Slavery to Freedom*, 347–48, 386; Chalmers, *Hooded Americanism;* Turner, *The Ku Klux Klan;* McVeigh, *The Rise of the Ku Klux Klan;* MacLean, *Behind the Mask of Chivalry;* Greenhaw, *Fighting the Devil in Dixie*.

72. Black and Black, *Mr. Justice and Mrs. Black*, 73.

73. The liberal voting percentages for the justices are found in Epstein and Mershon, "Measuring Political Preferences," 287.

74. Klarman, *From Jim Crow to Civil Rights*, 304.

75. Robert H. Jackson to Charles Fairman, 13 March 1950, RHJP, Box 12. See also Jackson, *The Nurnberg Case;* "Justice Jackson's Final Report to the President Concerning the Nurnberg War Crimes Trial"; "Nuremburg in Retrospect"; and "The Nurnberg Trial."

76. Robert H. Jackson to Charles Fairman, 13 March 1950, RHJP, Box 12 (emphasis added).

77. Memorandum by Mr. Justice Jackson, 15 February 1954, 3–4, RHJP, Box 184.

78. Jackson, Untitled Memorandum, 6 January 1954, RHJP, Box 184; Memorandum by Mr. Justice Jackson, 15 February 1954, 13–15, RHJP, Box 184; Memorandum by Mr. Justice Jackson, 15 March 1954, 18–23, Box 184.

79. Klarman, *From Jim Crow to Civil Rights,* 113, 188.

80. Memorandum by Mr. Justice Jackson, 15 March 1954, 4, 13, RHJP, Box 184; E. Barrett Prettyman, Jr., Re Nos. 104, 1, RHJP, Box 184.

81. Hockett, "Justice Robert H. Jackson and Segregation," 57–59; Rosenberg, *The Hollow Hope,* 97–100.

82. Jackson, Untitled Memorandum, 6 January 1954, 9–12 (quoted first through fifth), RHJP, Box 184; Memorandum by Mr. Justice Jackson, 15 March 1954, 18 (quoted sixth), RHJP, Box 184. See also Memorandum by Mr. Justice Jackson, 15 February 1954, 11–13, RHJP, Box 184. In chapter 5, I provide reason to believe that Cold War considerations might have played some role in Jackson's desegregation vote.

83. Jackson, Untitled Memorandum, 6 January 1954, 5, 12–13, RHJP, Box 184; Memorandum by Mr. Justice Jackson, 15 March 1954, 22 (emphasis added), RHJP, Box 184. See also Memorandum by Mr. Justice Jackson, 15 February 1954, 9, RHJP, Box 184.

84. From 1953 until his death in October 1954, Jackson supported civil rights litigants 62.5 percent of the time in 8 cases. Epstein and Mershon, "Measuring Political Preferences," 287.

85. See, e.g., Tushnet, *Making Civil Rights Law,* 194. Michael Klarman's instrumental account of Jackson's desegregation vote is vulnerable to a criticism he levels at others—that he provides a strained reading of the documentary record. See Klarman, *From Jim Crow to Civil Rights,* 301. Klarman argues that, in addition to the barriers Jackson mentioned in conference and detailed in his draft opinions for the case, the justice "had become skeptical of judicial supremacy, not only because he thought it was inconsistent with democracy, but also because he feared that courts were bad at it." Klarman emphasizes that "Jackson's rationale for invalidating segregation occupied just two pages [*sic*] near the end of a twenty-three-page opinion [that focused on the barriers to desegregation], and it read as if it were 'almost an afterthought.'" Quoting from Jackson's remarks in conference, Klarman declares, "Unable to 'justify the abolition of segregation as a judicial act,' [Jackson] agreed to 'go along with it' as 'a political decision.'" Ibid., 306–7. If Klarman's analysis were correct, Jackson's working papers for the case would have featured increasingly lengthy—and defeatist—discussions of the impediments to desegregation, along with a legal rationale that was conspicuous in its failure to justify Court action against segregated schools. As this section of the chapter demonstrates, Jackson's final legal memo, while lengthy, was anything but defeatist and legally unconvincing. It is thus reasonable to believe that Jackson's remarks in conference—which he made *before* he began writing his draft opinions—were *not* a reflection of a decision to support desegregation for political reasons (because he doubted that an acceptable legal argument could be found). Rather, a more natural interpretation of the justice's comments to his brethren is that, as a matter of politics, he supported desegregation, but that the Court should act only if it could provide a compelling legal argument for invalidating segregation.

5. THE RELEVANCE OF FOREIGN AFFAIRS

1. Clayton and May, "A Political Regimes Approach," 243, 234, 242, 241. See also Clayton, "The Supreme Court and Political Jurisprudence," 32–34.

2. Clayton and May, "A Political Regimes Approach," 242 (quoted); Clayton, "The Supreme Court and Political Jurisprudence," 35; Pickerill and Clayton, "The Rehnquist Court and the Political Dynamics of Federalism," 236. See also Dahl, "Decision-Making in a Democracy"; Shapiro, "Political Jurisprudence"; Gillman, "Martin Shapiro and the Movement from 'Old' to 'New' Institutionalist Studies"; Adamany and Meinhold, "Robert Dahl"; and Kritzer, "Martin Shapiro."

3. See chapter 6, below.

4. Clayton and May, "A Political Regimes Approach," 234, 242–45 (242–43 quoted); Clayton, "The Supreme Court and Political Jurisprudence," 35–37 (37 quoted).

5. Clayton, "The Supreme Court and Political Jurisprudence," 37–38 (quoted); Clayton and May, "A Political Regimes Approach," 246, 248–50 (250, 246 quoted). At this point, Clayton and May might have referred to certain studies, written prior to their call for a "political regimes" approach, which illustrate this form of institutionalism. The scholarship of Mary Dudziak (discussed in this chapter) and Mark Graber (see chapter 6, below) is especially noteworthy. See also Gillman, "How Political Parties Can Use the Courts"; Gillman, "Party Politics and Constitutional Change"; Whittington, "'Interpose Your Friendly Hand'"; and Whittington, *Political Foundations of Judicial Supremacy.*

6. Salokar, *The Solicitor General,* 3–4, 94, 177. See also Landsberg, *Enforcing Civil Rights,* 135–38, and Scigliano, *The Supreme Court and the Presidency,* 4, 197–98. The solicitor general's special relationship with the Court is reflected in his success rate in cases decided on the merits. In cases that the Court decided between 1925 and 1988 in which the government was a party, the government prevailed in approximately 69 percent of its cases. The government's rate of success was less than 50 percent in only the 1934 and 1935 terms. The government's success rate exceeded 80 percent in the 1939, 1953, 1981, and 1983 terms. Clayton, *The Politics of Justice,* 69–70.

7. Clayton, *The Politics of Justice,* 68; Krislov, "The Role of the Attorney General as Amicus Curiae."

8. Puro, "The United States as *Amicus Curiae,*" 223–29 (228–29 quoted). See also Clayton, *The Politics of Justice,* 68–69, and Segal, "Amicus Curiae Briefs by the Solicitor General."

9. Clayton, *The Politics of Justice,* 125. See also Ackerman, *We the People,* 105–6.

10. Dudziak, "Desegregation as a Cold War Imperative," 61–66, 89 (89, 63 quoted; emphasis added). See also Bell, "*Brown v. Board of Education* and the Interest-Convergence Dilemma," and Dudziak, *Cold War Civil Rights,* 79–114.

11. Dudziak, "Desegregation as a Cold War Imperative," 94–95 (quoting NAACP petition), 96–97; Dudziak, *Cold War Civil Rights,* 43–45, 63–66.

12. Dudziak, "Desegregation as a Cold War Imperative," 102 (quoting civil rights committee's report). See also President's Committee on Civil Rights, *To Secure These Rights,* 146–48.

13. Dudziak, "Desegregation as a Cold War Imperative," 81, 103.

14. Ibid., 101, 105–11; Layton, *International Politics and Civil Rights,* 27, 108; Brief for the United States as Amicus Curiae, *Brown v. Board of Education of Topeka, Briggs v. Elliott, Davis v. County School Board of Prince Edward County, Bolling v. Sharpe,*

Gebhart v. Belton, 1952, in Kurland and Casper, eds., *Landmark Briefs and Arguments,* 49:119, 121 (quoted). The relevant cases prior to *Brown* in which the Truman administration submitted *amicus curiae* briefs were *Shelley v. Kraemer,* 334 U.S. 1 (1948) (restrictive covenants); *Henderson v. United States,* 339 U.S. 816 (1950) (dining car segregation); *Sweatt v. Painter,* 339 U.S. 629 (1950) (segregation in higher education); and *McLaurin v. Oklahoma State Regents for Higher Education,* 339 U.S. 637 (1950) (segregation in higher education).

15. Dudziak, "Desegregation as a Cold War Imperative," 119 n.330, 117, 111 n.287.

16. Ibid., 113 n.299.

17. Dudziak, *Cold War Civil Rights,* 104–6. See also Douglas, *Strange Lands and Friendly People,* 296, 321, 326, and Douglas, *Beyond the High Himalayas,* 317, 321–23.

18. Warren, "The Law and the Future," 2, 9–12.

19. From 1953 until his retirement in 1969, Warren supported petitioners in civil rights controversies 82.8 percent of the time in 221 cases. Epstein and Mershon, "Measuring Political Preferences," 287.

20. From 1953 until his retirement in 1969, Warren supported petitioners in First Amendment controversies 79.9 percent of the time in 159 cases. From 1953 until his retirement in 1975, Douglas supported petitioners in First Amendment controversies 96.8 percent of the time in 249 cases. From 1953 until his retirement in 1975, Douglas supported petitioners in civil rights controversies 92.7 percent of the time in 397 cases. Ibid.

21. Bell, "*Brown v. Board of Education* and the Interest-Convergence Dilemma," 518–19, 522–24 (523 quoted); Dudziak, *Cold War Civil Rights,* 249–54 (251 quoted); Dudziak, "Desegregation as a Cold War Imperative," 117–20.

22. Baum, *The Puzzle of Judicial Behavior,* 20.

23. In Dudziak's words, "There does not appear to be direct evidence that members of the Supreme Court discussed the impact of racial segregation on Cold War foreign relations in their deliberations in *Brown.*" Dudziak, *Cold War Civil Rights,* 104.

24. Fassett, "Mr. Justice Reed and *Brown,*" 58 (emphasis added).

25. Epstein and Mershon, "Measuring Political Preferences," 287.

26. From 1953 until his retirement in 1957, Reed supported petitioners in First Amendment controversies only 20 percent of the time in 15 cases. Ibid. For relevant First Amendment cases prior to 1953 in which Reed participated, see *American Communications Association v. Douds,* 339 U.S. 382 (1950); *Gerende v. Board of Supervisors,* 341 U.S. 56 (1951); *Dennis v. United States,* 341 U.S. 494 (1951); *Garner v. Board of Public Works,* 341 U.S. 716 (1951); *Joint Anti-Fascist Refugee Committee v. McGrath,* 341 U.S. 123 (1951); *Adler v. Board of Education,* 342 U.S. 485 (1952); and Fassett, *New Deal Justice,* 475–502.

27. Jackson, Untitled Memorandum, 6 January 1954, 9–10, RHJP, Box 184. See also Memorandum by Mr. Justice Jackson, 15 February 1954, 11, RHJP, Box 184.

28. From 1953 until his death in October 1954, Jackson supported petitioners in civil rights controversies 62.5 percent of the time in 8 cases and petitioners in First Amendment controversies 50 percent of the time in 4 cases. Epstein and Mershon, "Measuring Political Preferences," 287. For relevant First Amendment cases prior to *Brown* in which Jackson deferred to the government, see *American Communications Association v. Douds,* 339 U.S. 382 (1950); *Gerende v. Board of Supervisors,* 341 U.S. 56 (1951); *Dennis v. United States,* 341 U.S. 494 (1951); *Garner v. Board of Public Works,*

341 U.S. 716 (1951); and *Adler v. Board of Education,* 342 U.S. 485 (1952). Cf. *Joint Anti-Fascist Refugee Committee v. McGrath,* 341 U.S. 123 (1951).

29. Clark, Conference Notes, n.d., TCCP, Box A27. See also Burton, Bench Memorandum Book on Segregation Cases, Conference Notes, 13 December 1952, HHBP, Box 337.

30. Epstein and Mershon, "Measuring Political Preferences," 287.

31. From 1953 to his retirement in 1962, Frankfurter supported petitioners in First Amendment controversies 49.9 percent of the time in 79 cases. Ibid. For examples of Frankfurter's deference toward the government in First Amendment controversies, see *American Communications Association v. Douds,* 339 U.S. 382 (1950); *Gerende v. Board of Supervisors,* 341 U.S. 56 (1951); *Dennis v. United States,* 341 U.S. 494 (1951); *Garner v. Board of Public Works,* 341 U.S. 716 (1951); *Uphaus v. Wyman,* 360 U.S. 72 (1959); *Barenblatt v. United States,* 360 U.S. 109 (1959); *Wilkinson v. United States,* 365 U.S. 399 (1961); *Braden v. United States,* 365 U.S. 431 (1961); *Communist Party v. Subversive Activities Control Board,* 367 U.S. 1 (1961); *Scales v. United States,* 367 U.S. 203 (1961); and Urofsky, *Felix Frankfurter,* 104–27. Cf. *Joint Anti-Fascist Refugee Committee v. McGrath,* 341 U.S. 123 (1951); *Adler v. Board of Education,* 342 U.S. 485 (1952); *Watkins v. United States,* 354 U.S. 178 (1957); and *Yates v. United States,* 354 U.S. 298 (1957).

32. Dudziak, "Desegregation as a Cold War Imperative," 62 n.4, 74 n.68.

33. McCoy and Reutten, *Quest and Response,* 67 (quoting Clark; emphasis added), 94; Segal, *The Race War,* 223 (quoting Clark). See also Dudziak, "Desegregation as a Cold War Imperative," 95, and Layton, *International Politics and Civil Rights,* 57.

34. 334 U.S. 1 (1948). See also Elman, "The Solicitor General's Office," 819.

35. Dudziak, "Desegregation as a Cold War Imperative," 101 (quoting government's *amicus* brief).

36. Elman, "The Solicitor General's Office," 818–19; Dudziak, *Cold War Civil Rights,* 276 n.24. See also Clark and Perlman, *Prejudice and Property.*

37. 339 U.S. 629 (1950) and 339 U.S. 637 (1950).

38. Dudziak, "Desegregation as a Cold War Imperative," 108–9 (quoting government's *amicus* brief); Dudziak, *Cold War Civil Rights,* 95–96.

39. Memorandum to the Conference from Mr. Justice Clark, *McLaurin v. Oklahoma State Regents for Higher Education* and *Sweatt v. Painter,* April 1950, 1, 3–4 (brackets with emphasis in original), TCCP, Box A2. In the version of the memorandum that he circulated to his brethren, Clark concluded, "If some say this [ruling against segregated graduate education] undermines *Plessy* then let it fall, as have many Nineteenth Century Oracles." Memorandum to the Conference from Mr. Justice Clark, *McLaurin v. Oklahoma State Regents for Higher Education* and *Sweatt v. Painter,* April 1950 (Circulated, 7 April 1950), 4, TCCP, Box A2.

40. Memorandum to the Conference from Mr. Justice Clark, *McLaurin v. Oklahoma State Regents for Higher Education* and *Sweatt v. Painter,* April 1950, 4–5, TCCP, Box A2. Clark continued, "The atmosphere of age and tradition at an established graduate school itself profoundly stimulates its students in achieving professional competence. And that atmosphere draws professors of stature—men who make an older University so different from a neophyte Negro academy. Further, the opportunities for discussion available in a larger school are literally invaluable—there surely can be no substitute for the exploration

and combat of ideas in a particular subject matter among maturing minds of varied backgrounds and opinions." Ibid., 5.

41. Ibid., 5–6. In the version of his memorandum that he circulated to his brethren, Clark stated, "[Oklahoma's] concern was the extension of the [desegregation] doctrine to the elementary and secondary schools. . . . Certainly this is not required now. I would be opposed to such extension at this time and would vote against taking a case involving same. Perhaps at a later date our judicial discretion will lead us to hear such a case." Memorandum to the Conference from Mr. Justice Clark, *McLaurin v. Oklahoma State Regents for Higher Education* and *Sweatt v. Painter,* April 1950 (Circulated, 7 April 1950), 1, TCCP, Box A2.

42. Memorandum to the Conference from Mr. Justice Clark, *McLaurin v. Oklahoma State Regents for Higher Education* and *Sweatt v. Painter,* April 1950 (Circulated, 7 April 1950), 2–3, TCCP, Box A2.

43. In his draft memorandum, Clark wrote,

There is fear that a flat overruling of the *Plessy* case would cause subversion or even defiance of our mandates in many communities. Intimidation, threats and riots are envisioned. A long and terrible step backward is forecast if we go too far forward with legal doctrines at this time. Taney's attempt, in *Dred Scott,* to resolve political and social issues of this magnitude is not comforting. I believe that those fears are relevant in resolving Constitutional issues of this type and of this magnitude. I would share those fears should we begin holding, today or tomorrow, that swimming pools may not be segregated; or should we decide that the fourth grade in schoolhouses in Mississippi must be open to Negro and white alike. But I feel confident that those fears are groundless should we rule that there can be no segregation in the college or graduate schools.

Clark, Memorandum to the Conference, *McLaurin v. Oklahoma State Regents for Higher Education* and *Sweatt v. Painter,* April 1950, 3, TCCP, Box A2. See also Memorandum to the Conference from Mr. Justice Clark, *McLaurin v. Oklahoma State Regents for Higher Education* and *Sweatt v. Painter,* April 1950 (Circulated, 7 April 1950), 1, TCCP, Box A2.

44. Supplemental Brief for the United States on Reargument, *Brown v. Board of Education of Topeka, Briggs v. Elliott, Davis v. County School Board of Prince Edward County, Bolling v. Sharpe,* and *Gebhart v. Belton,* 1953, in Kurland and Casper, eds., *Landmark Briefs and Arguments,* 49:1031–32, 1049, 1051 (emphasis added). See also Friedman, ed., *Argument,* 216, 254–55.

45. Brief for the United States on the Further Argument of the Questions of Relief, *Brown v. Board of Education of Topeka, Briggs v. Elliott, Davis v. County School Board of Prince Edward County, Bolling v. Sharpe,* and *Gebhart v. Belton,* 1954, in Kurland and Casper, eds., *Landmark Briefs and Arguments,* 49:748–49, 759–61, 763–67; Burton, Bench Memorandum Book on Segregation Cases, Conference Notes, 16 April 1955, HHBP, Box 337; Douglas, Conference Notes, 16 April 1954 [*sic*], WODP, Box 1150.

46. *Brown v. Board of Education of Topeka,* 349 U.S. 294 (1955). Members of the Court who favored moderate delays were encouraged by the opinion's statement that the district courts "will require that the defendants make a prompt and reasonable start toward full compliance with our May 17, 1954 ruling"; the directive that "the bur-

den rests upon the defendants to establish that [additional] time is necessary [and] in the public interest"; and the observation that "the vitality of these constitutional principles cannot be allowed to yield simply because of disagreement with them." Those justices who preferred indefinite delays approved of the opinion's emphasis on the need to accommodate "a variety of local problems" and the importance of "a practical flexibility" in formulating remedies; the statement that district judges "may properly take into account the public interest in the elimination of . . . obstacles" to desegregation; the pairing of the term "as soon as practicable" with the directive that desegregation occur "with all deliberate speed"; and the absence of a definite date for desegregation to be implemented. Addressing the concerns of both groups of justices, the opinion declared, "School authorities have the primary responsibility for elucidating, assessing, and solving [local school] problems; courts will have to consider whether the action of school authorities constitutes good faith implementation of the governing constitutional principles." Ibid., 298–301. See also Wilkinson, *From* Brown *to* Bakke, 61–65.

47. Wilkinson, *From* Brown *to* Bakke, 65–77; Rosenberg, *The Hollow Hope*, 42–57, 94–106.

48. The relevant cases are, respectively, *Yates v. United States,* 354 U.S. 298 (1957); *Scales v. United States,* 367 U.S. 203 (1961); and *Communist Party v. Subversive Activities Control Board,* 367 U.S. 1 (1961).

49. *Gerende v. Board of Supervisors,* 341 U.S. 56 (1951); *Garner v. Board of Public Works,* 341 U.S. 716 (1951); *Adler v. Board of Education,* 342 U.S. 485 (1952); *Keyishian v. Board of Regents,* 385 U.S. 589 (1967).

50. *Watkins v. United States,* 354 U.S. 178 (1957); *Uphaus v. Wyman,* 360 U.S. 72 (1959); *Barenblatt v. United States,* 360 U.S. 109 (1959); *Wilkinson v. United States,* 365 U.S. 399 (1961); *Braden v. United States,* 365 U.S. 431 (1961).

51. Abraham, *Justices and Presidents,* 237–38.

52. Klarman, *From Jim Crow to Civil Rights,* 299. See also Berry, *Stability, Security, and Continuity,* 91–104; Gugin and St. Clair, *Sherman Minton,* 197–210, 220–46; Atkinson, "Justice Sherman Minton and the Balance of Liberty"; and Wallace, "Mr. Justice Minton."

53. Berry, *Stability, Security, and Continuity,* 20–21. Unlike Warren and Minton, Burton was not a liberal on economic issues; Berry characterizes him as "a middle-of-the-roader with a conservative slant" whose "position [on labor relations issues] could be described as promanagement." Ibid., 12–13. See also Gugin and St. Clair, *Sherman Minton,* 87–114, and Atkinson, "From New Deal Liberal to Supreme Court Conservative," 373–77.

54. Atkinson, "Justice Sherman Minton and the Protection of Minority Rights," 101; Gugin and St. Clair, *Sherman Minton,* 57–86, 115.

55. Minton served on the Supreme Court from 1949 to 1956.

6. DOMESTIC POLITICAL CONSIDERATIONS

1. Dahl, "Decision-Making in a Democracy," 281, 293, 284, 285, 293. Although Dahl would strongly influence scholars who developed the noninstrumental "political regimes" model of Supreme Court decision making, his own approach to the Court (and to *Brown*) was instrumental, although not attitudinal, in nature. Adamany and

Meinhold, "Robert Dahl," 363–64; Epstein and Walker, "The Role of the Supreme Court in American Society," 320.

2. Dahl, "Decision-Making in a Democracy," 281–94 (282, 293–94 quoted). Jonathan Casper criticized Dahl for limiting his analysis to cases in which the Court declared federal legislation unconstitutional. Casper, "The Supreme Court and National Policy Making," 57–60.

3. Cf. Clayton, *The Politics of Justice,* 126–31, and Clayton and May, "A Political Regimes Approach," 246–47.

4. Burk, *The Eisenhower Administration and Black Civil Rights,* 15, 27, 46, 69, 92, 133, 205 (46, 205, 92 quoting Eisenhower); Berman, *The Politics of Civil Rights in the Truman Administration,* 204–5, 221.

5. Burk, *The Eisenhower Administration and Black Civil Rights,* 3–20; McCoy and Reutten, *Quest and Response,* 317; Berman, *The Politics of Civil Rights in the Truman Administration,* 209–10 (quoting Republican civil rights plank).

6. Berman, *The Politics of Civil Rights in the Truman Administration,* 230–31; McCoy and Reutten, *Quest and Response,* 331. Of the eleven states of the South, only two—Florida and Tennessee—went Republican twice in the eighteen presidential elections during the period 1876 to 1944. Five states—South Carolina, North Carolina, Louisiana, Texas, and Virginia—went Republican only once during that same period. Four states—Alabama, Arkansas, Georgia, and Mississippi—"maintained an unbroken record of Democratic loyalty" during that period. In 1948, four southern states—Alabama, Mississippi, Louisiana, and South Carolina—did not vote for Harry Truman; instead, they voted for Strom Thurmond, the States' Rights Democratic (Dixiecrat) party candidate for president. Key, *Southern Politics in State and Nation,* 10 (quoted), 329–44; Black and Black, *Politics and Society in the South,* 262; Sundquist, *Dynamics of the Party System,* 277–84; Tindall, *The Disruption of the Solid South,* 49–53.

7. Burk, *The Eisenhower Administration and Black Civil Rights,* 28, 44, 49, 69, 93, 95, 98, 205 (28, 49, 205 quoted).

8. Elman, "The Solicitor General's Office," 829, 832–33. See also Duram, *A Moderate among Extremists,* 59–64.

9. Elman, "The Solicitor General's Office," 833–36.

10. Warren, *Memoirs,* 291.

11. Philip Elman said that he "slipped [the brief's title] by [his] superiors." Elman, "The Solicitor General's Office," 835. See also Supplemental Brief for the United States on Reargument, *Brown v. Board of Education of Topeka, Briggs v. Elliott, Davis v. County School Board of Prince Edward County, Bolling v. Sharpe,* and *Gebhart v. Belton,* 1953, in Kurland and Casper, eds., *Landmark Briefs and Arguments,* 49:853, and Brief for the United States as Amicus Curiae, *Brown v. Board of Education of Topeka, Briggs v. Elliott, Davis v. County School Board of Prince Edward County, Bolling v. Sharpe,* and *Gebhart v. Belton,* 1952, in ibid., 49:142–46.

12. Friedman, ed., *Argument,* 250. Cf. Clayton, *The Politics of Justice,* 126–31, and Clayton and May, "A Political Regimes Approach," 246–47.

13. Clayton, *The Politics of Justice,* 129.

14. See the sources listed in ibid., 161–62 nn.51, 52. Aside from its involvement in *Brown,* "the Justice Department pushed the 1957 and 1960 Civil Rights Acts through Congress; and Eisenhower sent federal troops into the South to implement judicial in-

tegration orders." Ibid., 129. See also Duram, *A Moderate among Extremists,* 53–71, and Powe, *The Warren Court and American Politics,* 36. After reading Earl Warren's memoirs, it is clear that the chief justice would have rejected the view that Eisenhower used a "hidden-hand" strategy to promote civil rights. See Warren, *Memoirs,* 291.

15. Shapiro, *Law and Politics in the Supreme Court,* 1–49. See also Truman, *The Governmental Process.* Like Dahl, Shapiro would strongly influence scholars who developed the noninstrumental "political regimes" model of Supreme Court decision making, although his own approach to the Court was instrumental in nature. Kritzer, "Martin Shapiro," 387–91, 402–3, 406–9; Gillman, "Martin Shapiro and the Movement from 'Old' to 'New' Institutionalist Studies."

16. Scholars usually trace the "preferred position" doctrine to Justice Harlan Stone's opinion in *United States v. Carolene Products Co.,* 304 U.S. 144 (1938). In the fourth footnote to his opinion in that case, Stone suggested that there may be contexts in which the Court should abandon the presumption of constitutionality that it now (i.e., beginning in 1937) accorded to economic legislation: when challenged legislation appears to violate a specific prohibition of the Constitution, such as those of the first ten amendments; when legislation restricts effective participation in the democratic process; and when laws are directed at "discrete and insular minorities," that is, powerless groups against whom the majority is prejudiced.

17. Shapiro, "The Supreme Court," 188–94 (190, 193 quoted). See also Shapiro, "The Constitution and Economic Rights," 85, where he said, "Rarely has a Supreme Court doctrinal pronouncement been more transparently political." The "preferred position" doctrine "was especially to protect religious, national, and racial minorities—this uttered at a time when a major factor in the Democratic party's massive domination of the political process was its successful building of a coalition of ethnic and racial minorities."

18. For a noninstrumental critique of Shapiro's argument, see Kahn, *The Supreme Court and Constitutional Theory,* 3–104.

19. Brooks, *Walls Come Tumbling Down,* 17 (quoted); McAdam, *Political Process and the Development of Black Insurgency,* 79–80; Klarman, "Civil Rights Law," 456–57; Klarman, *From Jim Crow to Civil Rights,* 100.

20. Berman, *The Politics of Civil Rights in the Truman Administration,* 47–55, 77, 81; Burk, *The Eisenhower Administration and Black Civil Rights,* 6; McCoy and Reutten, *Quest and Response,* 97; McMahon, *Reconsidering Roosevelt on Race,* 184–85, 189 (quoting Clifford).

21. Berman, *The Politics of Civil Rights in the Truman Administration,* 50–57, 66–71; McCoy and Reutten, *Quest and Response,* 47–53, 79–95; President's Committee on Civil Rights, *To Secure These Rights,* 151–78 (166 quoted).

22. 334 U.S. 1 (1948).

23. Berman, *The Politics of Civil Rights in the Truman Administration,* 74–75, 83–84, 117–18, 157–58; McCoy and Reutten, *Quest and Response,* 99–100, 129–30, 178–80, 211–12; Franklin and Moss, *From Slavery to Freedom,* 461–62; Nieman, *Promises to Keep,* 141–42; Goldfield, *Black, White, and Southern,* 53–54; Elman, "The Solicitor General's Office," 817–27.

24. McCoy and Reutten, *Quest and Response,* 143–44; Berman, *The Politics of Civil Rights in the Truman Administration,* 129–33.

25. McCoy and Reutten, *Quest and Response,* 100–101, 116–17, 218–19, 340–43; Berman, *The Politics of Civil Rights in the Truman Administration,* 172–73, 240; McMahon, *Reconsidering Roosevelt on Race,* 193–94. The cases in which the Truman administration submitted *amicus curiae* briefs prior to *Brown* were *Henderson v. United States,* 339 U.S. 816 (1950) (segregation in interstate transportation); *Sweatt v. Painter,* 339 U.S. 629 (1950) (segregation in higher education); and *McLaurin v. Oklahoma State Regents for Higher Education,* 339 U.S. 637 (1950) (segregation in higher education).

26. Goldfield, *Black, White, and Southern,* 54; Berman, *The Politics of Civil Rights in the Truman Administration,* 157–78; Nieman, *Promises to Keep,* 142; Billington, *The Political South in the Twentieth Century,* 64–68; Bensel, *Sectionalism and American Political Development,* 152–53, 233, 371–73, 403–5 (372–73 quoted; emphasis added).

27. Shapiro, "Chief Justice Rehnquist and the Future of the Supreme Court," 146. On that same page, Shapiro added, "The only significant element in the New Deal coalition that the preferred position did not serve was conservative southern whites. But nobody in the New Deal was really fond of them anyway."

28. McMahon, *Reconsidering Roosevelt on Race,* 10.

29. Ibid., 7, 13–14, 16–17, 40–41, 65, 77 (40–41, 14, 16–17 quoted); McMahon, "Constitutional Vision and Supreme Court Decisions," 24. See also Katznelson, *When Affirmative Action Was White,* 25–141, and Milkis, *The President and the Parties,* 21–146. Franklin Roosevelt was not the first president to believe that the fulfillment of his constitutional vision required an expansion of executive authority at the expense of the influence of political parties. See Ceaser, *Presidential Selection,* 170–259.

30. McMahon, *Reconsidering Roosevelt on Race,* 99–100 (quoted); McMahon, "Constitutional Vision and Supreme Court Decisions," 25.

31. McMahon, *Reconsidering Roosevelt on Race,* 58–60, 102–3, 120–27, 144–76 (58, 102–3, 146 quoted); McMahon, "Constitutional Vision and Supreme Court Decisions," 25–27, 30–50.

32. McMahon also discusses the significance of President Roosevelt's Court-packing plan. McMahon, *Reconsidering Roosevelt on Race,* 61–96. See also Leuchtenburg, "The Origins of Franklin D. Roosevelt's 'Court-Packing' Plan."

33. McMahon, *Reconsidering Roosevelt on Race,* 107, 142. McMahon is able to identify only two civil rights cases—one involving the white primary (*United States v. Classic,* 313 U.S. 299 [1941]) and the other involving police brutality (*Screws v. United States,* 325 U.S. 91 [1945])—in which the administration argued before the president's appointees. Nevertheless, he contends that, overall, "the activities of the Roosevelt Justice Department did much to shape judicial doctrine in the postwar era. With its calls for activism to federally secure and protect the rights of African Americans, the department helped the Roosevelt Court—informed by its commitment to the principle of deference to the executive branch—to lay the precedential cornerstone of its new civil rights doctrine." McMahon, *Reconsidering Roosevelt on Race,* 150–56, 167–76 (175 quoted); McMahon, "Constitutional Vision and Supreme Court Decisions," 33–34, 43–48.

34. McMahon, *Reconsidering Roosevelt on Race,* 4–5, 265–66 n.24 (4–5 quoted).

35. Ibid., 60, 189–90.

36. Berman, *The Politics of Civil Rights in the Truman Administration,* 107–15; McCoy and Reutten, *Quest and Response,* 123–28; Key, *Southern Politics in State and Nation,* 329–44.

37. McCoy and Reutten, *Quest and Response,* 143–44, 331; Berman, *The Politics of Civil Rights in the Truman Administration,* 129–33, 230–31. McMahon recognizes that Eisenhower sought and secured the White House by "building on the ticket-splitting foundation laid by Strom Thurmond's bolting band of Dixiecrats in 1948." McMahon, *Reconsidering Roosevelt on Race,* 197–98.

38. Klarman, *From Jim Crow to Civil Rights,* 251, 291; Klarman, "Civil Rights Law," 449. The Supreme Court invalidated the white primary in *Smith v. Allwright,* 321 U.S. 649 (1944).

39. Bensel, *Sectionalism and American Political Development,* 405.

40. McMahon, *Reconsidering Roosevelt on Race,* 219–20, 217. The formal citation for the case in which the Court attempted to implement desegregation (i.e., *Brown II*) is *Brown v. Board of Education of Topeka,* 349 U.S. 294 (1955).

41. McMahon, *Reconsidering Roosevelt on Race,* 265–66 n.24

42. Ibid., 142.

43. See ibid., 150–56, 167–75.

44. Graber, "The Nonmajoritarian Difficulty," 36, 44.

45. Ibid., 39, 63–64, 66, 71 (63, 66 quoted).

46. See also Klarman, "*Brown,* Racial Change, and the Civil Rights Movement," 85–149, and Klarman, *From Jim Crow to Civil Rights,* 385–442.

47. See Rosenberg, *The Hollow Hope,* 97–100. Graber contends, "From 1936 to 1960, the public could not hold politicians accountable for judicial decisions condemning segregated institutions because neither the national Democratic party nor the national Republican party had any interest in overruling *Brown* and its progeny." Graber, "The Nonmajoritarian Difficulty," 67.

48. For case studies, Graber focuses on the issues of slavery, antitrust, and abortion. Graber, "The Nonmajoritarian Difficulty," 45–61.

49. Burk, *The Eisenhower Administration and Black Civil Rights,* 199.

50. Graber, "The Nonmajoritarian Difficulty," 64–65 (emphasis added).

51. In Michael Klarman's view, the justices' awareness of "the dramatic change in racial mores" that occurred in the middle of the twentieth century is evidence that these individuals were caught up in the current of history that was moving the nation toward racial egalitarianism. Klarman concedes that "southern justices . . . were more inclined to treat [recent changes in racial attitudes and practices] as a justification for staying their hand." Klarman, "Civil Rights Law," 458 (quoted); Klarman, *From Jim Crow to Civil Rights,* 308–10. But, as this book demonstrates, one cannot assume that *nonsouthern-ers* on the Court who commented on changes in race relations necessarily had a policy preference for desegregation.

52. Douglas, Conference Notes, 12 December 1953, WODP, Box 1150; Burton, Bench Memorandum Book on Segregation Cases, Conference Notes, 12 December 1953, HHBP, Box 337.

53. Memorandum to the Conference from Mr. Justice Clark, *McLaurin v. Oklahoma State Regents for Higher Education* and *Sweatt v. Painter,* April 1950, 3–4, TCCP, Box A2. Although he was not a New Deal justice, Harold Burton made reference in conference "to [a] trend away from separation of the races in restaurants, [the] armed forces, etc." Douglas, Conference Notes, 12 December 1953, WODP, Box 1150.

54. Douglas, Conference Notes, 13 December 1952, WODP, Box 1150.

55. Frankfurter, Memorandum, Written during the Summer, 1952 and Revised in September 26, 1952 by F.F., EWP, Box 571; Robert H. Jackson to Charles Fairman, 13 March 1950, 3, RHJP, Box 12; Memorandum by Mr. Justice Jackson, 15 February 1954, 3, 12–13, RHJP, Box 184. See also Jackson, Untitled Memorandum, 6 January 1954, 11, RHJP, Box 184, and Memorandum by Mr. Justice Jackson, 15 March 1954, 1, 21, RHJP, Box 184.

56. Key, *Southern Politics in State and Nation,* 664. See also Brief for Appellants, *Brown v. Board of Education of Topeka, Briggs v. Elliott, Davis v. County School Board of Prince Edward County,* and for Respondents in *Gebhart v. Belton* on Reargument, 1953, 58, NAACP Papers, Box II-B-142.

57. Myrdal, *An American Dilemma,* 514, xix (italics omitted), 4. See also Appendix to Appellants' Briefs, *Brown v. Board of Education of Topeka, Briggs v. Elliott,* and *Davis v. County School Board of Prince Edward County,* 1952, 3, 8, NAACP Papers, Box II-B-138; Brief for Appellants, *Brown v. Board of Education of Topeka, Briggs v. Elliott, Davis v. County School Board of Prince Edward County,* and for Respondents in *Gebhart v. Belton* on Reargument, 1953, 202–3, NAACP Papers, Box II-B-142; and *Brown v. Board of Education of Topeka,* 347 U.S. 483, 494 n.11 (1954).

58. Myrdal, *An American Dilemma,* 510–20, 1015–18 (518, 514, 1016, 510 quoted; italics omitted); Key, *Southern Politics in State and Nation,* 670.

59. Key, *Southern Politics in State and Nation,* 3–12, 551–54, 664–75 (8, 9, 553, 670, 673 quoted).

60. Myrdal, *An American Dilemma,* 401–2, 517. See also Kersch, "The New Deal Triumph as the End of History?" 190–91.

61. Myrdal, *An American Dilemma,* 517, 511; Key, *Southern Politics in State and Nation,* 670–74.

62. Key, *Southern Politics in State and Nation,* 674–75; Myrdal, *An American Dilemma,* 520, 519, 466 (italics in original), 1014–15, 1022.

63. Southern, *Gunnar Myrdal and Black-White Relations,* 128–29.

64. See Myrdal, *An American Dilemma,* 467, and Key, *Southern Politics in State and Nation,* 37, 365–67, 668.

65. Epstein and Mershon, "Measuring Political Preferences," 289.

66. Martin, *Civil Rights and the Crisis of Liberalism,* 53–59 (55 quoted).

67. Given Jackson's stated fears of judicial inefficacy regarding desegregation (discussed in chapters 1, 3, and 4), it is reasonable to doubt that his votes in other areas of law relevant to the South reflected a belief that the Court could do much to accelerate trends toward the liberalization of the politics of the region.

68. Kersch, "The New Deal Triumph as the End of History?" 190–209 (192 quoted). See also *Railway Mail Association v. Corsi,* 326 U.S. 88 (1944); *Steele v. Louisville and Nashville Railroad Co.,* 323 U.S. 192 (1944); *Tunstall v. Brotherhood of Locomotive Firemen and Enginemen,* 323 U.S. 210 (1944); *Graham v. Brotherhood of Locomotive Firemen and Enginemen,* 338 U.S. 232 (1949); and *Brotherhood of Railroad Trainmen v. Howard,* 343 U.S. 768 (1952).

69. See, e.g., Powe, *The Warren Court and American Politics,* 490, 494, where he contends that "the dominant motif of the Warren Court is an assault on the South as a unique legal and cultural region" and suggests that "the Court was a functioning part of the Kennedy-Johnson liberalism of the mid and late 1960s."

70. The ideological continuum that Segal and his colleagues used ranged from −1 (unanimously conservative) to 0 (moderate) to +1 (unanimously liberal). The ideological designations for the New Deal (i.e., Democratic or Independent) justices were as follows: Clark (0.0); Frankfurter (.33); Minton (.44); Reed (.45); Douglas (.46); Black (.75); Jackson (1.0). Segal et al., "Ideological Values and the Votes of U.S. Supreme Court Justices Revisited," 816.

71. Robert H. Jackson to Charles Fairman, 13 March 1950, RHJP, Box 12.

72. McMahon, *Reconsidering Roosevelt on Race*, 219. See also McMahon, "Constitutional Vision and Supreme Court Decisions," 50, where he says, "Those jurists who participated in [Roosevelt's] 'constitutional revolution,' . . . did so not because such conduct was consistent with their own policy preferences, as attitudinal theorists suggest (although at times it certainly was). Rather, they behaved in this fashion because they were part of an institution with an embedded mission."

73. Black and Black, *Politics and Society in the South*, 232–75, 292–316 (254, 255, 275 quoted). See also Billington, *The Political South in the Twentieth Century*, 131–85, and Bass and DeVries, *The Transformation of Southern Politics*, 3–56, 397–408.

CONCLUSION

1. Smith, "Political Jurisprudence," 104, 107.

2. Smith, "Ideas, Institutions, and Strategic Choices," 135. See also Gillman, "The New Institutionalism, Part I"; Epstein and Knight, "The New Institutionalism, Part II"; and Gillman, "Placing Judicial Motives in Context."

3. Baum, *The Puzzle of Judicial Behavior*, 20.

4. Hockett, "The Battle over *Brown*'s Legitimacy," 41–49.

5. Epstein and Knight, "The New Institutionalism, Part II," 5.

6. Graber, "Legal, Strategic or Legal Strategy," 45.

7. Ibid., 48, 60. See also Kahn and Kersch, "Introduction," in Kahn and Kersch, eds., *The Supreme Court and American Political Development*, 17–19; Kahn and Kersch, "Conclusion," in ibid., 455; and Kahn, "Social Constructions, Supreme Court Reversals, and American Political Development," 95–103.

8. See Kahn and Kersch, "Introduction," in Kahn and Kersch, eds., *The Supreme Court and American Political Development*, 13–21, and Kahn and Kersch, "Conclusion," in ibid., 443–63.

9. Smith, "Political Jurisprudence," 89, 91, 104–6. See also Gillman, "The New Institutionalism, Part I," 9–10.

10. It is wrong to assume that, in debating the legitimacy of the Warren Court's constitutional jurisprudence, scholars overlook differences among the justices. Even defenders of a constitutive account of Supreme Court decision making would not argue that the sense of mission that informed Warren's performance and the behavior of some of his colleagues in *Brown* necessarily would have led the justices to display a high degree of consensus in subsequent cases. The model's proponents concede not only that the Court's mission is open to judicial transformation in the face of changing political contexts but also that this sort of institutional influence guides decision making rather than dictates particular results. Justices are thus expected to differ with their colleagues when applying a general sense of mission to the specifics of individual cases, and, over time, even to alter their own views regarding what the Court's mission requires. Yet, in spite

of the fact that the disparate civil rights and civil liberties voting patterns of the justices involved in *Brown* more than adequately illustrate this point (see Segal and Spaeth, *The Supreme Court and the Attitudinal Model*, 245–47, 252–53), commonalities of belief and behavior that serve to distinguish these justices and the Warren Court generally (that is, all of the justices who served on the Court during Warren's tenure as chief justice) from the Court in preceding eras can be identified. Attitudinalists and constitutive model proponents alike acknowledge the Warren Court's unprecedented concern with the protection of civil liberties and civil rights. See ibid., 97–118, and Kahn, *The Supreme Court and Constitutional Theory*, 3–104.

11. John Hart Ely contends that, "as late as 1968," Alexander Bickel was "a Robert Kennedy liberal" although he was a judicial conservative. Ely, *Democracy and Distrust*, 71–72.

12. While conceding that the specific intentions informing the Fourteenth Amendment did not support school desegregation, Bickel argued, unconvincingly, that the framers may have used language that "was sufficiently elastic to permit reasonable future advances" in the area of civil rights. Bickel, "The Original Understanding and the Segregation Decision," 58–62 (61 quoted). For a criticism of Bickel's argument, see Berger, *Government by Judiciary*, 100–110.

13. Keck, *The Most Activist Supreme Court in History*, 54–55.

14. Bickel, *The Supreme Court and the Idea of Progress*, 7, 13. See also Kurland, "Foreword."

15. Kurland, "'*Brown v. Board of Education* Was the Beginning,'" 342, 346, 313, 315, 316. See also *Green v. County School Board of New Kent County*, 391 U.S. 430 (1968), and *Swann v. Charlotte-Mecklenburg Board of Education*, 402 U.S. 1 (1971).

16. McDowell, *Equity and the Constitution*, 98, 117, 10–11, 127–29, 11, 132, 122.

17. Caldeira and Wright, "Lobbying for Justice."

18. Bork, *The Tempting of America*, 73–79 (75, 77, 74, 79, 73 quoted).

19. Ibid., 75–76, 144, 82–83 (emphasis added). See also Bork, "Neutral Principles and Some First Amendment Problems," 14–15. Bork has some support for the proposition that the framers of the Constitution did not anticipate that judges would seek to discover the subjective intentions behind legal documents. See Powell, "The Original Understanding of Original Intent," and Gillman, "The Collapse of Constitutional Originalism," 206. But the notion that seemingly abstract constitutional language reveals that the framers of the Constitution or of the Fourteenth Amendment viewed judicial decision making as a discretionary exercise, or that they intended for judges to regard constitutional provisions as relative to time and circumstance (a notion that Bork simultaneously embraces and excoriates), is lacking in evidentiary support. Berger, *Government by Judiciary*, 283–311, 373–96; Perry, *The Constitution, the Courts, and Human Rights*, 70–75.

20. See also Bork, *The Tempting of America*, 78–81, 145–46, 169, 187–93, 213–14. As Ronald Dworkin notes, once Bork abandons an interpretive model that links constitutional meaning to the specific intentions of the framers, "then he has nothing left to which he can tether an opinion of what they wanted, except the exceedingly abstract language they used." Dworkin, *Freedom's Law*, 299. See also McConnell, "Originalism and the Desegregation Decisions," 951 n.11; Posner, "Bork and Beethoven," 1374–75; Posner, *The Problems of Jurisprudence*, 305–7; Berger, "Robert Bork's Contribution

to Original Intention," 1176–83; and Richards, "Originalism without Foundations," 1379–82.

21. For a recent attempt to demonstrate that *Brown* is more susceptible to originalist justification than the conventional wisdom suggests, see McConnell, "Originalism and the Desegregation Decisions." For critiques of McConnell's argument, see Klarman, "*Brown,* Originalism, and Constitutional Theory," and Maltz, "Originalism and the Desegregation Decisions." Cf. McConnell, "The Originalist Justification for *Brown.*" See also Maltz, "*Brown v. Board of Education* and 'Originalism,'" 142–45; Maltz, "A Dissenting Opinion to Brown"; and Berger, *Government by Judiciary,* 117–33.

22. McDowell, *Equity and the Constitution,* 11.

23. Bickel, *The Supreme Court and the Idea of Progress,* 180–81; McDowell, *Equity and the Constitution,* 130; Bork, *The Tempting of America,* 78.

24. Even originalists who seek to tether constitutional decision making to the subjective intentions of the framers must contend with, among other difficulties, the incompleteness of historical records, the question of whom to regard as framers (only the ratifiers?), and the multiple meanings that individual framers might have ascribed to the same constitutional language. Goldford, *The American Constitution and the Debate over Originalism,* 146–49; Hutson, "The Creation of the Constitution." More "sophisticated" forms of originalism, such as the form Robert Bork used (unsuccessfully) to square *Brown* with the framers' understanding of equal protection, require exercises of discretion, first, in determining an appropriate level of generality for a particular constitutional provision, and, then, in applying that abstracted constitutional principle to the circumstances of the present controversy. Goldford, *The American Constitution and the Debate over Originalism,* 154–75; Dworkin, *Freedom's Law,* 287–305; Dworkin, *A Matter of Principle,* 33–55; Whittington, *Constitutional Interpretation,* 182–87.

25. Goldford, *The American Constitution and the Debate over Originalism,* 74, 91, 50. Although Goldford is very critical of originalism, he emphasizes that his critique should not be regarded as an endorsement of non-originalism. Ibid., 15–17. See also Kahn, "Social Constructions, Supreme Court Reversals, and American Political Development," 90–91.

26. Kahn, "Social Constructions, Supreme Court Reversals, and American Political Development," 72 (quoted), 85, 87, 90 (quoted); Kahn and Kersch, "Introduction," in Kahn and Kersch, eds., *The Supreme Court and American Political Development,* 17–18 (quoted).

27. Kahn, *The Supreme Court and Constitutional Theory,* 4, 7–29, 67–104 (4, 91, 102, 82 quoted; emphasis added). Kahn examines the Warren Court's performance on the following equal protection issues: access to judicial process; the right to vote; the right to travel; the intent to discriminate and the fundamental right to marry; and residency requirements, welfare, and the right to travel. Kahn also provides constitutive interpretations of the Burger Court and, to a lesser degree, the Rehnquist Court. Ibid., 41–53, 105–208, 250–66. See also Dahl, *A Preface to Democratic Theory,* and Truman, *The Governmental Process.*

28. Kahn, *The Supreme Court and Constitutional Theory,* 30, 33, 251 (emphasis added). See also McConnell, *Private Power and American Democracy,* and Lowi, *The End of Liberalism.*

29. As noted in chapter 4, other factors, especially the violence that greeted

civil rights workers in the 1960s, also contributed to Warren's sense of mission in civil rights cases.

30. Kahn, *The Supreme Court and Constitutional Theory,* 65.

31. See, e.g., McDowell, *Equity and the Constitution,* 121, and Horowitz, *The Courts and Social Policy.*

32. Kahn, *The Supreme Court and Constitutional Theory,* 92, 91, 102–3, 251 (92, 91, 102 quoted).

33. Maltz, *Rethinking the Constitution,* 20; Bork, *The Tempting of America,* 143. See also Berger, *Government by Judiciary,* 316–18, 363–64, and Goldford, *The American Constitution and the Debate over Originalism,* 124–25.

34. Bork, *The Tempting of America,* 74.

35. Hockett, "The Battle over *Brown*'s Legitimacy."

36. Wilkinson, *Serving Justice,* 133. See also Black, "The Lawfulness of the Segregation Decisions."

37. Abraham Lincoln, "First Inaugural Address—Final Text," 4 March 1861, *The Collected Works of Abraham Lincoln,* ed. Roy P. Basler (New Brunswick, N.J.: Rutgers University Press, 1953), 4:271.

38. See Orfield and Eaton, *Dismantling Desegregation,* and Orfield and Yun, "Resegregation in American Schools."

39. Rosenberg, *The Hollow Hope,* 341.

40. Dudziak, *Cold War Civil Rights,* 251; Orfield and Yun, "Resegregation in American Schools."

41. Bell, "*Brown v. Board of Education* and the Interest-Convergence Dilemma," 523.

42. Ibid., 532, 533.

BIBLIOGRAPHY

MANUSCRIPT COLLECTIONS

Black, Hugo L. Papers. Library of Congress, Manuscript Division, Washington, D.C.

Burton, Harold H. Papers. Library of Congress, Manuscript Division, Washington, D.C.

Clark, Tom C. Papers. University of Texas at Austin, Tarlton Law Library, Austin, Texas.

Douglas, William O. Papers. Library of Congress, Manuscript Division, Washington, D.C.

Frankfurter, Felix. Papers—Harvard Law School Library. Frederick, Md.: University Publications of America, 1986. Microfilm.

Jackson, Robert H. Papers. Library of Congress, Manuscript Division, Washington, D.C.

National Association for the Advancement of Colored People. Papers. Library of Congress, Manuscript Division, Washington, D.C.

Warren, Earl. Papers. Library of Congress, Manuscript Division, Washington, D.C.

ARTICLES AND BOOKS

Abraham, Henry J. *Justices and Presidents: A Political History of Appointments to the Supreme Court.* 2nd ed. New York: Oxford University Press, 1985.

Ackerman, Bruce. *We the People: Foundations.* Cambridge, Mass.: Belknap Press of Harvard University Press, 1991.

Adamany, David, and Stephen Meinhold. "Robert Dahl: Democracy, Judicial Review, and the Study of Law and Courts." In *The Pioneers of Judicial Behavior,* edited by Nancy Maveety, 361–86. Ann Arbor: University of Michigan Press, 2006.

Amsterdam, Anthony G. "Telling Stories and Stories about Them." *Clinical Law Review* 1 (1994): 9–40.

———. "Thurgood Marshall's Image of the Blue-Eyed Child in *Brown.*" *New York University Law Review* 68 (1993): 226–36.

Atkinson, David N. "From New Deal Liberal to Supreme Court Conservative: The Metamorphosis of Justice Sherman Minton." *Washington University Law Quarterly* (1975): 361–94.

———. "Justice Sherman Minton and the Balance of Liberty." *Indiana Law Journal* 50 (1974): 34–59.

———. "Justice Sherman Minton and the Protection of Minority Rights." *Washington and Lee Law Review* 34 (1977): 97–117.

Balkin, Jack M., ed. *What Brown v. Board of Education Should Have Said.* New York: New York University Press, 2001.

Ball, Howard, and Phillip J. Cooper. *Of Power and Right: Hugo Black, William O. Douglas, and America's Constitutional Revolution.* New York: Oxford University Press, 1992.

Ball, William B. "Lawyers and Social Scientists—Guiding the Guides." *Villanova Law Review* 5 (1959): 215–23.

Bass, Jack, and Walter DeVries. *The Transformation of Southern Politics: Social Change and Political Consequence since 1945.* New York: Basic Books, 1976.

Baum, Lawrence. *The Puzzle of Judicial Behavior.* Ann Arbor: University of Michigan Press, 1997.

Bell, Derrick A., Jr. *"Brown v. Board of Education* and the Interest-Convergence Dilemma." *Harvard Law Review* 93 (1980): 518–33.

Bensel, Richard Franklin. *Sectionalism and American Political Development: 1880–1980.* Madison: University of Wisconsin Press, 1984.

———. *Yankee Leviathan: The Origins of Central State Authority in America, 1859–1877.* New York: Cambridge University Press, 1990.

Berger, Raoul. *Government by Judiciary: The Transformation of the Fourteenth Amendment.* Cambridge, Mass.: Harvard University Press, 1977.

———. "Robert Bork's Contribution to Original Intention." *Northwestern University Law Review* 84 (1990): 1167–89.

Berman, Daniel M. "Hugo Black, Southerner: The Negro." *American University Law Review* 10 (1961): 35–42.

———. "Hugo L. Black: The Early Years." *Catholic University Law Review* 8 (1959): 103–16.

Berman, William C. *The Politics of Civil Rights in the Truman Administration.* Columbus: Ohio State University Press, 1970.

Berry, Mary Frances. *Stability, Security, and Continuity: Mr. Justice Burton and Decision-Making in the Supreme Court.* Westport, Conn.: Greenwood Press, 1978.

Bickel, Alexander M. "The Original Understanding and the Segregation Decision." *Harvard Law Review* 69 (1955): 1–65.

———. *The Supreme Court and the Idea of Progress.* New Haven, Conn.: Yale University Press, 1978.

Billington, Monroe. "Civil Rights, President Truman, and the South." *Journal of Negro History* 58 (1973): 127–39.

———. *The Political South in the Twentieth Century.* New York: Charles Scribner's Sons, 1975.

Black, Charles L. "The Lawfulness of the Segregation Decisions." *Yale Law Journal* 69 (1960): 421–30.

Black, Earl, and Merle Black. *Politics and Society in the South.* Cambridge, Mass.: Harvard University Press, 1987.

Black, Hugo L. *A Constitutional Faith.* New York: Knopf, 1968.

———. "Justice Black and the Bill of Rights." Interview by Eric Sevareid and Martin Agronsky. CBS News Special. 3 December 1968. Printed in *Southwestern University Law Review* 9 (1977): 937–51.

Black, Hugo L., and Elizabeth Black. *Mr. Justice and Mrs. Black: The Memoirs of Hugo L. Black and Elizabeth Black.* New York: Random House, 1975.

Bork, Robert H. "Neutral Principles and Some First Amendment Problems." *Indiana Law Journal* 47 (1971): 1–35.

———. *The Tempting of America: The Political Seduction of the Law.* New York: Touchstone, 1990.

Brooks, Thomas R. *Walls Come Tumbling Down: A History of the Civil Rights Movement, 1940–1970.* Englewood Cliffs, N.J.: Prentice-Hall, 1974.

Burk, Robert Frederick. *The Eisenhower Administration and Black Civil Rights.* Knoxville: University of Tennessee Press, 1984.

Caldeira, Gregory A., and John R. Wright. "Lobbying for Justice: The Rise of Organized Conflict in the Politics of Federal Judgeships." In *Contemplating Courts,* edited by Lee Epstein, 44–71. Washington, D.C.: CQ Press, 1995.

Casper, Jonathan D. "The Supreme Court and National Policy Making." *American Political Science Review* 70 (1976): 50–63.

Ceaser, James W. *Presidential Selection: Theory and Development.* Princeton, N.J.: Princeton University Press, 1979.

Chalmers, David M. *Hooded Americanism: The History of the Ku Klux Klan.* New York: New Viewpoints, 1976.

Cho, Sumi. "Redeeming Whiteness in the Shadow of Internment: Earl Warren, *Brown,* and a Theory of Racial Redemption." *Boston College Third World Law Journal* 19 (1998): 73–170.

Clark, Tom C., and Philip Benjamin Perlman. *Prejudice and Property: An Historic Brief against Racial Covenants.* Washington, D.C.: Public Affairs Press, 1948.

Clayton, Cornell W. *The Politics of Justice: The Attorney General and the Making of Legal Policy.* Armonk, N.Y.: M. E. Sharpe, 1992.

———. "The Supreme Court and Political Jurisprudence: New and Old Institutionalisms." In *Supreme Court Decision-Making: New Institutionalist Approaches,* edited by Cornell W. Clayton and Howard Gillman, 15–41. Chicago: University of Chicago Press, 1999.

Clayton, Cornell, and David A. May. "A Political Regimes Approach to the Analysis of Legal Decisions." *Polity* 32 (1999): 233–52.

Cray, Ed. *Chief Justice: A Biography of Earl Warren.* New York: Simon and Schuster, 1997.

Dahl, Robert A. "Decision-Making in a Democracy: The Supreme Court as a National Policy-Maker." *Journal of Public Law* 6 (1957): 279–95.

———. *A Preface to Democratic Theory.* Chicago: University of Chicago Press, 1956.

Douglas, William O. *Beyond the High Himalayas.* Garden City, N.Y.: Doubleday, 1952.

———. *Strange Lands and Friendly People.* New York: Harper, 1951.

Dudziak, Mary L. *Cold War Civil Rights: Race and the Image of American Democracy.* Princeton, N.J.: Princeton University Press, 2000.

———. "Desegregation as a Cold War Imperative." *Stanford Law Review* 41 (1988): 61–120.

Duram, James C. *A Moderate among Extremists: Dwight D. Eisenhower and the School Desegregation Crisis.* Chicago: Nelson-Hall, 1981.

Dworkin, Ronald. *Freedom's Law: The Moral Reading of the American Constitution.* Cambridge, Mass.: Harvard University Press, 1996.

———. *A Matter of Principle.* Cambridge, Mass.: Harvard University Press, 1985.

Eisenhower, Dwight D. *Mandate for Change, 1953–1956: The White House Years.* Garden City, N.Y.: Doubleday, 1963.

Elman, Philip. Interviewed by Norman Silber. "The Solicitor General's Office, Justice Frankfurter, and Civil Rights Litigation, 1946–1960: An Oral History." *Harvard Law Review* 100 (1987): 817–52.

Ely, John Hart. *Democracy and Distrust: A Theory of Judicial Review.* Cambridge, Mass.: Harvard University Press, 1980.

Epstein, Lee, Valerie Hoekstra, Jeffrey A. Segal, and Harold J. Spaeth. "Do Political Preferences Change? A Longitudinal Study of U.S. Supreme Court Justices." *Journal of Politics* 60 (1998): 801–18.

Epstein, Lee, and Jack Knight. *The Choices Justices Make.* Washington, D.C.: CQ Press, 1998.

———. "The New Institutionalism, Part II." *Law and Courts* 7, no. 2 (spring 1997): 4–9.

———. "Walter F. Murphy: The Interactive Nature of Judicial Decision Making." In *The Pioneers of Judicial Behavior,* edited by Nancy Maveety, 197–227. Ann Arbor: University of Michigan Press, 2006.

Epstein, Lee, Andrew D. Martin, Kevin M. Quinn, and Jeffrey A. Segal. "Ideological Drift among Supreme Court Justices: Who, When, and How Important?" *Northwestern University Law Review* 101 (2007): 1483–541.

———. "On the Peril of Drawing Inferences about Supreme Court Justices from Their First Few Years of Service." *Judicature* 91 (2008): 168–79.

Epstein, Lee, and Carol Mershon. "Measuring Political Preferences." *American Journal of Political Science* 40 (1996): 261–94.

Epstein, Lee, and Thomas G. Walker. "The Role of the Supreme Court in American Society: Playing the Reconstruction Game." In *Contemplating Courts,* edited by Lee Epstein, 315–46. Washington, D.C.: CQ Press, 1995.

Fairman, Charles. "Foreword: The Attack on the Segregation Cases." *Harvard Law Review* 70 (1956): 83–94.

Fassett, John D. "Mr. Justice Reed and *Brown v. The Board of Education.*" *Yearbook of the Supreme Court Historical Society* (1986): 48–63.

———. *New Deal Justice: The Life of Stanley Reed of Kentucky.* New York: Vantage Press, 1994.

Frank, Jerome. *Law and the Modern Mind.* 1930. Reprint Gloucester, Mass.: Peter Smith, 1970.

Frank, John P. *Mr. Justice Black: The Man and His Opinions.* New York: Knopf, 1949.

Frankfurter, Felix. *Mr. Justice Holmes and the Supreme Court.* 1938. Reprint Cambridge, Mass.: Belknap Press of Harvard University Press, 1961.

Franklin, John Hope, and Alfred A. Moss, Jr. *From Slavery to Freedom: A History of African Americans.* 7th ed. New York: Knopf, 1994.

Freyer, Tony. *Hugo L. Black and the Dilemma of American Liberalism.* Glenview, Ill.: Scott, Foresman, 1990.

Friedman, Leon, ed. *Argument: The Oral Argument before the Supreme Court in Brown v. Board of Education of Topeka, 1952–55.* New York: Chelsea House, 1969.

Gallup, George H. *The Gallup Poll: Public Opinion, 1935–1971.* 3 vols. New York: Random House, 1972.

Garfinkel, Herbert. "Social Science Evidence and the School Segregation Cases." *Journal of Politics* 21 (1959): 37–59.

Gerhart, Eugene C. *America's Advocate: Robert H. Jackson.* New York: Bobbs-Merrill, 1958.

Gibson, James L. "Judges' Role Orientations, Attitudes, and Decisions: An Interactive Model." *American Political Science Review* 72 (1978): 911–24.

———. "The Role Concept in Judicial Research." *Law and Policy Quarterly* 3 (1981): 291–311.

Gillman, Howard. "The Collapse of Constitutional Originalism and the Rise of the Notion of the 'Living Constitution' in the Course of American State-Building." *Studies in American Political Development* 11 (1997): 191–247.

———. *The Constitution Besieged: The Rise and Demise of Lochner Era Police Powers Jurisprudence.* Durham, N.C.: Duke University Press, 1993.

———. "The Court as an Idea, Not a Building (or a Game): Interpretive Institutionalism and the Analysis of Supreme Court Decision-Making." In *Supreme Court Decision-Making: New Institutionalist Approaches,* edited by Cornell W. Clayton and Howard Gillman, 65–87. Chicago: University of Chicago Press, 1999.

———. "How Political Parties Can Use the Courts to Advance Their Agendas: Federal Courts in the United States, 1875–1891." *American Political Science Review* 96 (2002): 511–24.

———. "Martin Shapiro and the Movement from 'Old' to 'New' Institutionalist Studies in Public Law Scholarship." *Annual Review of Political Science* 7 (2004): 363–82.

———. "The New Institutionalism, Part I." *Law and Courts* (winter 1996–97): 6–11.

———. "Party Politics and Constitutional Change: The Political Origins of Liberal Judicial Activism." In *The Supreme Court and American Political Development,* edited by Ronald Kahn and Ken I. Kersch, 138–68. Lawrence: University Press of Kansas, 2006.

———. "Placing Judicial Motives in Context: A Response to Lee Epstein and Jack Knight." *Law and Courts* 7, no. 2 (spring 1997): 10–13.

Gillman, Howard, and Cornell W. Clayton. "Beyond Judicial Attitudes: Institutional Approaches to Supreme Court Decision-Making." In *Supreme Court Decision-Making: New Institutionalist Approaches,* edited by Cornell W. Clayton and Howard Gillman, 1–12. Chicago: University of Chicago Press, 1999.

Goldfield, David R. *Black, White, and Southern: Race Relations and Southern Culture, 1940 to the Present.* Baton Rouge: Louisiana State University Press, 1990.

Goldford, Dennis J. *The American Constitution and the Debate over Originalism.* Cambridge: Cambridge University Press, 2005.

Goldinger, Carolyn, ed. *The Supreme Court at Work.* Washington, D.C.: Congressional Quarterly, 1990.

Goldman, Sheldon, and Austin Sarat, eds. *American Court Systems: Readings in Judicial Process and Behavior.* San Francisco: W. H. Freeman, 1978.

Graber, Mark A. "Legal, Strategic or Legal Strategy: Deciding to Decide during the Civil War and Reconstruction." In *The Supreme Court and American Political Development,* edited by Ronald Kahn and Ken I. Kersch, 33–66. Lawrence: University Press of Kansas, 2006.

———. "The Nonmajoritarian Difficulty: Legislative Deference to the Judiciary." *Studies in American Political Development* 7 (1993): 35–73.

Greenhaw, Wayne. *Fighting the Devil in Dixie: How Civil Rights Activists Took on the Ku Klux Klan in Alabama.* Chicago: Lawrence Hill Books, 2011.

Gugin, Linda C., and James E. St. Clair. *Sherman Minton: New Deal Senator, Cold War Justice.* Indianapolis: Indiana Historical Society, 1997.

Gunther, Gerald. *Learned Hand: The Man and the Judge.* New York: Knopf, 1994.

Hackney, Sheldon. *Populism to Progressivism in Alabama.* Princeton, N.J.: Princeton University Press, 1969.

Hamilton, Alexander, John Jay, and James Madison. *The Federalist.* New York: Modern Library, n.d.

Hamilton, Virginia Van der Veer. *Hugo Black: The Alabama Years.* Baton Rouge: Louisiana State University Press, 1972.

Hand, Learned. *The Bill of Rights.* Cambridge, Mass.: Harvard University Press, 1958.

Hockett, Jeffrey D. "The Battle over *Brown*'s Legitimacy." *Journal of Supreme Court History* 28 (2003): 30–53.

———. "Justice Robert H. Jackson and Segregation: A Study of the Limitations and Proper Basis of Judicial Action." *Yearbook of the Supreme Court Historical Society* (1989): 52–67.

———. "Justice Robert H. Jackson, the Supreme Court, and the Nuremberg Trial." *The Supreme Court Review* (1990): 257–99.

———. *New Deal Justice: The Constitutional Jurisprudence of Hugo L. Black, Felix Frankfurter, and Robert H. Jackson.* Lanham, Md.: Rowman and Littlefield, 1996.

Holmes, Oliver Wendell. *The Common Law.* 1881. Reprint Boston: Little, Brown, 1963.

———. "The Path of the Law." *Harvard Law Review* 10 (1897): 457–78.

Horowitz, Donald L. *The Courts and Social Policy.* Washington, D.C.: Brookings Institution, 1977.

Horwitz, Morton J. *The Transformation of American Law, 1870–1960: The Crisis of Legal Orthodoxy.* New York: Oxford University Press, 1992.

———. *The Warren Court and the Pursuit of Justice.* New York: Hill and Wang, 1998.

Houston, Charles H. "Cracking Closed University Doors." *Crisis* 42 (Dec. 1935): 370.

———. "Educational Inequalities Must Go!" *Crisis* 42 (Oct. 1935): 301.

Hutchinson, Dennis J. "Unanimity and Desegregation: Decisionmaking in the Supreme Court, 1948–1958." *Georgetown Law Journal* 68 (1979): 1–96.

Hutson, James H. "The Creation of the Constitution: The Integrity of the Documentary Record." In *Interpreting the Constitution: The Debate over Original Intent,* edited by Jack N. Rakove, 151–78. Boston: Northeastern University Press, 1990.

Jackson, Robert H. "Justice Jackson's Final Report to the President Concerning the Nurnberg War Crimes Trial." *Temple Law Quarterly* 20 (1946): 338–44.

———. "Nuremburg in Retrospect: Legal Answer to International Lawlessness." *American Bar Association Journal* 35 (1949): 813–87.

———. *The Nurnberg Case.* New York: Knopf, 1947.

———. "The Nurnberg Trial: Civilization's Chief Salvage from World War II." *Vital Speeches of the Day* 13 (1946): 114–17.

———. *The Struggle for Judicial Supremacy: A Study of a Crisis in American Power Politics.* New York: Knopf, 1941.

Kahn, Michael A. "Shattering the Myth about President Eisenhower's Supreme Court Appointments." *Presidential Studies Quarterly* 22 (1992): 47–56.

Kahn, Ronald. "Social Constructions, Supreme Court Reversals, and American Political Development: *Lochner, Plessy, Bowers,* but Not *Roe.*" In *The Supreme Court and American Political Development,* edited by Ronald Kahn and Ken I. Kersch, 67–113. Lawrence: University Press of Kansas, 2006.

———. *The Supreme Court and Constitutional Theory, 1953–1993.* Lawrence: University Press of Kansas, 1994.

Kahn, Ronald, and Ken I. Kersch, eds. *The Supreme Court and American Political Development.* Lawrence: University Press of Kansas, 2006.

Katcher, Leo. *Earl Warren: A Political Biography.* New York: McGraw-Hill, 1967.

Katznelson, Ira. *When Affirmative Action Was White: An Untold History of Racial Inequality in Twentieth-Century America.* New York: Norton, 2005.

Keck, Thomas M. *The Most Activist Supreme Court in History: The Road to Modern Judicial Conservatism.* Chicago: University of Chicago Press, 2004.

———. "Party, Policy, or Duty: Why Does the Supreme Court Invalidate Federal Statutes?" *American Political Science Review* 101 (2007): 321–38.

Kellogg, Charles Flint. *NAACP: A History of the National Association for the Advance-ment of Colored People. Vol. 1, 1909–1920.* Baltimore: Johns Hopkins University Press, 1967.

Kelly, Alfred H., Winfred A. Harbison, and Herman Belz. *The American Constitu-tion: Its Origins and Development.* 6th ed. New York: Norton, 1983.

Kersch, Ken I. "The New Deal Triumph as the End of History? The Judicial Nego-tiation of Labor Rights and Civil Rights." In *The Supreme Court and American Political Development,* edited by Ronald Kahn and Ken I. Kersch, 169–226. Lawrence: University Press of Kansas, 2006.

Key, V. O., Jr. *Southern Politics in State and Nation.* 1949. Reprint Knoxville: Uni-versity of Tennessee Press, 1986.

Kirkendall, Richard. "Tom C. Clark." In *The Justices of the United States Supreme Court, 1789–1969: Their Lives and Major Opinions,* edited by Leon Friedman and Fred L. Israel, vol. 4, 2665–95. New York: Chelsea House, 1969.

Klarman, Michael J. "*Brown* at 50." *Virginia Law Review* 90 (2004): 1613–33.

———. "*Brown,* Originalism, and Constitutional Theory: A Response to Professor McConnell." *Virginia Law Review* 81 (1995): 1881–936.

———. "*Brown,* Racial Change, and the Civil Rights Movement." *Virginia Law Review* 80 (1994): 7–150.

———. "Civil Rights Law: Who Made It and How Much Did It Matter?" Review of *Making Civil Rights Law: Thurgood Marshall and the Supreme Court, 1936–1961,* by Mark v. Tushnet. *Georgetown Law Journal* 83 (1994): 433–59.

———. *From Jim Crow to Civil Rights: The Supreme Court and the Struggle for Racial Equality.* New York: Oxford University Press, 2004.

———. "An Interpretive History of Modern Equal Protection." *Michigan Law Re-view* 90 (1991): 213–318.

———. "Rethinking the Civil Rights and Civil Liberties Revolutions." *Virginia Law Review* 82 (1996): 1–67.

Kluger, Richard. *Simple Justice: The History of Brown v. Board of Education and Black America's Struggle for Equality.* 2 vols. New York: Knopf, 1975.

Krislov, Samuel. "The Role of the Attorney General as Amicus Curiae." In *Roles of the Attorney General of the United States,* edited by Luther A. Huston et al., 71–103. Washington, D.C.: American Enterprise Institute, 1968.

Kritzer, Herbert M. "Martin Shapiro: Anticipating the New Institutionalism." In *The Pioneers of Judicial Behavior,* edited by Nancy Maveety, 387–417. Ann Arbor: University of Michigan Press, 2006.

Kurland, Philip B. "'*Brown v. Board of Education* Was the Beginning'—The School Desegregation Cases in the United States Supreme Court: 1954–1979." *Wash-ington University Law Quarterly* (1979): 309–405.

———. "Earl Warren, the 'Warren Court,' and the Warren Myths." *Michigan Law Review* 67 (1968): 353–58.

———. "Foreword: 'Equal in Origin and Equal in Title to the Legislative and Exec-utive Branches of the Government.'" *Harvard Law Review* 78 (1964): 143–312.

Kurland, Philip B., and Gerhard Casper, eds. *Landmark Briefs and Arguments of the*

Supreme Court of the United States: Constitutional Law. Vol. 49. Arlington, Va.: University Publications of America, 1975.

Landsberg, Brian K. *Enforcing Civil Rights: Race Discrimination and the Department of Justice.* Lawrence: University Press of Kansas, 1997.

Layton, Azza Salama. *International Politics and Civil Rights Policies in the United States: 1941–1960.* New York: Cambridge University Press, 2000.

Leuchtenburg, William E. "The Origins of Franklin D. Roosevelt's 'Court-Packing' Plan." *The Supreme Court Review* (1966): 347–400.

Llewellyn, Karl. "Some Realism about Realism—Responding to Dean Pound." *Harvard Law Review* 44 (1931): 1222–64.

Longaker, Richard P. *The Presidency and Individual Liberties.* Ithaca, N.Y.: Cornell University Press, 1961.

Lowi, Theodore J. *The End of Liberalism: Ideology, Policy, and the Crisis of Public Authority.* New York: Norton, 1969.

MacLean, Nancy. *Behind the Mask of Chivalry: The Making of the Ku Klux Klan.* New York: Oxford University Press, 1994.

Maltz, Earl. "*Brown v. Board of Education* and 'Originalism.'" In *Great Cases in Constitutional Law,* edited by Robert P. George, 136–53. Princeton, N.J.: Princeton University Press, 2000.

———. "A Dissenting Opinion to Brown." *Southern Illinois University Law Journal* 20 (1995): 93–98.

———. "Originalism and the Desegregation Decisions—A Response to Professor McConnell." *Constitutional Commentary* 13 (1996): 223–31.

———. *Rethinking the Constitution: Originalism, Interventionism, and the Politics of Judicial Review.* Lawrence: University Press of Kansas, 1994.

Maltzman, Forrest, James F. Spriggs II, and Paul J. Wahlbeck. "Strategy and Judicial Choice: New Institutionalist Approaches to Supreme Court Decision-Making." In *Supreme Court Decision-Making: New Institutionalist Approaches,* edited by Cornell W. Clayton and Howard Gillman, 43–63. Chicago: University of Chicago Press, 1999.

March, James G., and Johan P. Olsen. "The New Institutionalism: Organizational Factors in Political Life." *American Political Science Review* 78 (1984): 734–49.

———. *Rediscovering Institutions: The Organizational Basis of Politics.* New York: Free Press, 1989.

Marshall, Thurgood. "An Evaluation of Recent Efforts to Achieve Racial Integration in Education through Resort to the Courts." *Journal of Negro Education* 21 (1952): 316–27.

Martin, Andrew D., and Kevin M. Quinn. "Dynamic Ideal Point Estimation via Markov Chain Monte Carlo for the U.S. Supreme Court, 1953–1999." *Political Analysis* 10 (2002): 134–53.

Martin, John F. *Civil Rights and the Crisis of Liberalism: The Democratic Party, 1945–1975.* Boulder, Col.: Westview Press, 1979.

McAdam, Doug. *Political Process and the Development of Black Insurgency, 1930–1970.* Chicago: University of Chicago Press, 1982.

McCloskey, Robert G. *The American Supreme Court.* 2nd ed. Revised by Sanford Levinson. Chicago: University of Chicago Press, 1994.

———. *The Modern Supreme Court.* Cambridge, Mass.: Harvard University Press, 1972.

McConnell, Grant. *Private Power and American Democracy.* New York: Knopf, 1966.

McConnell, Michael. "Originalism and the Desegregation Decisions." *Virginia Law Review* 81 (1995): 947–1140.

———. "The Originalist Justification for *Brown:* A Reply to Professor Klarman." *Virginia Law Review* 81 (1995): 1937–55.

McCoy, Donald R., and Richard T. Reutten. *Quest and Response: Minority Rights and the Truman Administration.* Lawrence: University Press of Kansas, 1973.

McDowell, Gary L. *Equity and the Constitution: The Supreme Court, Equitable Relief, and Public Policy.* Chicago: University of Chicago Press, 1982.

McMahon, Kevin J. "Constitutional Vision and Supreme Court Decisions: Reconsidering Roosevelt on Race." *Studies in American Political Development* 14 (2000): 20–50.

———. *Reconsidering Roosevelt on Race: How the Presidency Paved the Road to* Brown. Chicago: University of Chicago Press, 2004.

McVeigh, Rory. *The Rise of the Ku Klux Klan: Right-Wing Movements and National Politics.* Minneapolis: University of Minnesota Press, 2009.

McWilliams, Carey. "The Education of Earl Warren." *Nation* (12 Oct. 1974): 67.

Milkis, Sidney. *The President and the Parties: The Transformation of the American Party System since the New Deal.* New York: Oxford University Press, 1993.

Murphy, Bruce Allen. *Wild Bill: The Legend and Life of William O. Douglas.* New York: Random House, 2003.

Murphy, Walter F. "The Art of Constitutional Interpretation." In *Essays on the Constitution of the United States,* edited by M. Judd Harmon, 130–59. Port Washington, N.Y.: Kennikat Press, 1978.

———. "Constitutional Interpretation: The Art of the Historian, Magician, or Statesman?" Review of *Government by Judiciary: The Transformation of the Fourteenth Amendment,* by Raoul Berger. *Yale Law Journal* 87 (1978): 1752–71.

———. *Elements of Judicial Strategy.* Chicago: University of Chicago Press, 1964.

Murphy, Walter F., James E. Fleming, and William F. Harris. *American Constitutional Interpretation.* Mineola, N.Y.: Foundation Press, 1986.

Murphy, Walter F., and Joseph Tanenhaus. *The Study of Public Law.* New York: Random House, 1972.

Myrdal, Gunnar, with the assistance of Richard Sterner and Arnold Rose. *An American Dilemma: The Negro Problem and Modern Democracy.* New York: Harper and Brothers, 1944.

Newby, I. A. *Challenge to the Court: Social Scientists and the Defense of Segregation, 1954–1966.* Rev. ed. Baton Rouge: Louisiana State University Press, 1969.

Nieman, Donald G. *Promises to Keep: African-Americans and the Constitutional Order, 1776 to the Present.* New York: Oxford University Press, 1991.

Nowak, John E., Ronald D. Rotunda, and J. Nelson Young. *Constitutional Law.* 3rd ed. St. Paul, Minn.: West Publishing, 1986.

Orfield, Gary, Susan E. Eaton, and the Harvard Project on School Desegregation. *Dismantling Desegregation: The Quiet Reversal of Brown v. Board of Education.* New York: New Press, 1996.

Orfield, Gary, and John T. Yun. "Resegregation in American Schools." Civil Rights Project of Harvard University, course.cas.sc.edu/germanyk/post1945/materials/orfield_Resegregation_American_Schools99.pdf (June 1999).

Parrish, Michael E. *Felix Frankfurter and His Times: The Reform Years.* New York: Free Press, 1982.

Perry, Michael J. *The Constitution, the Courts, and Human Rights: An Inquiry into the Legitimacy of Constitutional Policymaking by the Judiciary.* New Haven, Conn.: Yale University Press, 1982.

Pickerill, J. Mitchell, and Cornell W. Clayton. "The Rehnquist Court and the Political Dynamics of Federalism." *Perspectives on Politics* 2 (2004): 233–48.

Pollack, Jack Harrison. *Earl Warren: The Judge Who Changed America.* Englewood Cliffs, N.J.: Prentice-Hall, 1979.

Posner, Richard A. "Bork and Beethoven." *Stanford Law Review* 42 (1990): 1365–82.

———. *The Problems of Jurisprudence.* Cambridge, Mass.: Harvard University Press, 1990.

Pound, Roscoe. "Mechanical Jurisprudence." *Columbia Law Review* 8 (1908): 605–23.

———. "The Scope and Purpose of Sociological Jurisprudence—Part III." *Harvard Law Review* 25 (1912): 489–516.

Powe, Lucas A., Jr. *The Warren Court and American Politics.* Cambridge, Mass.: Belknap Press of Harvard University Press, 2000.

Powell, H. Jefferson. "The Original Understanding of Original Intent." In *Interpreting the Constitution: The Debate over Original Intent,* edited by Jack N. Rakove, 53–115. Boston: Northeastern University Press, 1990.

President's Committee on Civil Rights. *To Secure These Rights: The Report of the President's Committee on Civil Rights.* New York: Simon and Schuster, 1947.

Pritchett, C. Herman. *Civil Liberties and the Vinson Court.* Chicago: University of Chicago Press, 1954.

———. "The Development of Judicial Research." In *Frontiers of Judicial Research,* edited by Joel B. Grossman and Joseph Tanenhaus, 27–42. New York: John Wiley, 1969.

———. *The Roosevelt Court: A Study in Judicial Politics and Values, 1937–1947.* 1948. Reprint Chicago: Quadrangle Books, 1969.

Purcell, Edward A., Jr. *The Crisis of Democratic Theory: Scientific Naturalism and the Problem of Value.* Lexington: University Press of Kentucky, 1973.

Puro, Steven. "The United States as *Amicus Curiae.*" In *Courts, Law, and Judicial Processes,* edited by S. Sidney Ulmer, 220–29. New York: Free Press, 1981.

Richards, David A. J. "Originalism without Foundations." Review of *The Tempting of America: The Political Seduction of the Law,* by Robert H. Bork. *New York University Law Review* 65 (1990): 1373–407.

Rogers, William Warren. *The One-Gallused Rebellion: Agrarianism in Alabama, 1865–1896.* Baton Rouge: Louisiana State University Press, 1970.

Rohde, David W., and Harold J. Spaeth. *Supreme Court Decision Making.* San Francisco: W. H. Freeman, 1976.

Rosen, Paul L. *The Supreme Court and Social Science.* Urbana: University of Illinois Press, 1972.

Rosenberg, Gerald N. *The Hollow Hope: Can Courts Bring about Social Change?* Chicago: University of Chicago Press, 1991.

Ross, B. Joyce. *J. E. Spingarn and the Rise of the NAACP, 1911–1939.* New York: Atheneum, 1972.

Ross, Dorothy. "The Many Lives of Institutionalism in American Social Science." *Polity* 28 (1995): 117–23.

Salokar, Rebecca Mae. *The Solicitor General: The Politics of Law.* Philadelphia: Temple University Press, 1992.

Schubert, Glendon. *The Judicial Mind: The Attitudes and Ideologies of Supreme Court Justices, 1946–1963.* Evanston, Ill.: Northwestern University Press, 1965.

———. *The Judicial Mind Revisited: Psychometric Analysis of Supreme Court Ideology.* New York: Oxford University Press, 1974.

Schultz, David A., ed. *Leveraging the Law: Using Courts to Achieve Social Change.* New York: Peter Lang, 1998.

Schwartz, Bernard. *Super Chief: Earl Warren and His Supreme Court—A Judicial Biography.* New York: New York University Press, 1983.

Scigliano, Robert. *The Supreme Court and the Presidency.* New York: Free Press, 1971.

Segal, Jeffrey A. "Amicus Curiae Briefs by the Solicitor General during the Warren and Burger Courts: A Research Note." *Western Political Quarterly* 41 (1988): 135–44.

Segal, Jeffrey A., and Albert D. Cover. "Ideological Values and the Votes of U.S. Supreme Court Justices." *American Political Science Review* 83 (1989): 557–65.

Segal, Jeffrey A., Lee Epstein, Charles M. Cameron, and Harold J. Spaeth. "Ideological Values and the Votes of U.S. Supreme Court Justices Revisited." *Journal of Politics* 57 (1995): 812–23.

Segal, Jeffrey A., and Harold J. Spaeth. *The Supreme Court and the Attitudinal Model.* New York: Cambridge University Press, 1993.

———. *The Supreme Court and the Attitudinal Model Revisited.* New York: Cambridge University Press, 2002.

Segal, Ronald. *The Race War.* New York: Viking Press, 1966.

Shannon, David A. "Hugo La Fayette Black as United States Senator." In *Justice Hugo Black and Modern America,* edited by Tony Freyer, 121–37. Tuscaloosa: University of Alabama Press, 1990.

Shapiro, Martin. "Chief Justice Rehnquist and the Future of the Supreme Court."

In *An Essential Safeguard: Essays on the United States Supreme Court and Its Justices,* edited by D. Grier Stephenson, Jr., 145–64. Westport, Conn.: Greenwood Press, 1991.

———. "The Constitution and Economic Rights." In *Essays on the Constitution of the United States,* edited by M. Judd Harmon, 74–98. Port Washington, N.Y.: Kennikat Press, 1978.

———. *Law and Politics in the Supreme Court: New Approaches to Political Jurisprudence.* New York: Free Press, 1964.

———. "Political Jurisprudence." *Kentucky Law Journal* 52 (1964): 294–345.

———. "The Supreme Court: From Warren to Burger." In *The New American Political System,* edited by Anthony King, 179–211. Washington, D.C.: American Enterprise Institute, 1978.

Silverstein, Mark. *Constitutional Faiths: Felix Frankfurter, Hugo Black, and the Process of Judicial Decision Making.* Ithaca, N.Y.: Cornell University Press, 1984.

Skowronek, Stephen. "Order and Change." *Polity* 28 (1995): 91–96.

Smith, Rogers M. "Ideas, Institutions, and Strategic Choices." *Polity* 28 (1995): 135–40.

———. "Political Jurisprudence, the 'New Institutionalism,' and the Future of Public Law." *American Political Science Review* 82 (1988): 89–108.

Somit, Albert, and Joseph Tanenhaus. *The Development of Political Science: From Burgess to Behavioralism.* Boston: Allyn and Bacon, 1967.

Southern, David W. *Gunnar Myrdal and Black-White Relations: The Use and Abuse of* An American Dilemma, *1944–1969.* Baton Rouge: Louisiana State University Press, 1987.

Sundquist, James L. *Dynamics of the Party System: Alignment and Realignment of Political Parties in the United States.* Rev. ed. Washington, D.C.: Brookings Institution, 1983.

Tate, C. Neal. "Personal Attribute Models of the Voting Behavior of U.S. Supreme Court Justices: Liberalism in Civil Liberties and Economics Decisions, 1946–1978." *American Political Science Review* 75 (1981): 355–67.

Tate, C. Neal, and Roger Handberg. "Time Binding and Theory Building in Personal Attribute Models of Supreme Court Voting Behavior, 1916–88." *American Journal of Political Science* 35 (1991): 460–80.

tenBroek, Jacobus, Edward N. Barnhart, and Floyd W. Matson. *Prejudice, War and the Constitution.* Los Angeles: University of California Press, 1954.

Thornton, J. Mills, III. "Hugo Black and the Golden Age." *Alabama Law Review* 36 (1985): 899–913.

Tindall, George B. *The Disruption of the Solid South.* New York: Norton, 1972.

Truman, David B. *The Governmental Process: Political Interests and Public Opinion.* New York: Knopf, 1951.

Turner, John. *The Ku Klux Klan: A History of Racism and Violence.* Montgomery, Ala.: Southern Poverty Law Center, 1982.

Tushnet, Mark V. *Making Civil Rights Law: Thurgood Marshall and the Supreme Court, 1936–1961.* New York: Oxford University Press, 1994.

————. *The NAACP's Legal Strategy against Segregated Education, 1925–1950.* Chapel Hill: University of North Carolina Press, 1987.

Tushnet, Mark, with Katya Lezin. "What Really Happened in *Brown v. Board of Education.*" *Columbia Law Review* 91 (1991): 1867–930.

Ulmer, S. Sidney. "Earl Warren and the Brown Decision." *Journal of Politics* 33 (1971): 689–702.

————. "The Longitudinal Behavior of Hugo Lafayette Black: Parabolic Support for Civil Liberties, 1937–1971." *Florida State University Law Review* 1 (1973): 131–53.

Urofsky, Melvin I. *Felix Frankfurter: Judicial Restraint and Individual Liberties.* Boston: Twayne, 1991.

Van den Haag, Ernest. "Social Science Testimony in the Desegregation Cases—A Reply to Professor Kenneth Clark." *Villanova Law Review* 48 (1960): 69–79.

Wallace, Harry L. "Mr. Justice Minton—Hoosier Justice on the Supreme Court." *Indiana Law Journal* 34 (1959): 147–57, 377–424.

Ware, Gilbert. "*Hocutt:* Genesis of *Brown.*" *Journal of Negro Education* 52 (1983): 227–33.

Warren, Earl. "'All Men Are Created Equal.'" *Record of the Association of the Bar of the City of New York* 25 (1970): 351–64.

————. "The Bill of Rights and the Military." *New York University Law Review* 37 (1962): 181–203.

————. "The Law and the Future." *Fortune* (Nov. 1955): 1–16.

————. *The Memoirs of Earl Warren.* Garden City, N.Y.: Doubleday, 1977.

————. Notre Dame Law School Civil Rights Lectures. *Notre Dame Lawyer* 48 (1972): 14–48.

————. "War-Time Martial Rule in California." *California State Bar Association Journal* 17 (1942): 185–204.

Weaver, John D. *Warren: The Man, the Court, the Era.* Boston: Little, Brown, 1967.

Wechsler, Herbert. "Toward Neutral Principles of Constitutional Law." *Harvard Law Review* 73 (1959): 1–35.

Westin, Alan F., and Trudy Hayden. "Presidents and Civil Liberties from FDR to Ford: A Rating by 64 Experts." *Civil Liberties Review* 3 (1976): 9–35.

White, G. Edward. *Earl Warren: A Public Life.* New York: Oxford University Press, 1982.

Whittington, Keith E. "Congress before the *Lochner* Court." *Boston University Law Review* 85 (2005): 821–58.

————. *Constitutional Interpretation: Textual Meaning, Original Intent, and Judicial Review.* Lawrence: University Press of Kansas, 1999.

————. "'Interpose Your Friendly Hand': Political Supports for the Exercise of Judicial Review by the United States Supreme Court." *American Political Science Review* 99 (2005): 583–96.

————. "Once More unto the Breach: Post-Behavioralist Approaches to Judicial Politics." *Law and Social Inquiry* 25 (2000): 601–34.

————. *Political Foundations of Judicial Supremacy: The Presidency, the Supreme*

Court, and Constitutional Leadership in U.S. History. Princeton, N.J.: Princeton University Press, 2007.

Wilkinson, J. Harvie, III. *From* Brown *to* Bakke: *The Supreme Court and School Integration, 1954–1978.* New York: Oxford University Press, 1976.

———. *Serving Justice: A Supreme Court Clerk's View.* New York: Charterhouse, 1974.

Woodward, C. Vann. *The Strange Career of Jim Crow.* 3rd rev. ed. New York: Oxford University Press, 1974.

Wyatt-Brown, Bertram. "Ethical Background of Hugo Black's Career: Thoughts Prompted by the Articles of Sheldon Hackney and Paul L. Murphy." *Alabama Law Review* 36 (1985): 915–26.

Yarbrough, Tinsley E. *Mr. Justice Black and His Critics.* Durham, N.C.: Duke University Press, 1988.

INDEX

Note: Page numbers in italics indicate tables and figures.

abolitionism, 24, 26

Acheson, Dean, 139

African Americans: changing attitudes toward, 8, 39–43, 57–58, 124, 125, 168–77; in Eisenhower's administration, 151; electoral power of, 104, 155–60; influence in New Deal coalition, 12, 148, 154; rural-to-urban migration and opportunities for, 41–42, 155; voter registration of, 42, 161–62, 163. *See also* civil rights

Alabama: Black as senator of, 115–17; convict leasing abolished in, 115, 117

American Bar Association, 134

amicus curiae briefs: higher education, 54, 157 (*see also* university cases); interstate transportation, 157; other civil rights cases under Truman, 42, 221–22n14, 228n25; restrictive covenant cases, 49, 139–40, 156, 222n14

—for Brown (Eisenhower administration, 1953): Court's interpretation of, 150–51; Court's invitation to provide, 152; decision to participate via, 151–54; on enforcement, 153–54; hopes to resolve racial issue as part of, 164–65; on indeterminacy surrounding Fourteenth Amendment, 27; political regimes model on, 12

—for Brown (Truman administration, 1952): on Cold War implications, 11, 127; desegregation plans in, 143, 211n33; desegregation rationale in, 133; hopes to resolve racial issue as part of, 164–65; political regimes model on, 12, 129–31

Anti-Convict Lease Association, 115, 117

Anti-Defamation League of B'nai B'rith, 106–7

attitudinal model: assessing validity of, 47–51, 55–58, 179–82; components and development of, 8, 36–39, 60; "current of history" approach in, 8, 39–43, 57–58, 133–34, 229n51; limits of, 9, 38, 183–84; strategic model compared with, 69–70; unresolved issues in, 77–78. *See also* public opinion

—measuring ideological values: ideological alignments of justices, 51–55, *52,* 206–7n42; ideological drift evidence and, 9, 56–58, 70, 77, 111, 119, 138, 146–47, 175–76, 180; newspaper editorials' assessments in, 50–51, 54–55, 207n45, 207n55; personal attributes of justices, 46–50, *48,* 206n39; problems of proof, 43–46. *See also* values

attorneys general, federal, 152. See also *amicus curiae* briefs; Clark, Tom C.; Jackson, Robert H.

attorneys general, state. *See* Warren, Earl
attribute models, 46–50, *48*, 206n39

bargaining in Court process, 61–63,
    85–91, 111–12, 184
barriers to desegregation: burden
    of proof and, 20–21; Court's
    separate-but-equal rulings, 29–30, 97;
    empirical findings to counter, 17–20,
    30; extralegal (enforcement), 31–32;
    judicial deference to segregationist
    legislatures, 20–21, 29, 31; precedents
    as, 15–17, 210n18; strict constitu-
    tional interpretation, 21–28. *See also*
    framers' intentions; implementation
    and enforcement
behavioralism, 60. *See also* attitudinal
    model
Bell, Derrick A., Jr., 131, 196
Bensel, Richard Franklin, 116, 157–58,
    162
Berry, Mary Frances, 225n53
Bickel, Alexander M., 76, 187–88, 190,
    193, 232nn11–12
Bingham, John, 24–25
Black, Charles L., 3, 214n70
Black, Earl, 177
Black, Hugo: cautions voiced by, 1;
    civil rights and First Amendment
    decisions summarized, 121–22, *144,*
    145; on constitutional interpretation,
    22; courts as "havens of refuge" and,
    115–22; on enforcement, 68; on
    framers' intentions, 119; ideological
    alignment of, *52,* 207n55; ideological
    drift of, 57, 119, 175–76, 180; judi-
    cial socialization of, 10–11; as KKK
    member, 10, 45, 46, 49, 92, 115, 117,
    180; *Korematsu* ruling, 200–201n19;
    liberal voting summarized, 173, *174;*
    "local control" argument of, 116–17;
    luncheon discussions of, 79; personal
    attributes of, *48,* 49; racial views sum-
    marized, 117; on remedy (relief) issue,

79–80, 80–81; on rule of law and
    desegregation, 65–66, 74, 210n18;
    segregation attitudes of, 45–46,
    65–66; as U.S. senator from Alabama,
    115–17
Black, Merle, 177
Black Codes (1860s), 98–100, 111, 120
Bolling v. Sharpe (1954). *See* District of
    Columbia case
Bork, Robert H.: on *Brown* and judi-
    cial activism, 188–90, 233n24; on
    Brown's effects, 5, 193, 194; critique
    of, 232–33n20; on judicial discretion,
    232n19
Brandeis, Louis, 31
Briggs v. Elliott. See South Carolina case
Brotherhood of Railroad Trainsmen,
    115
Brownell, Herbert, 152, 154
Brown II (1955), 143–44, 162, 224–
    25n46. *See also* implementation and
    enforcement
Brown v. Board of Education (1954):
    attempts at collegiality in Court
    discussions, 78–81; bargaining and
    loyalty appeals in discussions, 85–91;
    cases consolidated in, 197n1; consen-
    sus on issues, 81; decision announced,
    203n56; documentary record uneven
    for, 7–8; iconic status of, 2–4, 189,
    194–95; as judicial policy making
    (political), 4–5, 15, 33–35, 227n17;
    justices' multiple goals in, 177; jus-
    tices' opinions unchanged from 1952
    to 1953, 73–74; justices' separate
    written opinions on, 81–85; as limited
    to education (or not), 88–89, 214n72;
    nonaccusatory opinion sought for,
    114, 124; originalism in critique of,
    188–91, 233n24; post-announcement
    debates about, 32–35; remedy (relief)
    issue in, 79–80 (*see also* implementa-
    tion and enforcement); social and
    political context of, 8, 39–43, 57–58

(*see also* domestic policy issues; foreign policy issues). *See also* desegregation decision; domestic policy issues; unanimity (*Brown I*); Warren Court
—initial hearing (1952): burden of proof, 20–21; empirical findings, 17–20; external constraints concerning, 63–71; framers' intentions, 21–22; order of justices' speaking in conference on, 209n13; possible vote result if not delayed, 70–71; precedents, 15–17, 210n18
—rehearing (1953): concluding date of, 203n56; external constraints concerning, 31–32, 71–78; five key questions in, 201–2n27; framers' intentions, 22–28; judicial deference to segregationist legislatures, 20–21, 29, 31; order for, 152, 199n29; order of justices' speaking in conference on, 209n13
burden of proof: questions related to, 20–21, 29, 31, 97, 100, 113; in race cases, 112
Burger Court, 37, 187–88, 233n27
Burton, Harold H.: civil rights and First Amendment decisions summarized, *144,* 145; economic issue voting of, 225n53; on enforcement, 67, 72; foreign policy concerns of, 12, 45, 127, 138, 145–46, 147, 182; ideological alignment of, *52;* ideological drift of, 57, 146, 180, 182; limited experience with racial matters, 166; luncheon discussions of, 79; personal attributes of, *48;* on rule of law and desegregation, 66, 74; on segregation, 65; on trend away from segregation, 229n53
Bush, George H. W., 51
busing issue, 3, 187
Byrnes, James, 72

California: racial integration of National Guard, civil service, and judiciary, 103; Warren as attorney general of, 108–10;

Warren as governor, 103–4, 108. *See also* Japanese-Californians
Cameron, Charles M., 50–51
Cardozo, Benjamin, 83
Carpenters' Union, 115
Casper, Jonathan, 226n2
Chambers v. Florida (1940), 117–19, 121
Chicago Tribune, 51
Cho, Sumi, 109–10, 218n50
Civilian Conservation Corps, 146
civil rights: access to procedural justice as, 135; First Amendment concerning anticommunism and, 135–38, 222n20, 222n26, 222–23n28; limited newspaper coverage (Segal's study), 207–8n56; progressive politics and labor linked to, 169–77; restricted civil liberties vs. liberalized, 49, 138–39. *See also* civil rights movement; minorities
Civil Rights Act (1866), 24–25, 100
Civil Rights Acts (1960s), 226–27n14
Civil Rights Congress (CRC), 132
civil rights movement: brutality of southern response to, 112, 194–95; social and political context of, 8, 39–43, 55, 57–58, 133–34; as threat to New Deal and Democratic party, 160–68
Clarendon School district. *See* South Carolina case
Clark, Kenneth, 19
Clark, Tom C.: anti-segregation statement of, 140, 185; background and personal attributes of, *48, 49;* civil rights and First Amendment decisions summarized, *144,* 144–45; on enforcement, 68, 72; foreign policy concerns of, 12, 127, 138, 142, 144, 185; ideological alignment of, *52,* 54, 175; ideological drift of, 57, 77; liberal voting summarized, *174;* luncheon discussions of, 79; on *Plessy* and equality in education, 140–42, 224n41, 224n43; on racial progress in higher education, 168; on remedy

Clark, Tom C. (*continued*)
(relief) issue, 80; on rule of law and
desegregation, 76–77; on segregation,
racial harmony, and Mexicans in Texas,
65, 70–71, 209–10n16; segregation
and mixed feelings of, 45, 46, 142,
166; segregation defended by, 9, 138;
on segregation in historical record,
212–13n43; silences of, 181; as Truman's attorney general, 12, 45, 49,
138–40, 142, 144, 181–82; Warren's
bargaining with, 86
Clayton, Cornell W.: on enforcement,
153; on institutionalism, 127–28;
on missions and institutions, 94, 95;
political regimes model of, 128–29,
130–31; on Segal's measures, 207n45
Cleveland (Ohio), integration of nurses
in, 66
Clifford, Clark, 42, 155–56, 157, 161
Cold War: *Brown* as imperative in,
11–12, 45, 105, 107, 127, 131–34,
135–36, 142, 195; *Brown* decision
reconsidered in context, 134–38,
181–83, 185; changing attitudes to
race in, 41–42, 124, 125; economic
component of, 106, 134–35. *See also*
foreign policy issues
Coleman, William, 44, 64
Compromise of 1877, 98
Congress: involvement of (D.C. case),
69; justices' likely assumptions about,
166–67; pro-rights justices vs. civil
rights bills in, 165; suggested end of
segregation by, 66, 75, 83; Truman's
civil rights bills rejected by, 161, 165
Constitution: indeterminacy of, 1, 8,
27–28, 37, 38, 40, 113; as "living"
and dynamic, 23–27, 75, 101, 113–
15, 125, 131, 163, 188, 215–16n18;
originalism and strict interpretation of,
21–28, 188–91, 194, 233n24; separation of powers in, 61, 129–30, 194.
See also due process clause; equal pro-

tection clause; Fifteenth Amendment;
Fifth Amendment; First Amendment;
Fourteenth Amendment; framers'
intentions
constitutive model: assessing validity
of, 125–26, 128–29, 178, 180–81,
192; components and development
of, 10–11, 92–94, 186–87; constitutional interpretation and, 100–101;
courts as "havens of refuge" and Black
in, 115–22; historical-interpretive
methodology of, 94–97; Jackson's
decision making in, 122–26; judicial
mission and, 11, 231–32n10; racial
politics and, 97–100; socialization in,
215n3. *See also* institutions; judicial
mission
—Warren's decision making: impact
of hearing dialogue on, 110–15;
Japanese-Californians' internment
and, 108–10, 112; racial politics and,
103–8; view of Court's role, 101–3.
See also Warren, Earl
courts: discretion of judges in, 232n19;
as guardians of minorities, 99,
102–3, 111–12; as "havens of refuge,"
115–22; role in *Brown* implementation, 73, 79–80, 142–43, 211n29. *See
also* Supreme Court
Cover, Albert D., 50, 206n41
Craven, Avery, 34
CRC (Civil Rights Congress), 132

Dahl, Robert A.: on Eisenhower, 153;
limits of argument, 225–26nn1–2;
political jurisprudence model of, 128,
149–50, 154, 192
Darwin, Charles, 98–99
Davis, John: on enforcement questions, 32; on framers' intentions, 22,
25–27; on local control, 143, 153;
on separate-but-equal rulings, 29–30,
97; shocked at *Brown* decision, 33; on
social science evidence, 19, 20, 30

Davis v. County School Board of Prince Edward County (Virginia case, 1952), 18, 20–21, 197n1

decision making: bargaining in, 61–63, 85–91, 111–12, 184; dialectical interplay in, 114–15; documentary record on, 7–8, 95–96; institutional context of, 37–38, 94–97, 215n6; two types of models in, 6–7; Warren's view of, 101–3. *See also* desegregation decision; instrumental models; noninstrumental models

Delaware case (*Gebhart v. Belton,* 1952), 20–21, 197n1, 197–98n2

Democratic party: African American votes courted by, 104, 155–60; civil rights agenda as threat to, 160–68; Dixiecratic movement in, 13, 161, 171, 229n37; FDR's attempt to alter nature of, 12–13, 158–61, 171–72, 176–77; justices' earlier activities in, 8, 12–13, 15. *See also* New Deal coalition; Roosevelt, Franklin D.; Truman, Harry

desegregation: Court allegedly expected to resolve issue of, 164–67; diverse forces in support of, 179–86; limited support for, 43, 51–53; of military and civil service, 42, 54, 150, 151; of nurses, 66; public opinion on, 43, 53, 119; shift to integration from, 187–88. *See also* barriers to desegregation; implementation and enforcement; racial integration

desegregation decision: approach to studying, 5–14; as Cold War imperative, 11–12, 45, 105, 107, 127, 131–34, 135–36, 142, 195; "current of history" argument for, 8, 39–43, 57–58, 133–34, 229n51; extended to other cases and contexts, 214n72; multifaceted approach to, 178–86; resistance expected to, 31–32, 60, 67–69, 71–73, 142; resolution of

differences over, 59; scholarly attention to, 4. *See also* barriers to desegregation; *Brown v. Board of Education;* instrumental models; noninstrumental models; unanimity (*Brown I*); unanimity (*Brown II*)

Detroit Race Riot (1943), 146

Dewey, Thomas, 105–6, 157

dissenting opinions, as internal constraint, 62, 71, 81–82

District of Columbia: alleged framers' intentions evidenced in segregation in, 21–22, 25–26; desegregation's importance to, 133; treatment of foreign visitors in, 150, 151

District of Columbia case (*Bolling v. Sharpe,* 1954): controversy over, 2; Douglas on, 67; due process issue in, 2, 64, 66, 74–75, 88–89; Frankfurter on, 64; internment cases referenced in, 111–12, 120; judicial deference notion in, 20; judicial scrutiny defined narrowly in, 21; on racial discrimination by legislators, 99–100; reargument of, 67, 68–69; Warren on, 88–89

doll test, 19

domestic policy issues: administration's decision to participate in *Brown* and, 151–53; administration's stance interpreted by Court, 150–51; *Brown* and, 12–13; changing racial attitudes and, 169–77; courting African American vote and, 104, 155–60; under Eisenhower, 149–54; labor issues, progressive politics, and civil rights linked in, 169–77; restrictive covenant cases and, 49, 139–40, 156, 222n14. *See also* New Deal coalition; political regimes model

Douglas, Elsie, 85

Douglas, William O.: civil rights and First Amendment decisions summarized, 135–36, *144,* 145, 222n20; on enforce-

Douglas, William O. (*continued*)
ment, 67, 72; foreign policy concerns
of, 12, 127, 134, 135–36, 182–83;
ideological alignment of, 51, *52,* 175;
ideological drift of, 57; liberal voting
summarized, *174;* luncheon discussions
of, 79; multiple goal orientations of,
182–83; personal attributes of, *48;* policy preferences of, 9, 44, 90; question
concerning government's position, 153;
on remedy (relief) issue, 80; on rule of
law and desegregation, 66, 71, 74
Dred Scott case, 224n43
Dudziak, Mary L.: on *Brown* decision as
Cold War imperative, 11–12, 131–34,
135–36, 142; on Clark and *amicus
curiae* brief, 139–40; on Court decision making, 147; on loyalty investigations, 138
due process clause: to apply Bill of Rights
(against states), 3; coerced confessions
case concerning, 117–19; D.C. school
case and, 2, 64, 66, 74–75, 88–89. *See
also* equal protection clause
Dworkin, Ronald, 232–33n20

Eastland, James, 33
education. *See* public schools; university
cases; *and specific cases*
egalitarianism: framers' intentions linked
to, 23–25; *Plessy* as departure from,
28. *See also* racial equality
Eisenhower, Dwight D.: African Americans in administration of, 151; civil
rights actions of, 226–27n14; Committee on Government Contracts of,
151; decision to participate in *Brown,*
151–54; desegregation approach of,
32, 143–44, 150–51; electoral success of, 13, 104, 151, 161, 216n25,
229n37; involvement of and later
enforcement by, 68–69; justices appointed by, 51, 104–5. *See also amicus
curiae* briefs

Elman, Philip, 139, 152–53, 211n27,
226n11
Ely, John Hart, 232n11
enforcement. *See* implementation and
enforcement
Epstein, Lee: on bargaining and opinion
writing, 85; on editorial assessments of
judicial attitudes, 50–51; on external
constraints, 60, 61; ideological drift
study of, 56–57
equal protection clause: Bork's vs. Warren
Court's view of, 188–91; electoral
system restructured via, 3; *Gong Lum*
and, 15–17; *Plessy's* separate but
equal in conflict with, 75; reasonableness requirement for, 20, 64–65, 86,
123–24, 146, 181; Warren's civic
obligation and, 193–94. *See also* due
process clause
executive branch: *Brown* decision as Cold
War imperative for, 11–12, 45, 105,
107, 127, 131–34, 135–36, 142,
195; Court's relationship with, 127,
129–31, 164–67; expansion of authority of, 158–61, 168, 176, 228n29;
involvement of and later enforcement
by, 68–69. *See also amicus curiae*
briefs; domestic policy issues; foreign
policy issues; *and specific presidents*
external constraints. *See under* strategic
(or rational choice) model

Fair Employment Board, 156
Fair Employment Practices Commission,
139, 146, 156, 174
Fair Labor Standards Act (FLSA, 1938),
116
Fairman, Charles, 58, 122, 123
fascism, changing attitudes to race in face
of, 41–42, 124, 125. *See also* Nazism;
World War II
Fassett, John D., 136–37
FDR. *See* Roosevelt, Franklin D.
Federal Emergency Relief Board, 116

federal government: circumscribed power under Fifth Amendment, 121; desegregation plans of, 72, 211n33; grants-in-aid from, 157; living Constitution notion applied to powers of, 23–24; loyalty investigations of those in executive branch, 138; originalist ideas and, 191; restrictive approach to civil liberties in 1950s, 131. *See also* *amicus curiae* briefs; Justice Department; solicitor general

Fifteenth Amendment, 27, 100

Fifth Amendment: Court's role under, 11, 92; federal power circumscribed under, 120–21; wartime cases of, 20. *See also* due process clause

First Amendment: anticommunist tactics and, 135–36, 137–38; controversial uses of, 3; justices' voting on cases of, 37–38, *144,* 144–45, 147, 182–83 (*see also specific justices*)

Fiss, Owen, 94

FLSA (Fair Labor Standards Act, 1938), 116

foreign policy issues: *Brown* decision as imperative for, 11–12, 45, 105, 107, 127, 131–34, 135–36, 142, 195; Burton and Minton's concerns for, 12, 45, 127, 138, 145–47; civil rights and segregation as, 105, 107, 127, 131–32; Court discussions of, 136–38; racial discrimination's implications for, 139–40; torture as, 196; Truman-appointed justices and, 138–47. *See also* Cold War; political regimes model

Fourteenth Amendment: appropriate applications debated, 28–30; Court clerk's research on, 76, 187–88; Court's role under, 92; framers' intentions in, 21–28, 64, 86, 113, 189; petitioners vs. respondents on interpretation of, 100–101; Reed on segregation and, 63; separate but equal in conflict with, 75; strict scrutiny

under, 120–21. *See also* equal protection clause

framers' intentions: Black on, 119; Court clerk's research on, 76, 187–88; Frankfurter on, 27, 64, 100; indeterminacy of, 1, 8, 27–28, 37, 38, 40, 113, 189; judicial discretion and, 232n19; originalism and strict interpretation of, 21–28, 188–91, 194, 233n24; petitioners on, 22, 25–27, 100–101; petitioners vs. respondents on, 100–101; Warren on, 113. *See also* Constitution

Frankfurter, Felix: *Brown* memorandum of, 82–83; *Brown* rehearing questions of, 202n27; civil rights and First Amendment decisions summarized, 137–38, *144,* 223n31; on enforcement, 67–69, 72; foreign policy concerns of, 12, 127, 137–38, 182–83; on framers' intentions, 27, 64, 100; ideological alignment of, *52,* 175; ideological drift of, 57, 180; liberal voting summarized, *174;* luncheon invitation rejected, 79; miscegenation laws question of, 219n68; multiple goal orientations of, 182–83; on Myrdal, 173; personal attributes of, *48;* policy preferences of, 9, 44, 58, 71; on race relations trends, 168; on remedy (relief) issue, 79–80; on rule of law and desegregation, 64, 70, 76; on *Slaughter House Cases,* 29–30; social science evidence rejected by, 21–22, 64, 88; on university cases, 30

Franklin, John Hope, 98

Gebhart v. Belton (Delaware, 1952), 20–21, 197n1, 197–98n2

Genocide Convention (U.N., 1948), 132

Gillman, Howard, 94, 95, 209n10

Goldford, Dennis, 191

Goldman, Sheldon, 206n39

Gong Lum v. Rice (1927), 15–17

Graber, Mark A., 13, 164–67, 185, 229n47
Great Migration, 41, 155
Greenberg, Jack, 40
Gunther, Gerald, 34

Hamilton, Alexander, 61
Hand, Learned, 34
Hayes, George, 20, 29, 99–100, 120–21, 219n68
Henderson v. United States (1950), 222n14
Hirabayashi v. United States (1943), 20, 29, 99, 111–12, 200n18
Hoekstra, Valorie, 57
Holmes, Oliver Wendell, 31
Houston, Charles, 198n5
Howard, Jacob M., 25

ideological drift, evidence of, 9, 56–58, 70, 77, 111, 119, 138, 146–47, 175–76, 180. *See also* attitudinal model; values
implementation and enforcement: as barrier to desegregation, 31–32, 60, 67–69, 71–73; Court's agreement to delayed, 59, 69–70, 71–72, 143–44, 162, 184; District Courts' role in, 73, 79–80, 142–43, 153, 211n29; Jackson's memorandum on, 84; outlined in *amicus curiae* brief (1953), 153–54; special master for, 80, 213n50. See also *Brown II* (1955); strategic (or rational choice) model
India, international relations of, 134
Indiana, former Democratic senator from. *See* Minton, Sherman
industrialization, opportunities in, 41–42, 155
institutionalized racism concept, 14, 88
institutions: as constraint, 59, 61–63, 149–50; Court as one point in relationships among, 127–29; decision making in context of, 37–38, 56; FDR's constitutional

vision of, 12–13, 158–64, 168–70; historical-interpretive approach to, 94–97; new emphasis on roles of, 60, 92–94. *See also* constitutive model; political regimes model; strategic (or rational choice) model
instrumental models: assessing validity of, 69–71, 176–79; definition and focus of, 4–7; judicial role orientation in, 205n30, 214–15n3; limits of, 8–10, 36, 93, 180–81; in multifaceted approach, 179–86. *See also* attitudinal model; strategic (or rational choice) model
intentions of framers. *See* framers' intentions
"interest convergence" principle, 196
internal constraints. *See under* strategic (or rational choice) model
international affairs. *See* Cold War; foreign policy issues
interpretive community concept, 94

Jackson, Robert H.: anti-segregation statement of, 58, 122, 123, 176; *Brown* memoranda of, 83–85, 86, 123–25; civil rights and First Amendment decisions summarized, *144*, 220n84, 222–23n28; on decision making, 122–25; on enforcement, 31–32, 68, 69, 72; as FDR's attorney general, 44, 64; foreign policy concerns of, 12, 127, 137, 182–83, 185; ideological alignment of, 51, *52, 207n55*; ideological drift of, 57, 180; illness and death of, 81, 125–26, 175; judicial inefficacy fears of, 195–96, 230n67; judicial socialization of, 10–11; liberal voting summarized, 173, *174;* luncheon invitation rejected, 79; personal attributes of, *48;* policy preferences of, 9, 44, 122–23, 185; on race relations trends, 10, 168–69; on remedy (relief) issue, 80; on rule of law and desegregation, 64–65, 70, 71,

76, 181; as U.S. prosecutor at Nuremberg Trials, 44, 122; Warren's bargaining with, 86, 89–90
Japanese-Californians: internment of,
108–10, 112; racial classification of
and restrictions on, 20, 99. See also
*Hirabayashi v. United States; Korematsu
v. United States*
judicial activism (or policy making):
Brown as, 4–5, 15, 33–35, 227n17;
as means to avoid political stalemate,
164–67; New Deal electoral alliance
split by, 162–64; New Deal justices'
sensitivity to issue, 8, 15; normative
concerns and, 187–90
judicial deference: constitutive approach
to studying, 96–97; debates about,
20–21, 29, 31, 92, 97–100; industrial
regulation and, 88
judicial mission: concept of, 94–97,
215n6; early civil rights cases and,
160–64; as guardian of minority
rights, 99, 102–3, 111–12, 180–81;
individual protection from majority
tyranny as, 191; Jackson on, 231n72;
petitioners' reiteration of, 99–100;
Warren on, 102–3, 110–11. *See also*
constitutive model
judicial role orientation concept, 205n30,
214–15n3
judicial socialization concept, 10–11. *See
also* constitutive model
Justice Department: Civil Rights Section
established in, 159; Court's relationship with, 129–31, 221n6; postwar
judicial doctrine shaped by, 228n33;
reluctance to challenge southern
whites, 161–62; role in passage of
Civil Rights Acts, 226–27n14. See
also *amicus curiae* briefs

Kahn, Ronald, 94, 191, 192–94, 233n27
Kansas case. See *Brown v. Board of Education*

Key, V. O., Jr., 169–71, 172
KKK. *See* Ku Klux Klan
Klarman, Michael J.: on Burton's and
Minton's judicial restraint, 145; on
changing racial views and Court,
229n51; on civil rights in postwar
agenda, 55, 56; on Court's majoritarian culture, 40–41; on Jackson's
desegregation vote, 122, 124, 220n85;
on justices' motivations, 44–46,
57–58, 118–19, 135; limits of study,
9; on sociopolitical context of *Brown*,
8, 41–43
Kluger, Richard, 81, 90
Knight, Jack, 60, 61, 85
Korematsu v. United States (1944): findings of, 109, 200–201n19; judicial
deference and states in, 29; referenced
in *Bolling v. Sharpe*, 111–12; strict
scrutiny standard in, 20, 99, 120, 121,
180
Korman, Milton, 21
Ku Klux Klan (KKK): Black as member
of, 10, 45, 46, 49, 92, 115, 117, 180;
Minton's clash with, 146
Kurland, Philip B., 187–88, 190, 193

labor issues: Black's work on, 115–16;
New Deal, race, and, 157–59; progres-
sive politics and civil rights linked to,
169–77
LDF. *See* NAACP Legal Defense and
Education Fund
legislatures. *See* Congress; state legisla-
tures
Lincoln, Abraham, 76, 107–8
Los Angeles Times, 51
Lowi, Theodore, 192
lynching, 42, 52, 116, 146, 156, 159

Maltz, Earl, 194
March, James G., 92–94
Marshall, Thurgood: on desegregation
and international affairs, 133; em-

Marshall, Thurgood (*continued*)
pirical evidence used by, 2, 65 (*see also* social science evidence); leadership in desegregation suits, 198n5; questioned about enforcement, 71, 73; questioned about Fifteenth Amendment, 27; on *Slaughter House Cases,* 29; on speed of remedy, 80. *See also* NAACP Legal Defense and Education Fund
Martin, Andrew D., 56
May, David A., 127–29
Maybank, Burnet, 4
McAdam, Doug, 41
McCloskey, Robert G., 215n6
McConnell, Grant, 192
McDowell, Gary L., 188, 190, 191, 193
McLaurin v. Oklahoma State Regents for Higher Education (1950): *amicus curiae* brief for, 140, 222n14; empirical considerations in, 22; findings of, 16, 28, 101, 200n4; intangibles of education highlighted in, 87; larger, older vs. newer, smaller schools and, 223–24n40; racial classification and, 67; separate-but-equal idea weakened by, 74–75
McMahon, Kevin J.: on *Brown* and Democratic politics, 12–13, 158–60, 162; on *Brown II,* 162; on Eisenhower's election, 229n37; on individual action and social forces, 44; limits of argument, 176–77
Meany, George, 33–34
Mickum, George, 89
Miller, Samuel, 29
minorities: Court as guardian of, 11, 40–41, 92, 99, 102–3, 111–12, 149, 156, 163, 177, 179; courts as "havens of refuge" for, 115–22; Frankfurter as (Jew), 64; international relations and, 132–33 (*see also* Cold War); labor issues linked to, 13, 148, 160–61, 173, 183. *See also* African Americans; Japanese-Californians

Minton, Sherman: on behavioral changes, 67; civil rights and First Amendment decisions summarized, *144,* 144–45, 147; on enforcement, 73; foreign policy concerns of, 12, 45, 127, 138, 145–47, 182; ideological alignment of, *52,* 54, 175; liberal voting summarized, *174;* limited experience with racial matters, 166; luncheon discussions of, 79; personal attributes of, *48;* on race relations trends, 168; on rule of law and desegregation, 67, 74–75
miscegenation, 219n68
Moore, T. Justin, 18, 20, 31, 97
Morton, William, 117
Murphy, Walter F.: on delayed enforcement, 70; as influence, 92; strategic model of, 59–60, 61–63
Myrdal, Gunnar, 169–74, 217n45

NAACP (National Association for the Advancement of Colored People): early civil rights cases and, 163; U.N. petition of, 105, 106, 132, 138–39, 181; as voting bloc, 155
NAACP Legal Defense and Education Fund (LDF): barriers for, 8; cursory response to enforcement questions, 71, 73; on framers' intentions, 23–25; Frankfurter and, 58; *Plessy* rejected as precedent by, 16–17; restrictive covenant cases of, 49, 139–40, 156, 222n14; Truman administration's support for, 54. *See also* barriers to desegregation; Marshall, Thurgood; petitioners; social science evidence
Nabrit, James, 20, 29, 99–100
Nation, The, 108
National Association of Attorneys General, 139
National Education Association, 107

National Emergency Committee against Mob Violence, 156
National Youth Administration, 146
Nazism, 44, 122, 124, 125
New Deal coalition: African American influence in, 12, 148, 154; *Brown* decision as solicitous toward, 154–55, 158; civil rights agenda as threat to, 160–68; FDR's constitutional vision and, 12–13, 158–64, 168–72, 175, 183; judiciary and executive branch alliance in, 130–31; justices' earlier roles in, 8, 12–13, 15, 49, 116; opposition to, 103–4, 105. *See also* domestic policy issues; Roosevelt, Franklin D.
New Republic, 108
newspapers and media: on *Brown* decision, 34; editorial assessment of judicial attitudes in, 50–51, 54–55, 207n45; limited civil rights coverage in, 207–8n56; on NAACP's petition, 105
New York Times, 51
noninstrumental models: assessing validity of, 176–79, 184–86, 193–96; for decisions on racial equality, 13–14; definition and focus of, 4, 6–7; evidence for, 7–8; in multifaceted approach, 179–86; used to explain justices' motivations, 44–46. *See also* constitutive model; political regimes model
normative concerns: Court rulings and, 186–87; of critics of Warren Court, 3, 5, 187–90; of defenders of Warren Court, 190–96
norms of Court: Court rules, procedures, and, 61–63, 208–9n7; Court's adherence to rule of law and, 63–67, 73–77; as external constraint, 60; as internal constraint, 61–62; judicial activism and, 187–90. *See also* social science evidence
Nuremberg War Crimes Trial, 44, 122

O'Donnell, John, 108
Ohio: former Republican senator from (*see* Burton, Harold H.); integration of nurses in, 66
Olsen, Johan P., 92–94

Pakistan, international relations of, 134
Perlman, Philip, 140
Perry, Michael J., 2
personal policy preferences concept, 8–10, 36–39. *See also specific justices*
petitioners: Black's response to, 119–21; case law interpretation of, 113–15; on enforcement, 31–32, 71, 73; on framers' intentions, 23–25; on judicial deference, 20–21, 29, 97; sources cited by, 169–74; use of term, 197–98n4. *See also* Marshall, Thurgood; NAACP Legal Defense and Education Fund
Plessy v. Ferguson (1896): call to overturn, 140–41, 152, 153, 157, 224n43; as departure from Court's egalitarianism, 28; empirical findings and error in, 17; findings of, 87, 197n2; irrationality of theory underlying, 86; as precedent, 15; rejected as precedent in *Brown,* 1–2, 16–17, 74–75; social constructions of, no longer tenable, 191. *See also* separate-but-equal principle
pluralism, 192–96
political regimes model: assessing validity of, 145–47, 175–77, 181–83; attempt to change Democratic politics and, 12–13, 158–64, 168–70; components and development of, 127–31, 148; Court as policy maker in, 164–67, 192–96; influences on, 199n26, 225–26n1; legitimacy issues in, 149–50; political realism and, 157–58; preferred position doctrine and, 149–54, 227nn16–17. *See also* domestic policy issues; foreign policy issues; judicial activism

political socialization studies, 50
politics: development of preferences and meanings in, 93; hierarchical view of, 115–16, 117; judging process compared with, 101–2; racial, 97–100, 103–8, 122. *See also* Democratic party; institutions; Republican party
polity and rights principles: Court as guardian of minorities and, 99, 102–3, 111–12; development of, 94; respondents vs. petitioners on, 96–97; Warren Court's decision making based in, 190–96
Pollock, Earl, 87
poll tax issue: Eisenhower on, 150, 151; function of, 98, 159, 161–62; support for eliminating, 52–53, 104, 146, 169–70, 172
Powe, Lucas A., Jr., 230n69
preferred position doctrine, 154, 158, 227nn16–17, 228n27
President's Committee on Civil Rights (Truman), 42, 53, 54, 132, 156
President's Committee on Equality of Treatment and Opportunity in the Armed Forces (Truman), 156
President's Committee on Government Contracts (Eisenhower), 151
Pritchett, C. Herman, 36–37, 215n3
public opinion: assumptions about ideological attitudes, 51–52; of *Brown* as judicial activism, 4–5, 15, 33–35, 227n17; changing attitudes toward racial equality, 8, 39–43, 57–58, 124, 125, 168–77; of desegregation, 43, 53, 119; of Japanese-Californians' internment, 110; political elite views vs. general, 54; of Truman's civil rights program, 52–53. *See also* attitudinal model
public schools: challenges of equality in, 195–96; Clark on equality in, 140–41, 224n41, 224n43; desegregation of elementary and secondary, 43,

53, 54; racial integration of, 3, 74–75, 187, 211n33; Warren's prenomination comments on, 10, 103–4. *See also* racial segregation of schools
Puro, Steven, 130

Quinn, Kevin M., 56

race: classification by, 3, 8, 20–21, 29, 65–67, 84, 99, 112, 114, 120–21, 125; scientific evidence on, 124
race riots, Detroit (1943), 146
racial equality: changing attitudes toward, 8, 39–43, 57–58, 124, 125, 168–77; declining political interest in, 195–96; as liberal value (or not), 44, 53–54
racial integration: California National Guard, civil service, and judiciary, 103; of nurses, 66; of schools, 3, 74–75, 187, 211n33; shift from desegregation to, 187–88; social science findings on success of, 17–18
racial segregation: classification and, 3, 8, 20–21, 29, 65–67, 84, 99, 112, 114, 120–21, 125; as Cold War issue, 11–12, 105, 107, 127, 131–34, 135–36, 142, 195; Court's lack of authority to declare unconstitutional, 32–33; Court's perception of changing attitudes toward, 168–77; Eisenhower on, 150; elite calls to end, 54; foreign affairs impacted by, 139–40; hopes for Court to resolve issue of, 164–67; petitioners' review of, 97–100; psychological harm inherent in, 18, 86–88, 113–14, 214n68; as stamp of racial inferiority, 2, 3, 86–87, 89, 97–100, 124, 140–41. *See also* racial segregation of schools; racial segregation rationales; segregationists
racial segregation of schools: assumptions of equality in, disproved, 18–19; Clark's reluctance to jeopardize elementary, 140–42, 224n41, 224n43;

Eisenhower on, 152–53; framers' intentions concerning, 21–28; harms and inherent inequality of, 86–88; inferiority fostered by, 2, 3, 86–87, 89, 97–100, 124, 140–41; legal cases upholding, 15–17; little change in 1950s, 144; "local control" argument for, 116–17; as meeting the rule of law, 63

racial segregation rationales: as benefit for blacks, 30, 35, 75, 92, 97; black children as special education problem, 17, 84; to maintain white supremacy, 42, 45, 120–21, 127, 177, 180–81, 187; to preserve racial harmony, 2, 9, 11, 29, 65, 92, 111, 121, 126, 142, 197n2; southern laws of, 98–100, 111, 120. *See also* segregationists

Radical Republicans, 24–25

Rankin, J. Lee: on administration's position, 153; on Court's invitation to participate, 152; on indeterminacy of history of amendment, 27; questioned about enforcement, 31–32; on speed of remedy, 80

rational choice model. *See* strategic (or rational choice) model

Reagan, Ronald, 177

Redding, Louis, 20–21, 29, 97, 120

Reed, Stanley F.: civil rights and First Amendment decisions summarized, 137, *144*, 145, 147, 222n26; coerced confessions case and, 118; dissent drafted by, 81–82, 85; foreign policy concerns of, 12, 127, 136–37, 182–83; ideological alignment of, *52*, 175; ideological drift of, 57, 180; liberal voting summarized, *174;* loyalty to Court in voting against policy preferences, 10, 59, 89; luncheon discussions of, 79; personal attributes and background of, *48, 49*; policy preferences of, 46; on race relations trends, 168; on remedy (relief) issue,

80; on rule of law and segregation, 21, 63, 70, 75; segregation defended by, 9, 44–45, 71, 77, 79, 119, 180–81; on university cases, 30; Warren's opinion and, 86, 88, 89

Rehnquist Court, 37

Republican party: Burton's views and, 146; civil rights stance of, 107–8, 150–51; congressional control of (1946), 155; equalitarian principles of (Radical), 24–25; justices associated with, *48;* presidential candidates of, 105–6, 107–8, 180. *See also* Eisenhower, Dwight D.

respondents: as best able to implement desegregation, 143, 153; on enforcement, 31–32; on framers' intentions, 25–27; on judicial deference, 31, 97; on precedent, 8, 16–17; on social science evidence, 18–20; use of term, 197–98n4. *See also* Davis, John; racial segregation rationales

restrictive covenant cases, 49, 139–40, 156, 222n14

Robinson, Spottswood, 17, 20–21, 29, 97, 120

Rohde, David W., 37, 56

Roosevelt, Franklin D. (FDR): activist state legitimated under, 131; attempt to alter Democratic party, 12–13, 158–61, 171–72, 176–77; civil rights and labor issues linked by, 173–74; civil rights under, 148; constitutional vision of, 12–13, 158–64, 168–72, 175, 183; executive authority expanded by, 158–61, 168, 176, 228n29; Jackson as attorney general for, 44, 64; justices appointed by, 51, 123, 131, 155, 160, 183. *See also* Democratic party; New Deal coalition

Rosenberg, Gerald N., 39–40, 195

rule of law: bargaining and opinion writing concerning, 86, 90–91; constitutive dialogue concerning, 128–29; as

rule of law (*continued*)
external constraint, 63–67, 73–77. *See also* implementation and enforcement

Sakolar, Rebecca Mae, 129
Sarat, Austin, 206n39
Schubert, Glendon, 36–39
Segal, Jeffrey A.: civil liberties category of, 207n43; Clayton's critique of, 207n45; on editorial assessments of judicial attitudes, 50–51, 54, 175, 206n41, 231n70; ideological drift study of, 56–57; on institutional context of Court, 37–38; on Tate's attribute model, 49–50
segregationists: Black Codes of, 98–100, 111, 120; brutality of response to civil rights movement, 112, 194–95; Fourteenth Amendment ratification required for (Confederate states), 25–26; shocked at *Brown* decision, 33; underlying brutality exposed, 3; white supremacy goal of, 42, 45, 120–21, 127, 177, 180–81, 187. *See also* racial segregation; racial segregation rationales; southern whites
separate-but-equal principle: as barrier to desegregation, 29–30, 97; irrationality of theory underlying, 86; justices' vote against, 81; weakened in university cases, 74–75. See also *Plessy v. Ferguson*
separation of powers system, 61, 129–30, 194
Shapiro, Martin: on attitudinal model, 38, 39; on *Brown* and New Deal coalition, 154–55, 158; limits of account, 160, 163; political jurisprudence model of, 128, 227n15
Shelley v. Kraemer (restrictive covenants, 1948), 49, 139–40, 156, 222n14
Silverstein, Mark, 117
Sipuel v. Board of Regents of the University of Oklahoma (1950), 66, 210n20
Skowronek, Stephen, 94

Slaughter House Cases (1873), 28, 29–30, 75, 87
Smith, Rogers M.: on Court decision making, 6, 114–15, 128; on Court rulings and normative debates, 186; on multifaceted approach, 178, 185; on political institutions, 93–94, 95
social expectations. *See* implementation and enforcement; norms of Court
social science evidence: arguments concerning, 17–20, 30; Court's first use of, 2, 10, 35; Frankfurter's objection to, 21–22, 64, 88; implications of Court's use of, 187; Jackson on, 65; on psychological harms, 87, 113–14, 214n68. *See also* norms of Court
solicitor general, Court's relationship with, 129–31, 136, 139–40, 221n6
South Carolina case (*Briggs v. Elliott,* 1952): consolidated with *Brown,* 197n1; framers' intentions and, 22; segregation benefits to blacks claimed in, 30, 92; social science evidence in, 18–20
"Southern Manifesto" (1956), 33
southern whites: brutal response to civil rights movement, 112, 194–95; civil rights bills vs. pro-rights justices and, 165; Court's perceptions of changing racial views and, 168–77; desegregation attitude polls of, 46; Eisenhower's success among, 13, 104, 151, 161, 216n25; FDR's attempt to purge Democratic party of, 158–61, 171–72, 228n29; four political pillars of, 159; Fourteenth Amendment ratification required for (Confederate states), 25–26; Justice Department's reluctance to challenge, 161–62; justices from, *48,* 49; New Deal coalition and, 148, 154–58; one-party politics and restricted voting of, 155–56, 157; presidential voting summarized, 226n6; speed of remedy and, 80–81;

white primary of, 98, 159, 161, 228n33, 229n38. *See also* implementation and enforcement; segregationists

Soviet Union: collapse of, 195–96; racial segregation critiqued by, 105, 107, 127, 131–32. *See also* Cold War

Spaeth, Harold J.: on institutional context of Court, 37–38, 56; on judicial attitudes, 49–51; on justices' mutual influence, 57

Spencer, Herbert, 98–99

state legislatures: Black Codes of (1860s), 98–100, 111, 120; circumscribed power under Fourteenth, 121; enforcement issue and, 31–32; executive power vs., 158–61, 228n29; judicial deference to, 20–21, 29, 31, 97–100

Stern, Robert C., 152

Stevenson, Adlai, II, 151, 161

St. Louis Post-Dispatch, 51

Stone, Harlan, 227n16

strategic (or rational choice) model: assessing validity of, 89–91, 180–81, 184; components and development of, 9–10, 59–63, 93; critique of, 127–28. *See also* implementation and enforcement

—external constraints: extralegal issues, 60, 67–69, 71–73; implications of, 69–71; rule of law, 63–67, 73–77; separation of powers, 61; unresolved issues, 77–78

—internal constraints: agenda setting and opinion assignment, 208–9n7; bargaining to overcome, 61–63, 85–91, 111–12, 184; collegiality as means to overcome, 61, 78–81; justices' different opinions as, 62, 71, 81–85

Strauder v. West Virginia (1880), 28, 30, 75, 87

strict scrutiny standard, 20, 99, 120–21, 180

Sturges, Wesley, 5

Supreme Court: anti-New Deal decisions (1930s), 8, 15; first black clerk of, 44, 64; internment cases (see *Hirabayashi v. United States; Korematsu v. United States*); judicial inefficacy fears and, 195–96, 230n67; judicial restraint and, 145; loyalty to, 10, 59, 89; majoritarian culture of, 40–41; opinion writing process of, 85; originalism and limits on, 188–91, 233n24; *pur curiam* decisions concerning desegregation, listed, 214n72; restrictive covenant cases before, 49, 139–40, 156, 222n14; rules, procedures, and norms of, 61–63, 208–9n7; social and political context of, 8, 39–43, 57–58, 133–34; solicitor general's relationship with, 129–31, 136, 139–40, 221n6; Warren's view of role of, 101–3. *See also* institutions; judicial activism; judicial deference; judicial mission; separate-but-equal principle; Warren Court

Sweatt v. Painter (1950): *amicus curiae* brief for, 140, 222n14; empirical considerations in, 22; findings of, 16, 101, 200n4; intangibles of education highlighted in, 66, 87, 210n20; *Plessy* assumption belied in, 28; racial classification and, 67

Taft, William Howard, 15

Talmadge, Herman, 33

Taney, Roger B., 224n43

Tate, C. Neal, 39, 46–49, *48,* 50, 206n39

Texas: racial issues highlighted in, 65, 70, 209–10n16; racial segregation to maintain racial harmony in, 142, 144. *See also* Clark, Tom C.

Thurmond, Strom, 161, 226n6, 229n37

Tillman, Ben, 98, 111

transportation facilities (interstate), 156. See also *Plessy v. Ferguson*

Truman, David B., 154, 192

Truman, Harry: African American vote courted by, 104, 155–57; anticommunist efforts of, 132–33, 135; civil rights bills of, rejected by Congress, 161, 165; civil rights efforts of, 42, 52–53, 54, 150, 156–57; on civil rights vs. liberties, 49, 138–39, 144; Clark as attorney general for, 12, 45, 49, 138–40, 142, 144, 181–82; enforcement issues and, 32, *143*; justices appointed by, *48*, 51, 131, 138–47, 155, 182; political realism of, 157–58; presidential committees of, 42, 53, 54, 132, 156; solicitor general's office under, 152. See also *amicus curiae* briefs
Tushnet, Mark, 213n43

unanimity (*Brown I*): bargaining to obtain, 61–63, 85–91, 111–12, 184; obstacles to, 77–78; respondents' shock at, 33; significance of, 1, 10, 80–81
unanimity (*Brown II*), 143–44
United Mine Workers of Birmingham, 115
United Nations: charter of, 106–7; human rights orientation of, 131–32; NAACP petition at, 105, 106, 132, 138–39, 181
United States. *See* Congress; Constitution; Justice Department; Supreme Court
United States v. Carolene Products Co. (1938), 227n16
university cases: *amicus curiae* brief for, 54, 140; Clark's memoranda on, 140–42, 223–24n40, 224n43; constitutionality of educational segregation rejected in, 16, 101; decline to consider separate-but-equal in, 29–30; intangibles of education highlighted in, 66, 87, 113; intent not to reaffirm *Plessy* and, 140–41, 224n41, 224n43; racial classification and, 67; racial

progress and, 168; separate-but-equal idea weakened by, 74–75
urbanization, opportunities in, 41–42, 155
U.S. News and World Report, 108

values: civil liberties category of, 207n43; civil rights vs. liberties in, 49; ideological drift evidence and, 9, 56–58, 70, 77, 111, 119, 138, 146–47, 175–76, 180; liberal vs. conservative statements of, 206–7n42; measures of, 231n70; perceived vs. real, 50. *See also* attitudinal model
Vinson, Fred, 21, 23, 71, 104, 209n12
Virginia case (*Davis v. County School Board of Prince Edward County,* 1952), 18, 20–21, 197n1

Wall Street Journal, 51
Warren, Earl: appointed to chief justice, 23, 81, 104–5; background of, 45; bargaining for unanimity, 61–63, 85–91, 111–12, 184; on *Brown* decision, 1–2; as California governor, 103–4, 108; civil rights and First Amendment decisions summarized, 121, *144,* 145, 222n19; collegiality fostered by, 78–79; delayed vote recommended by, 71–72; democratic government analyzed by, 193–94; on economics and communism, 106, 134–35; Eisenhower's meeting with, 153; on framers' intentions, 113; Frankfurter's memorandum and, 82–83; ideological alignment of, 51, *52,* 54; ideological drift of, 57, 111; institutionalized racism recognized by, 14; Japanese-Californians' internment role of, 108–10, 112; judicial socialization of, 10–11; localism in education and, 166; luncheon discussions of, 79; opinion writing of, 77–78, 81, 85–91, 133; personal attributes of, *48;*

prenomination views of, 10, 103–8, 208n57; as presidential candidate, 105–6, 107–8, 180; on racial inferiority concept, 110–11; racial politics and, 103–8; on remedy (relief) issue, 79–80; on rule of law and desegregation, 73–74; view of Court's role, 101–3

Warren. C. J., 85

Warren Court (at time of *Brown*): awareness of sensitive nature of *Brown,* 1; bargaining process in, 61–63, 85–91, 111–12, 184; consensus on segregation matters, 39; dialogue before, 110–15; as expected to resolve racial segregation issue, 164–67; free speech and reapportionment rulings of, 155; influences on, 228n33; institutional context of decision making, 37–38; liberal voting summarized, 173–75, *174;* New Deal background of, 8, 12–13, 15; normative assessment of, 3–6; originalism in critique of, 188–91, 233n24; pluralism rejected

by, 192–93; political assumptions and, 154–55, 162–64; race relations trends perceived by, 168–77. *See also* Black, Hugo; Burton, Harold H.; Clark, Tom C.; desegregation decision; Douglas, William O.; Frankfurter, Felix; Jackson, Robert H.; Minton, Sherman; Reed, Stanley F.; Vinson, Fred; Warren, Earl; *and specific cases*

Washington Evening Star (newspaper), 34

Washington Post, 51

Wechsler, Herbert, 34–35

White, G. Edward, 105

White, Walter, 146, 155

white primary, 98, 159, 161, 228n33, 229n38

Wilkinson, J. Harvie, III, 3, 195

Wilson, Paul, 16–17

Woodward, C. Vann, 98

World War II: changing racial attitudes during and after, 8, 39–43, 57–58, 124, 125, 168–77; Nuremberg Trials after, 44, 122

Constitutionalism and Democracy

Kevin T. McGuire / *The Supreme Court Bar: Legal Elites in the Washington Community*

Mark Tushnet, ed. / *The Warren Court in Historical and Political Perspective*

David N. Mayer / *The Constitutional Thought of Thomas Jefferson*

F. Thornton Miller / *Juries and Judges versus the Law: Virginia's Provincial Legal Perspective, 1783–1828*

Martin Edelman / *Courts, Politics, and Culture in Israel*

Tony Freyer / *Producers versus Capitalists: Constitutional Conflict in Antebellum America*

Amitai Etzioni, ed. / *New Communitarian Thinking: Persons, Virtues, Institutions, and Communities*

Gregg Ivers / *To Build a Wall: American Jews and the Separation of Church and State*

Eric W. Rise / *The Martinsville Seven: Race, Rape, and Capital Punishment*

Stephen L. Wasby / *Race Relations Litigation in an Age of Complexity*

Peter H. Russell and David M. O'Brien, eds. / *Judicial Independence in the Age of Democracy: Critical Perspectives from around the World*

Gregg Ivers and Kevin T. McGuire, eds. / *Creating Constitutional Change: Clashes over Power and Liberty in the Supreme Court*

Stuart Streichler / *Justice Curtis in the Civil War Era: At the Crossroads of American Constitutionalism*

Virginia A. Hettinger, Stefanie A. Lindquist, and Wendy L. Martinek / *Judging on a Collegial Court: Influences on Federal Appellate Decision Making*

James R. Rogers, Roy B. Flemming, Jon R. Bond, eds. / *Institutional Games and the U.S. Supreme Court*

Vanessa A. Baird / *Answering the Call of the Court: How Justices and Litigants Set the Supreme Court Agenda*

Christine L. Nemacheck / *Strategic Selection: Presidential Nomination of Supreme Court Justices from Herbert Hoover through George W. Bush*

Barry Alan Shain, ed. / *The Nature of Rights at the American Founding and Beyond*

Mark C. Miller / *The View of the Courts from the Hill: Interactions between Congress and the Federal Judiciary*

Amy Steigerwalt / *Battle over the Bench: Senators, Interest Groups, and Lower Court Confirmations*

Martin J. Sweet / *Checkmate: The Persistence of Unconstitutional Laws*

Todd C. Peppers and Artemus Ward, eds. / *In Chambers: Stories of Supreme Court Law Clerks and Their Justices*

Jeffrey D. Hockett / *A Storm over This Court: Law, Politics, and Supreme Court Decision Making in Brown v. Board of Education*